A REMARKABLE COLLECTION OF ANGELS

BEATDOM

PUBLISHED BY BEATDOM BOOKS

ALSO BY THE AUTHOR

Scientologist! William S. Burroughs and the
'Weird Cult' (2013)
World Citizen: Allen Ginsberg as Traveller (2019)
High White Notes: The Rise and Fall of Gonzo
Journalism (2021)
Murakamian Magical Realism and Psychological
Trauma (2023)

A REMARKABLE COLLECTION OF ANGELS

A HISTORY OF THE 6 GALLERY READING

BY DAVID S. WILLS

Published by Beatdom Books

Copyright © 2025 by David S. Wills
Cover design © Matthew Revert

All rights reserved. No part of this book may be reproduced in any form or by any electronic or mechanical means including information storage and retrieval systems, without permission in writing from the author. The only exception is by a reviewer, who may quote short excerpts in a review.

ISBN: 978-1-0686980-2-6

First Print Edition

for Leang

Contents

Introduction   i

Bohemian Spaces
1.1 A Countercultural Capital   1
1.2 The Confusing History of a Strange Building   31
1.3 Arise, King Ubu   43
1.4 Five Painters and a Poet   59
1.5 The 6 Gallery   75

San Francisco is Beat
2.1 Allen Ginsberg Goes West   103
2.2 Writing Howl   127
2.3 Assembling Another Six   147

The 6 Gallery Reading
3.1 A Subterranean Celebration   175
3.2 Philip Lamantia and John Hoffman   183
3.3 Michael McClure   191
3.4 Philip Whalen   199
3.5 Allen Ginsberg   207
3.6 Gary Snyder   219
3.7 After the Reading   231

Aftermath
4.1 The Beginning of a Great Career   239
4.2 A Repeat Performance   271
4.3 Infamy, Infamy!   287
4.4 The End of the 6   311
4.5 Myth and Legacy   325

Appendices
Correcting Common Errors   347
The 1955 San Francisco Arts Festival   355
Timeline   377

Bibliography   389
Endnotes   333
Index   447

"It's all gotten kind of myth-like. Everybody remembers what they remember."

—Wally Hedrick

Introduction

On October 7, 1955, at the 6 Gallery in San Francisco, a group of poets gave a reading that proved so wildly successful the reverberations are still felt today. They stood on a tiny stage in a bizarre building in an unfashionable part of town, where a year earlier a group of misfit artists had established a co-operative gallery largely for the purpose of displaying their most experimental work—the sort of radical creations that were of no interest to the other galleries and museums in the city at that time.

The circumstances could hardly have been more modest. The poets were almost completely unknown and the venue was more like a studio than a gallery. Yet somehow the combination of poets, setting, and audience resulted in one of the most important literary events of the century. It would launch the careers of four of the poets on stage and bring about the publication of the most important poem of the late twentieth century. That evening arguably created the San Francisco Renaissance and publicly launched the Beat Generation, and both of these movements went on to influence the various countercultures that followed.

On that night, in that odd little gallery, Allen Ginsberg gave the first public reading of "Howl." It was an early and incomplete version of his poem, but it had a monumental impact on the people in the audience—a collection of artists, hipsters, professors, and others comprising the city's bohemian literati. Also on stage were Gary Snyder, Michael McClure, Philip Whalen, and Philip Lamantia, with Kenneth Rexroth acting as M.C. Aside from Rexroth, who was the city's most prominent writer and had a modest national reputation, these were young

A Remarkable Collection of Angels

and mostly untested poets. It was surprising enough that the event drew a capacity crowd but none of the poets had any right to expect that it would set them on the road to international acclaim, with Ginsberg soon becoming the world's most famous living poet.

Although they had published few works and possessed almost no experience reading in public, the poets' performances that night captivated their audience and their fates changed almost immediately. In the following months, Ginsberg, Snyder, Whalen, and McClure would read their work again and again before growing audiences. The only reason Lamantia did not was his lack of interest in fame or critical attention. The four Beat poets—as they would soon be identified—quickly began to find homes for their poems in little magazines and then with small publishing companies, riding a countercultural wave through the late fifties and into sixties hippiedom, thereafter becoming semi-respectable poets in the eyes of an establishment that had initially gasped in horror.

Looking back on that night, it is Allen Ginsberg's reading of "Howl" that stands out as not just the highlight of the evening but a landmark in American literature. Perhaps because of that reading, his poem was picked up by San Francisco's City Lights Bookstore, which published it the following year in *Howl and Other Poems*. This sparked an obscenity trial that not only made the poem nationally infamous but radically redefined what could be published in the United States by showing that a work seemingly containing obscene content could be recognized as possessing artistic merit. Generations of artists owe a tremendous debt to Ginsberg and Lawrence Ferlinghetti, the owner of City Lights, whose refusal to bow to government intimidation resulted in the case being fought and won.

It was Ginsberg who gained the most from the reading, becoming something of a local celebrity in the months after it, then building upon his success to achieve national and eventually international renown. Importantly, though, he used his growing fame to draw attention to his poetic peers, including his fellow 6 Gallery readers and old friends William S. Burroughs, Jack Kerouac,

Introduction

and Gregory Corso. Influenced by Walt Whitman, he recognized the importance of self-promotion and used the unexpected success of his 6 Gallery performance to create a literary movement around the disparate artistic styles and personal philosophies of his creatively inclined peers. Philip Whalen recalled many decades later:

> The thing that's wonderful is that Allen would always tell all these magazine editors who asked him for poems, "I will give you some poems, but I'd like you to print some poems by Gary Snyder and Philip Whalen, if you please." And they would say, "Oh, all right." So we got printed, which was a great break.

Whalen was perhaps exaggerating a little, for he was a terribly self-effacing man, but certainly Ginsberg pushed for his friends to be published and invited to read their work. Nor did he forget to mention their names and accomplishments when giving interviews, readings, or lectures, ensuring that they benefited at least to some extent from his rapidly growing stature. He did this out of friendship and loyalty but also because he recognized the strength that came from forming an alliance rather than taking on the world by himself.

Thus, a group began to form in San Francisco that would have an outsized influence on the culture. Rexroth, as the city's senior poet and a long-time supporter of rising poetic talents, championed these young upstarts, whilst Ferlinghetti published and sold their books. The city soon became a mecca for young creatives and a network of cafés, bars, galleries, and other venues emerged for these people to meet, share ideas, produce works of art, or give public performances. It was, for a time, synonymous with experimental art and poetry, causing Jack Kerouac to remark in 1958 that "San Francisco is the poetry center of America today."

Just two years after those virtually unknown poets stepped on stage at the 6 Gallery, "Howl" was declared not obscene and *On the Road* was published to great

A Remarkable Collection of Angels

acclaim, and the young Beat writers were practically household names. Ginsberg and Kerouac were the reluctant voices of a generation, authors of incendiary but usually misunderstood works. In 1958, the Beats spawned the beatniks and this would lead to the creation of San Francisco's next cultural export, the hippies, in the mid-sixties.[1] Generations of artists, poets, and musicians took influence directly or indirectly from the Beats. Fashions emerged. Laws changed. The culture was never the same again.

It is perhaps a fool's errand to ask whether all this could have happened without the reading at the 6 Gallery, but it does seem highly unlikely. Those poets reached the right audience in the right place at the right time, setting in motion a highly unlikely series of events. The combination of those young men and their enthusiasm for poetry and the support of this strange little gallery, coupled with the sentiment in a city that stood at odds with a national culture of conservatism and conformity, changed everything. What other venues would have given these young poets a chance? And, if they had been allowed such a reading, would they have attracted as large and enthusiastic an audience? Would that audience have contained so many influential people? Would Lawrence Ferlinghetti have published "Howl"? Would the poem have become embroiled in—and successfully contested—an obscenity trial of national importance? Without the trial and without the poem's infamy, would Kerouac's novel have had the impact it had? Would Ginsberg have

---

1   For those unfamiliar with the terminology, "beatnik" was a pejorative term Herb Caen coined to describe followers of the Beat Generation. His term connected the label "Beat" that the writers themselves used with "Sputnik," hinting at a communist connection. "Beatnik" quickly came to replace "Beat" among the uninformed, but the former was originally intended to refer to poseurs and followers rather than real artists. Today, most people who understand the distinction realize that labeling Ginsberg or Kerouac "beatnik" is inaccurate and insulting, but the legions of bongo-beating, beret-wearing hipsters who emerged in the late fifties, and who merely enjoyed the fashions associated with the underground whilst contributing little of value in terms of art, could certainly be labeled as such.

Introduction

found himself in a position to spread Eastern thought in the West, to argue passionately for gay rights, to lead anti-war marches and champion peaceful resolutions to potentially explosive situations? Finally, without all that, without the sudden rise of the Beat Generation, would it have been possible to have had the hippies and the free love and flower power movements, not to mention their impacts on wider society and bringing the Vietnam War to an end, all of which inspired subsequent generations of artists?

These are of course questions that are impossible to answer definitively but I believe that the 6 Gallery reading—more than any other event of its type or scale—has had an indescribably massive impact on late-twentieth-century culture, at least in the Western world. One need only look to the likes of Bob Dylan, John Lennon, David Bowie, Jerry Garcia, and other major creative minds to see how much they owed to the Beat writers. "If it wasn't for Kerouac and the Beats, there wouldn't have been any Doors," according to Ray Manzarek, and many a musician has made a similar claim. The emergence of the Beats and their inexplicable coherence as a cultural phenomenon prepared the world for the upheaval that followed.

Considering its vast impact, then, it is frightening to think of how unlikely the event's success was. Certain historical moments seem inevitable when looked back upon in retrospect, but the 6 Gallery reading came about and was carried off with no shortage of luck. Yes, there was an incredible amount of skill involved, but the mind boggles at how these young men were brought together in the right way and at the right time, how they formed such close bonds, and how they were able to collect such a large number of people of just the right disposition to listen to their poems—many of which were rather challenging and certainly would not have appealed to the average person. The poets themselves were shocked to step on stage and see such a large group of people awaiting them, and even though they believed in their art, they were pleasantly surprised to find that the audience understood and appreciated their words. One feels that had any variable been changed, the whole night might have gone very differently, altering the trajectory of modern Western literature.

Although most of the founders were not present that night, and although the event was largely organized independently of the gallery, through the efforts of the participating poets, the gallery nonetheless played an essential role in connecting artist and audience. Founded in 1954, the 6 Gallery had quickly become a hip, underground hangout for experimental artists and disaffected thinkers, but perhaps more importantly it had become famous for its exhilarating opening night parties, where any self-respecting artist or aficionado needed to be seen. And it wasn't only for social credit; these were events where people shared the latest ideas and ensured they remained on the cutting edge of contemporary art and philosophy. The gallery certainly didn't sell much, and you wouldn't find many connoisseurs of the arts inspecting the paintings and sculptures on a weekday afternoon, but come Friday night—which was typically when they chose to launch a new show—a big crowd of hipsters and bohemians and underground intellectuals was sure to show. If you weren't there, you were square.

The connection between the poets and their audience was truly special, and this was something that everyone in attendance who later spoke of the event agreed upon. (In fact, it was possibly the *only* thing they agreed upon.) The audience was plied with booze before and during the reading, and along with Jack Kerouac, who sat on the edge of the stage slugging from his jug of wine, they cheered and shouted encouragingly at the poets, who grew in confidence as their work—which had all seemed so personal and obscure before the event—was met with understanding.

All of the poets seem to have been well received but "Howl" was of course the standout success. Ginsberg's poem, which he had begun less than two months prior, struck listeners as original and brave. It is often described as a revolutionary work, yet the things he said were in part common complaints at that time. No one had said them in such a powerful way, though, and so "Howl" quickly became the poem of the era, speaking for a large but

Introduction

previously silenced segment of society. Ginsberg often spoke of taking the deeply personal and making it public as a way of reaching people, feeling that those unsayable personal truths were in fact universal, and by coupling these with the greater generational issues expressed in his poem, he articulated in an incredibly powerful way many of the ideas his audience already held. This united them, creating a sense of identity among the city's disparate groups. "I saw the best minds of my generation destroyed by madness," he began, looking out on that same generation, speaking directly to them, expressing something they knew but could not quite say. He ended not only to applause but to tears. There was a general sense that something monumental had occurred and that a new era had begun.

One of the few surviving documents written immediately after the event and describing it in any real detail shows just how well the poem had resonated with the people in the gallery that night. Composer Jack Goodwin[2] wrote that "Ginsberg's main number was a long descriptive roster of out-group, pessimistic dionysian young bohemians and their peculiar and horrible feats." This was a fantastic achievement, for Ginsberg had grown up thousands of miles away and had only been in San Francisco a year. His poem spoke not only to and for the people in the audience or his friends in San Francisco and New York, but it captured the feelings of millions of mostly young people throughout the country, expressing their frustrations and passions. Perhaps more than any poem of the modern era, Ginsberg's masterpiece spoke for a generation. How strange that seems... and yet seventy years later readers continue to read his long poem and see in it something of themselves and their own generations, which perhaps explains its stunning success.

"Howl" resonates with readers all these decades

---

2   Goodwin's work included *The Kiss-Off*, *The White Rabbit Caper*, and *The Pizza Pusher*. He was not a major participant in the events described in this book, but he was one of the best sources as he quietly attended many of these readings and wrote short but detailed accounts, seemingly aware of his proximity to a great historical movement.

later but at the time it was not just poignant; it was an indescribably daring work that challenged the oppressive social values of the era. For the people hearing it, there was a tremendous sense of liberation. As hard as it is to believe today, a poem—specifically an in-progress, avant-garde one detailing not just taboo but outright illegal activities—changed the world and made Ginsberg one of the most recognizable men in America, a public if controversial intellectual frequently invited to share his opinions on important issues, thereby shaping the public discussion surrounding drug use, gay rights, pacifism, and ecology. He not only captured his era and wrote its defining poem of resistance but came to change that era—and all of this stems from a poetry reading in a relatively new and largely unknown art gallery.

It is an inspiring story and one that is well-known in a sort of loose, semi-factual way. But the strange thing is that in spite of its tremendous importance, we know very little about it. A handful of people in attendance that night are still alive and of course it occurred at a time when recording equipment—though primitive compared to today—existed and was indeed used for literary events, but still the 6 Gallery reading is practically legend. This book aims to change that, yet I will admit up front that certain parts of the story are likely unknowable.

The lack of concrete information related to the reading largely stems from the fact that no one anticipated it being such a success. No one thought to bring a camera. No one made any video or audio recordings. No journalists were in the audience, scribbling notes. Given its subsequent importance, one might expect to look back and find mention of it in the cultural pages of the city's newspapers, which had been oddly supportive of the 6 Gallery, but there was nothing. The flurry of activity and the excitement of new friendships and exotic ideas and unexpected opportunities also meant that the poets themselves made little reference to it in their journals and correspondence. Word of mouth ensured that those who had not attended became aware of what had happened, and soon there were more readings—some featuring the original participants and others merely inspired by the success of the 6 Gallery reading—but of course oral

Introduction

transmission too often results in myth. Many who later tried to recall the reading in fact remembered other similar ones that took place around that time.

The poets' names became known around the city and eventually around the world, but there is little record of anyone discussing the 6 Gallery reading in the years immediately following it. It was two years later that Ginsberg wrote about it for a Dutch magazine and a few months after that Kerouac described it in *The Dharma Bums*, which was published in 1958.[3] Few outside of the Netherlands would have read Ginsberg's article but *The Dharma Bums* proved wildly popular both at home and abroad. The 6 Gallery reading had been "the birth of the San Francisco Poetry Renaissance," Kerouac told many thousands of readers around the world. But even then, his version—drawn from drunken memory two full years after the fact—was almost the only record of the reading until after his death in 1969.

In the seventies, when perceptions of the Beats had evolved beyond that of a hip, faddish movement and they were being taken seriously at least by a small number of young professors, Kerouac's novel provided an origin story. Of course, there had been the Columbia University group that first brought together the core Beat writers but it was the 6 Gallery reading that pushed them out of the shadows and into the glare of the public, simultaneously creating the San Francisco Renaissance, a related but distinct movement. Now seeking to make sense of recent history, scholars and journalists began asking Ginsberg, Snyder, and the other poets what had really happened that night and how it had come about. Of course, by then more than fifteen years had passed and memories had faded so that each participant gave a quite different account, and as the years went by they would contradict not only each other but themselves.

Since then, the 6 Gallery reading has become an accepted part of Beat history. It has even become a huge

---

3   The article to which I refer was co-written by Ginsberg and Corso, but the section concerning the 6 Gallery reading was clearly in Ginsberg's voice. This is discussed in more depth in Chapter 4.5.

part of the history of San Francisco, with one local writer remarking that it had become "nearly as much a part of the city's mystique as the 1849 Gold Rush or the 1906 earthquake." Yet its extraordinary importance has not led to any real understanding of how the event transpired or what exactly happened that night. There have been no books or documentaries about it, and whilst several hundred books mention it, along with an uncountable number of magazine articles and webpages, they are all conspicuously short on detail and nearly all of them have drawn their information from the same few sources.

The idea for this book first came to me many years ago when I tried to write an essay about the 6 Gallery and quickly realized that there was very little information available and that much of what had been written contradicted other accounts, and that all of it seemed to be interpretations of Kerouac's novel, mixed with Ginsberg's article and a number of things written by McClure, who kept contradicting himself and getting basic details wrong due to the fact he was writing several decades later. It seemed incredible that no one had written more than a few pages about it… but then again, how do you write about something like this? It is like writing the biography of someone who left no journals or letters, and whose family and friends are mostly dead, leaving behind only exaggerated, improbable anecdotes. It seemed like a doomed venture.

Part of me assumed that simply by investing more time and effort than others had done, I might soon find sources they had overlooked, and so I began my research by reading every written account I could find and comparing them, then scouring various archives for journals and letters that no one had found. This quickly showed me why no one had yet written a book-length account of the reading and why each shorter account had been so contradictory. The biggest problem was that the best sources had long ago been destroyed. Not only had no one recorded the event on film or tape, but the letters written about it by Ginsberg and Kerouac were lost or burned. Kerouac, in his own words, "wrote a huge letter to Burroughs about it" and had "no more energy to tell

Introduction

it" again in a letter to John Clellon Holmes on October 12. Burroughs burned the letter in a later fit of paranoia and so all that remains is a comment he wrote by way of response: "The reading sounds really great. Wish I could have been there." But what exactly had been said? We will never know, but the little he wrote to Holmes certainly sounded exuberant.

Philip Whalen's journal entries were destroyed in the early sixties and whilst Gary Snyder's journals are intact, he had so much fun during this period that he didn't bother writing any of it down. There is practically nothing between August and December except sparse notes. The period between meeting Ginsberg and Kerouac and the 6 Gallery reading is pretty much written off as "[a] wild week or two" and there's almost nothing else from the following month. Ginsberg's journals were no better. He wrote down fragments of dreams and ideas about poetry but the usual descriptions of his surroundings and social interactions are missing. The earliest of McClure's journals—or at least those that survive—is from May 1956. It seems everyone was too busy writing poetry and having fun to actually record what was happening. It was a time of incredible creativity, when brilliant young minds met and collaborated and encouraged one another, but whilst that makes it a time worth studying, it paradoxically makes it very hard to find reliable information.

I kept digging and finding the same problem. With no reliable sources to draw upon, those tasked with writing about the reading kept asking the participants or citing interviews with them, and all of these were conducted many years later. Reading these interviews side by side shows the extent to which memories can be trusted. By the time of the first interviews in the 1970s, there were inconsistencies and in later decades these grew increasingly absurd. Ginsberg kept changing his mind and contradicting himself, and nothing he said matched with anything Snyder said, whose stories differed from those of McClure's and Whalen's, while Ferlinghetti claimed Corso had been present even though he didn't visit the city until the following year... It was all just wildly incorrect. Almost everyone who spoke about it put himself at the center of the story and many of them had conflated multiple events. One almost illuminating interview with Philip Lamantia conducted in 2000 saw him ramble and digress so often that the tape ran out multiple times during his responses and so all the useful information about John Hoffman and the lead-up to the 6 Gallery is missing. He talked at great length on loosely related topics and then, when he finally got to the point, the tape clicked off. The same interviewer spoke to Whalen and just as he began to talk about the 6 Gallery, the same thing happened and the answers were not recorded. In 1997, that interviewer spoke with Gary Snyder and just as they turned to the topic of the 6 Gallery reading, the phone rang and that ended the interview. I spent years going through these documents and sometimes it felt as though the universe was conspiring to hide the information I needed.

Despite their best intentions, the biographers and historians who have taken on the unenviable task of describing the 6 Gallery reading have for more than a half century largely added to the problem. With a lack of reliable information, they have repeated or amplified falsehoods, often adding assumptions or creating new details to add color. Naturally, these people have had to make decisions for the sake of a coherent narrative. This often means privileging one account because it concerns a person who is the focus of their book or essay even when this account directly contradicts others or could have been disproven with a little more research. Regrettably, the most popular books have been cited by later generations of writers, so that those falsehoods or misinterpretations have become established truths. It seems to me that the whole history of the 6 Gallery and the reading that occurred there has been subject to a game of "Chinese whispers." Whereas some parts of Beat history have become clearer and better established over time thanks to the discovery of revealing documents, this event has become increasingly distorted.

Yet whilst this was off-putting from a research standpoint, it made me more interested in covering this topic. I knew it would be easy enough—albeit time-consuming—to clear up some basic mistakes. All I had to

Introduction

do was read more about the event than anyone else and avoid the trap of picking the most appealing versions, instead comparing the different accounts with each other and verifying them against the limited historical sources that could be found. I would need to track down every source cited by every author and find out what inferences and embellishments had been made in order to establish the basic facts and strip away the layers of myth. For one rather obvious example, I was able to confirm the date that the reading took place. Although it happened on October 7, about half of the books that mention it say that it was held on October 13. A look into the various archives of those present that night allowed me to find letters describing it dated *before* October 13 and referring to the previous Friday, which happened to be October 7, so that was an easy falsehood to dispel. Other parts of the story were harder. Much harder.

How, for example, can we determine what was read that night and in what order, without the existence of audiotapes? We simply cannot know for certain because no one was recording at the time. However, there are ways of figuring it out. Ginsberg and Kerouac wrote accounts in the next few years that gave the order of poets, and later Michael McClure, who was admittedly not a particularly reliable witness, wrote and spoke of this quite often and mentioned certain of the poems read. A letter written soon after the reading confirms the order of speakers, so we do not have to rely entirely on memories, and whilst it does not explicitly state what poems were read, it does contain some important clues. There are also contemporary documents that indicate what Snyder and Whalen might have read. Additionally, we can look to work done by Ann Charters in 1981, when she organized a reenactment of the 6 Gallery reading and attempted to find out exactly what poems were read and in what order. Her husband, Samuel Charters, wrote in his journal on November 6 of that year:

> Annie had written to McClure, Whalen, and Snyder, and they'd not only remembered the poems they'd read

twenty-five years earlier, they remembered something about each other's poems and the order they'd read in. The re-creation we performed had obviously come close to something still alive for the students and the people in the audience.

Again, this does not prove *beyond doubt* what was read but when all of these sources are combined and compared, it allows us to guess with a reasonable degree of certainty. I will speculate on what exactly was and was not read in Part 3 of this book, and my assessment of Allen Ginsberg's reading in particular will probably be of some surprise to those familiar with the story of the 6 Gallery reading.

In addition to establishing what happened that night, I wanted to find out the history of the building, for it was a very unusual place and its odd size and shape helped make the reading a success. Yet this was rather difficult and once again the challenge was compounded by dozens of writers merely repeating what others had said before them: it had been a car garage; it had been a stable for an old mansion; it had a dirt floor. Even finding the basic details of the building's history proved exhausting in part due to it having changed addresses several times and the occupants having used multiple variants of their address during their occupancy, but perhaps unsurprisingly a thorough investigation showed that most of what had previously been reported was untrue. (Just looking at photos of the 6 Gallery would have disproven the "dirt floor" idea that people have repeated so often, but again it is easier to simply take an interview answer as absolute truth and use it for a more colorful story.) Then we come to the tangled tale of organizing the reading... With so many conflicting accounts, each writer describing it before now has merely chosen the one that is most convenient to describe or which focuses on the writer who most interested them. All it takes is picking quotes that confirm one version of events and ignoring everything else. This book aims to avoid this sort of problem and for the first time provide an accurate account.

Introduction

With so many falsehoods and so much uncertainty, and with so few contemporary accounts even by those publicity-hungry young writers who constantly documented their own lives, I actually began to doubt whether the 6 Gallery reading really had been the event that it is so often portrayed as. Ginsberg had been the first to write about it in 1957, followed then by Kerouac, and then it had been resurrected when it was time to give the Beats academic legitimacy in the 1970s—a move again led by Ginsberg—so I started to wonder if it had been a sort of creation of his. After all, he devoted a lot of energy to chronicling the literary movement he had created, and it occurred to me that perhaps the 6 Gallery reading had been blown out of proportion, that maybe it made a nice, neat, exciting story and boosted their bohemian, outlaw credentials. Ginsberg was undeniably keen to place himself in what he saw as a literary lineage and he knew fine well the power of such narratives. The 6 Gallery reading would fit in with tales of the Columbia circle and his meetings with Burroughs and Kerouac, the murder of David Kammerer, Ginsberg meeting Carl Solomon in a mental hospital, Neal Cassady's Joan Anderson letter, the killing of Joan Vollmer, the marathon writing sessions that produced *On the Road*, the scattered manuscript of *Naked Lunch*, and various moments in the travels and travails of the nascent Beat Generation. All of these helped create a mythology that meant readers were not merely judging the Beats on the quality of their artistic output but viewing them as *literary figures*, their lives and art blurred together in exciting combinations emblematic of the era. I don't mean to suggest these events never happened, or that they were entirely exaggerated, but perhaps Ginsberg emphasized this, downplayed that, and pieced it all together in his own version of Beat history. The dozens of Beat biographies and books about the Beat Generation attest to the fact that, more than most writers, the Beats themselves were utterly fascinating characters.

However, I did not find anything that proved Ginsberg had elevated the 6 Gallery reading more than it should have been, and in fact the success of the 6 Gallery reading can be verified by other accounts. We have letters written just days later by Kenneth Rexroth and Jack Goodwin that confirm the rousing success of "Howl" (even if these lack the detail of Ginsberg's and Kerouac's accounts). *The Dharma Bums* depiction has been deemed reliable by those who were in attendance and even the people who hated or resented the Beat writers admitted that the event had been every bit the success Ginsberg claimed it had been. The final chapter of this book, titled "Myth and Legacy," goes into much detail about the veracity of Ginsberg's and Kerouac's accounts and discusses the extent to which they exaggerated the reading and shaped public perceptions of it. It is worth stating here, however, before you actually read this book, that both accounts are factually faithful even if Ginsberg's is preposterously exuberant.

Although this book will dispute many "facts" about the 6 Gallery reading, it will attest to its importance and affirm that it was a tremendous success that launched the poetic careers of four of the five participants and show that it was instrumental in making a success out of "Howl," thereby forming Ginsberg's reputation as a major poet. It will show that not only was the reading important for Ginsberg and the Beats, but it was a pivotal event in San Francisco's art history even if the city already had a vibrant arts scene—something people tend to forget or overlook. The San Francisco Renaissance did not emerge overnight but this reading occurred during the brief absence of the most influential local poets, resulting in a huge shift toward a more Beat-like literature.

In order to understand what happened at the 6 Gallery on October 7, 1955, we need to understand the context, and so this book will cover a lot of ground. The reading seems implausible without looking back to the beginnings of San Francisco and its emergence as a politically, culturally, sexually, and ethnically diverse city more conducive to radical artistic experimentation than any other in the nation. We need to understand the history of the building, too, to find out why the reading took place on a tiny stage at the back of a room measuring 100 by 20 feet and resembling a bowling alley combined with a horse stable. We need to see how these five poets—or six, including Rexroth the M.C.—met and befriended one another, forming a creative group that overlapped with many other artistic and social circles in the city, allowing for a mixing of ideas and also for the social networking required to spread word of this poetic revolution. We need to see how these people interacted and how they drew upon their esoteric interests to respond to the world of 1955 in such a way that their art resonated with the listeners in the audience and later a much wider public. Finally, to understand why its success proved so consequential, we need to see how the participants took advantage of the momentum generated by that night to launch one of the most vibrant artistic movements of the twentieth century.

Thus, this book will be divided into four parts. These concern 1) the history of the town, the building, and the gallery; 2) the arrival of Allen Ginsberg in San Francisco, his meeting the various participants, and the arranging of the reading; 3) an account of the reading itself; and 4) the aftermath, which shows how this small poetry reading rapidly spawned a nationwide literary movement. The last part includes a description of a follow-up reading from March 1956, often called a "repeat performance." This was fortunately recorded and thus we can use it to gain more insight into the poets' reading styles at that time and how they may have been received by a drunken audience of artists and hipsters. The narrative is largely chronological but occasionally there are small deviations in order to present certain parts of the story more coherently. For those who find these slight moves backward in time hard to follow, there is a detailed timeline included in the appendices.

Notes on the Text

As I have stated already, this is a story practically drowning in myth and uncertainty. Researching it took many years, yet even so there is much that cannot be said for certain. Most accounts of the 6 Gallery prior to this one were written with a degree of conviction belying the lack of research behind them. This resulted in very interesting,

A Remarkable Collection of Angels

readable accounts, but of course they were factually inaccurate. This book will be more honest and discursive. It will present the *likeliest* of facts, treating this historical inquiry as a matter of probability. It is impossible to say with 100% certainty whose idea the reading was, but by examining all the extant accounts and privileging those closest to the reading, which is to say the oldest ones, written before there was any effort to create a Beat mythology, we can come to the most probable of versions. This approach—which I believe is the only responsible one—is used throughout this book to avoid adding to the confusion surrounding the reading.

In the text, I will avoid speaking with the misleading certainty that too many before me have done, but I also want to present a readable narrative and I understand that spending two thousand words comparing two conflicting accounts of a relatively trivial matter may make this a dull book, so I will attempt to streamline such discussions. If the uncertainty is too great to ignore or if a particularly well-known myth needs to be dispelled, and this can be done so in a few short paragraphs, then I will do it in the text. Other issues may be dealt with in the footnotes if they are of some interest. I will also provide a short essay in the appendix that deals exclusively with falsehoods. This will contain what may seem like trivial discrepancies and I expect it will be of much interest to readers already well-versed in Beat history but perhaps less so to the general reader. There is one major issue that warranted a long discussion that is also given its own appendix and this concerns the San Francisco Arts Festival of September 1955.

I feel I also should point out here that although this book will drastically rewrite parts of Beat history and it will issue a great many corrections to previous accounts, nothing here is intended as an attack on any person in the world of Beat Studies. Where I have referred to earlier inaccuracies, I do so only for the sake of clarity, not to blame anyone for having made mistakes, and I hope these are not taken as a sign of disrespect. On the contrary, I owe a debt of gratitude to the Beat historians and biographers whose work has made my own possible. I have devoted

Introduction

many years to uncovering and piecing together the evidence required to write this book and those who have merely mentioned it in the context of a more general work did not have that luxury. I am also aware that the research for this book was conducted in an era of online databases and instant worldwide communication, so my job is easier than theirs. I have a great respect for the scholars who came before me even where I point out small errors in their work.

I should also explain the use of "6 Gallery" over "Six Gallery" in this book. The charm and success of the 6 Gallery came partly from the fact that it was run by poets and painters rather than businesspeople; however, this contributed to poor recordkeeping and that means certain details are not well established. Incredibly, this even extends to the name of the gallery. The vast majority of books that mention this place have called it "the Six Gallery," but the people who actually ran the gallery mostly used the numeral "6." This was used on the famous postcard to advertise the poetry reading that this book is about, on most other promotional materials, and it appeared above the entrance to the gallery, so I have elected for this form over the written version. During the editing phase of this book, I discovered a late interview with Deborah Remington, one of the gallery's founders, who made it very clear that it was meant to be "6" and not "Six." Unfortunately but understandably, writers have for decades used "Six" and so when I quote from these sources, I will use their precise wording; therefore, the reader of this book may encounter "the Six Gallery" or "Gallery Six" or "the Six" used in quotations whilst in the main narrative I have elected for "the 6 Gallery."

On that subject, the Beat writers and other bohemian artists of the era tended to talk and write in grammatically and lexically non-standard ways, so sometimes the quotations in this book may include what seem like errors. I have mostly kept these mistakes in order to preserve their words and to ensure accuracy rather than interpret their meanings. Enough mistakes have been made in Beat history due to such liberties being taken. Where words have been removed from quotations, I have used square brackets and ellipses: [...]. To replace a word or letter for the sake of grammar (something only done for coherence and intelligibility), I will also use square brackets.

In terms of referencing, this book contains nearly fifteen hundred citations as well as footnotes. Rather than mix footnotes and endnotes, I have chosen to cite everything at the back of the book by referencing a page number and then using a short quote. I trust that this will make the text more readable and avoid having extremely long and unsightly Roman numerals cluttering each line, particularly in later chapters. Having "MCCCXLVII" in the middle of a sentence is nothing more than an annoying distraction for the average reader. At the same time, it should be easy enough for scholars to track down my sources for each claim, should they wish to do so.

Finally, I should not have to explain this but most people get it wrong, so I feel the need to mention that "Howl" (in quotes) refers to the poem by Allen Ginsberg and *Howl* (in italics) refers to the book, whose full title is *Howl and Other Poems*. Whilst sometimes the word "Howl" could refer equally to either the poem or book, I have preserved this important distinction for the sake of clarity. However, in some quotes, people mistakenly use italics for the poem or quotes for the book. How frustrating! Even so, I will retain the original error because quotes should be faithful to the source.

Acknowledgements

For most of my previous books, the acknowledgements section has been limited because I had worked largely alone during the research and writing periods, using books and the internet to find the information I needed. However, this project was far more complex than those and required a great deal of help from many people around the world, provided over several years. I dread writing this because I know I will omit certain people who deserve to be thanked and I know that a few words of thanks are pitifully insufficient as a response to the immense help these people have provided.

Introduction

I will start with the librarians of various institutions across the U.S. and indeed some administrators who were able to help me with the unenviable task of sourcing archival documents, copying them, dealing with copyright and other legal issues, and then having them delivered to my house in rural Cambodia. Those people are truly saints. I have relied heavily on Tim Noakes at Stanford over the past years and I feel embarrassed every time I e-mail him: "It's me again... Sorry to bother you..." His patience is boundless. I must also thank Alison Fraser at the University of Buffalo. There were many more people who assisted me, often answering e-mails named only for the intuition at which they worked, and so I cannot thank them personally but I am immensely grateful to all of them.

Bill Morgan, who has written a tremendous amount about the Beat Generation, helped me to find a very important letter. For weeks prior to the e-mail he sent me, I felt this book was a failure, but that one letter resurrected the whole project. I am grateful for that and also for all the work he has done chronicling the Beats and arranging Allen Ginsberg's archives.

I would like to thank Ann Charters as well. In addition to her various books on the Beats, which I have cited many times, she was willing to answer my questions and provide suggestions. She also helped me catch a glaring error I had made and was eager to point out errors in her own earlier writings, stressing that I must correct these in this book for the sake of the historical record. Her encouragement particularly during a difficult period in was greatly appreciated.

David Simpson and his son helped me by answering my questions about the 6 Gallery and Kurt Hemmer, Matt Theado, and Stephen Duncan each helped me to source elusive documents that proved important for uncovering certain details related to the 6 Gallery reading.

Part One
Bohemian Spaces

A Countercultural Capital

Although defining the Beat Generation is notoriously difficult, there is little disagreement over the fact that it began on the East Coast, specifically around Columbia University in New York. It was here in late 1943 that the core Beat group first met, and over the coming few years they shaped their personalities, writing styles, and ideologies in the bars and cafés and dingy cold-water flats of Manhattan. Yet it was a decade later and on the other end of the continent—at the 6 Gallery in San Francisco—that they burst onto the literary scene. Ann Charters, one of the earliest and most influential Beat historians, called the 1955 reading the "moment that the 'Beat Generation' became part of the American Consciousness," and many other historians, biographers, and scholars have made similar remarks. Indeed, it is generally accepted that the 6 Gallery reading was the beginning of the Beats' rapid ascent to cultural relevance, but why was it that San Francisco allowed them to evolve from a group of talented friends into a literary movement that would change American art, culture, and even law?

At a cursory glance, it does seem rather strange that the poetry reading that publicly launched the Beat Generation took place on the opposite side of the country from where Jack Kerouac, Allen Ginsberg, and William S. Burroughs had met a little over a decade before. San Francisco was 2,500 miles from Columbia University and the New York City Beat haunts that played host to the youthful adventures of these young men. Moreover, it was considered somewhat of a cultural backwater. Lawrence Ferlinghetti, who would become one of the city's most important literary figures— and in 1998 its first Poet Laureate—said that when he arrived in 1951 "San Francisco was a very provincial place," a common refrain

1

among those who recall the city in the forties and early fifties. Compare this to New York, which was undoubtedly the center of publishing in the United States—the best place to find an agent, a mentor, a publisher, or organize a public reading—and it seems baffling that it was not on the East Coast that the Beats had their breakthrough.

In 1972, essayist Yves Le Pellec asked Allen Ginsberg why it was San Francisco where he began to find success and the poet replied that "there was a rigidity in the N.Y. literary world" that made writers, editors, and publishers there reluctant to consider new ideas. This contrasted, he said, with the much more open, experimental, and antiauthoritarian attitudes prevalent in San Francisco. He continued:

> For instance I took my poetry and Burroughs' *Junkie* and Jack's *On the Road* and other manuscripts around all over New York and nobody would publish them. I went to the big publishers, some of whom were friends of mine from Columbia by then, some of whom were even poets, and they rejected our books saying "The prose is bad" [...] So I took all the manuscripts to San Francisco and began circulating them there and found a much warmer reception. [Kenneth] Rexroth and [Robert] Duncan saw them and immediately understood them as being, you know, good writing, classic. [...] So that's why. San Francisco was not involved with the coldest aspects of American frozen consciousness.

He went on to explain that "from 1950 to 1960 the town that was most perceptive was San Francisco," by which he meant that poets and publishers were interested in new forms and subjects, and he referred to the culture of mimeographed publications that existed there, which would have been nearly impossible "in the more money-success-*Time*-magazine-oriented New York scene."

Ginsberg's answer is similar to comments made

A Countercultural Capital

by countless other writers and artists who called San Francisco home in the middle decades of the twentieth century. Jack Kerouac said it was "the last great city in America" and Philip Whalen concurred, saying, "As far as I was concerned, it was absolutely the greatest possible place to be at," citing the museums and libraries, as well as culturally rich Chinatown and the proximity to the ocean. One can argue over the timelines of the San Francisco Renaissance or the hippie era, or the definitions of the various literary and artistic movements of the time, but undoubtedly San Francisco was an unusually open and tolerant city, one at odds with the dominant post-war culture of conformity and materialism, where people were increasingly judged by the consumer appliances they could afford. It was a place where artists, bohemians, and even political radicals were more or less free to pursue their own interests and engage in dialog and collaboration, making it the perfect city for the Beat writers and their alternative lifestyles and groundbreaking art. Ferlinghetti, despite having called San Francisco "provincial," said that "this city has always been a poetic center, a frontier for free poetic life, with perhaps more poets and more poetry readers than any city in the world."

Looking back from the vantage point of the twenty-first century, we tend to associate San Francisco with a number of vital countercultural movements. It was a liberal enclave whose permissiveness allowed the Beats and beatniks, then the hippies, to emerge and to spread their messages across the land. It was not only at the far edge of the continent from New York, but the very opposite end of the cultural spectrum, too. If New York was the center of the dominant culture in the United States, San Francisco was the capital of the counterculture. It spawned poets and painters and rock bands that changed the world. It became famed for its tolerance, offering a diverse and progressive society, a bastion of open-mindedness in a conservative nation where racism, homophobia, and sexism ran rampant. Creativity and freedom became prized and the city became known as the home of jazz poetry, bongo-beating beatniks, free love, flower power, and City Lights Bookstore. It allowed an alternative press, too, in the form of *Rolling Stone*, *Ramparts*, the *San Francisco Oracle*, and others. Writers like Richard Brautigan, Ken Kesey, and Ron Loewinsohn moved to the Bay Area. Musicians such as Jerry Garcia, Grace Slick, and Janis Joplin found audiences there. Thinkers like Alan Watts made it their home, too.

Perhaps inevitably, the genuinely creative and talented were followed by the poseurs, followers, and scene-seekers—the ones who wore berets in the fifties and tie-dye in the sixties, but who made little to no contribution to those eras' artistic output. San Francisco became a victim of its own success, overwhelmed by young seekers in search of excitement. Local permissiveness was tested by free love, anti-war protests, LSD, and many more elements of countercultural lifestyles that offended mainstream sensibilities, but for a period of nearly two decades in the middle of the last century, the City by the Bay was undoubtedly the place to be for artists. Even after the counterculture was largely subverted and commercialized, there was an undeniable creative current in the city that continued to attract the genuinely artistic as well as the hangers-on. Of course, with the benefit of hindsight, there is often a feeling of inevitability, and perhaps it was true here, for in San Francisco the seeds that would grow a counterculture seem to have been there for a century prior to its blooming.

San Francisco became a part of the United States after the Mexican-American War of 1846–48, when the village of Yerba Buena, on the east side of what is now the San Francisco peninsula, was captured by the American Army. Although the peninsula had been colonized by the Spanish in 1776, the tiny settlement that would become San Francisco was settled by an English trader in 1835. He realized the potential of the sheltered bay and a commercial operation there. War broke out between the United States and Mexico in May and on July 9, 1846, the U.S.S. Portsmouth sailed into the San Francisco Bay and a small band of men rowed ashore and took control of the town without bloodshed. On January 30, 1847, the mayor of the town officially renamed it San Francisco and the following year California was ceded to the United States as part of the Treaty of Guadalupe Hidalgo.

Even before it officially became a part of the United States, Yerba Buena was under American control for almost two years and during this time it expanded at a rapid pace. Thanks to the natural harbor there, the military made it their new base in the region and a community grew around it, with a customs house and a quartermaster's store. Soon after, Mormons arrived en route to Salt Lake City, but several hundred stayed in San Francisco, which immediately doubled the population. This was nothing compared with the growth that followed, as the Gold Rush of 1849 brought vast numbers of people to the West Coast. Various estimates put the population in 1856 at around 50,000, meaning that in a period of just ten years it had grown one thousandfold. According to *San Francisco, 1846-1856: From Hamlet to City*, which drew upon census data and other sources, the population increase was as follows:

* 1844 – 50
* 1846 – between 200 and 300
* 1847 – 459
* 1852 – 34,000
* 1856 – 50,000 (estimated)
* 1860 – 56,000

During the second half of the century, San Francisco continued to grow, its population reaching 300,000 by 1890, making it the eighth largest city in the country.

Still, a booming little town was hardly unusual in this era, so what was it that set San Francisco apart from the rest of the country? What helped shape a culture conducive to free thought and artistic expression? For an art scene to flourish, there has to be a degree of openness to new ideas, and perhaps San Francisco was relatively open due to its being more ethnically, culturally, and politically diverse than most American cities of that time. Its location and history ensured that it was populated by people from across the world and with a wider array of backgrounds and perspectives than other cities, especially ones on the East Coast, which was far more influenced by Europe and particularly Great Britain.

In 1847, about half of the people in San Francisco were immigrants and despite the massive population change over the next thirteen years, this figure was roughly unchanged. In 1860, only two cities had higher proportions of their population born abroad than San Francisco, making it more diverse even than New York. What had changed was the ethnic makeup of the region, with huge numbers of Asian and black people arriving as the Native American and Hawaiian populations declined. The white population was a mix of Europeans and people from the various American states, as well as huge numbers from across the British Empire, resulting in a tremendous diversity of cultures almost right at the start of the city's history. As such, no one culture would dominate and San Francisco would evolve its own identity through a complex interplay of cultural influences.[1]

The fact that San Francisco was a Pacific Coast port city made it especially attractive to large numbers of Asian immigrants. Many of these people were Chinese, particularly from the south of the country. Like the white immigrants from Europe and the east of the United States, most of these Chinese people came in search of work, particularly in the gold mines and on the transcontinental railroad. By 1851, there were already 12,000 Chinese in San Francisco (fewer than ten of whom were women), and this number rose massively in the next decades. In 1860, for example, there were 35,000 Chinese in California, making up a tenth of the population. After the railroad was completed in 1869, many Chinese chose to settle in San Francisco's Chinatown, which provided a sense of community and some degree of protection against racism. Indeed, Chinese laborers, who had largely been welcomed upon their initial arrival in the city, were soon resented by white laborers. Anti-immigrant sentiment contributed to

---

1   It should be pointed out that in 1847 the city was almost half Mormon due to the small population combined with the arrival of one ship of Mormon immigrants. However, this was not followed up and they soon became a tiny minority within the city.

the 1882 Chinese Exclusion Act, which was renewed in 1892 and 1902.

Kenneth Rexroth, the city's best-known poet in the middle of the twentieth century, who claimed to speak a number of Asian languages and was reasonably well-versed in Asian literature,[2] spoke often of the influence of Eastern thought on San Franciscan culture. He called Buddhism "indigenous" to the city as it had been spread by Asian immigrants rather than Westerners. "The influence of Japanese and Chinese culture is direct," he wrote. "After all, the Pacific Ocean is just water [but a] thickly populated land mass is a barrier."

Although the logic in that statement is suspect, he was more or less correct. San Francisco was the main port of entry for Asian immigrants to the United States, and since the Chinese were quick to establish a huge Chinatown, it went on to become home to a large Asian population. In spite of various periods of racism, this population would have a substantial influence on the culture of the region and particularly on the views of artistically minded white people, who prior to the advent of cheap and easy international travel would sate their curiosity for foreign cultures by visiting "exotic" places such as this.

In addition to the large Chinatown in the north of the city, there were several Japantowns, including one in the Fillmore District, a few miles south of where our story takes place.[3] Japanese immigration to San Francisco began a little later than Chinese immigration, with the first immigrants known to have arrived in 1869. The following year, Japan opened its first consulate in the country,

---

2   Evidence suggests that Rexroth grossly overestimated his own language skills and indeed he had a reputation as a "bullshitter" who was good at pretending to know about esoteric subjects. However, he did read and speak at least some Chinese and Japanese.

3   For those unfamiliar with the layout of San Francisco, Fillmore *Street* runs through a huge chunk of the city but only a small portion of it is called Fillmore *District*, and of course that district includes various streets other than Fillmore Street. The 6 Gallery was located near Fillmore and Union, which is fourteen blocks north of the upper limits of Fillmore District.

choosing San Francisco as the location. Immigration was initially minimal due to the Meiji government's comparatively strict laws concerning emigration but these were repealed in the 1880s. By 1890, there were about 500 Japanese people in San Francisco, a figure that had increased almost tenfold by 1910. By then, there were 72,000 Japanese in the United States and more than half of them resided in California, with San Francisco having the largest population of any city. To begin with, most Japanese settled on the outskirts of Chinatown and several very small Japantowns were established, but following the 1906 earthquake, which levelled Chinatown and the smaller Japantowns, most Japanese in the city migrated to the Western Addition, which is the location of the Japantown that still exists today.

Japanese influence in the city grew with its population. At the turn of the century, there were 90 Japanese-owned businesses in San Francisco and this had grown to 545 by 1909, with a substantial number of them in the Fillmore District. Naturally, a number of institutions arose to support the growing population, with Japanese organizations of all sorts being founded. One historian noted that "[b]y 1898, San Francisco was headquarters for Buddhist churches and social organizations located throughout the West, including prefectural associations, or *kenjin-kai*, benevolent associations, and newspapers." Japanese monk Nyogen Senzaki founded a "floating zendo" in Japantown in the mid-twenties, which the Fillmore Museum claims was "the first regular instruction in Zen offered to western students." Before that were several Buddhist "churches" and in 1894, for the California Midwinter International Exposition, a tea garden was built. It was the first Japanese public garden in the United States. These sorts of attractions drew curious white Americans and in particular artists and intellectuals who wanted to learn from another culture. One newspaper account from 1902, however, warned that visitors may be disappointed that Japanese people dressed in "European costume," unlike the Chinese of Chinatown, who wore "national dress of gorgeous colors." The article was progressive for its day, yet disturbing by later standards, simultaneously celebrating the city's diversity whilst treating its Asian

A Countercultural Capital

inhabitants rather like animals in a zoo.

The Fillmore Japantown grew through the early part of the century to become the second biggest population of ethnically Japanese people outside Japan. However, after the Pearl Harbor attack in December 1941, Executive Order 9066 was signed, requiring the internment of many persons of Japanese birth or descent for the duration of the war. The Fillmore Japantown, which was by now the main one in San Francisco, became a ghost town. These empty homes and businesses were soon filled by large numbers of African Americans migrating from the Deep South. Between 1940 and 1950, the number of black people in San Francisco increased almost tenfold, with the majority living in the Fillmore District and on Fillmore Street, which ran north from there to the top of the peninsula. Although many Japanese residents would return after the war, and many other Japanese would move into the area, the Fillmore District became a largely black part of the city.[4] By 1949, there were only about 100 Japanese-owned businesses, compared to the 400 that were found there prior to the war.

With the increasing black population came yet another culture that would shape the city. Once again, racism was rife but some white people found black culture inspiring, particularly the proliferation of musical forms such as jazz, blues, and bebop. In 1949, the Nippon Drugs building, a decades-old Japanese-owned business, became Vout City, a club operated by the charismatic jazz musician Slim Gaillard. His wild performances were legendary and were famously celebrated by Jack Kerouac in *On the Road*. The two-mile-long Fillmore Street and many of its side streets were now home to dozens of black-owned businesses, including many bars and nightclubs, which in the late forties and early fifties hosted some of the finest musicians of the era. Soon, this section of San Francisco was one of the country's major jazz hubs, known as "the

---

4   Many Japanese chose not to return and moved instead to other parts of the country. The U.S. census of 1950 showed an almost 7% decrease in the Japanese population of the West Coast. However, California still had a Japanese population about eight times higher than the next most populous state, Illinois.

Harlem of the West." Visiting musicians included Charlie Parker, John Coltrane, Miles Davis, Dizzy Gillespie, Billie Holiday, and Dexter Gordon. Kerouac said he "never saw such crazy musicians. Everybody in Frisco blew. It was the end of the continent; they didn't give a damn." The area remained a focal point of jazz music for about a decade and a half until racially motivated urban renewal projects saw it dismembered.

By the early fifties, then, San Francisco was an ethnically and culturally diverse society where Asian religions and philosophies, as well as black music, could easily be found. In a nation whose population was 89.5% Caucasian, it offered an alternative to mainstream white American culture. There was undoubtedly a tendency for ethnic groups to cluster in certain enclaves, and in many cases a justified reluctance to mix with other groups, but nonetheless it was a city where people coexisted in a comparatively peaceful state and where multicultural friendships, businesses, and artistic collaborations could and did take place. Demographic changes—even those that brought about collective trauma—happened so regularly that the city never developed a fixed identity and instead was always a place with a changing culture. To the sort of people who shaped the mid-twentieth-century art scene, this atmosphere was liberating and so writers and painters began to flock to the city in the forties and fifties, keen to learn about Buddhism, Asian painting, haiku, and jazz.

San Francisco was not only a culturally diverse city; it was politically diverse, too. This seems to have been true from the very beginning for as one historian put it: "Between the years 1846-56, San Francisco was a noncooperative community [in which m]any refused to be taxed, to obey the laws, to fix the streets, to serve on juries, to participate in politics and government or even to vote." Already, San Francisco was bursting with anti-authoritarian sentiment. Although the city became better governed and its citizens developed some sense of civic duty, in the century after its incorporation into the United States, San Francisco developed a reputation for tolerance toward radical and unpopular political positions. Socialists, communists, and anarchists were comparatively common and they were free to assemble and even—to some extent—agitate. Rexroth attributed this to the city's unique history, claiming that

> San Francisco is the only major city in America except New Orleans not colonized by the overland spread of the Puritan ethos. It was settled by the rascally and anarchistic types attracted to any gold rush, by North Italians who became one of the elite groups of the city, and by a small number of Jewish families mostly from northern Bavaria [...] Until the city was caught up in the population explosion, the racial conflicts and the crooked politics of the 1960's, it was one of the last homes of *la vie midterranée*, of persona *laissez faire* and *dolce far niente*, certainly a more Mediterranean city than post-War Two Barcelona, Marseilles, or Genoa.

Ferlinghetti agreed with Rexroth's assessment, saying the city "had been founded, not by bourgeoisie, but by prospectors, sailors, railroad workers, gold diggers, ladies of good fortune, roustabouts and carney hustlers." Arriving by train in January 1951, he found himself in "a burning bed of anarchism, pacifism, and a wide open, non-academic poetry scene, provincial but liberating." He claimed San Francisco had an "island mentality" because it was largely detached from the rest of the North American continent and Rexroth said the same thing, writing that San Francisco's culture was not a regional one like the Midwest, but rather "[i]t was more like the culture of a different country whose inhabitants happened to speak American." Allen Ginsberg, meanwhile, claimed that poets were attracted by "the long honorable San Francisco tradition of Bohemian-Buddhist-Wobbly-mystical-anarchist social involvement and a local literary consciousness in terms of Western woodsmanship and a kind of competent communal outdoor life." These are opinions echoed by countless writers and artists of the era, including Gary Snyder, who—admittedly expanding the region from just San Francsico—said that "the West has this enormous tolerance for deviants" that one does not find on the East Coast or in the South. He went on: "People can be pretty conservative in some cases, but they're usually tolerant of everybody else, too."

During World War II, Rexroth was registered as a conscientious objector and spent the war working in what he called "concentration camps," attempting to help the interned Japanese whom he believed were victims of a monstrously racist policy. Conscientious objectors were given various non-military roles throughout the war as a means of fulfilling some kind of national service and the West Coast had a number of camps for them that were often attached to the U.S. Forest Service or National Parks Service. Rexroth claimed that these men would frequently visit San Francisco when on leave and that "a majority of these people settled in the San Francisco Bay Area" after the war. In his view, they had an outsized influence on music, painting, sculpting, and theater. He was likely exaggerating when he said that "a majority of" them came, but certainly many of them did, including his good friends, the poets William Everson (later Brother Antoninus) and Kenneth Patchen.[5] Although they were sent to a camp in Oregon, both settled in San Francisco after the war and were influential in the city's burgeoning literary scene, contributing to the development of an anarcho-pacifist ethos. Jack Goodwin seemed to agree with Rexroth, claiming that "most of the local poets [were] paranoid anarchists, rendered the more so by Conscientious Objector camps and Senator McCarthy."

---

5   Patchen was, alongside Rexroth, one of the best-known poets in the city during the late forties and fifties. However, although many sources suggest he was an influence on the Beat poets, there is no real evidence for this and much to the contrary. Ginsberg is on record as stating "Patchen [...] had NO influence on 1) Kerouac 2) Corso 3) Burroughs 4) Myself much less Snyder Whalen McClure." Patchen also had no interest in them and so his world rarely intersected with the younger, more avant-garde poets and artists. He will be mentioned a few times in this book but perhaps surprisingly little given his stature.

A Countercultural Capital

Quite a few of these artists were homosexual, too, and again this is no coincidence. Although homosexual intercourse was illegal throughout the United States until 1962, when it was decriminalized in Illinois, San Francisco again had a comparatively permissive attitude and was home to a large number of gay people. This arguably stems from the Gold Rush, when up to 95% of the city's population was male, and among the aforementioned Chinese and Japanese communities this sort of disparity continued much longer, with around twenty times as many males as females at the turn of the century. Reliable evidence about homosexual relations in the nineteenth century is admittedly lacking, but given how common it was in similar environments, most people who write about LGBT history in the American West tend to speculate that it was prevalent here as well. Alfred Kinsey, for example, wrote:

> There is a fair amount of sexual contact among the older males in Western rural areas. It is a type of homosexuality which was probably common among pioneers and outdoor men in general. Today it is found among ranchmen, cattle men, prospectors, lumbermen, and farming groups in general—among groups that are virile, physically active. These are men who have faced the rigors of nature in the wild. They live on realities and on a minimum of theory. Such a background breeds the attitude that sex is sex, irrespective of the nature of the partner with whom the relation is had. Sexual relations are had with women when they are available, or with other men when the outdoor routines bring men together in exclusively male groups.

Certainly, there were all-male dances called "stag waltzes" and much cross-dressing around this time. Whilst the motivations here were not necessarily related to sexuality, it shows a willingness among the male population to eschew certain norms regarding gender. It was illegal for men to dress as women and so arrests were made, with the defendants usually claiming they had worn women's clothes as a joke. Likewise, in cases of homosexual intercourse people were sometimes charged but these were not so easily documented due to ironically conservative attitudes that meant the authorities and media were reluctant even to mention the crimes they were willing to punish. Still, San Francisco seems to have been more permissive in such matters than other parts of the nation and crackdowns against gay and cross-dressing communities tended to come intermittently, likely as the result of periodic moral panics.

Between these crackdowns, San Francisco's now-famous gay scene began to develop. At first, gay-friendly businesses opened in waves and were temporary fixtures, such as Dash, which was established in 1908 and closed soon after. It featured men dressing as women, supposedly with waiting staff performing public sex acts. It was partly owned by a judge, who attempted to interfere in a police investigation, but nonetheless the bar closed the same year that it opened. After its closure, one newspaper called it "one of the vilest saloons and dancehalls ever maintained in San Francisco." Eventually, more prominent and long-lasting establishments would open, such as Finocchio's Club in North Beach, which presented itself as a drag club and attracted an ethnically diverse audience that included both gay and straight people but was primarily considered a gay bar. The Sailor Boy Tavern opened in 1938 and is described in numerous publications as being "rough," perhaps due to it being one of the first leather bars or maybe due to the large number of off-duty military men who frequented it. Jack's Turkish Baths and Third Street Baths provided spaces for gay men to meet in a more overtly sexual context.

There were lesbian establishments, too, and these tended to draw a more diverse crowd as perhaps they seemed more appealing to the heterosexual community. Mona's 440 Club was allegedly the first, founded in 1936, and in the late forties 12 Adler Place opened, becoming a double bar operating together with Tommy's Place.[6] These venues featured women dressing in men's clothes, with Mona's advertising itself as a place "where girls can be boys" and 12 Adler Place featuring female-to-male cross-dressing acts and female staff in tuxedos. This brought scrutiny in 1954 during the homophobic crackdown known as the Lavender Panic and 12 Adler Place was shut down after a long police investigation that turned into a media frenzy. It has been called "[o]ne of the most publicized police raids in San Francisco history."

The city's gay scene developed rapidly in the middle of the century. According to the book *Gay by the Bay*, "World War II was a transformative event in the history of modern queer communities and identities" around the world, but perhaps more so for San Francisco than other places. Noting the practice of dishonorably discharging gay servicemen, it explains:

> As one of the primary departure points for troops headed to the Pacific theater, San Francisco's wartime population swelled with government-certified homosexuals—many of whom were none too anxious to return to their hometowns and only too eager to remain in the Bay Area.

As the gay population grew, so too did the number of bars and restaurants serving them, which in turn drew more queer people to the region, and an attitude of relative tolerance emerged. By the late forties, there were many gay writers and artists living and working in the city, and by the mid-fifties their ranks had swelled to include Robert Duncan, Jack Spicer, James Broughton, Allen

---

6   These were technically separate businesses but they shared a building and had multiple connection points so that patrons of one could freely move through to the other. One had a liquor license and the other did not, so that partly explains the connection. 12 Adler Place tended to be more popular among the non-lesbian patrons. In fact, Jack Goodwin, who spoke of 12 Adler Place as "the main neighborhood bar" in North Beach, was never even aware that it was a lesbian bar.

Ginsberg, John Wieners, Stan Persky, George Stanley, and Robin Blaser. Painter Deborah Remington said of the mid-fifties scene:

> Remember that you had a lot of gay men here. A great preponderance of the men, of the poets anyway, not all of them, were gay. It wasn't something that was discussed or talked about too much. It was just accepted. No one came out and said, "Are you straight or gay?" You just did what you did. [...] Everyone had a mate, whether you were married or not. There were plenty of boyfriends-and-girlfriends and lots of boyfriends-and-boyfriends. And that was—I mean it sounds strange today because everyone is so involved with gender identification—but it just was not an issue. In those days, it just wasn't. This was a community that if you excelled at what you did, you were accepted.

In addition to the comparatively progressive attitudes of San Franciscan artists regarding race, politics, and sexuality, this was a world relatively open to women as well. "There was none of that macho bullshit," recalled painter Sonia Gechtoff. "When I came to New York I was horrified at how the female artists were being disregarded." Remington agreed, saying, "If they respected you, you were one of them and they treated you like an equal," and noted that she "was winning prizes at the museums and so was Sonia." She added that "if you were serious about your work, if you were able to make good paintings in their eyes, let's say, you were treated absolutely on an equal basis. [...] I never felt discriminated against because I was a woman." Indeed, although female poets would often find it harder than their male peers to have their work published, the growing number of small art galleries in San Francisco were markedly less sexist, and out of this environment came the likes of Gechtoff, Remington, Joan Brown, and Jay DeFeo. In fact, Remington reflected toward the end of her life that female painters and even poets in San Francisco "were all held up as goddesses" by the male artists of the city.

Particularly among the artistic communities of the city, there was a move away from Western rationalism and an embrace of non-Western concepts. As well as the aforementioned Asian philosophies brought to San Francisco by diaspora communities, there were elements of the indigenous cultures of the region, with various West Coast writers fascinated by Native American life and lore. Above all, the Beats and other bohemian artists on the West Coast felt that neither European nor East Coast thought and form should be taken as their model. In their personal lives, as well as in their art, San Francisco's bohemians began exploring the occult, astrology, and mysticism, all of which were generally scoffed at by the writers, publishers, and editors of the East Coast establishment. There was sometimes a dilettantism to these areas of inquiry and many white writers have been criticized for picking and choosing convenient elements of other cultures, but their enthusiasm was often authentic and the influence of their esoteric interests was not insignificant.

The atmosphere of open-mindedness and tolerance toward different lifestyles, beliefs, and behaviors meant that artists and writers tended to feel more comfortable in San Francisco than in other parts of the country, where they were frequently ostracized for failing to conform to societal expectations. In San Francisco, Rexroth wrote,

> nobody cared what you did as long as you didn't commit any gross public crimes. They let you alone and however much you might have puzzled them they respected you as an artist. At no time in all the years I have lived in San Francisco have I ever met with anything but respect verging on adulation from neighbors, corner grocers, and landladies. They were proud to be associated with an artist or poet. With Greenwich Village landladies or Left Bank concierges, this is simply not true at all.

Gary Snyder, who came to San Francisco in the early fifties and looked to Rexroth as a mentor, said that the place possessed a quality that brought out the best in artists. "[T]here was something about the city," he said, "that encouraged poets and novelists to draw creative work from their innermost depths." Poet Weldon Kees, who lived in San Francisco from 1950 until his death in the middle of 1955, said, "Perhaps no other area [...] is so densely populated with architects, designers, ceramicists, interior decorators, landscape gardeners, and entrepreneurs of modern furniture."

Kees attributed this to San Francisco having "the most equable climate in the entire country" but as we have seen, there were myriad factors, not the least of which was the fact that San Francisco—as hard as it is to believe now—was an astonishingly cheap place to live in the middle of the last century. Rents were affordable, there were good restaurants that even indigent artists could afford, and one could easily procure a gallon of red wine for next to nothing. All of this was conducive to the artist's way of life and made San Francisco reminiscent of Paris in the twenties. In fact, that is a comparison many have made, including Lawrence Ferlinghetti, who had lived in Paris prior to moving to San Francisco. "I used to make up all these literary reasons why I came out here," he said, "but I realize that it was really because it sounded like a European place."

From the mid-forties on, San Francisco and the wider Bay Area became a hub of creative activity as people moved there for the various reasons discussed in this chapter. It is true that there had been a creative scene prior to this (Jack London, Ambrose Bierce, Bret Harte, Mark Twain, and Gertrude Stein had all lived in the area at one point or another), but it was during and after World War II that it truly became a center of the arts. In 1944, *Circle* magazine was established by George Leite at Daliel's Bookstore and Gallery in Berkeley, publishing the work of local writers such as Henry Miller, Philip Lamantia, and Bern Porter, the latter of whom was the magazine's initial publisher. The first two issues were mimeographed and after that they raised the necessary funds to print a more professional-looking magazine. According to Lamantia, Leite founded *Circle* "mainly to print Miller," who was respected but nonetheless struggled to get his work in print. In the coming years, it would include poems by Rexroth and Everson, as well as William Carlos Williams,[7] Anaïs Nin, Weldon Kees, Robert Duncan, and Kenneth Patchen. It ran for ten issues between 1944 and 1948. It "was the first distinguished literary magazine since the turn of the century in San Francisco," Lamantia said. *The Ark* was another "little magazine," as these hand-printed publications came to be known, which existed for a single issue in 1947. Its contributors included many of the same names that had appeared in *Circle*.

The loose artistic community that formed was markedly different from those found on the East Coast and particularly New York. While some felt that the distance from major publishers and prestigious art galleries signaled a lack of opportunity, it was partly this that allowed more experimentation and helped elevate San Francisco into the role of a true rival. Many artists and writers working in San Francisco in the late forties and early fifties commented upon the lack of expectation of commercial, critical, or popular success as the reason for their development of original forms. Remington said, "I think it was different in San Francisco because there were no commercially viable galleries.... It gave us permission to be more experimental." With no reasonable expectation of being published or having their paintings hung in a gallery, these men and women did not have to adhere to popular trends and could instead pursue their own interests. They could explore wild new concepts without fear of failure. They were able to create with astonishing freedom and this resulted in the plethora of overlapping movements of that time. Lawrence Ferlinghetti even attributed this to his success with City Lights Bookstore:

> I came here because New York was all sewed up, because there was no hope in

---

7   Williams was based in New Jersey but exerted a tremendous influence over many of the most important San Francisco-based poets.

New York of a young guy getting anything that was interesting. It was too hard to live there and make it. I would never have dared to open a book store in New York because it would have had to be too commercial and the only way to make it in New York is to be commercial on one level or another. There was no room for anything new. Things are still open out here. It's still the last frontier.

Rexroth agreed, saying that "[n]ot only did local poets develop quite independently of the infighting of New York literary cocktail parties, but writers came to Northern California from other parts of the country to escape the factional, ultimately commercial, pressures of the East."

These "pressures of the East" included the expectation to conform to popular modes of expression and express accepted political or artistic views. This was an era of rather oppressive conformity and pushing against social and artistic norms could be dangerous. Dashiell Hammett's left-wing views earned him a stint in prison and caused his books to go out of print, so that he died poor and largely forgotten. Those who wrote on controversial topics or used what was considered offensive language were frequently censored, limiting their ability to express themselves. Norman Mailer famously avoided censorship by using "fug" where "fuck" had been intended in *The Naked and the Dead* but other writers were less willing to make changes, with some of Henry Miller's novels banned across the United States. So much has been made of the conformity of the era, particularly in books about the Beat Generation, that it has become rather a cliché even to mention it, but it is impossible to deny that it was a staid time in American history, when stability and conformity were prized and dissent could be truly dangerous. Many were willing to go along with this because standards of living were improving rapidly and America was becoming the pre-eminent power in a new world order, the old powers of Europe rent by the war, their empires crumbling at an astonishing speed, but others, and particularly young, left-wing, artistic types, were dissatisfied with a materialistic culture that afforded little spiritual nourishment and few opportunities for honest expression. Michael McClure called it "a bitter, gray" world and connected it with America's role as the new superpower, armed with world-ending bombs and a willingness to meddle—even at the expense of untold numbers of lives—in all sorts of geopolitical matters:

> The country had the feeling of martial law. An undeclared military state had leapt out of Daddy Warbucks' tanks and sprawled over the landscape. As artists we were oppressed and indeed the people of the nation were oppressed. [...] We saw that the art of poetry was essentially dead—killed by war, by academies, by neglect, by lack of love, and by disinterest.

He did not truly believe that poetry was dead. It was merely that the old forms were no longer useful and that a new poetry was needed to contend with the new world. Almost from the moment he arrived in San Francisco, he saw that this was a place inhabited by people like him—creative and brave and willing to stand up against all that they perceived as wrong. But they were not out to change the whole world; they had simply found a space where they were free to create as they pleased, and they did so on a small scale.

In San Francisco, poems and manifestos were typically hand-printed, read aloud, or pasted on the walls of bars and cafés, which meant that they could more easily evade censorship as they were too difficult to police. Their reach was limited but they were not subject to the same constraints as those faced by writers at big publishing companies, allowing their creators yet more freedom to express themselves. This freedom to express challenging ideas, and without the temptation to appeal to major gallery curators or publishers, resulted in a move away from traditional aesthetics and toward conceptual art. Artists like Wally Hedrick and Jess[8] began using found objects in welded sculptures or collages, with Hedrick's artworks expressing strong political views, while poets began to tear up conventional ideas regarding the form and content of their work. Hedrick went as far as to say, "I'm a politician. I'm trying to make these paintings do what politicians should be doing." According to Beat historian Bruce Cook, poetry at this point was supposed to be

> [c]rabbed, pinched, elliptical, and oblique things, often rhymed and metered and in exotic forms such as the ballade or the sestina. It was academic poetry, not merely in fact, for it was written almost without exception by [professors]. It was the kind that was written for other [professors] not merely to be read, but to be deciphered. "Difficulty," preferably of the learned, pedantic kind, was quite generally considered a most desirable virtue among academic poets.

In San Francisco, however, this style of writing was not viewed favorably. What the city offered, Rexroth said, was a "total rejection of the official high-brow culture" through the creation of its own alternative artist society with more of an emphasis on individual expression and original, experimental creation free from the rigidity of East Coast traditions.

Rexroth claimed that San Francisco "was jumping from the end of the war to 1955" but others, such as Professor Thomas Parkinson,[9] an early supporter of

---

8   Jess was born Burgess Franklin Collins, but used "Jess" as a mononym, and this book will refer to him as such from here on.
9   Parkinson had been associated with the Berkeley Renaissance in the 1940s and had poems published in *Circle* and *The Ark*. He later helped Ginsberg have his poetry read on BBC radio and put together the first academic study of the Beat Generation in 1961. That same year, he survived an assassination attempt by a former student looking to kill liberal professors.

the Beat writers, have suggested that there was a period of stagnation between approximately 1950 and 1953. Certainly, one can look at the innovations in the various art forms and see that there was a surge in creative output during this period, with a slight reduction in the years Parkinson highlighted. Perhaps this was due in part to Douglas MacAgy, who served as director of the California School of Fine Arts[10] from 1945 to 1950.

 C.S.F.A. had struggled coming out of the Great Depression and in 1942 it lost its director after the institution was unable to pay his salary. In 1944, the board seriously considered closing the school and selling off its real estate, but then MacAgy, who at just thirty-two years old was the curator of the San Francisco Museum of Art, appeared and convinced them to hire him, with his tenure beginning on July 1, 1945. It was the beginning of an immensely important era and one that would have a lasting influence.

 MacAgy was a stubborn but visionary man who passionately supported artists, and at C.S.F.A. he sought to assemble "a faculty [...] which would emphasize vision over craft, and spirit over method," according to his biographer, David Beasley.[11] In the words of Richard Cándida Smith, author of *Utopia and Dissent: Art, Poetry, and Politics in California*, "MacAgy was convinced that only by making the school the center for the most advanced thinking in the visual arts would it be able to survive," and he not only succeeded in helping the school survive but in creating a vibrant arts scene that allowed the development of numerous talented individuals who would have outsized influences on American culture. MacAgy was

---

10 This was renamed the San Francisco Art Institute in 1961. It closed in 2022.

11 The fact that MacAgy, who was an art school director and then later a museum curator, has a biographer at all is testament to his incredible vision. On the first page of his biography, this is noted: "A biography of an art curator is unusual, but then Douglas MacAgy was an unusual man. [...] He was not only an innovator in ways of bringing art to the public but a catalyst for artists during that extraordinarily creative period in American art after World War Two [...] A narrative of his life is really the story of modern art."

given a substantial amount of freedom and so he set about hiring a whole new faculty and drawing up an entirely new curriculum. Indeed, the staff who worked for him reads like a *Who's Who* of the era's art scene. These included Ansel Adams, William Gaw, Charles Howard, Elmer Bischoff, Dorr Bothwell, Edward Corbett, David Park, Hassel Smith, Clyfford Still, and Richard Diebenkorn. Mark Rothko, Salvador Dali, and Man Ray also taught classes at MacAgy's invitation.

Beasley argues that MacAgy created a curriculum that impressed upon his students one of his core values: "a sense of rebellion against the past which he saw as essential if the artist was to find self expression." He loathed academia and referred to art as "a living creature in flight," which is why at C.S.F.A. and in his various roles as museum curator, he sought to move away from classicism and to allow artists to develop unique styles and views based upon an understanding of art history as well as the world around them. This entailed a thoroughly multidisciplinary approach. He wrote that he wanted his students to:

> investigate city plans, architecture, sculpture, printing, music, literature, politics, economics, and the social role of the artist in cultures from the late medieval to our own. In the process, they construct three-dimensional models, "perspective machines," and formal studies of the conceptual arrangements of each period. When they emerge from these courses they have a substantial leverage for their continuing essays into the undiscovered regions of the mind.

In the modern parlance, he wanted to provide a *holistic* education, allowing students to achieve their full potential through exposure to a wide range of thoughts and styles. At the time, such an idea was radical. Weldon Kees complained in 1952 that art had followed most other areas of the capitalist economy by engaging in "specialization."

He said, "Surely one of the more disquieting aspects of our culture is the bland and unquestioning acceptance of [specialization]. 'I never read anything,' says the painter. 'I don't see what the painters today are up to,' says the novelist." This was precisely what MacAgy fought against. One particularly notable effort came when he brought together, for a two-day round-table event on April 8–9, 1949, the philosopher George Boas, the artist Marcel Duchamp, the critic Alfred Frankenstein, the composer Darius Milhaud, the architect Frank Lloyd Wright, the anthropologist Gregory Bateson, and others to discuss modern art. It was by all accounts a huge success.

His tenure was brief but astoundingly important and he gained international recognition, being featured in publications like *Harper's Bazaar*. Art critic Kenneth B. Sawyer claimed that "between 1946 and 1949—the San Francisco Bay Area was the most aesthetically advanced region in the United States," a period that aligns closely with MacAgy's time as director. It was in this period that San Francisco came to develop its own form of abstract expressionism, the in-vogue style usually associated with a few New York artists, and other styles that would be associated with the West Coast began to emerge.

In 1949, MacAgy encouraged Clay Spohn (another C.S.F.A. teacher) to produce "The Museum of Unknown and Little Known Objects." He had been a supporter of Spohn's work for some years, even writing about it in *Circle No.5* in 1945. He agreed with Spohn's notion that "Art is not only free of anything that has to do with the dogmatic, but it is the essence and spirit of freedom. It can be developed only when the mind and spirit are completely free and released. Limitation is the enemy of free expression." "The Museum of Unknown and Little Known Objects" attacked the pretentiousness of art and has been cited as an early—and perhaps the first—example of Pop Art or Funk Art. Certainly, it is not hard to see its influence in the various experiments with junk, found objects, and assemblage that were so common in the city during the fifties. MacAgy, commenting on the success of Spohn's work, said that it "located mines of meaningful imagery in the refuse and wreckage of civilized neglect."

Shortly after MacAgy's departure, several of the teachers at C.S.F.A. (including David Park, Elmer Bischoff, and Richard Diebenkorn) would move toward a new style of painting and form what is known as the Bay Area Figurative movement. Although this happened after his time as director, it can reasonably be asserted that it emerged from the environment he created there. This movement could be broken down into multiple generations, with the third generation comprising some of the artists involved with the running of the 6 Gallery.

MacAgy not only hired talented teachers but opened the school to creatively inclined ex-servicemen. These veterans—who in 1949 made up a staggering 87% of the school's full-time students—embraced abstract expressionism as a means of expressing trauma while their fraternal bonds helped give the San Francisco art scene a more cohesive atmosphere than its New York counterpart. A 1971 inquiry into the San Francisco arts scene of the forties and fifties explained:

> Most of these men and women were older than the average art student, more experienced, more sophisticated and some were better educated. Quite a few of them had been college students, some in the sciences, before they entered the services. As the student body of an art school, they were an exceptionally serious and vital group of people. They were concerned with the search for values on a level of maturity quite different from that of the usual student, perhaps because of their war experiences. [...] The combination of these two factors, mature students and exceptional instructors, resulted in a solar flare in San Francisco's art history.

MacAgy made sure that the school's facilities were open all day and night and that there were facilities available for all art forms, from music to sculpture and from film to painting.[12] Such was the impact of his time there, as well as the teachers who worked under him, that he directly and indirectly fostered an atmosphere of multidisciplinary experimentation that would shape the city in the next decade and beyond. Wally Hedrick said that "MacAgy was going toward the ultimate art school where there would be one department, and it would be art. There would be no degrees, no lecture classes, probably only had painting, sculpture, and drawing." This idea spilled out of C.S.F.A. and into the wider city.

Rebecca Solnit, author of *Secret Exhibition: Six California Artists of the Cold War Era*, said that "what distinguishes this period in Bay Area art is the spirit of coexistence, a spirit in which inspirations were drawn from many sources and multimedia collaborations were common." In and around C.S.F.A., these people would collaborate and socialize in this uniquely open atmosphere and soon the city began to attract artist visitors from abroad. Word spread across the country that there was a scene forming inside and outside of C.S.F.A. and young artists began heading west. If you had something to say, San Francisco was becoming *the* place to go.

By the halfway point of the twentieth century, then, San Francisco was becoming—at least for those in the know—a hip place for creative types. It was a multicultural city with a multidisciplinary art scene that was developing a collaborative environment populated by political radicals. Its vibrant art scene was, Rexroth said, "the one community in the United States which had a regional literature and art at variance with the prevailing pattern."

What San Francisco lacked, though, were venues for artists to gather, collaborate, and display their work. In spite of all the expression, there was a conspicuous lack of places for artists to put their work before the general public. The city's museums and galleries catered to established artists and generally did not offer space

---

12   One history of art on the West Coast, noting the explosion of creativity and attributing it partly to MacAgy and partly to these ex-military students, also mentioned the facilities, praising "its old halls [and] cavernous, friendly studios conducive to expressive experiments."

to newcomers or the radically experimental. There were two annual art fairs that attracted hundreds of artists, but these were temporary events. Hedrick complained that "[i]n San Francisco in the late '40s, early '50s, there was no venue for artists like us, or anybody really. There were a couple of galleries that showed contemporary work, but they were sort of holdovers from the Depression." This was a problem not just for visual artists but for poets. Gary Snyder complained that there had been no sense of community among poets, nor any sort of audience, in the early fifties. Rexroth hosted weekly poetry readings at his apartment, where politics and art were discussed and poets could recite their latest work, and in the early fifties several notable cafés and bars would open, putting on poetry readings and showing paintings and drawings on their walls, but they could only hold a limited number of people. It was not enough for a growing, vibrant art scene.

This began to change when, in 1949, Clyfford Still encouraged his students at (and several graduates of) C.S.F.A. to open their own art gallery, which they did, founding Metart in two rooms of a small building at 527 Bush Street. It was a small, short-lived, and flawed venture but it was an important one for it was San Francisco's first artist-run gallery. Metart was run by twelve student artists, each of whom was given a one-month window to show their work: Ernest Briggs, William Huberich, Jeremy Anderson, Hubert Crehan, Jack Cohantz, Jack Jefferson, Jorge Goya, Zoe Longfield, Kio Kiozumi, Edward Dugmore, Horst Trave, and Frann Spencer. Although details are hard to come by, it seems other artists showed their work there, including Knute Stiles and Bruce McGaw. Ernest Briggs' show was first, opening the gallery in April 1949. The final show was by Francis Spencer in April 1950, prior to a break of several months, and between June 17 and July 14 Still had his own exhibition there. He resigned from C.S.F.A. shortly after and moved to New York, so the exhibition was a farewell show.

Metart was a liberating and empowering venture. A handful of surviving photos show highly experimental work including unusual sculptures in a small, dark room, the walls of which are covered in dark wires or string.

According to Trave, "Each member had full control of selection and arrangement of his or her show for one month." Most importantly, though, it "was an attempt to put on shows without commercial consideration or restrictions and presenting a more compact picture of production and direction." This would be the direction of art in San Francisco over the next decade and would be precisely what allowed it to flourish to the extent that it did.

Metart received positive reviews but closed less than a year and a half after it opened. There had been some bickering between the members, who were unprepared for the effort required to run a functioning gallery, even if it was a non-standard, non-commercial venture, but more than the gallery, more even than the artists who showed there, Metart was important for being the first in a revolutionary series of venues in San Francisco that would forever change the city and shape the counterculture. Despite its short existence and limited scope, it was frequently cited in the sixties and seventies as an important venture, the first in succession of co-operative, artist-run galleries open to the wildly experimental. Like the galleries we will look at next, an unusual number of the people who showed there went on to have successful careers.

The same year that Metart opened, Bern Porter founded the Contemporary Gallery just across the Bay from San Francisco, on the waterfront at Sausalito. Porter was an artist but he is best remembered for his various efforts supporting other artists. He knew Gertrude Stein in Paris in the thirties, then worked next to Albert Einstein on the Manhattan Project after being drafted. He was a scientist but also drawn to the creative world, where he passionately supported those whom he admired. Through his imprint, Bern Porter Books, he published many works by and about Henry Miller, as well as the first books by Robert Duncan and Philip Lamantia. He also published works by Kenneth Rexroth, Lawrence Ferlinghetti, William Faulkner, Pablo Picasso, and Charles Henri Ford. These included books and broadsides, mixing poetry, prose, painting, sketching, and photography. He was also the publisher for *Circle* magazine.

In Sausalito, Porter turned part of his house, which he called Schillerhaus, into a gallery before founding the Contemporary Gallery in 1949. Like his efforts in publishing, he sought as a gallerist to exhibit groundbreaking works in a range of disciplines. Porter worked in various media and felt that a gallery should not be limited to paintings and sculptures. He thus showed experimental films, held poetry readings, and hosted live music performances. He was particularly fond of energetic abstract art and showed the large-scale works of C.S.F.A. teachers including Richard Diebenkorn, Hassel Smith, Edward Corbett, and Jean Varda. When asked years later about his connection to so many influential artists, Porter replied that he sought out or was sought out by "pioneers in producing [whose] work is such that has never been created before."

It is easy to dismiss the importance of the Contemporary Gallery, for no one involved in the galleries this book mostly concerns ever went on record as acknowledging its existence, but Porter was thoroughly enmeshed in that scene. Not only did he publish Duncan's first book and put on shows by numerous C.S.F.A. teachers, but he was close friends with the man who first turned 3119 Fillmore into an art gallery, tried to coax one of the founders of the King Ubu into showing his work in Sausalito, and was poised to publish "Howl" before Ginsberg read it at the 6 Gallery. Altogether, Porter was an influential and much-loved figure in the Bay Area arts scene and his gallery was more than likely an inspiration to those who later championed wildly original artists with no thought to commercial gain.

The Confusing History of a Strange Building

The artists who flocked to San Francisco in the middle of the twentieth century did not settle in an even distribution across the city. Rather, like the various ethnic groups, they tended to cluster in certain areas and form small communities there. In fact, this had been going on long before the 1940s. In the late nineteenth century, writers in San Francisco often stayed at Montgomery Block, affectionately known as Monkey Block. Until the 1880s, it was an expensive place to live but when rents dropped artists began to move in and it gained a rather bohemian reputation. Mark Twain, George Sterling, Bret Harte, Robert Louis Stevenson, Ambrose Bierce, and Jack London all lived there, and Frieda Kahlo and Diego Rivera stayed when they visited San Francisco. One website devoted to San Franciscan history said, "Name any writer, poet, or painter associated with or visiting the city between the 1870s and the 1940s [...] and you will invoke someone who walked its halls, worked in its windows, ate, and probably drank too much, at its tables." It was a vast building, taking up an entire block, with the ground floor housing many bars and restaurants. It survived the great earthquake of 1906 and countless fires, as well as a number of economic disasters, but it was eventually torn down in 1959 to build a car park. Later, the Transamerica Pyramid was built on the ground where once "the most famous literary and artistic structure in the West" had stood, in the words of Lawrence Ferlinghetti. Even in those final years, long after its heyday, Monkey Block housed artists such as Elmer Bischoff, David Park, Richard Diebenkorn, and Adaline Kent.

Monkey Block stood at the very southern edge of the area known as North Beach and in the 1950s it was this district that became the primary destination for creatives in San Francisco. Here, a poet could sit with a beer and talk to a musician underneath a painting by an artist living just down the street. North Beach, with its cheap Chinese and Italian food, as well as low rents, was home to many artists, some of whom were students at the nearby C.S.F.A. It was, according to McClure, "like a reservation in which there was a free space for bohemians and oddballs of all stripes to meet in between the Italian and the Chinese districts in what was still a remarkably inexpensive part of town with lots of [residential] hotels." Although McClure said that it was "between" those two districts, North Beach was in fact primarily Italian and Jack Goodwin suggested that this was a contributing factor in it developing into such a favorable location for artists. "[A]s in every city in the world," he wrote, "this Italian section included a certain amount of sub-standard low-cost housing for students, writers, painters and opera singers, plus a certain permissive atmosphere" that he attributed to "the eternal Italian landlady."

Ferlinghetti was amazed when he first arrived in San Francisco to find such a beautiful, progressive city, but it was North Beach in particular that captivated him. "I certainly saw North Beach especially as a poetic place," he said, "as poetic as some quartiers in Paris, as any place in old Europa, as poetic as any place great poets and painters had found inspiration." He founded City Lights Bookstore there in 1953 and a number of North Beach bars and cafés catered to artists throughout the fifties: The Place, the Anxious Asp, Miss Smith's Tea Room, the Co-Existence Bagel Shop, The Cellar, Paper Doll, and Vesuvio's among them. Although the beatnik fad and the resulting influx of gawking tourists would push out many of the true bohemian artists, North Beach remained home to a number of poets well after its mid-fifties heyday.

Over on Fillmore Street, about a mile west and also just a short walk from the C.S.F.A., yet more artistic types clustered in an area that would for much of the fifties become another cultural hub. Fillmore Street runs from the very north of the San Francisco peninsula through the affluent and predominantly white Pacific Heights, via

The Confusing History of a Strange Building

the largely black Fillmore District, via Japantown, to the Lower Haight. It is, as Rebecca Solnit has said, "like a core sample" of the city. The street was mostly left intact after the 1906 earthquake and fire, becoming a major recreational destination for the city's inhabitants from the 1920s until the 1970s. It was briefly the primary shopping district when businesses temporarily moved there, and photos from 1908 show a densely packed street lined with commercial enterprises. From 1895 to 1941, it was served by a unique counterbalanced tram whose cars were known as "dinkies" due to their unusually small size. These helped people up and down the steep street in the Pacific Heights area.[13]

About a quarter of the way down this two-and-a-half-mile road, there is a block that is edged in by Fillmore to the east and Steiner to the west, by Greenwich to the north and Filbert to the south. Unlike most city blocks in this part of San Francisco, which are roughly square shaped, it is split in half by Pixley Street to make two narrow rectangles. On the eastern edge of the southern rectangle is a line of five two-story buildings, each about twenty feet wide and one hundred feet deep. They are strange properties, their narrowness belying their depth. Today, as when they were built about a hundred and twenty years ago, they look rather nondescript, particularly the middle of the five buildings, which is smaller and simpler in design than the others. It lacks the little architectural flourishes that mark its neighbors, such as bay windows, elaborate entablatures, and even spires. Were it not for a small blue plaque outside it, which itself is rather inconspicuous at just about three feet high, one would not suspect that an event of incalculable cultural significance took place here. The plaque contains the first few lines of Allen Ginsberg's epochal "Howl" and an image of the poet as a young man. Beneath, the text reads:

---

13 If one stepped out of the 6 Gallery and turned right, one would see an extremely steep hill rising toward Broadway. The street grade here is a little over 24% in places, with a rise of about 200 feet from 3119 Fillmore to the top of the hill at Broadway.

Bohemian Spaces

Presented to San Francisco on the 50th Anniversary of the first reading of HOWL at the Six Gallery.
October 7, 2005
San Francisco salutes the Beat Generation poets Jack Kerouac, Philip Lamantia, Michael McClure, Kenneth Rexroth, Gary Snyder, and Philip Whalen.
By Supervisor Michela Alioto-Pier and Lawrence Ferlinghetti of City Lights Bookstore.

Cities change hugely over time and that includes the individual buildings that comprise them, yet this particular building and indeed the ones surrounding it look much the same as they did in 1955, which is to say that its narrow, flat-faced façade not only continues to hide its depth but is incongruous with its role in American literary history. The 6 Gallery reading was not only a surprise success due to the inexperience of its participants but also due to the absurd modesty of the building, which had little history of holding such events and certainly does not look like the kind of place one would choose to host an era-defining reading. Even at its gussied-up best, it looked more like a shabby studio than an art gallery with its concrete floor and clapboard walls and a plywood "6" wrapped in fairy lights hung above the front door. The building was not intended to be a gallery nor was it extensively overhauled for this purpose. Rather, it was just a cheap space converted with minimal effort to display the work of local artists, then had been temporarily adapted for a one-night poetry reading. In that sense, it was not unlike the found objects that became funk art or the snatches of real conversation from the streets that became Beat poetry.

Researching the history of the building that was in 1955 home to the 6 Gallery was surprisingly difficult. For one thing, most publications that discuss the 6 Gallery have relied heavily upon the flawed memories and egotistical mythmaking of the participants, resulting in decades of inaccurate reporting. Rather than trying to find out what the building had actually housed, the authors of these texts have repeated various rumors

The Confusing History of a Strange Building

and misremembered fragments of stories, resulting in a strange list of falsehoods. To be fair, that situation has come about because so many people from the 1950s were willing to share their memories whilst more reliable sources of information are difficult if not impossible to uncover. Official records and other contemporary documents are scant, confusing, and often contradictory. Still, it is possible, by utilizing city maps, directories, legal documents, and newspaper records, to more or less trace the occupants and owners of this building.

The confusion begins with what should be a simple matter: the address. The building has had multiple addresses throughout its history, with the one used by the 6 Gallery having only come into existence a few years prior to the founding of the gallery. Those who have read about the 6 Gallery before will know that it was located at 3119 Fillmore Street; however, that same building is listed today as 3115 and 3117, the former referring to the commercial downstairs space and the latter to the residential upstairs space. The numbers 3115 and 3117 were used when the building was constructed in 1905 and these addresses remained until 1952, when the building became 3119, a number that was used until the early twenty-first century, at which point it reverted to the original numbering. If this were not confusing enough, 3115 and 3117 were not the only addresses used in the half century between its construction and the founding of the 6 Gallery. Many of the residents and business owners who occupied these spaces alternated between 3115 and 3105 and 3117 and 3107. They might use 3115 as their address one year but then switch to 3105 the next. This is complicated by the fact that today the numbers 3105 and 3107 belong to its southern next-door neighbor. Whilst it seems that 3115 was the primary business address and 3117 was the residential one, the building was often occupied by a business owner who lived upstairs and used the two (or sometimes four) addresses interchangeably.

Adding to the confusion, various people are registered as having lived at all of these address variants during the late nineteenth century, prior to the construction of the building that would later house the 6 Gallery. It is unclear

35

whether they lived in a building that existed there earlier or whether these numbers referred to other locations on that street before 1905.[14] The latter seems more logical of an assumption, but in fact some of these people then occupied the later addresses, suggesting continuity. It is particularly odd that 3119 Fillmore was used by various people for ten years before the construction of the building but that this number ceased to exist around the time the building was constructed and remained unused until 1952.

Early maps of San Francisco show a neat, grid-ironed town ending a little further west than Fillmore Street, whereafter the peninsula was filled by ranches. The block on which the 6 Gallery would be located was then known by town planners as "343" but would later become known as "515." As early as 1894, Block 343 was outlined on maps with the address that would become 3115–3117 listed as belonging to "Thos Magee." This refers to the prominent real estate agency, Thomas Magee & Sons, which owned much land around the city, and it is quite likely that the property was at this point undeveloped land. Certainly, a photo from 1886 shows it to have been empty although the roads around it had already been marked out and another map from 1895 shows little had changed, with the area still predominantly undeveloped. City maps and sales documents show the lot measured as 24 feet by 100 feet, part of a line of five plots of equal dimensions on Fillmore Street. Buildings on these plots would be constructed intermittently between 1900 and 1913, with 3115–3117 the middle of them and constructed in 1905. It would be known by city administrators as property 8 of this block.

Whilst the two buildings south of 3117 are three stories tall and rather eye-catching, with their almost embarrassingly ornate Edwardian architecture, the middle building is short and squat, its front about as tall as it is wide. It looks almost the same today as it did in 1914 (the earliest photo I can find of the building), although its white-painted wooden slatboard façade has been replaced

---

14   It is tempting to think this confusion could be traced to the 1906 earthquake but this part of the city was unscathed.

The Confusing History of a Strange Building

by a grey stone one. It was simple and resembled the sort of building one found in old western towns, which San Francisco was at the turn of the last century. Upstairs, there was one single window and another double. Unlike the ostentatious bay windows of its neighbors, surrounded by intricate millwork, these were flat and unadorned, and they remain that way more than a century later. The one feature of design that stands out even slightly is the cornice, although it appears to have been remodeled and increased in size since 1914, when it protruded less.

In 1906, the plot was still listed on maps as belonging to Thomas Magee & Sons but it had been sold to Andrea Moni in 1904 for $1,500. In fact, records show that Moni had lived in this building from as early as 1903 (casting doubt on the official construction date), and that he sold wood and coal from what was then registered as 3107. By 1905, he was listed in various directories as selling coal from 3115 Fillmore, an address shared by an organization called Bruschera & Tognoli. Over the next few years, Charley Bruschera would be listed as the occupant of both 3115 and 3117, selling hay, wood, and coal. It is unclear whether he rented the property from Moni or whether Moni was involved in the business, but records show that in 1908 the police brought charges against Bruschera for operating a stable, which went against city ordinances, and that appears to have ended his tenancy.[15] In any case, Moni remained the owner of the building.

In 1908, Andrea Moni paid $200 to have the building altered so as to be fit for use as a store. From 1909, he and his wife Armida occupied this building for both business and residential purposes, living upstairs and running the shop at street level. Around this time, he appears to have begun using the Americanized name Andrew Moni, a common practice at the time due to anti-Italian discrimination. Under this name, he ran Greenvalley Wine & Grocery with Pasquale Civiletti, who then sold his share

---

15 Certain publications have claimed that the building was once a stagecoach house and it is possible its brief period as an illegal stable may be the origin of this falsehood. The stagecoach ceased to be a viable mode of transport about a half century prior to the construction of this building.

to Moni later that year. Another wine shop briefly existed in 1909: Civiletti & Compagno Wines. However, just two years later the Monis were embroiled in a legal feud with Lorenzo Compagno, who along with various other claimants disputed the Monis' ownership of the building.

It was not only this building that was owned and occupied by people of Italian origin. The area around it was largely occupied by Italian-American businessowners during this period and oftentimes they seem to have engaged in shared business ventures. Those who described the few blocks around 3119 Fillmore in the early decades of the century spoke of grocers, shoemakers, druggists, delicatessens, candy shops, pool rooms, bakeries, and butchers frequently possessing names of Italian origin: De Vecchi, Pellegrini, Stiranetti, Solari, Cavalli, Briglia, Pezolo. However, it was not exactly another Little Italy. Although Italians seem to have owned many of the businesses, this part of San Francisco was quite diverse, with many people of Chinese, Irish, Spanish, and German descent living there. One man who lived in the Fillmore-Union area in the first half of the twentieth century recalled various Chinese businesses, including two laundries; a Mexican street-food vendor; German bands; and gypsy fortune tellers.

Even as the city grew and places like Fillmore Street became increasingly metropolitan, it had an oddly rural feel, with stables and vegetable gardens. People sold goods—including live chickens—from horse-drawn carts. There was no shortage of saloons, either. This was still the West, after all. Immediately surrounding 3119 Fillmore were Mecchi & Co. Produce,[16] Starck's Delicatessen, and the Jersey Creamery. The latter alludes to the fact that even into the twentieth century this part of San Francisco had cows grazing and a number of dairy operations still working, hence the name "Cow Hollow." This is the name of a district beginning just one block west of Fillmore Street. Some people who remember the Fillmore-Union area recall it being part of Cow Hollow, but in fact it is about a hundred meters outside the boundaries of that

---

16   Mecchi also seems to have been a business partner of Moni's prior to the construction of these buildings.

The Confusing History of a Strange Building

area. The use of "Fillmore-Union" came about because that area fell in between a number of named districts.

The Monis lived at the 3115–3117 Fillmore address for several years but seem to have rented part of the space to Georgi Antero, an arrangement lasting at least from 1910 to 1913. In 1914 and 1915, the building was partly occupied by a restaurant. Spanish-language newspapers advertised it as being a Spanish restaurant but a photo of the building shows a sign reading "French and Spanish Restaurant." The other half of the downstairs area has a sign above it that simply says "Painting."

Moni still owned the building as late as 1917; however, he now lived at 2118 Greenwich Street, just a few minutes' walk away. That same year, he paid $700 to have the Fillmore building converted so that it had a private garage, after which he rented the space to a chauffeur called Albert Swartz from 1917 to 1921. Almost every text that mentions the 6 Gallery refers to it as having been a commercial garage at some point, yet there is no record of it ever being one. Perhaps Swartz was registered as a chauffeur and worked as a mechanic on the side, but no records exist to verify this, and the license Moni obtained was for a "private garage," not a commercial one. No business directories from any point during the building's history show a commercial garage existing at any of the variants of its address. The closest thing to evidence is a "too late to classify" advert from 1919 stating rather ambiguously "Garage or repair shop, upper floor for painting, suitable bldg. Call at 3107 Fillmore."

Despite the downstairs area seemingly having been converted into a garage, it was occupied from 1921 to 1930 by a plumber called Stenger, and in 1931 another plumber, Michael Desiano, moved in. He spent a great deal more on adverts than previous business owners here, suggesting that his business was rather successful and it occupied both stories. He operated out of the 3115–3117 address from 1931 to at least 1937, after which an assortment of people moved in—L. B. Dixson in 1938; real estate and insurance agents Mary and Louis Flecchia in 1940; Lim D. Sam also in 1940, operating what was listed perhaps erroneously as the San Laundry. Oddly, most of these businesses used 3117 or 3107, which was the upstairs address, rather than 3115, which referred to the commercial space on the ground floor. The upstairs space was divided into two individual flats and a large number of mostly young families occupied them at different times during the half century after its construction. In 1946, former baseball player Italo Chelini was arrested there for operating an illegal betting agency.

As of 1948 and 1949, the building was home to Paramount Pest Control and the company stayed at this address until 1952, thereafter moving to Gough Street. When the Paramount Pest Control company vacated 3117 Fillmore, the whole building became known as 3119 and it would retain this number for about half a century. Interestingly, it was when the numbering changed that the building—or at least its downstairs space—took on an entirely new purpose.

In July 1952, the San Francisco Community Theater was founded by poet, painter, playwright, and occasional actor W. Edwin Ver Becke at 3119 Fillmore Street. Ver Becke was a good friend of Bern Porter and quite possibly saved his life after Porter suffered from a particularly bad case of depression when he first moved to Sausalito in the forties. Ver Becke gave him a place to stay and forced him to eat. Later, Porter put on an exhibition of Ver Becke's paintings and in 1954 did the design work for Ver Becke's book, *Line in Painting*. Ver Becke had run his own gallery in Sausalito, which served as an inspiration for Porter, and it was here that he founded the Sausalito Little Theater, acting as the group's director. He was singled out for praise several times in Bay Area newspapers, including the *San Francisco Examiner;* however, Ver Becke tended to move from place to place quite often and by 1952 he was living in San Francisco.

That summer, the San Francisco Community Theater announced its formation with a media blitz and attempted to garner interest by performing a popular play, *Angel in the Pawnshop*, which had debuted on Broadway in 1951. In stark contrast to the two arts venues that would follow it, the San Francisco Community Theater aimed "to stage clean plays with family appeal to please audiences of every age group," and gave the media an ambitious list of future works they intended to perform.[17] However, it was a short-lived venture. Their first show premiered at the California Palace of the Legion of Honor in September and they earned "a rather unfavorable reception," with one reporter calling it "a disappointment" featuring "exceedingly amateurish" acting, bad writing, and generally terrible production values. By October, the local press was already querying whether or not the organization still existed and soon after Ver Becke was living in Laguna Beach, teaching drama and founding yet more dramatic groups.

The San Francisco Community Theater, despite its obvious ambition, did not recover from this inauspicious beginning. Its life was so short that records are scant and confined only to a handful of newspaper articles. It would be little consolation for Ver Becke, but his doomed effort in San Francisco had an important if largely unnoticed impact: it set precedence in the use of this building for artistic purposes. For almost fifty years, the Fillmore building had been used for commercial purposes but Ver Becke had overseen a minor conversion, turning it into a "workshop gallery." For a short period of time, they opened the space from 11 a.m. to 5 p.m. each day and used it for "exhibitions of theater designs." Their main attraction was a collection of drawings and sketches by San Francisco's "Artist Laureate" Antonio Sotomayor. As a "workshop gallery," it was also used for rehearsals and may even have been used for performances after the catastrophic failure of their opening show at the California Palace of the Legion of Honor. This is evidenced by an advertisement that appeared in the *Educational Theatre Journal*, which claimed the organization had an impressive 800 members and that the Fillmore Street building could hold 250 people—an unlikely number for daytime attendance at "exhibitions of theater designs."

Unfortunately for Ver Becke and his group, by the

---

17   Unlike his friend Porter, Ver Becke was quite conventional and had little interest in radical new art forms. In both his Sausalito and San Francisco theater ventures, he put on versions of already popular plays and generally attempted to avoid offending or confusing audiences.

time this listing appeared in May 1953, the group had long since disbanded. By December 1952, less than half a year after they moved in and just a few months after turning 3119 Fillmore into an art gallery, the San Francisco Community Theater had vacated the premises and the building had new tenants.

Arise, King Ubu

Not long after the San Francisco Community Theater moved out of the building at 3119, another non-commercial, artist-run enterprise was established there. Perhaps also fitting the description "workshop gallery," the King Ubu Gallery aimed to host both theater and visual art, and it was founded by three young men who dabbled in an array of disciplines: Robert Duncan, Jess, and Harry Jacobus.

Born in Oakland in 1919, Duncan was the oldest of the three founding members and also the most experienced and renowned. He was a prominent figure in the Bay Area literary scene of the 1940s and was friends with writers such as Helen Adam, Madeline Gleason, Lyn Brockway, and Kenneth Rexroth. Duncan was known for his radical politics, his intelligence, and his poetic abilities, publishing his first book in 1947 through Bern Porter. He lived as an openly gay man and wrote a courageous, landmark essay called "The Homosexual in Society" in August 1944, in which he admitted to being gay. This made him one of the first prominent Americans to publicly admit his homosexuality and unsurprisingly it cost him various publishing opportunities. However, Duncan was fearless in life and in art, and he reflected positively: "So I was *out*, just read out, out, out, at a point when I would have been *in* at the wrong place." Duncan, like many of the bohemian artists and writers of San Francisco in that era, realized that it was better to be an honest outsider pursuing one's own creative goals than to give oneself over to the establishment and merely produce the same work as everyone else.

In 1949, Duncan met Jess, who was then a student at C.S.F.A., and they exchanged vows on New Year's Day, 1951, thereafter living as a married couple some sixty-three

43

years prior to the legalization of homosexual marriage in California. One writer who knew both men described Jess as "thin and shy, a pallor like someone who stays indoors a lot. Quiet-spoken, when he did speak, he seemed like a vulnerable and sickly adolescent, although he was then in his 30s." Others have gone as far as to call him a recluse, and by all accounts he was by far less social than Duncan, preferring to stay home as much as possible. Jess had originally trained as a chemist, and like Bern Porter he had worked on the Manhattan Project during World War II. Both men were horrified after the destruction of Hiroshima and Nagasaki. In 1948, after a nightmarish vision of nuclear apocalypse, Jess quit his job and moved to San Francisco to become an artist. At C.S.F.A., he studied under various influential teachers, including Still, Corbett, Smith, Bischoff, and Park, and consequently began his art career in the mode of abstract expressionism. However, Jess soon switched his focus to collage, which he called "Paste-Ups," as a means of differentiating his efforts from surrealist and Dadaist collage. These involved mixing text, photographs, comic strips, jigsaw pieces, and other items, often to create homoerotic images in scenes of nuclear holocaust. "Visual and verbal puns organize the intricacies," according to a description on the Jess Collins Trust website, "as the viewer's attention is drawn inward to Jess's constellations of myth and imagination." His interest in this had been partially inspired by the book *Une semaine de bonté* (1934), a gift from Duncan.

These days, Harry Jacobus—the youngest of the trio—is the least well known of the King Ubu founders. Whilst Duncan became one of the most important poets of his era and Jess was significant in avant-garde circles, possessing a minor cult following but never achieving popular acclaim, Jacobus' legacy has faded. Today, he lacks even a Wikipedia page, is merely a footnote in publications by California art museums, and is largely remembered as a friend of Duncan and Jess. Having served in World War II, he moved to the Bay Area, enrolling first at the Oakland School of Arts and Crafts, then at C.S.F.A., where he studied under Still and Park alongside Jess. He worked with paint, pencil, and crayon, usually producing simple works in soft, washed-out colors. Like many of the artists of that time and place, his work was playful and childish, but perhaps lacking in originality. Whereas Jess's work could seem primitive at times, it was daring and thought-provoking. Jacobus' crayon patterns, on the other hand, were—as one modern critic put it—"unbearably twee, even trite."

What brought these three artists together was not a similarity in style or form but rather an interest in celebrating and combining the various arts. In 1952, Duncan began planning a publication that would bring together not just poets or different kinds of writers, but which would present an array of art forms. To his friend and fellow poet Charles Olson, he wrote:

> MEANWHILE we are starting a critical "four sheets" type format out here, a journal for THE ARTIST'S VIEW, painters and poets writing on their work. It is going to be done by a photolithographic process—quite cheap and anything can be reproduced... a page of handwriting, a typescript, a painting, etc.

This can be viewed as a prototype for the gallery the three men would found later that year. Jess, who had been a student during Douglas MacAgy's tenure and had absorbed the concept of a holistic art education, would switch between painting styles throughout his life and also write poetry and fiction. His early collages, which he called "picture-poems," blended text and visual elements in an effort to break down the barriers between forms. Duncan devoted himself primarily to writing poems, plays, and essays, but he did some painting and illustration and was also a supporter of various art forms. "Second only to his love of Fine art was Robert's interest in music and theater," wrote Ekbert Faas in his book on Duncan, *Young Robert Duncan: Portrait of the Poet as a Homosexual in Society*. Lyn Brockway, a friend of the three founders and a painter whose work was exhibited at King Ubu, wrote that Duncan "always had time to discover and encourage and involve himself with other poets and painters and musicians [...] He created a strong feeling of concern and respect for the individual and the diversity of personal expression." Whereas Metart had been conventional in that it showed only paintings and drawings, King Ubu would bring together various art forms. They imagined a venue that would have paintings on the wall, sculptures in the corner, poetry both printed and read aloud, and music played by live performers. Art historian Seymour Howard put it succinctly when he wrote: "Metart was an *art* gallery; King Ubu was an *arts* gallery."

The origins of King Ubu are rather unclear, for no one bothered to document it. According to Rebecca Solnit, it was Jacobus who came up with the idea of starting a gallery and who found the space at 3119 Fillmore Street, newly vacated by the San Francisco Community Theater, but she gives no citation for this claim and it does not seem the likeliest of explanations. It seems the idea grew out of Duncan's planned publication and a number of letters indicate that Duncan and Jess were responsible for renting the building on Fillmore Street, too. These documents show that Edwin Ver Becke, founder of the San Francisco Community Theater, visited their home in October 1952. They may have met through Bern Porter, who was a friend of all three men, but Ver Becke was also a regular on the mid-forties poetry scene and so he could have met Duncan elsewhere. Two months after this meeting, King Ubu was opened, and whilst this does not conclusively prove that this is how they came to occupy the building, it does seem rather too much of a coincidence to dismiss. Letters from Ver Becke also show that he had sold them the lighting equipment he had brought from Sausalito and installed at 3119 Fillmore, which further supports my theory. Admittedly, Ver Becke knew Jacobus but they seem to have disliked one another and had little contact.

Regardless of whose idea the gallery was, the 3119 Fillmore Street address was newly vacant, had already been adapted for small-scale art shows and stage performances, and was in a wonderful location. It was only a half hour's walk from C.S.F.A. and provided views of the harbor, Sausalito, and Tiburon. The rent was very modest, too. Numerous sources state that they paid $50 per month but the 6 Gallery founders only paid $40 when they took over the following year, so it is likely that the rent for King Ubu was also $40 per month.

Duncan originally wanted to call the gallery "Aurora Rose," a reference to the goddess of dawn, but the group opted instead for King Ubu, inspired by Alfred Jarry's infamous play, *Ubu Roi*, which the *Paris Review* called

> a play so contentious that its premiere, in December 1896, was also its closing night. It lives in the annals of drama because it offended almost everyone who saw it. In this, it prefigured modernism, surrealism, Dadaism, and the theater of the absurd.

The first word was a misspelled curse word and it featured a king carrying a scepter that was in fact a toilet brush. Characters wore cardboard masks and the background featured scenes painted together in a confusing hodgepodge of imagery. Altogether it was so obscene, scatological, and absurd that after just a few seconds the audience began booing and continued to boo for fifteen minutes. When the play finally finished, a riot ensued.

By the 1950s, the play's name acted as a cultural touchstone—something a learned bohemian appreciated. Jack Goodwin remarked decades later that "[s]omeone was always putting on 'Ubu Roi' in those days." Naming their gallery after this play also signaled the intention of the three artists to create a venue that would not shy away from the shocking or absurd, embracing the seemingly juvenile, lampooning the overly pretentious, and ultimately pushing visitors to question the very concept of art itself.

Whilst there are scant records concerning the San Francisco Community Theater's use of the building, we have a number of descriptions and even photographs that show the King Ubu gallery. As we have established, the building was 24 feet wide and 100 feet deep, but there was a stairway leading up to an apartment above, and so the first floor—the actual gallery space—was narrower even than its stated dimensions suggest. Artist Jay DeFeo called it a "big deep wide very funky space" although it certainly

47

was not wide, and her husband Wally Hedrick said it was "sort of like a bowling alley" that ran from the Fillmore Street entrance through a relatively narrow entrance area that opened up into a bigger room at the back of the building. Elsewhere, he said "the 6 Gallery was like a stable. It was about 100 ft. long but it was only about 10 feet wide. And then at the end of the corridor, it opened up and there was a stage." Deborah Remington, fifty years after the 6 Gallery closed, described it:

> There was a narrow opening; it had a garage door in front, and it would just go up and down. About the width of a car. And you'd walk in about 15 ft., and then it widened out into a fairly wide, largish room, I'd say about 30x30 ft or 30x20, something like that, I can't remember the exact dimensions. Then it narrowed again in the back. There was a little bathroom on the right. Then it narrowed into a little hallway maybe about 6 or 8 ft. long, and then the building ended.

It was also divided in two by pillars and a wall running down the middle. For a gallery, this was no bad thing as four walls provided more display space than two. Although the three founders did little to their gallery space prior to opening it, one notable change was the installation of a pair of ten-foot-tall, beveled-glass doors discarded by the Mark Hopkins Hotel. Jacobus, who had some skill as a handyman, installed them. These seem to have been located behind the rolling garage doors.

One might assume this lack of effort to create a conventional gallery space was due to the financial constraints of the founders, but whilst that was likely a consideration, the aesthetics came more from their personal philosophies vis-à-vis life and art. Like the Beat artists and others before them, Jess and Duncan felt that separating life from art was an artificial distinction.[18] In

---

18   This was a view also shared by the 6 Gallery artists. Deborah Remington, one of the founders and an acquaintance

several of their homes, they transcended the boundaries between accommodation, studio, and gallery space. These were also communal spaces. At 1350 Franklin Street, known as the Ghost House, they lived with other artists and writers. They occupied the large ballroom there for about a year before moving to 1724 Baker Street, which they borrowed from James Broughton and Kermit Sheets, with experimental filmmaker Stan Brakhage living in their basement. Jacobus often came over to paint, and his work inspired Jess and Brakhage. With artists coming and going, the place became—in the words of Liza Jarnot, Duncan's biographer—a "household salon bursting at the seams." However, it should be noted that not just *anyone* was welcome. Duncan said, "We are bourgeois. We like to live in a nice house, we like to have nice things," which meant Jack Spicer was banned as he tended to be clumsy, whilst Allen Ginsberg was not welcome due to his preference for sitting on the floor rather than using chairs.

In their Baker Street home, they held shows as though the apartment were a gallery. Here, they not only put art on the walls, but attempted to make art of the house itself. Duncan wrote to Broughton, who was in Europe:

> At Baker St. gradually the temper of the old manse is changed; last month the kitchen was transformed by Jess into a Collins painting: today he is at work on the bathroom. [...] Intense, brilliant Collins paintings in the dimensions of four walls, ceiling and floor. Two walls in hot tangerine orange, one wall in soft orange-pink and one in white; ceiling in white; floor in what the paint company with poetic inspiration calls Bermuda blue; woodwork in white and gold; center medallion in gold; from which a large Japanese lantern. The walls

---

of Jess and Duncan, and whose work they showed at King Ubu, said shortly before her death that "a strong social rebellion" underpinned the life and work of the artists in that scene and that "It's also important to realize— with respect to rebellion— that our lifestyle wasn't different from our work."

49

crowded with canvases and smaller pieces; two Norris Embrys; the Virginia Admiral; three Lyn Browns; one Lili Fenichel; three Jess Collins.

The home was not only a living space combined with a gallery; it also functioned as a literary salon where poets read their work, and it was used as the film set for multiple independent movies.

In the above quote, Duncan mentioned Jess being "at work on the bathroom" and at least one photo of this survives in the University of Buffalo's Harry Jacobus Collection. Jess had indeed covered the walls in drawings. These are titles or squares. One would be plain white and the next a unique geometric painting. The effect is rather like a chessboard except instead of plain black, there are mandalic patterns. In the gallery, Jess more or less replicated this. These images were much larger in scale and appear to comprise dozens of eyes. Perhaps the effect was to have the walls looking back at the gallery viewer.

Despite some sources claiming that there was a sawdust or dirt floor, photos show it to have been bare concrete. One of the later 6 Gallery founders confirmed this, saying, "It had a real funky cement floor, real dirty, I can't remember ever painting it, maybe it was, but it was a grey." Indeed, the building by this point had stood for a half century in the middle of a modern city, so it was hardly a barn. Some of the walls were stone and others were made of wood, making one half of the gallery look like a derelict building and the other more like a garden shed. The wooden parts were mostly painted white except for one single red wall, and paintings were hung directly on the wooden beams. It had a pitched roof with exposed trusses, yet in some parts concrete supports reinforced the old wooden structure of the building. Bedsheets were hung from the trusses, perhaps to diffuse the glare of the spotlights the theater group had left behind. Works of art were positioned haphazardly up and down the long room. There were paintings on butcher paper (the cheapest medium available and thus a fairly common choice for penurious painters), as well as sculptures and large canvases.

Some of these were nailed directly to the wooden beams. As the gallery also hosted many poetry readings, there was a small, movable stage, which Remington described:

> Well, the Ubu was primarily a place for 10 poets to read. There was a little podium that was on rollers that was in the middle of the gallery, and it was maybe 8 x 8 feet square, and it stood about 15 inches off the ground. It was painted black or dark gray or something. When we needed to use it, we'd just wheel it into the gallery. Otherwise, we'd stand it up and put it in the back against the wall in the very back beyond the restroom! So, if we were having an art show we wouldn't want that thing around, but sometimes people would sit on it.

The setup, then, was simple to the point of absurdity. It was about as far from a slick, commercial, big-city gallery as it was possible to be. No doubt this partially stemmed from limited resources, but it was nonetheless a fitting location for what would happen at the Ubu and the more famous gallery that would replace it a year later. Seymour Howard, in the book *The Beat Galleries and Beyond*, says it was

> a place where anything, anything creative, could and did happen. [It had] a communal atmosphere of play, reciprocity, commitment, and optimism [and] attracted a coterie of dedicated followers. King Ubu was alive, a place to be oneself—a life-enhancing emancipating alternative to a pervasive and spiritually deadening grey-flannel-suit ethos. It celebrated the joyful life-giving process in creativity; it promoted health and healing in the unburdened heart by proving experiential sensation and a knowing beyond reason.

Even the announcements for shows were charmingly simple. These hand-drawn, hand-printed, black-and-white fliers and posters "introduced a crude and vital Zen-like high taste of enlightened primitivism," according to Howard. Some of their publicity materials used the slogan "The Vanguard of Uncivilization," further showing that their adoption of apparently primitive art was deliberate. Some were drawn by Jess, others by Duncan, and most of the individual artist shows had fliers drawn by the artists themselves. Due to budgetary constraints, a printer friend made copies for them to distribute. One big event about halfway through the gallery's lifespan was promoted with a red, yellow, and black silkscreen poster. Whilst eye-catching, it was extremely crude—perhaps even ironic, given it promoted an art gallery—with doodles reminiscent of cave paintings and text poorly spaced, as though the illustrator had forgotten how long a word was and had to rotate and squeeze it to fit. In that regard, and others, it looks not unlike a birthday card drawn by a young child. Yet perhaps these also owed something to Alfred Jarry, who drew the promotional materials for *Ubu Roi* by hand. Those were crude, confusing sketches that seemed to add the performers' names as an afterthought, rotated 90 degrees so as to highlight the characters rather than the actors.

King Ubu opened on December 20, 1952, with an exhibition of "large scale" work by Jess and Jacobus, alongside David Park, Elmer Bischoff, James Weeks, and Hassel Smith, and also sculptures by Miriam Hoffman. The founders put up a sign and informed some of their friends, but otherwise they put little effort into promoting the gallery. They made no attempt to court reviewers but nonetheless Alfred Frankenstein—one of the country's leading art critics—reviewed their opening show for the *San Francisco Chronicle*. Unusually open-minded for the era, he was a supporter of young, underrepresented artists and a big believer in the importance of artist-led galleries and communities. He frequently toured new and small galleries and gave them exposure in his *Chronicle* column. He was moderately positive about the new gallery, although Jess felt his reviews were "inane" and responded by utilizing them in his collages. Meanwhile, Lawrence Ferlinghetti, who was then writing reviews for *Art Digest* (a job that Rexroth helped him to get), said the gallery featured "the most interesting non-objective art of the season." During its short life, King Ubu had most of its shows announced quite prominently in the *San Francisco Examiner*, so in spite of its founders' lack of promotional effort, it became relatively well known.

In total, King Ubu held fifteen shows lasting about three weeks each. There were seven solo shows, three shared ones, and five group shows. Similar to the C.S.F.A. philosophy, there was no effort to present a particular style of art or to impose any uniformity across the displayed work. On the contrary, there was a deliberate effort to juxtapose contrasting styles and ideas. From the outset, it was intended to be multidisciplinary. Jess wrote that it was "a showplace for artworks and stage for drama and poetry. Shows paste-ups, paintings and junk assemblies." Exhibitions of paintings and sculptures were broken up with poetry and theater and music. There were even experimental films shown there, including two by Stan Brakhage. It has been described as being like a cabaret and had "manifestation nights" that included poets and painters performing spontaneously. The poetry nights were apparently more successful than most other events, with readings by Duncan and Jess, as well as Jack Spicer, Robin Blaser, Weldon Kees, Kenneth Rexroth, Philip Lamantia, and—according to Ferlinghetti, in his report for *Art Digest*—"other yeasty poets." Jay DeFeo, looking back on the period many years later, could not recall much about King Ubu except that "[i]t was very poetry oriented" and that it drew a lot of poets in spite of ostensibly being an art gallery. Remington agreed, saying that it "was primarily devoted to poetry reading, but you had to have something on the walls! I mean people weren't going to just stand around and stare at blank walls!"

Duncan, who was going through a year-long obsession with Gertrude Stein at this point, which he later reflected had "obliterated every possible trace of [his own] originality," directed a performance of her play, *The Five Georges*. Using crayons and brown butcher paper, he drew five large panels that functioned as the backdrop to the performance, which was given on November 5,

1953. Duncan also gave a performance of his own play, *Faust Foutu* (which loosely translates to "Faust Fucked"), for which he also produced scenery panels. Although this performance is mentioned almost nowhere, and his biographer claims the play was only given its "debut" in 1955, he explained in 1962 that "[i]n 1953 when this play was completed, I rented a mimeograph machine and ran off, 100 copies I think it was [...] Which furnished acting copies for the cast and for some of the audience." One might think perhaps he had forgotten the exact year, but "1953" was printed on the manuscript, showing that a performance indeed occurred that year.

Lyn Brockway, whose work featured in the opening night show, recalled King Ubu many years later:

> It was indeed very different from other galleries which were, and are, essentially businesses. I suppose each of us hoped to fill the place with his or her work and have the crowds standing in line to purchase [it]. But (that remote hope aside) I think our main excitement and pleasure were in seeing so many paintings and sculptures in one place instead of viewing them in the artists' usually cramped quarters. Paintings were hung whichever way the artist chose; nothing was hung in a straight, horizontal line at the King Ubu... and sculptures filled the floor. The idea of a casual and artist-involved gallery was certainly not new, but the King Ubu was the only one of that size and stature in San Francisco at the time.

King Ubu was never intended as a money-making venture, and its founders' disinterest in monetary matters meant it struggled from the outset.[19] Just a few months

---

19   Duncan had a $100-per-month inheritance that allowed him to devote his life to the arts, but he "was a notorious pinch-penny," according to Jack Goodwin and even though $100 went a long way in 1950s San Francisco, he clearly did not feel the need to invest much of it in King Ubu.

after opening, the fire department inspected it and condemned the building's wiring, which cost $260 to have redone. They held a raffle of their artwork, selling pieces by Park, Bischoff, and others, but this brought in a paltry $48. Fortunately, William Roth of the Matson Navigation Company, a wealthy friend of Duncan's, paid their bill and covered their rent, but the gallery was closed for two months as the necessary electrical work was done. Even when it re-opened, they made little profit because their visitors were primarily impoverished artists who could barely afford their own materials, never mind the luxury of buying artwork. The gallery also took only ten percent of sales instead of the industry standard of thirty.

"Mailings, and openings, utilities and props eat into our monthly income," Duncan wrote to a friend, "and I am going to have to go to work again to keep things going well rather than poorly." The three men opened a restaurant called Pere Ubu—named for the main character in *Ubu Roi*—a few miles west at 321 9th Avenue. Jess and Duncan designed the menus and Jacobus ran the kitchen. However, this merely spread their energies and King Ubu closed at the end of 1953 with an "Exhibition of Pictures in Various Mediums Using Traditional and Exploratory Techniques" by David Moore, starting on December 6. "His esthetic majesty, King Ubu, has vacated his quarters," the *Vallejo Times-Herald* reported. The gallery had lasted exactly one year.

According to Wally Hedrick, King Ubu shut down because "they ran out of money; they were going to lose the gallery." Whilst this is a plausible explanation, the gallery closed exactly one year after it opened, which of course suggests that they had simply taken on a one-year lease and felt they had pushed their idea as far as they needed to. This view is supported by a comment Deborah Remington made in an interview with Beat historian Nancy M. Grace: "Jess and Robert did their gallery for one year, and they told everyone they were going to do it for a year, and the minute the year was up they closed the gallery." Like the art they produced and displayed, the gallery they operated had been an experiment, and perhaps by now one that had run its course. There was also the fact that Duncan had begun teaching a workshop at the newly opened San Francisco Poetry Center. He may have felt that King Ubu diverted his energies from poetic matters with little compensation. The fact that his letters from this period mostly failed to mention the gallery but were filled with references to his own developing poetics and interest in ventures such as the Poetry Center and his play, *Faust Foutu*, suggests that for Duncan at least the gallery had become little more than an interesting distraction.

The man who had rented the building at 3119 Fillmore Street before them was aware of its impending closure several months before the fact. Although he lived in Laguna Beach by late 1953, Edwin Ver Becke was in contact with Duncan and Jess and knew by the end of September that the gallery was about to close. His letters imply that perhaps Jacobus was responsible. Implying that Duncan considered Jacobus "shiftless," Ver Becke wrote asking, "Is it MONEY or is it ART that Harry is after?" Perhaps with Duncan's interests lying elsewhere, Jess generally being a homebody, and Jacobus now disinterested or distracted, there was no point in renewing the lease. Ver Beck congratulated them on their experiment and told them to push forward with their individual artistic pursuits:

> About the UBU, it is sad that it cannot continue with vitality. Nothing is greater than its leadership and S.F. could certainly stand such a place. But the sacrifice for you is not worth the value received. [...] So do not grieve UBU. Thank God for its all too lovely birth and its sacred passing. You must think of your LIFE. Never look back! The salt pillar doesn't last very long in the rain."

King Ubu was a short-lived venture that may appear in certain regards to have been a failure, yet the three founders created something that succeeded in forming a small community and inspiring their peers. It may not have lasted long or made money, but in that time and place, these were not the chief concerns for artists. Art was viewed as ephemeral and largely removed from financial considerations, which is precisely why it was such a stunningly creative environment. Most importantly, though, King Ubu served as an example of what was possible when artists ceased trying to get into mainstream galleries and simply opened their own. "The King Ubu really set the stage," said William Morehouse, who had been involved with Metart several years prior. Deborah Remington, one of the last artists to show at King Ubu, said, "That's where we got the idea. The Ubu had come along and spoiled us, and when it closed we were all disappointed. [...] we'd all been very encouraged by having that gallery."

The "idea" she was referring to was the 6 Gallery.

Five Painters and a Poet

It would not be long before the building at 3119 Fillmore Street was occupied again. King Ubu closed in December 1953 and was replaced, less than a year later, by another enterprise that built upon its legacy: the 6 Gallery. Its name came from the fact that it had six founders: Wally Hedrick, John Allen Ryan, Deborah Remington, Hayward King, David Simpson, and Jack Spicer.

Excluding Spicer, whom the other five met in 1953, the group had been friends since the forties. Hedrick, Simpson, and Remington (who was a few years younger than the rest) had known each other since junior high while King and Ryan joined their social group at Pasadena Junior College, which was at the time an experimental educational institution for high-I.Q. students that combined high school and university education. There they all formed a group called the Progressive Art Workers. "The only reason we made this little club," Hedrick later recalled, "was because we entered as a group in our first competitive show at the Pasadena Museum." That was in 1946, when they were all in their late teens. "We wore black Navy sweaters and Irish wool caps, and Calder-inspired bent-wire pendants on black silk cords around our necks," Ryan remembered. "Like young art students everywhere, we were rebellious, but harmlessly so. We were simply high-spirited and deeply engaged in what we were doing."

At school, they spent half the day in class and then went out to paint landscapes. They were all passionate about art, learning about Picasso and Cubism, about Dali and Paul Klee, and their work tended toward abstraction, but they dabbled in other forms, including collage. They also loved jazz and opera, and in their early artistic experiments they tended to bring together different forms. "We were always trying to marry the arts," Remington recalled. She remembered one of Wally Hedrick's inventions:

> I remember Wally Hedrick made a light machine. It was very crude, and it had Christmas tree lights, it had this board on it, and if you pushed a button, a string of lights would go on. At some point, he hooked it up to a hi-fi, or stereo we called it then, so we'd listen to music and somehow these lights, primitively, would go on and off to the bass and treble. Then you could override that, push other things, and so we made this light symphony.

Hedrick would continue to make these sorts of devices throughout his life, combining an understanding of technology with a penchant for creation and specifically the fusion of different forms—painting, music, light, sculpture.

The group of friends spent a lot of time at the home of a sculptor in Sierra Madre Canyon, not far from Pasadena, listening to new records and talking about opportunities in the art world. Unfortunately, "there wasn't any art activity in Pasadena to speak of in a community sense," Remington said. Even in the wider Los Angeles area, they felt there was little to get excited about. In the fall of 1947, they went to the Otis Art Institute in Los Angeles but hated it. "After a couple of months, the instruction was mediocre, pedantic," Remington said. "It wasn't interesting enough. It wasn't revealing enough, strong enough, hard enough for kids who were really serious, as we were. [...] it was just dumb and boring, and it simply wasn't strong enough to hold our interest." The group asked Leonard Edmundson, a friend and teacher at their college, what they should do and he replied, "The first thing to do is to get out of Pasadena and go to San Francisco."

In 1947, Hedrick and John Stanley, a potter friend, jumped in Wally's Ford Model A and drove up the coast, arriving in San Francisco in the middle of the night. The next morning, they showed up at C.S.F.A. and ran into Douglas MacAgy, who mistook them for high-school students. After the misunderstanding was cleared up, MacAgy personally showed Hedrick and Stanley around the impressive Russian Hill campus, where they met Clyfford Still, David Park, and Elmer Bischoff. They did not know enough about the art world to be impressed by these artists, who were already quite well known, but they were amazed by the scale of the paintings some students were working on and the fact that artists seemed to be throwing paint at these giant canvases. "We immediately went back to Pasadena with a new viewpoint," Hedrick recalled. "Here was this really good place, it seemed like heaven, full of these crazy artists."

Separately, Remington and her mother visited the school and were similarly blown away by the abstract expressionist art on display. She said, "I fell in love with it immediately," adding that "it was like a step into another world all of a sudden." She explained:

> I looked at all the art hanging on the walls around the patio, and a lot of it, I didn't understand. I had just walked into something called abstract expressionism, right straight smack in the face. It fascinated me. I loved it. I hated it. It interested me all in the first impact. [...] I can't tell you. It was like a step into another world all of a sudden. Anyway, in the next few hours, I registered, signed up, the whole thing. I felt like well, my future is sealed here. Went back to Pasadena and packed up and came back to San Francisco.

With Hedrick raving about San Francisco and Remington enthusing over the school, and both of them excited about the experimental art being done there, the rest of the Progressive Art Workers were soon convinced and began gathering materials for their applications.

In February 1949, Ryan, King, Remington, and Simpson all enrolled at C.S.F.A. but Hedrick—who came from a poorer background—merely dropped in on classes. "The idea of moving to San Francisco so I could go to college was just unthinkable," he said, adding that no one in his family had ever gone into tertiary education. Hedrick maintained a studio in Pasadena and drove back and forth, spending more time in the bars and cafés of North Beach than the classrooms at C.S.F.A., but he did hang around the school enough to join the Studio 13 Jass Band,[20] named for a room in the northeastern corner of the old school building at C.S.F.A. that was open to anyone who wanted to use it for art practice. The band used it regularly for rehearsals and it was where Clay Spohn's famous "Museum of Unknown and Little Known Objects" had been shown in 1949. It included MacAgy, Park, Bischoff, and various other musically inclined artists, with Hedrick playing the banjo. They were originally called "Picasso 5," but Park had complained, preferring Matisse to Picasso. The band would stay together, albeit with a rotating membership, for about a half century.

For the five friends, their first months in San Francisco and at C.S.F.A. were illuminating. They hung out in North Beach, talking with other artists at 12 Adler Place and across the street at the newly opened Vesuvio Cafe, run by Henri Lenoir, a beret-wearing Frenchman who was proud to have so many artists for customers. They were, he said, attracted "by the non-bourgeois atmosphere created by the avant-garde paintings [he] hung on the walls." At the Black Cat and the Iron Pot, they could see the latest in local art as the owners allowed young painters to display their work on the walls. Ryan said it "was an exciting time to be in the city, and to be in school there." He continued:

> During the first three semesters, we studied under Jean Varda, Zigmund Sazevich, David Park, Elmer Bischoff, Ernest Mundt (who placed before us the Bauhaus version of Dada, Surrealism and Existentialism, and made it part of our thinking), James Budd Dixon, Richard Diebenkorn, & many

---

20   "Jass" was an early spelling of what is now more commonly known as "jazz."

others. Clay Spohn and Ansel Adams were still there, and even if we didn't study with them, we were aware of their presence and their work.

The style of teaching at C.S.F.A., however, was more in line with twenty-first-century pedagogy than the traditional methods found in other institutions in the 1940s. Rather than a teacher-centered environment comprised of instruction and lectures, students learned from each other and embarked upon their own journeys of artistic discovery according to their personalities and individual inspirations. Hedrick said, "In this little community, we didn't have to have art teachers. It sounds egotistical, but we were our own teachers and we taught each other." This happened on campus and off it—in houses that doubled as studios and galleries, and in the bars and cafés where the creatively inclined gathered to share their philosophies, their works, and their aspirations. In this time and place, artistic education was not merely a classroom affair; it was an organic and holistic learning process that occurred in a range of locations and arose as much from interactions between students as between students and teachers.

As we saw in a previous chapter, this "holistic" education was largely due to C.S.F.A. director Douglas MacAgy, who pushed for a curriculum that did not distinguish between the arts. Remington remembered it being "just a great nurturing ground for everybody" due to the mixing of disciplines in both a teaching and social context. She said, "this integration with all the arts was taking place, and it's not like today where the arts are separate—you know, the theatre people have their own world and the dance people and literature, the poets, then the visual arts—it wasn't like that. We all socialized together, we went to the same parties, we talked to each other."

In 1950, Hedrick, King, and Ryan were called up for military service (Simpson was exempt for having already done a stint in the Navy) and they trained for duty in the Korean War. Before being sent to Korea, however, Ryan was stationed for a year in San Francisco and continued to see his friends, paint, and enjoy the cultural scene. He lived with Knute Stiles, a student at C.S.F.A. and later the owner of The Place, where Ryan would end up bartending for a period. Stiles introduced Ryan to Robert Duncan, who "became a kind of poetic mentor to" him. Ryan already knew Duncan's lover Jess from their time at C.S.F.A. Already, the young painters were enmeshed in a complex socio-artistic network that would produce a number of regionally and later nationally renowned artists of all sorts—painters, models, conductors, ballet dancers, and musicians. "There wasn't a place we could go," he said, "where we didn't run into people we knew, and San Francisco seemed like a mighty small town then." All of this led to collaborations—painters writing poems, poets reading to jazz, musicians crafting sculptures. "There was a good melting pot of people and ideas," Remington recalled.

When the three painters were discharged from the military in late 1952, King and Hedrick moved into "the Ghost House" at 1350 Franklin. Ryan did not move in with them, instead moving to a home on Davis Street with a friend or possibly a lover. The Ghost House on Franklin was the same building where the King Ubu founders—Duncan, Jess, and Jacobus—had lived in 1951, and it would be occupied at various times by a number of other creatives, including Philip Lamantia; filmmaker Christopher Maclaine; the photographer Nata Piaskowski, who took some of the only surviving photos of King Ubu and the 6 Gallery;[21] and Piaskowski's husband, a painter called Martin Baer. Solnit described the building as "a decrepit, cavernous Gothic-Victorian on Franklin at Sutter Street whose three floors of rooms were rented out as studios and illegally inhabited by young writers and artists [...] conveniently located between North Beach and the

---

21   Remington said that Piaskowski, who had been a student at C.S.F.A. in the late forties, "documented almost every party" and that she may have even photographed the 6 Gallery reading, but there is no evidence of this. If the photos ever existed, they are sadly now lost. She took photos of both the opening shows at King Ubu and the 6 Gallery and these can be found in the books *Lyrical Vision* and *The Beat Generation Galleries and Beyond*.

Fillmore, a place where Thelonius Monk or Miles Davis might drop in, where drugs and parties were common." She was exaggerating somewhat, for the building was not "illegally inhabited." The residents may have done various illegal activities whilst living there, and they certainly treated the old building as though they were squatters, but they in fact paid rent to whoever had divided it into individual apartments. The city was dotted with such "pads," as they later became known, where artists would cohabit, the lines between home, hangout, studio, and gallery blurring.

The painters received their certificates of completion from C.S.F.A. in 1953. Remington was briefly married and moved away from San Francisco while Hedrick, Ryan, and a friend called Bill Morehouse, who had known Hedrick in Korea, moved to Oakland and entered the degree program at the California School of Arts and Crafts, where they could make use of their G.I. Bill benefits. "We couldn't keep our benefits unless we were enrolled in an accredited degree program, and C.S.F.A. didn't have one at that time," Ryan explained. It was a disappointment for them—"a catastrophe" in the hyperbolic words of Hedrick—because C.S.A.C. turned out to be far more conventional than C.S.F.A. and none of them were cut out for the academic rigor of regular higher education. At C.S.F.A., they had spent four mornings a week drawing and painting but at C.S.A.C. they were expected to attend various lectures, including art history, which they disliked.

Thankfully, C.S.F.A. started its first accredited program in September 1953 and so Hedrick and Ryan moved back to San Francisco, subletting their Oakland house. Through a combination of G.I. Bill benefits and academic scholarships, all five of the painter friends were able to enroll for the '54–'55 academic year at C.S.F.A. They already had credits for their artwork but "what [they] really basically needed were all the academic things," Remington said. "The history, the English, the art history. We actually had to take physics and chemistry." This would allow them to receive a Bachelor of Fine Arts. They no longer had to do art classes and so they painted at home instead. It would be their final year and they knew that to become professional artists they would need exposure, and this raised the question of what venue would allow them to exhibit their work.

There had been a handful of small venues that allowed some of these artists to display their paintings. Remington had shown hers at King Ubu and Simpson showed his at Studio 44, a gallery one block south on Fillmore. Hedrick and Ryan (as well as many other local artists, including Jess) had been given one-person shows at a newly opened bar called The Place,[22] but they felt there were no dedicated gallery spaces available to them. A bar was better than nothing, but they wanted something bigger, particularly as their skills developed and it seemed there might actually be a modest audience. "There was nowhere in San Francisco we could show our work," Hedrick said. "There was nothing. We weren't known well enough to approach the museums, they didn't want us." Remington said they were "kind of obstreperous kids" with "a sense of anti-establishmentism" who were "interested in rebel positions and that kind of stuff, and we couldn't get into shows anywhere else. Nobody would have us, so we had to make a place of our own. It never occurred to us that we couldn't do it. We just did it." Over the next few months, they began to plan the running of their gallery.

John Allen Ryan took credit for the group renting the property at 3119 Fillmore Street, explaining many years later, "I knew Duncan and Jacobus, and so we got the place." Jay DeFeo, however, believed that it was Deborah Remington who connected the group. Remington had in fact shown her work at King Ubu in November 1953—one of the last shows before the gallery closed. She had known Duncan and Jess well enough for them to invite her to exhibit her work. She also believed that the two groups were quite close, saying that Duncan and his "coterie" of poet friends "were all part of our group, and it just wasn't separate."

---

22   The Place opened in 1953 and was run by Knute Stiles and Leo Krikorian. On its opening night, Ryan placed a toilet in the window with a draft notice above it. The police came and forced them to remove the installation. This event has been frequently misattributed to the opening of the 6 Gallery. There is more information about The Place in Chapter 2.3.

Five Painters and a Poet

Both are plausible explanations but Wally Hedrick remembered it being Ryan who came up with the idea. Interestingly, he said this was because Ryan was primarily a poet and the others were visual artists. Certainly, Ryan wrote poetry and sent it to friends, including Allen Ginsberg. Jack Goodwin said he wrote "sad poems about his bohemian life" and claimed to have written music to perform alongside Ryan's work at a public reading. David Simpson, however, disagreed. He told me that "John Ryan was more of a painter than a poet, although I guess he had a circle of friends that included poets. He was never known as a poet and I don't recall him ever really writing any poems. He certainly never had anything published." As we have seen many times now, it was common for artists to dabble in different forms and undoubtedly Ryan liked to express himself in both poetry and painting, but it is interesting that Hedrick pointed to Ryan as more of a poet than painter and claimed that was what linked him to the King Ubu founders. He explained this in a 1985 interview:

> I admire poetry, but poets are a very strange group of people, and I never had too much contact with them. But, anyway, John did. He knew Jess, Robert Duncan, and that whole crew. He was also going to school at the same time I was, and Jack Spicer [...] was teaching then. Anyway, they ran out of money; they were going to lose the gallery. That's why this group that I knew got together, and—I think the rent was $35[23]—we managed to scrape it together, and we took it over.

His recollection of the transition period between the two galleries makes it sound rather smooth. In fact, "they were going to lose the gallery [...] and we took it over" sounds as though the painters stepped in to replace the poets, but King Ubu closed in December 1953 and the 6 Gallery opened at the end of October 1954, which

---

23   The rent was in fact $40/month.

meant the property sat vacant for more than ten months. Moreover, it was only in June 1954 that the group decided they were interested in running their own gallery.

In the above quote, Hedrick also made reference to Jack Spicer, the sixth founding member. He had been employed to work in the English department of C.S.F.A. upon their establishing a degree program, which is how the painters from Pasadena met him. David Simpson called him "a faculty advisor" but the others mostly remember him teaching English and history. His biographers called him "head of the new humanities department." Spicer himself seemed somewhat unclear. When asked what he taught at C.S.F.A., he simply replied, "Everything." Remington recalled:

> There was a wonderful teacher who showed up at school, a poet named Jack Spicer, who was a very strong influence on us in terms of—oh, he was very interested in us as a group and as individuals in our work. He taught us, oh, let's say, Dante, a great excursion into Dante. And when you have this man for literature, for history, he was hired—at that time, the faculty was very small. So one had him for art history, world history, world literature, communications. You probably would have took every class you had from him. [...] The man, I think, really taught us how to think. He was a very strong influence on us all. We loved him.

Although he was their teacher, Jack Spicer was only a few years older than the Progressive Art Workers. Born in Los Angeles, he was also from the same part of the country as these five painters, and so a friendly relationship emerged between them. This was unusual because Spicer was an aggressive alcoholic who tended to have more enemies than friends. "All of the bartenders thoroughly disliked Spicer," Jack Goodwin remembered, "even though he spent most of his salary on them. They got sick of the everlasting carping and nagging and pissing and moaning." He claimed to live on a diet of whisky and peanut butter and was known locally as "Queen of the put-down" for his consistent stream of creative invective. He was certainly admired for his intelligence and his poetic abilities, as well as his lofty principles, but he had a long history of pushing people away, especially those who could have helped him become more successful as a poet.

Spicer had been friends with Robert Duncan and Robin Blaser in the forties, forming what they called the Berkeley Renaissance. He was—like Duncan—openly homosexual and he wrote about his sexuality in his poems, which made them hard to publish. Extremely principled, he refused to sign a McCarthyist loyalty oath at U.C. Berkeley in 1950 and this cost him dearly as he had hoped to become a teacher there after completing his graduate studies. Despite the professional setback, his stance endeared him to other poets. He was not one to capitalize on such bohemian credit, though, and he found himself constantly at odds with other writers and artists. Those who liked him tended to tolerate his bad habits out of respect for his intelligence, his bravery, and his creative capacity, but among the people whom he despised were many who could have helped him—Ginsberg, Ferlinghetti, and Charles Olson to name but a few. If he disliked someone, even for the pettiest of reasons, he would make it known and refuse to cooperate with them. When the Beats became successful, they earned his purest hatred. Ginsberg once denied this and said, "I think he thought that my own method was much too involved with personal statement and ego," but Spicer loathed everything about Ginsberg, from his poetry to his success to his promotional abilities. It didn't help that Spicer was hugely antisemitic. After the success of "Howl," he was sometimes heard shouting "FUCK GINSBERG" in public.

He constantly refused acceptance and then railed against perceived rejection. This likely stemmed from his insecurities. He was physically quite unattractive and believed he had a very small penis, which led to envy and sexual frustration. Feeling constantly inferior to those around him and unable to socialize normally, he lashed out often and viciously. Ginsberg and others frequently reached out to him, hoping to expand their poetic community and achieve greater success through a united front, but Spicer refused and continued to alienate himself. He was his own worst enemy and avoided the sort of professional associations that benefited other poets, so that in spite of his talent and reputation his first book was only published in 1957.[24] He died in the poverty ward of a local hospital less than a decade later. Ultimately, his reputation as a poet would undergo a minor resurrection in death, when he was no longer capable of self-sabotage.

The painter friends found Spicer's classes fascinating and inspiring. He taught history and literature, making these subjects—which the artists were reluctant to learn—incredibly engaging, even "magical" in the words of one student. She said, "He was a wonderful teacher, a very innovative teacher [...] and taught us how to relate art history to the political and social history of the times." He told his students, "I'm not teaching you what to think. I'm teaching how to think," and they respected that. It fit with their personal educational journeys and allowed them to appreciate even the more challenging parts of his lessons. One person who knew him and was highly critical of his numerous personal flaws admitted that "when he was teaching classes [a] supportive, constructive side came into action [and p]rojects were tailored to the interests of individuals."

Even in a place like C.S.F.A., filled with unusual ideas and methods, his lessons were unconventional. He brought tarot cards into class and told his students to pick one, then he would say, "Your assignment is to write an interpretation of the card." He would make them produce art and then describe it and shuffle the descriptions to see if students could correctly identify the works described. Remington remembered:

---

24   This was *After Lorca*, published by White Rabbit Press and with a cover designed by Jess. One of the poems was dedicated to John Allen Ryan.

Well, in a three-hour period he taught us that we didn't know what we were talking about! We couldn't communicate, we couldn't write, we were dumbfounded! The guy was just fabulous. In that same class, he would have us writing ads for Ivory soap and Clorox bleach and stuff like that. There again, the same thing; we'd have to write slogans, and you'd read the slogan and he'd say, "What product is that about?" And we'd go "Gasoline? Motor oil? We don't know!" We couldn't write! So that taught us a lot about writing.

He taught Shakespeare but would not let them do whole plays; rather, they would study the play within a play in Hamlet. He made them learn Middle English to read Chaucer. Spicer, who vacillated between difficulty and accessibility in his own poems and pondered the notions of high-brow and low-brow art, attempted to utilize pop culture in the classroom as he sometimes did in his poems (which were also used as study materials), and he would bring a strobe light into the room, turn off the lights, and have his students improvise monologues about a coming nuclear apocalypse. They were made to write screenplays and he pushed and pushed them to think creatively about every conceivable angle.

To pass his class, students had to write letters to the editor of the *San Francisco Chronicle* and have them published. Spicer—who had begun his course by saying, "I plan to be my own best student"—participated in his own assignment and was annoyed when he was beaten by Ryan, whose letter appeared in the *Chronicle* just four days later. Remington said everyone thought it would be easy, but it took her four attempts before her letter was published, and some students couldn't manage it at all. True to his word, Spicer failed them.

Spicer's classes became famously raucous, sometimes involving alcohol, and his students even came to class high on occasion. Eventually, the five painters began taking him to The Place, where he began to hold court, lecturing informally on life and art for those who would listen, or simply playing Scrabble when the bar was too quiet for his proclamations. According to one regular, he found "disciples" there and began his "poet factory" by insulting young poets, forcing them into defending themselves, which usually led to them becoming part of his circle. In the bathroom, an "ongoing epic" was graffitied with Spicer at the center of it. Both inside the classroom and out, he was a local character of great interest. No wonder when the students got a new history teacher, Jan Von Werloff, who strolled into class in a suit and began lecturing in the traditional mode, they all laughed out loud.

Spicer soon began sleeping with Ryan and the two men created their own private language and secret society, the Interplanetary Services of the Martian Anarchy. Spicer's biographers called Ryan Spicer's "fuck buddy" but it seems the two had a more substantial relationship than that, albeit not a monogamous or particularly long-lasting one. Ryan tried to help Spicer with his insecurities, but Spicer probably felt some degree of envy and frustration here, too, for Ryan was a very handsome man and socially gifted. Bisexual, he floated freely between gay and straight communities, generally getting along well with those he met. This was the very opposite of Spicer, who seems to have taken an immediate dislike to most of the people around him and pre-emptively shunned them. One observer said that there was "a love-hate thing going on" between them possibly due to Spicer's disapproval of Ryan's bohemian friends.

The relationship between teacher and students grew close enough that Spicer not only encouraged the Progressive Art Workers to establish their own gallery but eventually joined them in the effort. In fact, Wally Hedrick claimed that the idea of a gallery bringing together all the arts, including poetry, was Spicer's. David Simpson concurred. He told me that Spicer "came in as a poet, as a full-fledged member, and was influential in expanding away from just painting and sculpture [and it was under] his influence that we accepted readily that poetry readings would be a good idea." Spicer joined the five painters and encouraged them in their efforts to establish an art gallery, but it was not an easy relationship. Even with his young poet friends, who were tolerant and respectful, there were repeated fallouts and they excommunicated him from their group several times, resulting in tearful reunions when he was forgiven.

The 6 Gallery

With Jack Spicer on board, the five painters had become a group of six and now that they were intent on opening their own gallery, this number would be used for its name. In fact, the naming of the gallery is one of the only parts of this story upon which all the participants agree. It was Deborah Remington who came up with it, and this is how she recalled the decision being made:

> We sat there one afternoon right in the beginning before we opened, we sat there from about 3 o'clock to 6 o'clock, all of us thinking about what to name this place. We went through name after name. Finally, David Simpson had to get to work at about 6 because he had a job pumping gas at a gas station.[25] So, we had to wrap it up. Well, I guess most of us had jobs. And so I remember—clearly as if it were yesterday—just out of desperation, I said, "Listen, there's six of us. Let's call it the 6 Gallery." And fine, okay, goodbye. So that's what we did!

After renting the empty space at 3119 Fillmore, they made several efforts to raise funds. The first was a rummage sale at the San Francisco Arts Festival at Aquatic Park in late September. They did not sell art; rather, the artists gathered random items to sell and then attracted customers with their bohemian antics. Hedrick claimed that the man who invented the concept of a "Happening," Allan Kaprow, was there that day, the implication being

---

25   Simpson's job started at midnight. He was going home to sleep rather than going to work.

that this was a proto-hippie happening, the first of what would become a countercultural trend. There is no evidence to suggest that Kaprow was in attendance that day (or even in that part of the country) and Hedrick, speaking several decades after the fact, also appears to have conflated multiple events related to the 6 Gallery, but certainly quite a few of the group's antics and artistic creations pre-figured those more commonly associated with the sixties counterculture.

Herb Caen, who would several years later coin the term "beatnik," and who also popularized the word "hippie," visited the festival and made note of the unconventional group, writing about them briefly in his column for the *Chronicle*. He wrote in a fairly mocking tone, seemingly viewing the artists at the festival as flea-ridden. However, he seemed somewhat positive about the group. On September 26, several days after his visit to Aquatic Park, he reported:

> Stopped by booth called "Six," sponsored by six people interested in art, music, poetry, integrity and other worth-while things. Several young ladies with long blonde hair and leather sandals, several young men with bare chests and beards gathered in circle, listening intently to record of avant garde poem, recited against background of polytonal music.

The music was the Dave Brubeck Trio[26] and the poetry was Spicer's "California Poems" played on a loop for three consecutive days, which annoyed people in nearby booths. Caen reported one young painter complaining, "That stuff is driving me nuts." In spite of aggravating the other artists, the group raised about $80 for plasterboard,

---

26   Brubeck was not well known at this point, but a successful album in June led to him unexpectedly appearing on the cover of *Time* in November, hugely elevating his status. He was surprised and embarrassed, recognizing that his selection was largely due to his being white. Brubeck and his group would play at the 6 Gallery at least once.

The 6 Gallery

according to Hedrick, which they would use to give the gallery some proper wall space—something King Ubu had lacked.

There was also "a well-attended poetry reading" on October 26 at the Opus One, a North Beach café, gallery, and gay bar that often hosted classical music performances.[27] Ryan said it "was a big success," helping them raise another "$30 or $40." In the middle of October, Remington and Spicer appeared on local radio station K.P.F.A. to talk about their new gallery. K.P.F.A. was an influential, left-leaning media outlet that began broadcasting in 1949. It was allegedly co-founded by Kenneth Rexroth, who described it as "devoted to the reeducation of its audience on what you might call libertarian principles." It featured a great deal of poetry and in 1953 gave a platform to Alan Watts, who at the time was largely unknown. Spicer had hosted a show in 1949 and 1950 but was fired after too many complaints about his rude language. Ferlinghetti was a keen K.P.F.A. listener, saying that it "was a total political, social education for [him]," and many people tuned in to Rexroth's book-review show, which he described as focused on "mature non-fiction, high-brow literature, scholarly works, fine arts, orientalia, poetry." However, listeners may have been tuning in more for his "outrageous pronouncements on the state of contemporary intellectual life" than his literary insights, according to his biographer Linda Hamalian. He seems to have treated his radio show much like his Friday-night salons, which is to say he viewed it as his personal soapbox and ranted freely on his favorite topics. Ferlinghetti recalled that "he didn't review just literature. He reviewed every subject—geology, anthropology, astronomy, philosophy—and it seemed as he had this encyclopedic knowledge."

It is clear that, unlike the King Ubu founders, the

---

27   Given that gay bars were illegal at the time, there is little contemporary evidence but it has been well established since, through the testimony of patrons such as biographer Lewis Ellingham, that it was a gay bar that simply advertised itself as a classical music venue as a coded term. Like the various lesbian bars of North Beach, it drew a large and naïve straight crowd as well.

six poets made an effort to spread word of their venture. The promotional leaflets sent out to advertise the new gallery and its pre-opening fundraiser emphasized the multidisciplinary nature of the gallery but interestingly put poetry first:

> A new gallery of poetry, painting, sculpture, and photography [...] New poetry tapes, experimental music, color organ

Despite the fact that five of the six founders were painters, who had opened the gallery largely to show off the work they would create as final-year art students, poetry was still listed first on most promotional materials. This was likely due to Spicer. According to his biographers, Lewis Ellingham and Kevin Killian, "Spicer, who knew he had no talent for curatorial work, contented himself with writing press releases—'propaganda'— and beating the drums among the 'literati.'" No doubt he chose to put his preferred art form at the top of the bill. The experimental music and color organ, meanwhile, were Hedrick's domain. A thoroughly multidisciplinary artist with an array of hands-on skills, such as welding, he often created wondrous contraptions by utilizing unconventional materials. In this case, he had built an electric piano that he and Ryan both played, and which emitted different lights according to the notes chosen.

The six founders also put more effort into decorating their new premises than Duncan, Jess, and Jacobus had done with King Ubu. With the money they raised, Hedrick and Ryan installed some plasterboard wall panels that did not quite reach the ceiling and in other places they merely hung white canvas over bare walls, with paintings hanging from black wires that attached to pipes and beams on the ceiling. The plasterboard was then painted white, one of the few conventional aspects of the gallery. However, even the best walls only rose about eight or nine feet, with bare concrete beneath them and the building's wooden frame exposed above, alongside an array of pipes and wires. These pipes may even have leaked, with DeFeo calling the gallery "very damp." "The ceiling was open," Remington

The 6 Gallery

said, and so "you could see the rafters and that stuff." In this regard, it prefigured the wave of art galleries located in reclaimed industrial facilities in the twenty-first century, which make no attempt to hide the pipes and beams that make up the buildings' interior structures.

They managed to find a desk to put by the entrance and installed a phone line to give the gallery some semblance of professionalism. A small number of mismatched chairs were also procured so that patrons had someplace to rest. The space was lit by the theater lights left over from the tenants before King Ubu, with the same exposed-wood walls, beams, rafters, and columns. Near the back of the gallery, there was a small, raised stage or dais. A photo from the opening night shows it to have been about ten inches high.[28] Here, the bare walls were still covered in graffiti, with a number of paintings affixed or hanging from the rafters. However, now that there was much white wall space, the 6 did more closely resemble a conventional gallery than King Ubu, which had largely seemed like a derelict building with a number of artworks strewn randomly throughout.

Outside, above the big doors Jacobus had installed, they hung a large plywood "6." Hedrick, who often covertly used school equipment for private projects, had cut it using a machine at C.S.F.A. and they wrapped it in fairy lights for some degree of visibility in the evening. The handful of surviving photos show the gallery to have been tidier and marginally more conventional than the King Ubu had been. Most importantly, though, the six artists were delighted with their new gallery. Ryan later wrote:

---

28   Earlier in the book, we saw Deborah Remington recall an 8-foot-by-8-foot movable stage on rollers that she remembered being about 14 inches high. This was a different size and shape from the stage at the 6 Gallery, which was not movable and still existed in the 1990s, so although it is tempting to view them as the same stage, perhaps slightly adapted, they do appear to have been quite different. However, it is not impossible that the movable stage was altered or that Remington's memory of its dimensions was substantially off.

> It was exactly what we wanted. Anything that we wanted to have happen could happen. We had no set schedule, and we could do anything, as long as we met the costs. [...] From the very beginning, the "6" had everything, but operated on nothing: we had painting, poetry, sculpture, 3-D movies by Hy Hirsch and others, jazz (traditional & progressive), & Dada "happenings," but no money.

The group agreed that the gallery should be run as a cooperative and adhere to certain principles of fairness. Part of this meant that the position of gallery director would rotate, with Hedrick being the first to assume the role. The gallery director would not be allowed a one-person show during their tenure but would be exempt from the $5/month membership fee. In 1955, though, it became apparent that no one else would take responsibility and Hedrick's position was made permanent.[29] That year, he painted a work called "I'm the Director," a mixed-media painting on canvas that depicts a totem-pole-like structure made of scrap. My interpretation is that it shows a struggle for balance, which is likely a reflection of Hedrick's feeling as he ran the gallery, took classes at C.S.F.A., joined the Council of the San Francisco Art Association and also served as Chairman of Annual Exhibitions, competed in competitions, showed at other galleries, served on juries for yet more art competitions, and was put in charge of creating an "Art Bank" at C.S.F.A. When talking about his role three decades later, he said, "I was the director of the gallery, and I didn't even know what was going on," saying that his role was mostly to "sweep the floor and lock the door at the end of the night." However, he might have been somewhat self-effacing here, as others have referred to him as the "ringleader," "chief organizer," and "unofficial head." Hedrick retained this position until

---

29 The exemption from dues appears to have been quickly changed as well, for all the founding members were paying double the amount owed by other members by November, and that included Hedrick.

1957, when the original founders had mostly drifted away and Manuel Neri took over as director.

The collective's secretary, meanwhile, was Ryan, which Hedrick explained was "because he was a poet and could write." Jay DeFeo, who was not one of the founders but was a member from a very early stage, was the group's treasurer and also its secretary whenever Ryan was out of town, which he often was.[30] Remington was put in charge of early P.R. work, which involved contacting people in the arts and media world of San Francisco. She was afraid of speaking with these people, so she "would just send penny postcards" that Hayward King mimeographed at work. She said that Ralph Gleason and Kenneth Rexroth were early supporters of their venture. Rexroth in particular "was very supportive. He'd always come to the poetry readings. [...] And he was very involved. He loved us and supported us, and whenever he could he'd mention us in critiques or reviews." Being a cooperative endeavor, the labor was shared, and so the six founders would pick letters from the alphabet and then take turns addressing letters to people on their mailing list.

For the opening show, all five poets displayed their work alongside pieces by Leo Valledor, Robert Bachman, Jack Davis, James Weeks, Robert Carrigg, Peter Shoemaker, Joel Barletta, Madeleine Dimond, Peter Forakis, and Lynn Williams.[31] In total, there were thirty-six pieces by sixteen artists. Photos supposedly taken on the opening night

---

30   Confusingly, Beverly Pabst (of the Pabst Brewing family) was also the group's sometime secretary and sometime treasurer. Although dates are hard to confirm due to a lack of documentation, it appears she may have held these roles toward the end of the gallery's existence and DeFeo was more involved early in its short life. In any case, positions could be rather fluid and no one was legally contracted.

31   A number of the artists in this show had displayed their work at King Ubu. Several books report that only three artists exhibited at both galleries (Wasserstein, Remington, and Jess) but this is completely untrue. There were many artists who participated in exhibitions at both King Ubu and the 6. This is hardly surprising given the overlapping social circles and the lack of other venues particularly during the time when King Ubu was open.

appear to show works by Dimitri Grachis and Fred Martin, neither of whom is listed as having contributed but would show at the 6 Gallery several times in the future.[32] Spicer—who was an excellent and dramatic performer of his own work—read poems backed by the Dave Brubeck Trio and some of his other poems were printed on the walls. These were interspersed with Chinese or Chinese-style calligraphy. However, "[f]ew sold," as one observer noted, and Frankenstein, who was generally very kind toward the gallery, scoffed at this "forced and even sentimental" juxtaposition, saying, "The poetry displayed is by Jack Spicer, and while it is outside my province, it struck me as notably skillful and very rich in content, but the visual comments whereon which hung next to the manuscripts were almost uniformly feeble, not to say embarrassing."

Although it was a small gallery with laughably limited resources, the efforts of the six founders were successful in gaining local attention and the gallery was popular from its first day. The media mentioned it often and local arts publications took an interest. Soon after their opening night, the *San Francisco Art Association Bulletin* reported:

> A new gallery has opened at 3119 Fillmore Street in San Francisco that will exhibit works of painting, poetry, sculpture and photography. The first exhibition featured

---

32   Martin was not a paid member of the 6 Gallery in October but paid double in November, so it is possible that he was a late addition to the show. Paying membership fees entitled an artist to contribute to group shows but, as with much at the 6 Gallery, it was not a strict rule and various artists contributed without showing and vice versa. David Simpson told me that he "was one of the only members who had money [and so he] occasionally paid a little extra." Looking at the limited remaining financial records, this does seem to have been normal. When a member had some extra cash for whatever reason, they paid more than their share. However, it should be noted that the alleged photos from the opening night show the same parts of the gallery with different paintings in place, indicating that the photos in fact came from different events and thus it is possible the Martin and Grachis works might have been from a later exhibition.

The 6 Gallery

a show by SFAA artist and associate artist members. The Gallery is open from 2:30 to 10:00 p.m. on Saturday and Sunday and from 1:00 until 5:00 p.m. on weekdays.

Even a few hundred miles south, in Los Angeles, where the five painters had grown up, there were notices in the media. The *Los Angeles Times* highlighted this story of local artists making it in another town:

> Southland Artists Open S.F. Gallery
>
> A group of South California artists have opened the Six Gallery at 3119 Fillmore St., San Francisco. It will cater to painters under 30.

Of course, these are merely announcements and they mostly rehashed press releases and repeated key details, but in the coming days and weeks, the 6 Gallery was visited by a number of critics. Although their reviews were mixed, they almost always applauded the intentions and enthusiasm of the founders. *Fortnight* magazine gave a full page to the "[s]ix youthful pioneers, in revolt against commercial art galleries and living by rote and caution." The article refers to the gallery as a studio, which it certainly looked like and sometimes functioned as. (A photo of Manuel Neri and Bruce McGaw shows the artists lying on the floor of the gallery, covered in paint splatters, looking as though they are amidst their ongoing work.) The article's author, Alan Tory, understandably failed to grasp that Spicer (the group's poet) was part of the six and claimed that Bill Eichel, a photographer, made up the numbers. To be fair, Eichel was the seventh member of the cooperative even if he was not part of the founding six. The article highlighted the fact that the student artists worked regular jobs (sewer worker, secretary, gas pump attendant, cafeteria manager) to pay the gallery's bills and emphasized the more unusual elements of the gallery: its cooperative nature, the placing of photography on an equal footing with painting, being a studio where people could listen to poetry for twenty-five cents, and a series of "poetry concerts" planned for the coming year. "It was from similar beginnings that Picasso and Matisse shaped their careers," the article concluded.

Most of the 6 Gallery's shows would be announced in local newspapers and art journals with periodic reviews by Frankenstein and others, including Lawrence Ferlinghetti,[33] who was then writing for *Arts Digest*. Given that Ferlinghetti later made his name as a poet and publisher of poetry, it is perhaps unsurprising to note that he was most interested in the concept of an art gallery open to poetry, among other art forms:

> When the "6" Gallery opened late this past fall with a declaration that it intended to combine the showing of painting with music and poetry and, moreover, to make poetry "pay," it was viewed with skeptical monocles by most of the local press, as well as by a good many other people who otherwise heard about it. Tried before in many a brave garret gallery, the idea of public synthesis of the arts was loaded with the usual yawning pitfalls.

This "synthesis of the arts," he felt, was the main selling point of the 6 Gallery. Whilst ambivalent regarding some of the paintings shown, he was extremely impressed by a series of "2-D and 3-D abstract movies by Hy Hirsh [sic], movies which were as beautiful and as interesting, from an experimental point of view, as any seen this year in this region, which is saying quite a bit."

Ferlinghetti's review alluded to a promise made by the founders of the 6 Gallery to "make poetry pay," something that other critics mentioned in their reviews. In this initial statement, they also said that their gallery would undoubtedly "make grievous errors in taste and grievous

---

33   Ferlinghetti believed criticism was itself a form of art and he took his job seriously. Wally Hedrick said, "One of my favorite art critics was Lawrence Ferlinghetti" because he made "a critical statement, but in a poetic image that everyone can interpret in his or her own way."

The 6 Gallery

errors in tone but will never be dull." In the *San Francisco Chronicle*, art critic Alfred Frankenstein said that the 6 had been "neither grievous in taste nor grievous in tone, but it was not too incredibly exciting."[34] Overall, though, he felt the 6 was interesting even if there had been "a few wrinkles." This was something the artists never shied away from. Indeed, in another statement posted on the gallery's wall, they made a promise to themselves and their visitors:

> We commit ourselves to exhibiting not only successes and matured achievements, but half-steps, blunders and fumblings by the way.

We have already seen that the 6—as King Ubu had done—looked like a hybrid of a studio and a gallery but here we have a public acknowledgement that this was a deliberate part of its function. It was tied in with the artists' anti-establishment views on art, their rejection of convention and niceties. The 6 Gallery was not only for finished, polished works but a place to demonstrate process and concept, even if these were never fully realized. Given that the gallery would later become famous for an early, incomplete reading of the most important poem of the late twentieth century, it is safe to say that they succeeded.

Interestingly, it was this approach that Frankenstein—normally so enthusiastic about the gallery—found off-putting. Calling the idea of spontaneous composition and deliberately unfinished works a form of "workshop demonstration," he said, "The spontaneous, unpremeditated action is always revealing, but a planned program of spontaneity can be a little wearisome, and when Manuel Neri fixes a pair of overalls to a canvas and covers it with a film of paint [... t]he whole thing is both fascinating and a little appalling." Looking back, Remington said that "he was very supportive of what we

---

34   The repetition of "grievous" here appears to refer to a press release or public statement made by the gallery founders. Other phrases are similarly repeated in a strange way, suggesting that the various critics were making uncited references to this document, which has been sadly lost to time.

were doing, although he didn't fully understand what we were doing."

Regardless of how he felt about the works shown there, Frankenstein—like most of the people who reviewed the 6—was very enthusiastic about the core concept and the founders' ambitions, writing:

> No self-respecting art community is ever complete without a small, informal gallery run by the artists themselves and dedicated to emerging talent and experimental ideas. These galleries seldom last forever but the idea behind them never dies. Many of the things they display are half-baked and scarcely survive their initial exposure; on the other hand, some of the most important people in the history of art have been introduced to the public by ventures of this kind.

This was extremely similar to what he had said about King Ubu, shortly after it had opened:

> In every town that calls itself an art center there ought to be a gallery of the informal, only mildly commercial kind, somewhere off the beaten track, and run entirely at the caprice or convenience of its owner.

However, Frankenstein acknowledged that the 6 was better run than its predecessor: "One of the most extraordinary things about this gallery is that it actually seems to be open when it is supposed to be open." This would change as the months went by, but initially the 6 was run by extremely enthusiastic artists who understood that a certain degree of professionalism might be beneficial even in a thoroughly unconventional endeavor.

The 6's opening show was followed by more films, photography, and paintings, including work by the young student artists and their teachers (including Hassel Smith,

The 6 Gallery

David Park, Elmer Bischoff, and Richard Diebenkorn). Music was frequently provided by the Studio 13 Jass Band, which also played at a Dadaist Christmas event, the postcard for which read "I'M DREAMING OF DADA!" and promised "a real live three headed Santa Clause [sic] and all sorts of Art." The artist members of the 6 Gallery were instructed to "bring at least 5 pieces of your work to be priced under $24 [...] bring your ideas and electric trains and decorations to be hung on the hanging Xmas tree. Also bring some burgundy wine if you can." This cooperative, communal atmosphere further set it apart from other galleries, fostering an atmosphere of positivity and creative collaboration, an extension of the shared living spaces and café culture that marked the city's art scene. In *Lyrical Vision*, Bruce Nixon wrote:

> The artists remember the gallery was always packed with people. There was continual talk and wine and the charged excitement of the new art and poetry. It was an era of declamations. Readings almost always took place during openings, and young student jazz bands often turned up to play or accompany the poets.

Hedrick concurred, saying, "it was easy. I mean, all we had to do was [...] have our little meetings once a month and people would come and say, 'Well, we have, you know, we have this 3D movie we want to put on or we have some dancers, we have some avant-garde music.' We were overwhelmed by people asking us to use the facilities."

The gallery was popular but even by December its opening hours had been reduced, partially due to the six founders being in school on weekdays and partially because the gallery only really attracted visitors on weekends and on opening nights. Even though it was not a commercial operation, it seemed wasteful to have the place open when there was little chance of anyone stopping by. As the owners of Metart and King Ubu had discovered, running a gallery was more of a hassle than they anticipated. The six founders plus some of the members took turns watching the gallery, something that Jay DeFeo called "babysitting." She did it one night a week with her husband, Wally Hedrick, and said that it was generally viewed as an unwelcome chore.

Within just a few months, the 6 had made a good name for itself and had even helped in forging a new artistic district within the city. In the *Chronicle*, columnist R.H. Hagan wrote: "Art is busting out all over west of Van Ness avenue, and nowhere so much as in the general area whose main intersection is Union and Fillmore streets." He wrote that the 6 was on "the experimental fringe of the local art world" but seemed impressed by certain of their shows. Another few months later, Frankenstein would report in the same paper on the further expansion of the Fillmore-Union area:

> Things are cooking in the Fillmore-Union neighborhood, where there are now at least six galleries devoted to the exhibition of art and where the local avant-garde now has its headquarters. The latest manifestation in that area is the re-opening of the East and West Gallery, 3108 Fillmore, under a new director, Mrs. Leonid Gechtoff, who used to run a gallery in Philadelphia and seems determined to give the 6 Gallery across the street a run for its money.

The East and West Gallery[35] sat opposite the 6 and was run by the mother of artist Sonia Gechtoff. It is claimed in various places that Ethel "Etya" Gechtoff—widow of painter Leonid Gechtoff—coined the term "beatnik," though these claims seem unlikely and whilst they are occasionally repeated, no one has yet offered any proof. Ethel Gechtoff had, as Frankenstein noted, come from Philadelphia, where she had been the director of

---

35   As with the 6 Gallery, there is some uncertainty over the name of East and West. It sometimes appeared in contemporary documents as "East-West," "East West," and "East & West." It does seem that "East and West Gallery" was the intended presentation of the name, however.

The 6 Gallery

the Beryl Lush Gallery, and East and West, despite her lack of funding, presented itself in a more professional, conventional light than the 6 Gallery. Dimitri Grachis, owner of the Spatsa Gallery (which opened just around the corner, several years later), said that Gechtoff "gave focus and stability to the area." Not far away was Studio 44, which opened in 1952 and showed "avantgarde and primitive art" in a range of media until its 1956 closure.

Just six months after its founding, then, the 6 was at the heart of a burgeoning arts district. It was just far enough from C.S.F.A. and from North Beach to possess its own identity, one that grew with each new gallery and the migration of various artists. Many of these people lived a fifteen-minute walk south at 2322 Fillmore, a block of apartments known as "Painterland." Hedrick and DeFeo, who had married shortly before the 6 Gallery opened,[36] moved there in October 1955, their apartment soon becoming a gathering place for artists. James Weeks, Paul Beattie, Joan Brown, and Sonia Gechtoff lived there too and in the late fifties it would become home to Michael and Joanna McClure, Bruce Conner, Manuel Neri, and Robert Duncan. The $65 rent was, when shared between enough people, more or less affordable even for these often-indigent artists.

Through these first months, the 6 Gallery continued in its mission to exhibit the *arts* rather than just *art*. It became particularly well known as a venue for experimental film, with filmmakers such as Jordan Belsen, Sidney Peterson, Stan Brakhage, Fred Hobbs, Frank Stauffacher, and Hy Hirsch showing their work. "The Bridge," a film made by Weldon Kees and William Heick, was shown there in 1956 and this became rather infamous for Kees had disappeared during the shooting of it, probably jumping from the very bridge featured in the film.[37]

---

36   Wally Bill Hedrick and Mary Jay DeFeo were married August 26, 1954, just a month before the fundraising events they ran for the 6 Gallery.

37   His car was found near the bridge in July and he was never seen again, so it is generally assumed that he jumped. He had confided in friends that he was suicidal and had even driven to the bridge several times with the intention of jumping, but

Another infamous event occurred when Kenneth Rexroth invited Walter Lowenfels to read in San Francisco. Less than a year earlier, he had been charged with conspiracy to overthrow the U.S. government, but due to his poor health he was allowed periods of leave from the maximum-security Holmesburg Prison in Philadelphia. On one such occasion, he took the chance to travel across the country and read to a packed audience in the 6 Gallery. "The proprietors of the gallery were delighted at the chance to defy authority," Rexroth recalled. Even the gallery director, Hedrick, was shocked at times, with a nude dance performance standing out in his mind many years later. Speaking about a performance by choreographer Anna Halprin and her dance troupe, he said, "That was the first time in my life that I saw a group of dancers stark naked. I mean, I'm just a kid from Pasadena. That was far-out for me." Halprin had a dance studio nearby at 1833 Union Street.

Not everything was controversial, though. Much was simply enthusiastic, experimental, or unusual. One man brought dozens of birds on stage and proceeded to talk to them, apparently convinced he was having a two-way conversation. Some shows began with wet paint because the artist, working at the gallery, had painted through the night to achieve a degree of spontaneity. Bizarre contraptions were devised, such as an inflatable dome with a light machine in the center and dancers around it, whose shadows were cast outward for the viewers outside to see. And these are just the performances people remembered well enough to describe years later. Unfortunately, no one at the gallery was particularly interested in documenting any of this and records are notoriously poor, with almost no photos or written reports. "I think the people who were involved in it were too involved [for record-keeping]," Hedrick said later. "If I'd gotten hung up with tape recorders and cameras, it would have never gotten done because it was so impromptu." Once again, it was the spontaneity of the scene and the lack of interest in

---

changed his mind in the end. "We all saw it coming—but what can you do?" Rexroth wrote to James Laughlin soon after the news broke.

The 6 Gallery

humdrum business concerns that pushed artists into new territory.

In this era of wild experimentation and improvisation, where artists pursued ideas over aesthetics, one did not find much in the way of traditional art—picturesque landscapes, still lifes, realistic portraits, and so on. No one was interested in *nice* or *beautiful*. Rather, the emphasis was on the expression of ideas through unconventional means or whatever was at hand. It was in a sense conceptual art a decade before the term was coined. Remington said:

> The spirit of Dada was very strong. We set this thing up as an anti-cultural thing, coming on the heels of the Ubu, and some of us were very influenced by Dada literature. We all had that sense. We talked about ideas and poetry and painting, and a lot of that was prompted by our interpretation of what Picasso had done in the '20s, and the '30s with Dada and their literature and their dialogues. [...] We were trying to hit what we considered a stuffy community—we wanted to say that there's something happening here, and it's interesting.

Many of the artists in and around the 6 Gallery aimed to convey a message or ask a question rather than please the eye. Hedrick was particularly enamored of Marcel Duchamp, who had famously rejected "retinal art" (that which only pleases the eye) and consequently began using "readymades," by which he meant manufactured objects reframed as works of art. The most famous example was a urinal labeled "Fountain" in 1917. Similarly opposed to "retinal art," Hedrick painted the word "peace" on an American flag in either 1953 or '54, and later he began sourcing broken TV sets, refrigerators, and other household appliances for use in his various sculptures. "Hedrick liked working with junk," wrote Richard Cándida Smith, author of *The Modern Moves West*, "because he found it an accurate and offensive symbol of an American society in love with waste and war." Junk was cheap and plentiful, making it a great source of material for poor artists, but often it possessed a deeper meaning as the detritus of an affluent society reclaimed and repurposed.

There were many other artists in the area doing similar work but with their own motivations and creative interpretations, and not all of them resisted the "retinal" to the extent that Duchamp had. Jess created "Necro-facts" from objects he found outside or in thrift stores by assembling them in interesting ways, but these were seldom permanently constructed and he routinely rearranged them. He explained: "In general, the parts are not permanently joind, rather they are balanced, intertwined, jammd, lockd, screwd, hung, loopd, linkd, tied; rarely cemented, taped." Bruce Conner and Wallace Berman would become well known for their use of found objects in assemblies later in the decade but their efforts differed greatly from Jess's. Ingrid Schaeffer, in a guide accompanying an exhibition of Jess's work, said, "Where Berman's sculptures are characterized by inscribed surfaces, and Conner's by erotic and fetishized materials, what binds Jess's assemblies is simply a love for putting things together." Other artists used found art and assemblage as temporary forms of creation partly as a means of inspiration, with Richard Diebenkorn saying, "If you're not getting it in paint, and you start putting [objects] on paper, and you're successful there, the next time you work in paint you're influenced by your success the day before."

The use of junk and other found objects was one method of pushing the boundaries of what art could be and this was thoroughly explored through the fifties and into the early sixties, but there were other, related experiments. The process of producing collages from varied printed sources was another, with Jess's "Paste-ups" proving particularly successful.[38] He often took material from comic books but had a vast library of printed material to draw from, including advertisements for feminine hygiene products, tarot cards, and puzzle

---

38   Jess used "Paste-ups" and "Necro-facts" to highlight the fact that he viewed his work as distinct from wider art styles, namely Surrealist collage and Assemblage movements.

pieces. These efforts became more complex over time and some of his paste-ups included thousands of fragments. This was again similar to Hedrick, who in paintings took elements of his own provincial upbringing and used them to subvert the pretensions of high art. He applied comic book illustration to classical scenes such as *Virgin and Child*, for example. Comics were thought of as decidedly low-brow and almost the antithesis of art, but for Jess, Hedrick, and a great many others, this was perfect. It brought elements of real life into art—something Hedrick then reversed when he turned his toilet into an installation by rigging it to play music and produce a lightshow whenever someone sat on it. As a jazz musician, painter, and sculptor, whose artistic creations often moved into the technological and kinetic realms, Hedrick was constantly questioning the meaning and purpose of art. Like so many other creatives in San Francisco at the time, he produced work in a range of media, defying categorization. This is why, in a joint interview with his wife, Jay DeFeo, he said, "I would rather not be called a painter or sculptor but an artist."

DeFeo, who became one of the most celebrated artists to emerge from the 6 Gallery, also worked in multiple fields. She was a painter, sculptor, photographer, collagist, and jewelry maker. She used paint almost as a sculptor would use clay or marble, seeking not to produce pictures but to create layered, structured, texturally complex artworks. Her most famous work, *The Rose*, took eight years to complete as she applied paint to a canvas until it weighed almost two thousand pounds. It was, she said, "a marriage between painting and sculpture." Richard Cándida Smith said her "sculptural manipulation of paint as a material substance" was highly regarded, reaching an audience far larger than most of her 6 Gallery peers, and related it to "the ambitions of young painters at the time, touching on a desire that a genuine practice of art could 'restore' humanity's understanding of the basic laws governing all natural phenomena." Adding to the challenge of labeling the different movements and styles of the era, artists like DeFeo posed the question of what constituted a painting and what differentiated it from a sculpture. Writing in the *Chronicle*, art critic Alfred Frankenstein called one of DeFeo's paintings "an event in itself," which is a reasonable assessment of such an original and provocative work. The term "event" could in fact be applied to various works from this period and reflects a prevalent attitude concerning the purpose and composition of art. Robert Duncan tied it to poetry in 1959, arguing that "Poems are events of Poetry, of our consciousness of making a universe of feeling and thought in language."

Fred Martin, who showed often at the 6, came closest to convention with his landscape paintings of Rome and Venice, which he based on images in travel books from the early nineteenth century. However, he painted dozens or even a hundred of these pictures on tiny pieces of wood or slate that he had acquired for free from work as offcuts. He priced them very cheaply, so unlike most of the work that hung in the 6 Gallery, they actually sold well. Some people recall them selling for five or ten cents, but Martin remembers them being between fifty cents and a few dollars. The diminutive size of these works may have been an attack on the contemporary notion of huge canvases denoting more serious and challenging art, particularly when accompanied by a huge price tag.

Bruce Nixon wrote that "conventional notions of aesthetic enterprise gave way to a new image of the artist as an idea-giver, commentator, moral critic; here, in its own new-found role, art became the rough, immediate, hand-hewn application of idea and emotion, and an aesthetic of ugliness soon emerged around it." This attitude extended—by necessity as much as anything—to the ongoing advertising campaigns the gallery ran for new shows. As had been the case at King Ubu, cheap postcards, flyers, and posters were used to announce events. These were often made by the artists themselves and they were typically crude. They were usually comprised of basic information, such as dates, the gallery address, and the artist's name, alongside either a sketch or simple pattern. "We did things cheaply in those days," Martin explained. "The picture postcard gallery announcements of today did not exist, and I mimeographed the text and marbelized the cards myself." These postcards were often ironic or self-effacing, sometimes stating or implying the artists' stance against convention. One of Martin's postcards, for example, stated that he was "on the way to the ivory tower" before referring to his paintings as "cheap souvenirs of a disputed passage."

Of course, this all added to the charm of the gallery, which was—we must remember—a cooperative run by idealistic young artists. It was not a traditional, professional gallery and did not pretend to be one. It looked and functioned somewhere between a gallery and a studio, and it was also a sort of social club, where creative types could gather to share their ideas and work and discuss what had been created elsewhere in the city. It was exciting, McClure said. "[T]he very smallest bit of new communication was like gold and it got passed around and became a common ground of interest." This only worked because the group was open enough to admit newcomers. When painter Dean Fleming arrived in the city, having heard about the 6 Gallery on a trip to Mexico, he showed up and seemed to miraculously assimilate into the group:

> [T]here was a bunch of people there, and they were all cleaning up and getting ready for the next show. So I just grabbed a broom, and I was helping—cleaning and that was nice. And we finished, we got some beer, and we're sitting there. And I said, "This is really, really neat, you know. How do you become a member?" And they said, "Oh, you're already a member." That's weird. They haven't seen my paintings, my breaking chains or anything. [...] it was all about temperament. That's what they taught me. That's all temperament. You don't have to paint anything or do anything. You just have the right attitude.

As Fleming alludes to here, the 6 Gallery had already garnered a number of active supporters and a communal if rather disorganized dimension. Many of these people made small financial contributions but others simply helped with setting up and cleaning up. This was important because openings were usually wild events. Hedrick said, "part of the thing was to get loaded and just act outrageous." This naturally meant there was a large clean-up operation the following day. Remington pointed out that the gallery also hosted "rent parties" for which people would pay a small amount of money, then receive food and wine in exchange, with the leftover cash going toward paying the gallery's rent and bills.

All of this led to an unusually welcoming and open-minded atmosphere, making the 6 Gallery diverse not only in an artistic sense, but bringing people of different backgrounds together in a friendly and creative space. Hayward King, one of the founders, was black and gay. Leo Valledor, one of the earliest members, was Asian, as were Bernice Bing, Carlos Vela, and JoAnn Low—all close associates of the 6 Gallery. It must be emphasized that this sort of inclusive atmosphere was not common at the time. The 6 Gallery was founded the same year as Brown v. Board of Education, which can be seen as the beginning of the Civil Rights movement, and this was in the midst of a long and painful process of desegregation. Anti-miscegenation laws were being repealed but still existed in many states, and even though San Francisco was comparatively progressive, racism was prevalent. "Sometimes we as a group would go somewhere," Remington recalled, "and they wouldn't allow Hayward into a bar or restaurant. That was only occasionally, but it did happen. So we'd say, 'Okay, if he can't come in, we're not coming in.' So, we would all leave."

This was a problem they sometimes encountered in bars or restaurants, but at the 6 Gallery, and in the other artistic enclaves of San Francisco, your race, gender, and sexual orientation did not matter. You were judged by your artistic talent. Everyone was welcome, and this led to an entirely different arts scene than one found on the East Coast.

*

The 6 Gallery

In late January 1955, almost three months after its founding, the 6 Gallery ventured into the realm of theater. As we saw in a previous chapter, the King Ubu gallery had hosted several performances by Robert Duncan, and it was Duncan who returned once again to the tiny stage at the back of 3119 Fillmore. Although it is frequently stated that *Faust Foutu* was debuted here, he had in fact performed it on this very stage two years prior and then a partial reading was given at Black Mountain College in 1954. However, this performance would be incendiary, one that was talked about across the city for years.

Whilst the visual artists of the 6 Gallery often claimed to have no artistic influences and instead reacted spontaneously and originally to the contemporary environment, Robert Duncan was unashamedly influenced by his forebearers—poets and playwrights including Gertrude Stein. He is often lumped together with the Beats and San Francisco Renaissance poets, but he despaired of their pure-expression poetry and believed strongly in art as a serious discipline. He studied his influences religiously in an effort to further his own art. However, one work that had surprisingly not influenced him was Goethe's *Faust*, which he had not yet read when he sat down to work on a play called *Faust Foutu*.[39] Well educated, he would have been aware of the story behind this classic tale, and he set about updating the ancient tale for modern times, filling it in particular with references to the Korean War. The result was a wildly inventive play that his biographer, Mark Johnson, called "excessively clever, at times impossible to follow, downright silly, pretentious, highly self-reflexive, and a good deal of fun." Laden with countless puns and absurdities, the play began with the Master of Ceremonies saying:

---

39   He did, however, read it some months after completing the play. He referred to Goethe's version and other iterations of the Faust tale many times in *The H.D. Book*, written between 1959 and 1964 but only published in 2011. I shall also note here that Duncan never mentioned *Ubu Roi* as an influence on *Faust Foutu* but there are numerous similarities and he certainly was a fan of Jarry's play, so it is highly likely that he was consciously influenced.

> Dear lower world, cigarettes, convertibles, lazies and generalmen. I announce the Devil of Fun and all his pomps. My argument? Well it's all an old song…

Duncan attempted to defy all expectations, with certain sections of his play utterly disconnected from others, parts seemingly out of order, and comical self-references, such as critical commentary on the work of Robert Duncan himself. In Act III, one character asks, "do you really like Robert Duncan's work," to which another replies, "O I know it's not absolutely first rate. He's terrible uneven you know." There is—seemingly apropos of nothing—a letter to a dentist, followed by a final section that is hard enough to read when written down but would have been utterly impossible to understand when read aloud because five characters speak at the same time.

Like so much in the arts world of San Francisco at that time, it was not only experimental but brought together people from various backgrounds in order to complete it. For several months, Duncan recruited friends and held rehearsals for what would become, in the words of his biographer, "a collaborative theater experience." He gave them the script and some instructions, but he left much to the actors he had chosen. One of them, the poet Ida Hodes, later wrote Duncan:

> At the end I did understand what you wanted—but you had not said enough about what you wanted before then—and in a way that was good because it was in the nature of an experiment to say "here is one of my songs— sing it" and I believe you were really pleased with the total response to such a request. I think, Robert, that it would have been impossible for you not to have a "plan"… for Faust…— but… you also wanted even more a creative participation— and that made it exciting for all of us.

The 6 Gallery

On January 20, 1955, Duncan gathered his ensemble of artists and together they read his play in the strange, long room on 3119 Fillmore Street. Duncan played The Poet and Jack Spicer was A Muse. Larry Jordan was Faust, Michael McClure played A Boy, and Helen Adam played Greta Garbo. Ida Hodes was Marguerite. Jess and Harry Jacobus also had roles, so all three of King Ubu's owners were present on stage. None of them acted; they just sat and read the script aloud before an audience. "A couple of people stood up while they read their lines," McClure remembered, "but mostly it was a play reading, not a performance. There were no costumes or sets." He said that "Jess spoke his lines with the immense clarity and irony that we see in his collages. Faust chanted out his songs with loud, untrained voice. The whole place was held together with the thread of Duncan's presence."

McClure remembers the participants being nervous partly because they had almost no experience reading in front of an audience and partly because they so badly wanted Duncan's approval. Already, he was an influential figure in the city's literary scene. They tried their best to please him and the result, McClure said, "was a magical quality" in part due to the mix of people reading—poets, painters, composers, filmmakers. "[W]e all believed in the play," he said, "and we all believed in the beauty and intelligence and the awesomeness of it as an act of language and wit."

In the end, though, the play was remembered largely for Duncan's performance. When reading lines at the end of the play, he stripped naked in front of the audience and proclaimed, "This is my body." This was generally seen as a courageous act—the poet standing naked before the world both literally and figuratively—and it gave the venue "an aura of notoriety," as one historian put it. The little gallery that was becoming a center of the arts in an already experimental, bohemian city now had a landmark event in its history. The play would never become a great success either performed or printed,[40] and even in books about Duncan it figures as an extremely minor work deserving

---

40   Small print runs were sold in 1958 and 1959. It was printed in slightly larger editions in 1960 and then in 1985.

of a few paragraphs at most, but oddly it became an important moment for the 6 Gallery and the literary-artistic movement that was developing in the city. That is partly because of an audience member and the inspiration that he is said to have taken from Duncan's bold move.

Part Two
San Francisco is Beat

Allen Ginsberg Goes West

As Robert Duncan stripped off his clothes whilst reading the final lines of *Faust Foutu* on January 20, 1955, Allen Ginsberg sat in the audience with his boyfriend, Peter Orlovsky. They had met Duncan a week earlier at The Place and he had invited them to attend. According to Michael McClure, this was the germ of the idea for the 6 Gallery reading some eight months later, and at least one of Ginsberg's biographers credits it as the inspiration for Ginsberg's infamous disrobing the following year at a poetry reading in Los Angeles.[1]

Ginsberg was a relative newcomer to San Francisco. Originally from Paterson, New Jersey, the shy, sensitive, and curious young man had met Jack Kerouac and William S. Burroughs at Columbia University in New York in late 1943, forming the core of what would become known as the Beat Generation. In the following decade, he traveled widely, experimented with numerous substances, worked an assortment of jobs, underwent various therapies, and through all of this he sought to become a great poet. He was a perpetual student, attempting to learn from everyone he met and every place his visited, but although his ideas regarding life and art were in a continual process of revision and development, he never strayed far from this 1944 statement: "The most individual, uninfluenced, unrepressed, uninhibited expression of self is the true expression and the true art." For a decade, he struggled to find an authentic voice until in the jungles of Mexico in 1954 he made several breakthroughs, resulting in the long poem "Siesta in Xbalba," a milestone in his poetic development. In the two years after returning from Mexico—a period he spent primarily in San Francisco—he would produce some of the most important poetry of

---

1   See Chapter 4.3 for more on this incident.

103

the mid-twentieth century.

After crossing the border from Mexico in June 1954, Ginsberg visited his old friend and lover Neal Cassady, who was then living in San Jose. He stayed with Neal and his wife, Carolyn, for two months, journeying into San Francisco on Mondays. In July, he wrote his father:

> I'm glad I'm in San Jose where I can be protected from the temptation to run around to wild surrealist movies, art shows, jazz bands, hipsters, parties, cellar lounges filled with hi fidelity Bach etc. All in all a very active cultured city the rival of NY for general relaxation and progressive artlife.

In spite of his enthusiasm for the city and the fact that San Jose allowed him the freedom to enjoy San Francisco without being overwhelmed by it, his time with the Cassadys was generally unpleasant. Allen had been in love with Neal for years and this led to a great deal of frustration for him. Neal had occasionally engaged in sexual activity with Allen but much preferred women. Neal was also, at this point in his life, obsessed with the teachings of a quasi-mystic charlatan called Edgar Cayce, whose brand of bullshit failed to impress Ginsberg, who was just beginning his studies into Buddhism. He felt alienated from Neal, and there was some friction between Ginsberg and Carolyn, who knew of his feelings for her husband. On August 19, she went to Ginsberg's bedroom to ask him a question and found the two men having sex on Allen's bed. According to her memoir, she was not so much angry as embarrassed. In fact, she even apologized and felt guilty about appearing homophobic. In typical form, Neal refused to acknowledge the incident and Ginsberg failed to see what he had done wrong. Even so, it was obvious that the situation could not be allowed to continue and so Carolyn convinced Allen to leave, saying, "I'll be glad to pay your way anywhere you want to go, Allen. I'll help all I can, but you will have to go… as soon as possible." He was allowed to stay another few days to figure out his future and then Carolyn drove him five miles north to San Francisco. "On the way I apologized and begged his pardon a dozen different ways," she wrote later. "He was kind and understanding, but I wondered what inner turmoils he was surmounting."

Carolyn left him outside the Marconi Hotel in North Beach. They kissed goodbye and she gave him twenty dollars. In spite of how badly he had hurt her, and the fact that Ginsberg saw nothing wrong with his actions, she cared for him and didn't want him to starve—and after more than eight months of travel, relying on handouts from friends and strangers, starvation was not unthinkable. Located near the intersection of Broadway and Columbia, in the heart of the city's bohemian district, surrounded by the cheap cafés and restaurants of Chinatown and Little Italy, the Marconi was run by two friendly and permissive lesbians who gave him a room beneath Al Sublette, a friend of his, for six dollars a month. They told Allen he could do as he pleased and said they were drunk most of the time. Ginsberg felt that they were giving him permission to indulge in whatever sex and drugs he enjoyed, and perhaps he was right, for the previous year the hotel had been the scene of a large police raid, resulting in the arrests of one of the owners, two of her female guests, and ten male patrons. The police called it a "house of prostitution." Whilst Ginsberg appreciated the freedom to indulge himself, he was perhaps more interested in what lay across the street: a small and recently opened bookshop called City Lights.

City Lights was located in a pie-shaped building on Columbus, just south of Broadway. The Artigues Buildings, as it was originally called, was built in 1907 on the ruins of an earlier building destroyed in the 1906 earthquake and in the next half century was home to various businesses including another bookshop, called Cavalli's.[2] Peter D. Martin rented the mezzanine level above the ground-floor space, which was then occupied by a flower shop, and from here he ran *City Lights*, a pop

---

2   Cavalli's is still open at a nearby location; however, in 2007 it stopped selling books and became a café. Founded in 1880, it has occupied several locations throughout the city.

culture magazine. The first issue was published in June 1952 and co-edited with Norma Swain and Richard Miller. It aimed "to publish original writing of insight and power in any form on any subject of contemporary interest and concern [...] as long as they are honestly written at the top limits of the writer's ability and understanding." As with much San Francisco art at the time, it was aimed at breaking with convention. The journal's content would "demonstrate that intelligent people must deal with the totality of experience, and not solely with particular areas that have come to be regarded as the Proper Arts or the Established Sciences." The editors welcomed that which most would consider low-brow: content from or relating to comic books, films, pop music, and so on. The initial call for submissions addressed issues pertaining to the San Francisco cultural scene, highlighting earlier problems and showing the same sort of interest the Fillmore-Union galleries did in overcoming these—namely, through community effort:

> Starting a magazine in San Francisco is like striking up a conversation among strangers; there are the same doubts and hesitations, and often the same false beginnings that end in discouraged silence. We are a wary crowd, and previous attempts in the Bay Area have only added to our cautious reserve. But maybe we are not strangers after all—we who are introducing CITY LIGHTS, and you who we hope will become our contributors and readers. We are all—intermittently, at least—thoughtful, responsive people living in the same city in the same tough and stubborn time, and we are all engaged in a common attempt to comprehend and define a contemporary experience that is exclusive and difficult. Because we are not strangers and because the need for communication among us is so plain, the editors of CITY LIGHTS feel that still another beginning should be made.

By 1953, *City Lights* had included poems by Philip Lamantia and the first film criticism by Pauline Kael, and the spring 1953 edition included several translations of Jacques Prévert poems by Ferlinghetti.

Ferlinghetti, who at the time was known as Lawrence (or Larry) Ferling,[3] was a well-traveled painter, poet, would-be novelist, French teacher, translator, and art critic. He had discovered Prévert's work in Paris several years earlier and had been enthralled by its anti-establishment message. Witty, intelligent, and brave, Prévert's collection, *Paroles*, had sold half a million copies in France but the poet was unheard of in America. Ferlinghetti attempted to sell his translations of this book but found resistance from major New York publishers, who believed the only people willing to read them would already speak French. Ferlinghetti thought of this as "first class assininity" and wrote, "These are public poems." In Prévert, Ferlinghetti saw a similar attitude to what later became known as the Beat Generation—a disaffected youth struggling to find meaning in a rapidly changing world but responding artfully and with great wit.

When Ferlinghetti was walking down Columbus Avenue one day, he saw Martin standing out front of the oddly shaped building at 261 Columbus, where the downstairs space was now empty after the flower shop had closed. He introduced himself and Martin replied, "Oh, you're the one who sent me the Jacques Prévert translations!" The two men soon got to talking about the possibility of opening a bookshop. For Martin, it was a great idea because *City Lights* journal had been intellectually stimulating but not financially profitable. He viewed a bookshop as a potential means of subsidizing the little magazine. Meanwhile, Ferlinghetti saw the opportunity to import more than just translations of Prévert. In Paris, he had seen up close the city's wonderful bookstores, which functioned as literary hubs and sometimes as publishing houses.

They soon agreed to invest $500 each in order to open a paperback bookshop. Like many San Francisco ventures

---

3   He changed his name to Ferlinghetti in 1954, but I will use "Ferlinghetti" for the sake of clarity.

of the era, it was a radical concept and City Lights was quite likely the first paperback-only bookshop in the country.[4] Back then, paperback books were not considered proper literature and so they tended to comprise pulp fiction sold in drugstores rather than real bookshops. However, Martin and Ferlinghetti recognized the snobbishness in this view and believed in making literature accessible, so they aimed to sell affordable paperback books rather than expensive hardback editions. Many of their titles sold for twenty-five cents and when in June 1954 they held a book-signing event, one prominent columnist quipped, "This is undoubtedly the first autograph party for a 25-cent book in the history of literature and the ballpoint pen." They also courted controversy from the outset, posting a "Pocket Book of the Month" sign in their window that resulted in legal action by the Book-of-the-Month Club.

Despite its popularity, City Lights was not a financial success and for the first several years it struggled to break even. About a year and a half after the shop opened, and with the journal also shuttered due to financial pressures, Martin sold out to Ferlinghetti and moved back to New York, leaving the latter in charge of the business. This left Ferlinghetti free to pursue something he had wanted since the beginning: to turn City Lights into a publishing company. Martin had viewed the idea as foolish but Ferlinghetti saw the potential and importance of publishing radical, original, often dangerous art. Just as the city's artist-led galleries had taken chances on non-commercial art, Ferlinghetti would put literature above profits in his own business venture.

A mere eight months after Martin left, Ferlinghetti published his own *Pictures of the Gone World* as the first in the company's "Pocket Poets" series.[5] Few people—Martin

---

4   A few newspapers speculated that this may be true around the time the shop opened and by the early 1960s City Lights was advertising itself as "[t]he first paperbook store in the land."

5   Although this was the first in the Pocket Poets series and published by the owner of a paperback bookstore, the first edition was split between a run of 500 paperback copies and 25 hardback ones. The paperback version sold out quickly and was reprinted in March 1956 and then again in June 1957.

included—knew then that Ferlinghetti was a poet, and indeed he thought of himself more as a painter at this point than a poet, but this book was an incredible debut. Some reviewers snootily called it too accessible but Kenneth Rexroth wrote in the *Chronicle* that it was "a remarkable first book, because it speaks with an achieved personal idiom—something it usually takes years to develop. He is completely independent of influence from any other poet writing in English." They continued to publish important books, including many by the Beat and San Francisco Renaissance poets, in a distinctive format. The concept was inspired by Pierre Seghers' *Poètes d'Aujourd'hui* poetry series and the iconic covers clearly replicated Kenneth Patchen's *An Astonished Eye Looks Out of the Air* (1945), published in a conscientious objector camp by William Everson's Untide Press. City Lights' books, however, would be smaller and nearly square—supposedly shaped to fit the pockets on a pair of workman's jeans.

City Lights was open from 10 a.m. to midnight every day and aimed to introduce to America the Parisian café-bookshop concept, wherein visitors could sit and relax and read without the pressure to buy anything. Ferlinghetti said that even with the late opening hours they "literally could not shut the doors at closing time," saying that they "seemed to be responding to a deeply felt need." Some people have suggested that it was more like a library from which you could—if you felt like it—occasionally purchase a book. In that sense, like the 6 Gallery, it was a gathering place as well as a place of business, blurring the lines between artist and viewer. Ferlinghetti explained in 1975:

> When I first came to town in the early fifties there was no book store to walk into to browse, to just hang out. I remember going into downtown bookstores and immediately being approached by clerks who wanted to know exactly what I was looking for. One of the original ideas of the store was for it to not be an uptight place, but a center for the intellectual

community, to be non-affiliated, not tied up with, not belonging to any official organization.

Unsurprisingly, it was "Allen's favorite spot in the neighborhood," according to Bill Morgan. In those first weeks in San Francisco, he often stayed there until midnight, reading or talking with people, including Ferlinghetti and Shigeyoshi (or, more commonly, "Shig") Murao, the charismatic clerk who had offered to work there unpaid before becoming a full-time staff member and ultimately manager of the store. Essentially taking over from Peter Martin to allow Ferlinghetti to focus on the publishing side of the business, Murao quickly became more than just an employee and one newspaper report from the seventies even claimed that "Shig more than anyone else is responsible for the store's continuing success." He would work at City Lights for more than twenty years and became close friends with Ginsberg.

As much as he would have loved to have sat around reading and writing and talking all day, Ginsberg had a hotel and food to pay for, and so on September 13, 1954, he began working for market research firm, Towne-Oller & Associates, which specialized in tracking shipments of health and beauty products from warehouses to stores. He earned a surprisingly good salary, which allowed him to pay off all his debts within about six months of starting, but he hated working full-time in a job that sapped his energies without allowing him to think creatively. He also felt that marketing was "basically the technology of brainwashing, that is, picking people's brains for money." He found it interesting and it helped him to better understand—and therefore resist—methods of control, but he soon realized that he did not want to be a part of what he perceived as a fundamentally unethical industry.

In addition to a full-time job, he found himself a girlfriend, Sheila Williams,[6] and began a heterosexual

---

6   In books about the Beats, Sheila is usually noted as "Sheila Boucher," but she only took this surname in 1956, after leaving Ginsberg and marrying Paul Boucher. When she was with Allen, she went by her maiden name, Williams.

relationship. He felt it was time for him to settle down and perhaps even have children, despite having known for many years that he was a homosexual. He moved into her Pine Street apartment and they split the rent, but it was a relationship doomed to failure. Although he initially seemed very enthusiastic about Williams, a jazz singer who appreciated his poetry and enjoyed smoking pot, Ginsberg was soon to accept his homosexuality. This was partially due to his new psychiatrist, Dr. Philip Hicks, a young, progressive therapist who eschewed traditional attitudes to homosexuality. Ginsberg began seeing him on October 25 "to overcome a block in his writing." Hicks helped Ginsberg accomplish this but first they worked through other issues. When he asked Ginsberg what he really wanted, Ginsberg said that he wanted to "do nothing but write poetry and have leisure to spend the day outdoors and go to museums and see friends. And I'd like to keep living with someone—maybe even a man—and explore relationships that way. And cultivate my perceptions, cultivate the visionary thing in me. Just a literary and quiet city-hermit existence." Dr. Hicks then told Ginsberg to do just that and not worry so much about the consequences. It was a revelation for Allen, who had previously felt there was something profoundly wrong with him and that pursuing an unconventional lifestyle was simply out of the question.

In San Francisco, it did not take Ginsberg long to meet the local poets and painters and thinkers. In fact, it rarely took him long to meet such people regardless of location or even language. Here, he had letters of introduction from William Carlos Williams and Philip Lamantia, whom he had known back on the East Coast. Williams was a hugely influential poet nationwide and many of the writers in San Francisco had tremendous respect for him, while Lamantia was considered one of the most promising young poets in the country, having been hailed by André Breton as "a voice that rises once in a hundred years" when he was only fifteen or sixteen years old. At just seventeen, he was published in the first two issues of *Circle* alongside the likes of Henry Miller and Bern Porter, and Porter published Lamantia's first book, *Erotic Poems*, when he was only nineteen. Originally born in San Francisco, he moved around often and is rarely considered a local poet, but he was a presence in the city during parts of the forties and fifties and was highly regarded by many of the more established poets.

Within a few weeks of arriving, Ginsberg had met with both Kenneth Rexroth and Robert Duncan, recognizing them as influential figures on the local scene. Throughout his whole life, he gravitated toward well-known writers partly so he could learn from them and partly to see if they could provide publishing opportunities for him, and he knew that both Rexroth and Duncan were highly respected. He had been corresponding with Rexroth since June 1952 for these reasons, but soon after arriving and meeting the older poet in person, he began to feel that he was not quite as gifted as he had been led to believe. To Cassady, Ginsberg said Rexroth was "not really great as writer," and he told Kerouac he was a "poor poet with big ego." Even so, he admitted that Rexroth was "a nice guy" and "the only real brain around here." To his brother, he wrote the following, which is more or less in line with what others have said about Rexroth:

> I met Kenneth Rexroth who is the big cheese poet here [...] A real learned man, translates Chink, Jap, Greek, Latin, French and is an editor at New Directions.[7] Also an anarchist self-professed with a whole line of dreary self pitying ARTIST hangups. I'm no one to talk but he makes a profession out of it which is really embarrassing to listen to. However he knows a lot about literature when his taste is not corrupted by this kind of hangup.

Ginsberg's views on Duncan were similarly mixed. When they first met, Ginsberg gave the impression of being rather impressed, with Duncan later recalling that "[e]ven meeting me, and I was nothing, was to him

---

7   Rexroth was not an editor for New Directions but was a close friend of James Laughlin and often read manuscripts and recommended poets for publication.

overwhelming," and indeed many years later Ginsberg said, "When I first came to San Francisco, the King, or Prince, or Queen Poet, was Robert." Ginsberg liked to tell the story of Duncan coming to his hotel room and seeing Kerouac's "Essentials of Spontaneous Prose" taped to the wall, and remarked that "Robert I think was the first person who recognized the high literary quality of Kerouac's instructions." However, Duncan recalls the meeting quite differently, suggesting that Ginsberg had answered his door half-naked and explained that he had "probably looked at what was on the wall in order to show 'I'm not going to be looking at your shorts!'"

In personal correspondence, however, Ginsberg was less enthusiastic. To his father, he said Duncan was "smart but sort of a pathetic type, tries to browbeat these poor nowhere would-be student poets at round table workshop type meetings, admission 50¢ and not worth a nickel." He told Kerouac that Duncan "runs a crappy tho sincere Pound type poetry circle" and that "his poetry also is no good because too aesthetically hung up all about his sensibility."

The workshop Ginsberg refers to was probably the one Duncan ran for the San Francisco Poetry Center, which he had been doing since early 1954. This group met once a week for a two-and-a-half-hour session and by January Duncan himself was none too enthusiastic about it, feeling as though he was only showing off his poetic knowledge but not really imparting any wisdom. Despite his doubts, and Ginsberg's criticisms, Duncan's workshop was popular and was attended by a number of important poets. Such was his intelligence and poetic ability that he was viewed as a mentor by the likes of Michael McClure and John Allen Ryan, and generally admired by the poets of the city. McClure said of him:

> As brilliant and "major" as Rexroth was it was Duncan who seemed to be even more international. It did not matter that Duncan was unknown or that he said he'd be happy to have just five hundred readers—the scope of intention and

smoldering liveliness in his poems made Duncan seem to be the most international among us. We could imagine Robert speaking with Picasso and Cocteau and Stein and D. H. Lawrence.

Ginsberg's initial dislike of Duncan's workshop may have been due to the fact that it focused heavily on the technical side of poetry. He believed first and foremost that poetry was a matter of personal expression. Gary Snyder perhaps put it best, just a month after the 6 Gallery reading, when he wrote in his journal:

> Poetry-function, for Ginsberg, is to reveal yourself to others thus revealing them to themselves & thus revealed—naked—finding a community without fear, & can love freely.

On the other hand, Duncan believed in the supremacy of form, and this difference of opinion persisted for years. They even debated it in public on several occasions, including at the 1963 Poetry Conference in Vancouver. However, it's also likely that Ginsberg was upset that Duncan had not appreciated his poetry. Looking over the work that would later be published as *Empty Mirror*, Duncan felt it was self-absorbed, an opinion he retained well after Ginsberg had become famous. In fact, this perhaps explains Ginsberg's criticism of Rexroth, too, for both elder poets found *Empty Mirror* to be rather weak. Still, they appear to have viewed Kerouac's work positively, which ensured that Ginsberg did not completely lose faith in their judgment. He showed them parts of *Visions of Neal* (later published as *Visions of Cody*) and they were impressed by Kerouac's style. "Any man who can write down fifty pages of description of a car bumper is a great genius," Duncan said.

Although Duncan was influential over a number of prominent local poets and his workshops were popular, it was Rexroth's Friday-night salons that were unequivocally the main draw for aspiring poets in the area. Rexroth was about fifty years old and had been living in the city for several decades, cultivating a reputation as a man of letters. By no means a modest man, he boasted to Laughlin that he was "de facto cultural minister of San Francisco," which to be fair is not an entirely inaccurate claim. In the mid-forties, "his home became a mecca for local and visiting artists and writers," according to his biographer, with his Friday-night literary salons becoming a highly regarded feature of the burgeoning literary scene. Even rival poet-mentors looked to him, with Duncan once saying, "We were all brought up on Daddy Rexroth's reading list." By the time Allen Ginsberg arrived in town, there was no question who "the big cheese poet" was.

Rexroth had grown up in Chicago, where he badly wanted to attend the exclusive "Little Room" literary salon but was too young, poor, and inexperienced. Likewise, he was influenced by the Washington Park Bug Club, an open-air forum for political discussion. When he came to the West Coast and began to gain a reputation as a writer, he set up an anarchist discussion group called the Libertarian Circle, out of which came what he called the "Poetry Forum." This was a Wednesday event and was more formal than his Friday night salons. He charged a dollar for entry and taught classes on poets like Eliot, Pound, and Yeats.

The Friday night gatherings began as an informal get-together for local intellectuals but they turned into a more coherent literary salon, where poets would read their work and receive feedback from whoever attended that week (if they could get a word in edgewise—no easy task when Rexroth was around). They were held twice a month and usually between twelve and seventeen people would attend. Permission needed to be sought in advance if one wanted to attend, but a polite phone call would almost always elicit an invitation. Many of the most important names in mid-twentieth-century American poetry were attendees, with the likes of Ferlinghetti, Snyder, Ginsberg, Spicer,[8] Duncan, Lamantia, Kees, Everson, Broughton,

---

8 Spicer and Rexroth may have respected one another to some extent as poets, but they disliked each other. Spicer liked to "bandy bitcheries" and torment the older poet whilst Rexroth

and Parkinson frequently in attendance.

Rexroth held court in his Potrero Hill apartment, a setting that lent a feeling of intimacy and community. Not only was he a voracious reader for his own pleasure but he reviewed books for his radio show and for publications including *The New York Times Book Review*, *Art News*, *The New Republic*, and *The Nation*, so the walls were lined with an extraordinary number of books. Of course, to keep his bohemian credentials, he ensured they were arranged on shelves made of salvaged apple crates. The walls were covered in art—mostly his own Mondrian-inspired paintings. Philip Whalen described the apartment as having "great chambers with high ceilings and a very luxurious feeling of space, and a lot of chairs and tables and a vast library."

Coming from an underprivileged background, Rexroth was largely self-educated. Like many autodidacts, he was both proud of and insecure about his education and he used his intellect and knowledge to act superior toward others. He was probably unaware that many of his more intelligent listeners knew that he was not always as knowledgeable as he asserted. Ginsberg soon realized that he was "a bullshitter" while Gary Snyder said Rexroth talked about everything "in a very knowledgeable way" but that he "learned eventually that sometimes he didn't know what he was saying." Ferlinghetti, who was a regular at Rexroth's salon, said, "Many times he made up things and exaggerated things," citing as an example Rexroth claiming to have met Oscar Wilde in 1912, even though Wilde had died in 1900 and Rexroth had been born in 1905. Snyder gave another amusing example, highlighting just how extreme Rexroth's lying could be:

> James Laughlin, he said that Kenneth got so bad about name dropping and knowing every famous writer and having slept with every famous woman writer, he said that it finally got so bad that he would just make

---

issued rather backhanded compliments when reviewing Spicer on his radio show, once saying "*Whatever else* Spicer may be, he is a poet of some stature."

up some name and say, "What did you think of so-and-so?" And Rexroth'd give you a wonderful lecture on that person.

McClure remembers him forcing discussions into his personal areas of interest—anarchism, pacifism, Chinese poetry—but said, "You didn't know what to believe and you didn't know what not to believe."

Many others who attended those sessions made similar remarks, often commenting on his views as outrageous and toxic. Snyder, one of his most ardent supporters, said, "I wouldn't say that he was exactly homophobic, but he talked like he was," referring to what he called Rexroth's "rough language." Although a great many of the city's gay poets went to his Friday-night salons, they often went elsewhere when Rexroth's vicious side came out and they were made to feel unwelcome. People were also appalled by his sexism, especially the horrendous behavior he showed his wives. Snyder often defended Rexroth, calling him "a great mentor" but admitted that "he was very bitchy and he could be very cruel to people." Jack Goodwin meanwhile spoke of "Rexroth's paranoid fantasies," comparing them to *Mein Kampf*. Philip Whalen said, "He was annoying to many people—they thought he was a bore who talked all the time," and went on to speak of the countless fights he started that would last for years. Rexroth claimed to speak numerous languages that he had taught himself but even here his knowledge was rather limited. For the book *Hip Sublime*, Gideon Nisbet investigated Rexroth's comically bad translations of Greek poetry, arguing that he had only a "superficial knowledge" of the various languages he claimed to have mastered. Even so, he had the confidence to publish many translations from Greek and Japanese, and Nisbet acknowledged that "as a poet and bullshitter alike" Rexroth had "considerable talent." Similarly, McClure noted Rexroth's flaws and the fact that most of the group still maintained a certain love and respect for him by explaining that "you have to be tolerant of his arrogance, and have to think it's funny, and you have to see what an anarchist philosopher really is, what this one truly is."

Even if he dominated the Friday meetups and had a tendency to lecture on subjects he only pretended to understand, Rexroth was engaging and entertaining and there was plenty of real wisdom to be gained, making him an important local figure and ensuring that his salon remained popular. He was undeniably intelligent and poetically talented, and he was generous with his time and energy, doing much to foster a sense of community in the city's art scene and frequently helping young poets. William Everson, also known as Brother Antoninus, said, "Though others picked up his mantle and received the plaudits, it remains true that today we enjoy the freedom of expression and lifestyle we actually possess largely because he convinced us that it was not only desirable but possible, and inspired us to make it be." By the time Ginsberg arrived in San Francisco, his salon was a vital meeting place for poets, with many of the area's most famous writers meeting there and developing close friendships. Newcomers to the city would attend and soon become plugged in to the literary scene, meeting other writers and even publishers.

Most importantly, though, Rexroth offered the possibility of an artistic scene very different to that found on the East Coast or in Europe. "He vigorously and relentlessly reiterated his opposition to the Eastern establishment," according to Linda Hamalian, "thus clearing the way for the counterculture that would break out in the next decade." When young poets showed up and read their work, Rexroth wanted to hear something original, not couched in Old World vernacular. This is why, when Ginsberg read it on January 14, 1955, he found Kerouac's *Visions of Neal* so thrilling. Many Kerouac scholars would say this was his finest work, yet its wildly unconventional style meant that it remained unpublished in Jack's lifetime. Rexroth's enthusiasm shows that—his numerous flaws aside—he was ahead of his time.

As one might expect from a young poet, and particularly one so dedicated to the craft and eager to ingratiate himself into poetic communities, Ginsberg attended Rexroth's salon several times, but even so he did not meet Gary Snyder, who called himself "a student of

Kenneth Rexroth" and was a regular attendee. He did, however, meet Philip Lamantia at one of these events and the two men reconnected, having not seen each other in several years. Their meeting was fortuitous because Lamantia traveled frequently. He was married to the photographer Gogo Nesbit, and they stayed together in the city, but he often took off on long trips alone. The two men stayed up all night talking about visions and religion after one Friday session in 1955. Lamantia was just back from a stay in Mexico, where he had lived with the Cora (or Nayarit) people of Mexico, hoping to experience a special peyote ceremony, but his two-month stay had not overlapped with one of the "thirty secret rituals" they had over the course of each year.[9]

Through Rexroth, Ginsberg also met Ruth Witt-Diamant, the director of the San Francisco Poetry Center. The Poetry Center had been founded by Witt-Diamant and Madeline Gleason at the start of 1954 with a donation from W.H. Auden and its first reading occurred in February of that year. Duncan and Rexroth had helped in its inception, and unsurprisingly Rexroth claimed credit for the whole idea, but it was Witt-Diamant who ran the organization and made it a success.[10] She would book famous poets and bring them to San Francisco, then set them up with West Coast tours. For two decades prior to founding the Poetry Center, she had been a professor at San Francisco State University and through her position there had come to know many of the era's most important poets. W.H. Auden, William Carlos Williams, Dylan Thomas, and T.S. Eliot had all read for her and numerous famous poets stayed with her when they visited San Francisco. She was

---

9   An interesting sidenote: Lamantia had become interested in the Cora Indians through the work of early anthropologist Jaime d'Angulo, whose daughter later appeared at the 6 Gallery reading and "fell in love with Allen [Ginsberg]."
10   In 1965, Rexroth recalled, "For years the Poetry Center was in fact the poetry readings and seminars at my house. When this activity became unmanageable, Robert Duncan, Madeleine [sic] Gleason and I set up the Poetry Center and got Ruth Witt Diamant to sponsor its readings at S. F. State College which was then downtown." This may have some truth to it, but as always it is wise to take Rexroth's words with a pinch of salt.

also close friends with Anaïs Nin.

After Auden read at the San Francisco Museum of Modern Art on October 7, 1954, Ginsberg attended the party Witt-Diamant gave for him and found himself surrounded by academics and old people. Feeling bored, he approached a handsome young man and introduced himself. His name was Michael McClure, a young poet and painter from Kansas who had recently moved to San Francisco, ostensibly to study painting with Mark Rothko and Clyfford Still. In truth, he had probably moved in pursuit of the woman whom he would soon marry, Joanna Kinnison, with whom he was now living in an apartment on Telegraph Hill, just around the corner from The Place. After taking classes under Robert Duncan at San Francisco State, he became more focused on poetry than painting and would ultimately become famous as a poet and playwright, but he exemplified the spirit of multidisciplinary experimentation and collaboration that was prevalent in the city at that time. Like Duncan, Jess, Ryan, Ferlinghetti, and others, McClure actively created in both written and visual form, but more than most he moved between the different social groups with ease. The fact that he was handsome and thus popular with the city's numerous gay poets helped. Later, Michael and Joanna would move to the Painterland apartments near the 6 Gallery and become a part of that wild socio-artistic scene.

At the Auden party, Ginsberg and McClure felt an immediate connection. Within just a few minutes of meeting, they were engaged in a long conversation about dreams and poetry and particularly William Blake. Ginsberg had experienced a vision of Blake some years earlier that was a terribly important moment in his life and he was surprised to learn that McClure had dreamt of *being* Blake as a child. The two men quickly bonded and remained life-long friends. "We felt simpatico at that moment," McClure later recalled. As he had done on the East Coast in the forties, Ginsberg was assembling a small group of artistically inclined friends with whom he could discuss important matters, expanding his views on life and art. He noted in his journal: "Art is a community effort—a small but select community." But it would not be easy for him to balance a social life and a creative one. Personal dramas—though he would later use them as the basis for certain poems—made it hard for him to find the time or energy to write.

In December 1954, Ginsberg walked out on his girlfriend Sheila after a fight and went to Foster's Cafeteria, an all-night restaurant that was popular with artists. He approached a bearded man to ask the whereabouts of a friend called Peter Duperu.[11] The man did not know Duperu—a North Beach junkie—but instead introduced himself as Robert LaVigne, a painter. The two men "got into a big, interesting, artistic conversation about [...] New York painters" and LaVigne invited Ginsberg back to his apartment to see his paintings, one of which was a large, brightly colored portrait of a naked young man sitting above some onions. Ginsberg instantly fell in love. When he asked who the model was, LaVigne said, "Oh, that's Peter" and in from the next room walked Peter Orlovsky, a handsome young man. LaVigne pushed the two men together and they came to occupy an apartment on Gough Street in the same building as Neal Cassady and his girlfriend Natalie Jackson,[12] a living situation that reminded Ginsberg of the old New York Beat scene of the mid-to-late forties.

In San Francisco, then, Ginsberg found a relatively hip town with a number of talented poets, creative minds, and oddball characters. Like Columbia had been for him a decade earlier, it was a stimulating environment full of ideas and conversations, people to learn from, and new experiences. In spite of this, during his first six months in the city he wrote relatively little except for journal entries and letters. He was working, socializing, and attempting

---

11   His name is always capitalised "Du Peru" or "DuPeru" in books about the Beats but historical records, including census and housing data, as well as what appears to be his signature on a draft card, indicate that the above ("Duperu") is correct.
12   Neal was still married to Carolyn Cassady and would attempt for months to go back and forth between the two women. In May, he would leave Carolyn but returned to her shortly after Natalie's death later that year.

to stay in contact with his Beat peers in other parts of the world. At work, he was evidently quite skilled and his boss offered him a promotion with the possibility of a move to New York City, but increasingly Ginsberg felt he wanted unemployment again. Poverty was an unpleasant prospect but at least it would bring him the freedom to write, something he struggled with when working a nine-to-five job. He had learned during his Mexico trip, whilst staying in the jungles of Chiapas, that great poetry tended to come when he devoted whole uninterrupted days to thinking and experimenting with sounds and ideas.

Despite all the positive qualities of his new environment, throughout the first half of 1955 Ginsberg was in a period of heavy depression. He had been through several of these in his life, sometimes pushed almost to the brink of suicide, and this bout was a particularly bad one. "I can't stand life," he told Kerouac. He said that there was no one in the city that he liked except for Orlovsky and Cassady, and wrote that "SF is empty." He was even thinking about leaving for Los Angeles. His relationship with Orlovsky brought not only feelings of love and happiness but also intense pain, for Peter was primarily straight and Ginsberg felt he was pressuring him into a gay relationship. He also felt guilty about taking Orlovsky from LaVigne, who had initially broken up with Peter but later felt regret. It was "[t]he first time in life [he felt] evil," Ginsberg wrote in his journal. His relationship with Peter would bring much grief in addition to the love and happiness it provided, with the deeply disturbed Orlovsky often falling into "a very dark, Russian, Dostoevskian black mood" and sometimes locking himself away for days, weeping or despondent. Back east, Carl Solomon, a friend Ginsberg had met in a mental hospital in the late forties, was again institutionalized, news that deeply upset Allen. Solomon had struck him as a beautiful soul and the fact that his unique worldviews and general temperament were viewed as symptoms of mental illness requiring such medical intervention seemed proof that the country was uncaring and that the social systems in place simply punished the individual and suppressed the artistic mind.

Ginsberg was angry at everyone and everything. After

he moved into his own apartment in February, a pleasant space on Montgomery Street, he was inconvenienced and enraged as Cassady borrowed his bed to screw Natalie Jackson. Through much of his life, he found himself loving and lusting over straight men, anguished as they found love and sex with women. At work, meanwhile, he was tasked with compiling statistics about sales of toiletries in supermarkets and had to make up a marketing plan to boost sales. Gifted though he surely was in this profession, he disliked it and felt it sapping his creative energies. He felt that his days were occupied with meaningless work and his nights were filled with too many social obligations. No doubt he felt envy at the bohemians of North Beach and the artists of Fillmore-Union, who were free to devote themselves to their work as so many of Ginsberg's heroes had done.

To cope with all this, he drank heavily and took too much codeine, and he felt everything he wrote was "egocentric slop." Something was missing. In his journal, he discussed his troubles with poetry and concluded that "[t]he lines are not yet free enough." Looking back some years later, Rexroth agreed with this assessment, saying:

> Ginsberg had been a rather conventional, witty poet influenced by his New Jersey *Landsman* William Carlos Williams, and taught his letters at Columbia by Mark Van Doren, Lionel Trilling, and Jacques Barzun. He was very much a catecumen [sic] of the highly select Trotskyite-Southern Agrarian Establishment, and destined by his elders to step into the thinning ranks of their youth brigade alongside Norman Podhoretz and Susan Sontag and others of like ilk and kidney. He inhaled the libertarian atmosphere of San Francisco and exploded.

Still, San Francisco would not change him until he invested the necessary time and that meant quitting his job.

Testament to his gift for marketing, when Ginsberg told his employers that he wanted to be made unemployed, they offered him more money, a promotion, and even a move to the East Coast. However, he was now determined to be made redundant so that he could claim unemployment and use it to live as a poet, figuring he could survive on $30 per week for six months. Feeling old and unproductive, he wrote, "I've lost too much time as it is and will pass my free days at leisure as I really want to." He was successful in this attempt and on May 1 he began receiving unemployment payments, the first of which was spent on Bach records. Another went toward buying Peter a car that looked like a hearse, which they used to explore the area surrounding the city.

Despite all this, his depression worsened and by his twenty-ninth birthday, in June 1955, Ginsberg was at one of the lowest points of his life—an existence he called a "monstrous nightmare"—and hoping that he might be able to find the right words to describe it, to turn his pain into art. "Great art learned in / desolation," he wrote in a journal. Previous battles with depression had yielded this much, at least, with early works sporting titles like "Dakar Doldrums" and "Denver Doldrums." Now, however, he seemed to be suffering from a rare bout of writer's block. Thankfully, it lifted after Orlovsky went on a trip to the East Coast and Ginsberg began sleeping with John Allen Ryan. It is not exactly clear where, when, or how they met but Ginsberg had certainly visited the 6 Gallery and was a regular at The Place. They had overlapping social circles and frequented the same bars, cafés, and restaurants. He called Ryan "a beauty [...] with droop sinister gamblers mustache & thin body & secret cool love of God, pure sentimentalist."[13] One night, as they lay in bed, he had a dream. He wrote about it in his journal and later turned the journal entry into a poem called "Dream Record: June 8, 1955." It begins:

---

13   Ginsberg's relationship with Orlovsky was never a conventionally monogamous one. Allen was happy for Peter to screw women and both were content with Allen screwing men. Ryan, as I have already mentioned, slept with men and women.

Allen Ginsberg Goes West

> A drunken night in my house with a
> boy, San Francisco : I lay asleep :
> darkness:
> > I went back to Mexico City
> > and saw Joan Burroughs leaning
> > forward in a garden-chair, arms
> > on her knees.

Ginsberg often used his journals to note his vivid dreams and sometimes turned these into poems. This is a particularly successful effort and also an example of his taking a painful memory and making art of it. In the poem, he documents a dream of seeing Joan Vollmer in Mexico City. He meets her returned to the prime of her life, prior to the ravages of alcoholism and "the bullet in her brow" that had ended her short existence. Joan asks him about their Beat friends, scattered around the world and struggling to find success or happiness. He asks her about death and whether the dead care for the living, but she fades and he is left beside "her rain-stained tombstone [in] an unvisited garden in Mexico." It is a sad poem, of course, but at least his depression was once again yielding artistic output. For the Beat writers, great art was the ultimate aim in life and this, they believed, stemmed from intense experience, regardless of whether that was euphoria or despair.

The poem was criticized by Rexroth as "stilted & somewhat academic" but Ginsberg cared far more for Burroughs' opinion and Burroughs felt the concrete imagery practically brought him into Ginsberg's dream, saying, "Baudelaire remarked on this when he spoke of poetry as a form of ritual or incantation, magic words to evoke an image or series of images in the reader's psyche." The poem was strong enough to lift Ginsberg out of his brief writer's block and it marked the beginning of a productive period for him. Over the summer, he revised (in spite of Kerouac's advice to rely upon spontaneity) poems that would one day be printed in his collected works: "Green Automobile," "Malest Cornifici Tuo Catallo," and the aforementioned "Dream Record: June 8, 1955."[14] But it was not easy and he struggled to sit and produce whole poems. For much of July, he spent ten hours per day at his desk, working on poems he had written between 1952 and 1955. Ideas for new material tended to come to him as single lines rather than whole poems and he found it hard to expand these into anything meaningful.

In his journal, on an unknown date later that summer, when pondering his new poem, he wrote, "Note for Joan Dream: What consciousness in oblivion?" Although this line never made it into his poem, it was arguably its theme and he approximately paraphrased his journal note when he wrote, "Joan, what kind of knowledge have / the dead?" At yet another later but unknown date, he expanded upon this:

> I saw the best mind angel-headed hipsters damned.
> What consciousness in oblivion, Joan?

His dream of Joan had not only led to breaking his writer's block; it had pushed him into the first version of the first line of his most famous poem, "Howl."

---

14   Interestingly, "Dream Record" was finalized pretty early but he continued to tinker with it in tiny ways. One notable revision was the removal of the statement "I got / tired of San Francisco." Certainly, he had felt negatively about the city at times, but with this poetic breakthrough his feelings would change, and one wonders if he removed that line because the poem helped transform his views.

Writing Howl

Written in 1955 and 1956, "Howl" quickly became a sensation, often referred to as the defining poem of its era. As such, in the seven decades since its publication it has been studied intensely, with several books devoted to it as well as a vast number of essays, with a particular focus on its cultural significance and its literary influences. Ginsberg himself frequently spoke of writing his poem, explaining its meaning and composition carefully to interviewers and students. One particularly valuable resource, put together by Ginsberg and his biographer, Barry Miles, is the cumbersomely titled *Howl: Original Draft Facsimile, Transcript & Variant Versions, Fully Annotated by Author, with Contemporaneous Correspondence, Account of First Public Reading, Legal Skirmishes, Precursor Texts & Bibliography*.[15] In the introduction to this valuable book, he gave this version of the writing process:

> I sat idly at my desk by the first-floor window facing Montgomery Street's slope to gay Broadway—only a few blocks from City Lights literary paperback bookshop. I had a secondhand typewriter, some cheap scratch paper. I began typing, not with the idea of writing a formal poem, but stating my imaginative sympathies, whatever they were worth. As my loves were impractical and my thoughts relatively unworldly, I had nothing to gain, only the pleasure of enjoying on paper those sympathies most intimate to myself and most awkward

---

15 The title appears to have been inspired by *The Waste Land: A Facsimile and Transcript of the Original Drafts Including the Annotations of Ezra Pound*, published in 1971.

in the great world of family, formal education, business and current literature.

What I wrote that afternoon, printed here in facsimile, was not conceived as a poem to publish. It stands now as the first section of "Howl." Later parts were written in San Francisco, and in a garden cottage in Berkeley over the next few months, with the idea of completing a poem.

This account, written in the mid-eighties, is a little fanciful in that it suggests Ginsberg sat down and suddenly began work on a poem (or part of a poem) that he completed in a single sitting. In that sense, he is continuing the Beat myth of spontaneous composition begun with Kerouac, who it is sometimes claimed wrote the manuscript of *On the Road* in a series of marathon sessions at the typewriter lasting about three weeks. In fact, both works were partially the result of spontaneous composition but substantially rewritten and edited at later dates. As we have seen already, Beat history is often jazzed up for the sake of a better story.

Ginsberg began with a line in his journal that acted as the starting point for Part I of "Howl." It is unclear when exactly he wrote the first line or when he sat at his typewriter and expanded upon it. I strongly suspect, too, that he had written various lines and then later used these as the basis for his first typed version, which was produced at some point between August 7 and 12,[16] and Dr. Hicks, his therapist, said many years later that Ginsberg had indeed shared an in-progress handwritten manuscript that predated the first-known typed version, which he brought

---

16   Establishing the timeline is extremely complex and involves comparing various manuscripts, journal notes, and letters. It is quite frankly beyond the scope of this particular book as it would take thousands of words just to establish a loose date range for one of many drafts. For those interested in this textual history, in 2024 I wrote a very long essay about it called "First Draft, Best Draft," which can be found here: https://www.beatdom.com/howl-first-draft/

to his therapy sessions to help work through both poetic and personal problems. There is other evidence to suggest that he did not write the whole of Part I as spontaneously as he later claimed, but it is impossible to say for certain. He likely did have one major writing session as described in the previous quote, but this probably involved compiling and developing lines he had previously drafted. In any case, the poem came to him quite easily compared to others and perhaps that was because he had stopped trying so hard. "I thought I wouldn't write a *poem*," he explained, "but just write what I wanted to without fear, let my imagination go, open secrecy, and scribble magic lines from my real mind."

He often noted ideas and phrases in his journals, to which he might return for poetic inspiration, but never did he write a line that would morph into something quite so impactful or infamous. "I saw the best mind angel-headed hipster damned" became, in mid-August, "I saw the best minds of my generation destroyed by madness starving, mystical, naked." A handwritten correction to the first-known typed draft changed "mystical" to "hysterical" before it was sent to Jack Kerouac in Mexico for his opinion. His "angel-headed hipsters" became the less effective "hipsters with angelic heads" before moving to different parts of the poem and settling in the third line as "angelheaded hipsters burning for the ancient heavenly connection to the starry dynamo in the machinery of night." For the rest of August, he continued to revise the first part of his poem, adding and removing many lines, substantially rewriting the ones he had first written, and constantly changing their order.

Ginsberg had long since moved away from traditional verse but for several years had been mining his journals for "prose seeds" to adapt into short-line poetry in a style similar to William Carlos Williams, his primary poetic inspiration. By early 1955, however, he felt that these poems were lacking something and he filled his notebooks with ideas about poetry, trying to determine what it was. The breakthrough finally came when he sat down to type "Howl" and he knew it almost immediately. In the middle of the month, he wrote his brother Eugene to say he was "writing in a new style now, long prose poem strophes, sort of surrealist." These "strophes" as he called them, "came as a surprise solution to a metrical problem that preoccupied [him] for a decade" and he found them liberating.[17] This was the cure for what he had identified several months earlier when he complained that his "lines are not yet free enough." This new style, based around a long "Hebraic-Melvillean bardic breath" meant he could say what he wanted more easily and more accurately, and as he wrote and rewrote his poem, he produced what was in a sense a long list of images based upon the lives of his Beat friends. He was cautiously confident in his work and shared parts of it with his friends and family, in spite of its radically personal, often sexually explicit content.

After all his years of struggle, after all his studies and explorations, he had found his voice, but it was not just his own voice; it was a Beat poem, a poem for his era, a poem for his generation. It was not only a response to the world around him and a depiction of his peers; it utilized a new method in poetry and one that had been pioneered by Kerouac. Ginsberg even felt that it sounded like his friend's work. In a letter accompanying the earliest known draft of "Howl," he wrote Kerouac:

> I realize how right you are, that was the first time I sat down to blow, it came out in your method, sounding like you, an imitation practically. How far advanced you are on this. I don't know what I'm doing with poetry. I need years of isolation and constant everyday writing to attain your volume and freedom and knowledge of the form.

Here, he is playing up both the supposed spontaneity of its composition and the musicality that had resulted therefrom. It may sound like self-effacement coupled

---

17   It seems he may have temporarily called his poem "Strophes." A version mailed to Burroughs in Tangier had this title although ones before and after it were called "Howl for Carl Solomon."

with flattery for a man he loved perhaps more than any other, but Ginsberg had taken Kerouac's ideas seriously. To his brother Eugene, he said that his latest work was "more or less Kerouac's rhythmic style of prose" and to William Burroughs he said, "Started a poem, came to me like inspiration, reads like Kerouac style."

This claim may sound strange to those who read "Howl" and then Kerouac's poetry, for there is little similarity on the surface. In fact, one of the reasons why defining the term "Beat Generation" is so difficult is that most of the writers grouped under this label had unique styles of writing and subject matter. Even the Beat triumvirate of Burroughs, Kerouac, and Ginsberg differed hugely from one another. When we throw in others, like Gregory Corso, Diane di Prima, Bob Kaufman, Michael McClure, and Gary Snyder, we see that thematically and stylistically they differed tremendously. They didn't even comprise a generation in the truest sense. Yet as we saw in the previous chapter, Ginsberg had with him in San Francisco a copy of Kerouac's *Visions of Cody*, which he had showed to Rexroth, Duncan, and others, and here perhaps we can see what Ginsberg meant when he said, "This is more or less Kerouac's rhythmic style of prose." One of the earliest Beat scholars, John Tytell, observed in *Naked Angels* that when Kerouac's prose is broken into poetic lines, it is more than a little similar to "Howl":

> I've pressed up girls in Ashville saloons,
>   danced with them in roadhouses
>   where mad heroes stomp one
>   another to death in tragic driveways
>   by the moon:
> I've laid whores on the strip of grass runs
>   along a cornfield outside Durham,
>   North Carolina, and applied bay rum
>   in the highway lights;
> I've thrown empty whiskeybottles clear over
>   the trees in Maryland copses on soft
>   nights when Roosevelt was President;
> I've knocked down fifths in trans-state trucks
>   as the Wyo. road unreeled;

> I've jammed home shots of whiskey on Sixth
> Avenue, in Frisco, in the Londons of
> the prime, in Florida, in L.A.
> I've made soup my chaser in forty-seven
> states;
> I've passed off the back of cabooses,
> Mexican buses and bows of ships in
> midwinter tempests (piss to you);
> I've laid women in coalpiles, in the snow,
> on fences, in beds and up against
> suburban garage walls from
> Massachusetts to the tip of San
> Joaquin.

If this does not convince the reader of a similarity, then perhaps they might wish to listen to a 1960 reading from *Mexico City Blues* given by Ginsberg at the Hotel Sherman in Chicago, which sounds remarkably similar to the poet's reading of his own work. Even though, at their most basic, Kerouac's poem had short lines and Ginsberg's had very long ones, when Ginsberg read "230th Chorus"[18] and then followed them with "Howl," he chanted them both in a very similar cadence and one can see how he viewed his own work as rhythmically inspired by his friend's.

Then, of course, there is the influence of spontaneous composition. Whether or not he actually wrote a draft of "Howl" Part I in a single sitting, Ginsberg certainly claimed to have done so and likely attempted it. The following year, in a famous letter explaining his own work, he said that "[t]hese long lines or Strophes as I call them came spontaneously as a result of the kind of feelings I was trying to put down" and variants on the word "spontaneous" appear again and again in his letters and journals from this period. He had Kerouac's "Essentials of Spontaneous Prose" taped above his typewriter and probably at least took some inspiration. Yet a key

---

18   On tape, he refers to it as "228th Chorus" and says there are a total of 280, when actually what he read was "230th Chorus" and there were 242 in the published version.

difference is that Ginsberg massively rewrote his poem and then continued to edit it until he was satisfied. This was in spite of Kerouac's admonishment that he didn't "want it arbitrarily negated by secondary emendations made in time's reconsidering backstep."

From Kerouac's "Essentials of Spontaneous Prose," Ginsberg also seems to have taken an interest in replicating musical forms in poetry. Although Kerouac's short text mentions jazz twice and never speaks of blues, he arguably put this writing style to best use in *Mexico City Blues*, which he was writing at the same time Ginsberg composed "Howl." These excerpts came after Ginsberg had written a draft of "Howl" and so they cannot be said to have directly influenced its initial composition,[19] but certainly Kerouac's method of writing did, and *Mexico City Blues* was one of Ginsberg's favorite literary works. Years later, he cited it frequently when teaching classes on poetry and once called it "one of the great seminal books of poetry of midcentury because it's the loosest and most open free form of all poetry written at a time when people were experimenting with open form." After initially reading parts of Kerouac's book, Ginsberg responded that he wanted "to get piano and study basic music, write blues poems," and expanded upon this in a letter to his brother a few days later:

> I have been looking at early blues forms and think will apply this form of elliptical semisurrealist imagery to rhymed blues type lyrics. Nobody but Auden's written any literary blues forms, his are more like English ballads, not purified Americana. Blues forms also provide a real varied syncopated meter, with many internal variants and changes of form in midstream like conversational thought.

---

19   Ginsberg sent Kerouac a draft of "Howl" Part I and in Kerouac's next letter he responded with a few poems from *Mexico City Blues*. It is very clear from the context that Kerouac was sending samples of *Mexico City Blues* for the first time and that Ginsberg had not read any of them before.

However, "Howl" was more inspired by Kerouac's assertion that "sketching language is undisturbed flow from the mind of personal secret idea-words, blowing (as per jazz musician) on subject of image." In other words, "Howl" was more jazz than blues. It had grown out of the Fillmore jazz scene and the jazz records Ginsberg played on his good three-speed Webcor phonograph. He seemed to confirm this when explaining his poem during a reading in February 1956: "You might think of [the lines] as a bop refrain, building chorus after chorus after chorus, the ideal being say Lester Young in Kansas City in 1938."

For Ginsberg and Kerouac, jazz was tied to speech and they believed that literature—whether poetry or prose or a hybrid form—ought to capture the American vernacular, and ideally the hippest subcultures. Ginsberg believed that developments in jazz mirrored those in prose and particularly innovations by his mentor, William Carlos Williams. He said:

> It was [in the 1940s] that William Carlos Williams was introducing the notion of the variable measure of speech in poetics while saxophonists such as Lester Young and Charlie Parker and trumpeters such as Dizzy Gillespie and later Miles Davis were doing the same thing in jazz. The saxophone echoed the breath of speech and it was as if it was speaking in accents of conversation or excited rhapsodic talk. There was an element introduced into music of the actual voice as spoken through the saxophone or trumpet that echoed the oddities of rhythm of black speech. This was important to Kerouac because it influenced his prose line. [...]
>
> Now William Carlos Williams wasn't listening to this, he was listening to common pattern Rutherford speech, ordinary talk. People saying, "I've eaten the plums which you left in the icebox and which you were probably saving for

breakfast, forgive me, they were delicious, so sweet and so cold." But the musicians were talking to each other on the street, so jazz is more like urban street talk with very stylized gestures and accents. They were getting it from and feeding it into the music. This was Kerouac's conscious theory beginning in the 1940s and he applied it in some passages of *The Town and the City* and consciously applied it later in *Mexico City Blues*. This was the basis of his style [...]

The musicians were imitating the humor of actual speech phrasing and transferring it right into the music and taking inspiration for the musical phrasing and rhythm from human speech. They refreshed the whole mainstream of American jazz with the rhythms of actual talk just as the mainstream of American poetry, through William Carlos Williams, was being refreshed, rhythmically, through the hearing and imitation of actual spoken speech. It was all going on simultaneously. There was nothing more American than jazz, and in American poetry nothing more American than Williams.

"Howl" was new and exciting in part because it responded to the modern world and built upon revolutionary cultural developments such as these, but at the same time the poet looked back to the past, to his poetic forebearers, and found ways of incorporating concepts that would align with his jazz-inspired rhythm and hep-talk lexis. Specifically, and perhaps of greatest influence, he began borrowing from Walt Whitman and Christopher Smart. From Whitman he developed "a long catalogue" akin to "Song of Myself" and from Smart he borrowed the concept of long lines rooted in anaphoric referencing, based on a starting point of "who...," which helped him to "keep the beat":

> who poverty and tatters and hollow-eyed
> and high sat up smoking in the
> supernatural darkness of cold-water
> flats floating across the tops of cities
> contemplating jazz,
> who bared their brains to Heaven under
> the El and saw Mohammedan
> angels staggering on tenement roofs
> illuminated,
> who passed through universities with radiant
> cool eyes hallucinating Arkansas
> and Blake-light tragedy among the
> scholars of war,
> who were expelled from the academies for
> crazy & publishing obscene odes on
> the windows of the skull
> who cowered in unshaven rooms in
> underwear, burning their money in
> wastebaskets and listening to the
> Terror through the wall,
> who got busted in their pubic beards
> returning through Laredo with a belt
> of marijuana for New York[20]

This was based upon Smart's "Jubilate Agno," which after two opening lines returns to a fixed base of "Let" (later switching to "For"):

> Rejoice in God, O ye Tongues; give the glory
> to the Lord, and the Lamb.
> Nations, and languages, and every Creature,
> in which is the breath of Life.
> Let man and beast appear before him, and
> magnify his name together.
> Let Noah and his company approach the
> throne of Grace, and do homage to
> the Ark of their Salvation.

---

20   This is from the published version of "Howl." These lines differ somewhat in early drafts.

> Let Abraham present a Ram, and worship the
>   God of his Redemption.
> Let Isaac, the Bridegroom, kneel with his
>   Camels, and bless the hope of his
>   pilgrimage.
> Let Jacob, and his speckled Drove adore the
>   good Shepherd of Israel.

Smart had not constrained himself to lines of equal measure but rather had allowed his meaning to dictate length, something Ginsberg copied as he found this allowed him free expression. In the first part of Smart's poem, the shortest line had just thirteen syllables and the longest is seventy-two whilst the shortest line in Part I of "Howl" is also just thirteen syllables and its longest is one hundred and eleven. "The form is exactly the same as 'Howl"s form," Ginsberg told a group of students during a lecture several decades later and indeed it is easy to see that they were very similar.

There were other similarities beyond just the form of their respective opening sections. Smart had written this poem when locked up in a mental institution between 1759 and 1763, but it was not discovered until 1939 and only published in 1943. "Howl" was associated with madness in a number of ways. Its first line of course mentions "minds destroyed by madness" and also Carl Solomon, whom Ginsberg met in a mental hospital, many times, with Solomon the focus of Part III. Ginsberg even said that "these forms developed out of an extreme rhapsodic wail [he] once heard in a madhouse." Their vast lengths, wit, and anti-authoritarianism also unite them. In 1959, Ginsberg referred to Part I of his poem as "a lament for the Lamb in America with instances of remarkable lamblike youths." Whilst "lamb" could of course be a reference to another of Ginsberg's poetic influences, William Blake, "Jubilate Agno" is Latin for "Rejoice in the Lamb," the title Ginsberg usually used when referring to the poem.

Looking at Ginsberg's literary inspirations, we see a distinctly East Coast and European influence on the poem. Walt Whitman and William Carlos Williams were from New Jersey, as was Ginsberg himself, whilst Kerouac came from Massachusetts and Smart was English. Others whom I have not yet mentioned or said much about include William Blake, Antonin Artaud, Catullus, Ezra Pound, Arthur Rimbaud, and Guillaume Apollinaire. Most of the events recounted and people mentioned are from the East Coast and one that did occur on the West Coast is transplanted onto the East—Philip Lamantia's Koran-inspired vision that Ginsberg locates in New York rather than San Francisco. Yet although "Howl" was written and edited over a period of many months, its composition took place entirely in San Francisco and Berkeley and it must thus be viewed as a product of its immediate environment. In other words, even if Ginsberg was not a San Francisco poet, "Howl" was undeniably a San Francisco poem. As we have seen, it grew out of a dream that came whilst he was in bed with John Allen Ryan, one of the founders of the 6 Gallery and a reasonably well-known artist in the city at that time. The first part of the poem was then largely written in his Montgomery Street apartment, with the second part written in Foster's cafeteria and "Footnote to Howl" written on a city bus. Much of the poem was revised in a little cottage in Berkeley after Ginsberg moved there in September, and it would be read aloud for the first time in San Francisco, then changed according to the reactions given by San Francisco audiences, before ultimately being published in San Francisco.

San Francisco and the wider Bay Area afforded Ginsberg an environment conducive to creation and gave him access to a socio-artistic group of an unusually experimental nature. He had been to the 6 Gallery; he had spent nights in The Place and Foster's cafeteria, chatting with poets and painters and photographers, discussing new ideas and styles, critiquing old ways, and sharing visions; and he had attended readings and openings and soaked up the city's burgeoning cultural scene. He was depressed and struggled with writer's block at times, but he was still inspired and constantly wrote in his journal about how he needed to change his poetic voice and what he wanted to say. Although he bitched about them in private, he learned a lot from his interactions with the likes of Rexroth and Duncan, and he was able to discuss art with educated, worldly figures like Ferlinghetti. He could take in avant-garde painting and theater, witness the communal living spaces of true bohemians, and listen to authentic jazz. All of it to some extent shaped his poetry, politics, and personality.

We tend to view Ginsberg as a singularly gifted poet and "Howl" as a work of original expression, but whilst both of these are largely true, it is also easy to see connections between what he achieved with the writing of this poem and what the artists of King Ubu, the 6 Gallery, and other San Francisco galleries and studios were attempting to create. They inhabited a new and rapidly changing world in which old ideas and methods seemed feeble, if not redundant. As he wrote "Howl," he made radical innovations in terms of content, lexis, and rhythm. He wrote openly of cocksucking and narcotic use, pioneered a pared-down grammar, and employed a distinctly contemporary American idiom. Like the collagists, assemblists, found artists, funk artists, experimental filmmakers, and other creatives active in that time and place, he was making art out of material that had not previously been thought of as suitable. Where Jess clipped from comic books and Hedrick made sculptures of beer cans, Ginsberg listened for turns of phrase that comprised the American vernacular, even if these included expletives. The point was not to be crude or explicit—at least, that was not the whole point—but rather to be *real*, to say something about the world through capturing a part of it and using it in an original creation. This was something he had pursued on and off since the forties, partly inspired by Williams, but in the creative environment of San Francisco, surrounded by like-minded artists, he had pushed this concept further. He seems to have known this throughout most of his adult life, but shortly after visiting San Francisco for the first time, already immersing himself in the art scene and socializing with erudite hipsters, he noted in his journal that "art is a community effort—a small but select community living in a spiritualized world endeavoring to interpret the wars and solitudes of the flesh."

Ginsberg was not just creating new art but

challenging the very notion of what art could be. He was saying something about the world by drawing upon the deeply personal and creating an original form that was incomprehensible to those bound by the strictures of traditional poetry. It was a concept that would be explored thoroughly by his Beat peers, Jack Kerouac and William Burroughs, and it is this penchant for originality that is why many of the painters working in San Francisco at that time are often lumped in as part of a wider "Beat movement." Looking at the provocative, experimental art and bohemian lives of people like Jay DeFeo and Fred Martin and Manuel Neri, there are undoubtedly similarities that make it tempting to expand the Beat label. Perhaps Ginsberg was more talented, or maybe he was just better at self-promotion. Perhaps it all came down to luck. But certainly what he managed with "Howl" was something that dozens of other artists were attempting in San Francisco in the mid-fifties.

In an environment where artists sought to make something wildly new, there was nonetheless a shared reverence for select elements of the past. The most obvious was the influence of Dadaism and surrealism. We have seen already that the artists of King Ubu and the 6 Gallery were to varying degrees influenced by Dadaism and that artists like Picasso and May Ray were admired in the city. Although Ginsberg's interest in visual art tended toward the classical, or toward the works of Paul Cézanne, he found value in Dadaism and its concept of absurdist humor as a valid reaction to the horrors of war and the rationalist, materialist, capitalist value system that had produced wars resulting in tens of millions of deaths. "Howl" was, he said, "a tragic custard-pie comedy of wild phrasing, meaningless images for the beauty of abstract poetry of mind." He often talked about his poem as a form of surrealism, particularly his seemingly incongruous combinations of words like "hydrogen jukebox." Explaining "Howl" for a group of students many years later, he explained that he had differed from the long lines of Whitman through the inclusion of "crazy poetic juxtapositions within the line, phrasings within the line, like 'angry fix,' or 'Mohammedan angel.'" This jarring juxtaposition, this thought-provoking imagery, was not unlike the art hanging in the galleries of San Francisco at that time and shares some spirit and technique with the likes of Robert Duncan's *Faust Foutu*, albeit Ginsberg's was a more effective statement, more carefully crafted and coherent. (Of course, Dadaism made its way more obviously into the poem in the line beginning: "who threw potato salad at CCNY lecturers on Dadaism.")

Parts I and III of "Howl" were written in San Francisco and perhaps achieved something similar to the goals of the various artists operating in the city, but it was Part II that was the most immediate product of its environment. In mid-October 1954, not long after he moved to the city, Ginsberg took peyote and had a vision in front of the Sir Francis Drake hotel, seeing it change before him into a terrifying form, monstrous and even demonic, with its windows transformed into eyes. He could not name it then, unsure of whether it was "the tower of Baal or Azriel" or "The Tower of Lucifer," but in August of the following year, he took peyote again and this time was able to give the building a name. He wrote to Kerouac that he "saw Moloch Molochsmoking building in red glare downtown St. Francis Hotel, with robot upstairs eyes and skullface, in smoke, again." After his second vision, he sat in Foster's cafeteria, several blocks west of the hotel, and wrote a draft of Part II that began:

> Moloch! Moloch! Whose hand ripped out their brains and scattered their minds on the wheels of subways?
> Molloch! Filth! Ugliness! Ashcans and unobtainable dollars! Beauties dying in lofts! Harpischords unbuilt! Children screaming under the stairways! old men weeping in the parks!

The published version would read very differently:

> What sphinx of cement and aluminum bashed open their skulls and ate up their brains and imagination?

> Moloch! Solitude! Filth! Ugliness! Ashcans
> and unobtainable dollars! Children
> screaming under the stairways! Boys
> sobbing in armies! Old men weeping
> in the parks!

This part of "Howl" underwent more revisions—and of a more substantial nature—than the other sections. From an initial 194 words, three of which were "Moloch" (with three different spellings), this part of the poem grew to 385 words, with Moloch used 39 times. According to Jonah Raskin in *American Scream*, these revisions often came after the public readings that he gave around the city:

> The more he performed the poem, the more it turned into a performance piece. Accordingly, he wrote Parts II and III with verbal pyrotechnics, rhetorical flourishes, and dramatic phrases. Lines like "Moloch! Moloch! Nightmare of Moloch!" and "Carl Solomon! I'm with you in Rockland"[21] were meant to be performed aloud before a live audience.

As we shall see, Ginsberg would find audiences receptive to his poem and as Raskin suggests he modified it to make "Howl" even more effective. If parts of it fell flat, he would reconsider them. If they were well received, he felt validated. The poem ultimately became famous as a cry of discontent among Americans of his generation in the post-war era, yet it was his San Franciscan audiences that helped shape it with their responses. But again, this returns to the fact that "Howl" was not only one poet's vision and voice reflecting the sentiments of a nationwide or worldwide movement; it was one conceived in San

---

21 Ginsberg had met Solomon in New York State Psychiatric Institute and Solomon was never at Rockland, a place Ginsberg chose more for its sound than for historical accuracy. Ginsberg similarly said Solomon had been to C.C.N.Y. when in fact he had attended Brooklyn College. "I used poetic license," he said, explaining this in a lecture.

Francisco, emerging from its streets and cafés and bars and galleries, and then honed in those same places, discussed and read aloud and then edited to make it yet more of a product of its environment. With Part I, Ginsberg described the destruction of America's youth and its creatives and independent thinkers; with Part II, he pointed his finger at Moloch, embodiment of a mechanized, uncaring society and declared it guilty; and with Part III, he celebrated the supposedly mad, turning away from the negative and toward a message of solidarity and hope. "The title notwithstanding," he explained, "the poem itself is an act of sympathy not rejection." As Snyder once wrote, "The poet articulates the semi-known for the tribe," and with "Howl," Ginsberg eloquently stated what the people around him were saying or what they thought but could not quite put into words.

One final connection to explore, particularly in light of the perhaps surprising use of "Moloch" in "Howl," is the link between Ginsberg's poem and one written by San Francisco's cultural *éminence grise*, Kenneth Rexroth. Although one typically does not think of Ginsberg as being influenced by Rexroth, it is quite possible that he was, and particularly by a poem Rexroth had written in 1953 after the death of Dylan Thomas: "Thou Shalt Not Kill."[22] Most notably, Rexroth wrote the line:

> Three generations of infants
> Stuffed down the maw of Moloch.

Comparing the two poems, it is hard to deny that Ginsberg borrowed ideas. Both poems discuss people destroyed by modern society. They both mention lobotomies, madhouses, communism, psychoanalysts, locomotives, *Time* magazine, and the Canaanite deity Moloch. Both contain long lists—Rexroth's poem a list of questions and Ginsberg's a list of relative clauses.

---

22   In 1953, Rexroth wrote "Lament for Dylan Thomas." He revised and expanded it substantially so that by 1955, when Ginsberg seems to have first read it, the poem was called "Thou Shalt Not Kill."

In fact, there are a great many similarities including uncommon vocabulary that strongly suggest Ginsberg had read Rexroth's poem prior to or during the writing of "Howl" and borrowed not only the concept but some key language. This did not go unnoticed. Poet Bob Kaufman offered a satirical comment at The Place one evening, posing as "Ginsroth Rexberg" for Blabbermouth Night and reading a work called "Who Killed Gene the Scrounge?" It included the lines:

> You killed him, with your 90-cent jugs of wine,
> You killed him, with your Thunderbird-and-Quinine Water,
> You kill him, you son of a bitches.
> I've seen your North Beach Parties, where all the men get raped and all the girls get off scot-free!
> I've seen your North Beach parties, where all the cops come and John Ryan gets all the cute ones!

It is an odd and astute mix of the two poems and shows that it was not only scholars poring over these poems decades later who noticed similarities. It is unclear why Ginsberg refused to acknowledge a link between the poems but perhaps he felt embarrassed by the similarities. A suggestion of this comes from an unpublished poem in a journal that features the line "You you dirty son of a bitch I sound like Kenneth Rexroth paranoiac." In spite of this awareness, for years he denied that "Thou Shalt Not Kill" had any influence on him and even dismissed the poem as "not very classy, not very strong as poetics," calling it a "beatnik poem." Another possibility is the complex relationship between the two poets. In private, Rexroth told Ginsberg never to mention their relationship even though Rexroth himself often wrote about the Beats almost as his students. He was an irrational, paranoid man and Ginsberg's letters to him show frustration and uncertainty for someone he respected but who was deeply unpleasant.

Over the next decades, several others pointed out connections, including Ann Charters, who chastised Ginsberg for failing to credit Rexroth and this seems to have led to a temporary falling out between them. However, in 1987 Ginsberg admitted in an interview with Regina Weinrich that Charters had been right. Now calling it "a really terrific poem," he explained:

> Rexroth in his poem also used the word "Moloch." I probably picked it up from Rexroth. But I had forgotten that. I think that was a neurotic block out partly because I thought Rexroth's poem was too crude, too accusatory, negative in a sense. It was in a sense the classical beatnik poem, ingenious poem, right-minded and right-hearted, but it lacked an elegance that I wanted to see in my poetry or maybe I'm being too snobbish. [...] it made a big imprint on me, impression on me because it was even more bohemian than my bohemian or more beat than my beat. [...] I certainly should give him credit. I'm sorry I didn't in this book but that's another thing a scholar can amplify.

Like any artist, Ginsberg took influence from various sources. These have been explored in this chapter and there are a great many books and essays that go into far more detail, particularly regarding those unrelated to San Francisco. None of that detracts, however, from the fact that "Howl" was a fiercely original poem and one only Allen Ginsberg could have written. He may have borrowed elements of style or even ideas for content, and he littered it with stories from his friends' lives, but it was authentically his. He took disparate influences and used them to respond to the world of the 1950s and did so more effectively than any other poet, Rexroth included. Even when he had only written a single draft of Part I, he recognized that "Howl" was an "[e]legy for the generation." Indeed, it was an eloquent articulation of anti-conformity, anti-capitalist, anti-conservative sentiment, and found a wider audience than he could have imagined. It became the most famous poem of the second half of the twentieth century, taught in schools around the world for its poetic power and the ideas it expressed.

As of August and September 1955, however, "Howl" was merely words on paper, shared among a few select friends. We shall see in the next chapters how the writing of this poem gave rise to the reading of the century, which would in turn help "Howl" to change the world.

Assembling Another Six

On September 1, Allen Ginsberg moved out of his Montgomery Street apartment and into a cottage at 1624 Milvia Street in Berkeley. He had enrolled at U.C. Berkeley to study poetry, feeling that he wanted to devote his life to it, yet recognizing that living on a poet's royalties was not a realistic goal. He reasoned that if he spent a few more years studying in a formal environment, he might be able to become a professor, which would provide money, travel opportunities, and access to research materials for his ongoing poetic investigations. Even Kerouac, who was no fan of the academy, supported this move and urged Ginsberg to become a "big college professor savant about literature and Buddhism and Oriental Art poet." However, he suggested Ginsberg should "not study Greek and Prosody at Berkeley" and instead study Sanskrit and translate sutras because "it's a Buddhist, AN EASTERN FUTURE ahead."

The Milvia Street cottage was, for Allen, a small slice of paradise and, coupled with his new poetic breakthrough, it helped lift him out of the depression that had gripped him for most of 1955. To Kerouac, he wrote that it was:

> a Shakespearean Arden cottage with brown shingles and flowers all about, big sweet garden, private, apricot tree, silence, a kitchen and bathroom too, windows on sunlight, near Shattuck (Key System trolley) Avenue, six blocks from school, perfect place to retreat be quiet, which is my desire since I am more absorbed in writing than before.

He now had his own private and peaceful home,

where he could write as much as he wanted, yet it was only a short walk from the university and not far from San Francisco, where Peter stayed with his brother Lafcadio, allowing Allen the freedom to return when he felt like socializing but without the distractions of actually living in the city. It was the perfect location and almost immediately he had a burst of creative energy, writing a number of new poems, including "Strange New Cottage in Berkeley," "A Supermarket in California," "Four Haiku," "Sunflower Sutra," "Transcription of Organ Music," and "Sather Gate Illumination." Each of these would end up in his *Collected Poems*, many years later.

A "small magazine in Southern California" called *Variegation* had published two of his poems ("Sunset" and "Fragment of a Monument") and one had been republished by the *New York Herald Tribune*, which further boosted his confidence,[23] and then on September 16 he gave his first public poetry reading at the San Francisco Arts Festival. It was the same festival where, one year earlier, the founders of the 6 Gallery had held their fundraising event; however, this year the poetry readings were held indoors at the Nourse Auditorium. On September 15, Jack Goodwin's play, *The Pizza Pusher*, was performed before Maya Angelou danced as part of the BooBam Drum Ensemble, and the next day, at 6 p.m., Ginsberg read alongside Jack Gilbert, Guy Wernham, and Jack Nugent.

Although Goodwin later claimed Ginsberg read Parts I and II of "Howl," he appears to be mistaken and a letter Ginsberg sent ten days after the event mentions only that he read "A Supermarket in California."[24] Writing to Robert LaVigne, who was then in Mexico, he said that there had been "much laughter and applause" and that he was

---

23   The poem published as "Fragment of a Monument" had been written about five years earlier, so it was not new work. It was eventually published in his *Collected Poems* as part of a longer poem—one of two titled "The Shrouded Stranger."

24   Whilst it seems to me extremely unlikely that Ginsberg read any of "Howl" at the Arts Festival, it is not possible to totally discount it. In fact, Goodwin's account is detailed enough that I have devoted a short discursive essay to it at the end of this book (Appendix #2), so that readers can make up their own minds.

"[a]mazed to hear how virile it sounded," adding that he "had been afraid it was too much [of a] fairy poem."

Had Ginsberg read "Howl," the poetry part of the event might have garnered more publicity but local papers simply noted that the location had been "a flop," and the festival was primarily discussed in the media due to a controversial depiction of Vice-President Richard Nixon. Even so, it seems to have been reasonably well attended and Ginsberg's letter to LaVigne shows he felt his work had been enthusiastically received. It was an important step in his poetic development and proved to him that his work not only possessed value but may even have an audience. Privately, he read parts of "Howl" for close friends but never for more than a handful of people at any one time. This would soon change, however, for during September he was busy organizing a poetry reading that would take place in early October.

There are multiple versions of how the 6 Gallery reading of October 7, 1955, came about. In recalling that summer—and specifically the planning of the event—various participants tended to put themselves at the center, taking credit for the idea or the organization or both. McClure spoke and wrote about it the most and, perhaps unsurprisingly given the nature of human memory, he contradicted himself a great many times whilst usually providing an entertaining story. In one telling, he claimed that he proposed the whole event, saying to Wally Hedrick, "Hey wow, that was real nice, that thing we had with Robert Duncan.[25] You wanna have a poetry reading? Can you arrange a poetry reading here?" Elsewhere, he said the opposite, which is that Hedrick asked him. In this version of events, McClure agreed but was soon too busy with work and a pregnant wife. When he ran into Ginsberg on the street, he said, "I've been asked to set up a poetry reading, but I'm in a bit of a crunch of time and life at this moment," to which Ginsberg immediately

---

25   He is referring to the *Faust Foutu* performance that had taken place earlier in the year. This is a claim he made elsewhere. For example, in *Lighting the Corner*, he wrote: "the Six Gallery reading was probably given because of the performance of Faust Foutu earlier in the year."

volunteered to handle the organization of the event. Gary Snyder and Kenneth Rexroth similarly claimed much of the responsibility for organizing the event, yet all three men gave wildly contradictory versions, and none of them managed even to correctly recall *when* the event took place. Snyder's accounts are the easiest to disprove and bear absolutely no resemblance to what really happened but all of them have their various problems.[26] Even Allen Ginsberg, who was in fact the one who primarily organized the event, gave contradictory accounts in later years, sometimes changing his mind mid-interview.

Given the problems of myth, memory, and ego, it is necessary to find contemporaneous sources to help verify later claims. There are two letters Ginsberg wrote around this time that can help us figure out whose idea it was and who organized the event as well as providing clues about the timeline. One of these letters was sent to Kerouac in the middle of August. It is undated but considering postal times, it must have been written between August 10 and 13. In this letter, he wrote:

> An art gallery here asked me to arrange poetry reading program this fall, maybe you and I and Neal one night give a program; also we can record and broadcast whatever we want on Berkeley radio station KPFA.

---

26 See, for example, his interview with Junior Burke in 2011 or the interviews conducted by John Suiter for *Poets on the Peaks*. Almost everything Snyder said put himself at the center of the narrative, coming up with all the ideas and doing much of the work, yet it is easily disproven by contemporary documents and he is unable to get dates right or even the order of events. He claims to have come up with the whole idea for the reading and then contacted the 6 Gallery, before asking Rexroth to be M.C. and writing the postcard text. Elsewhere, he said that he met Ginsberg several times to discuss their poetry before jointly coming up with the idea of a reading, yet we can see from Ginsberg's letters that the idea had been established before they met and Snyder's participation was agreed during their first meeting.

The other letter was dated September 9 and was sent to John Allen Ryan, who like Kerouac was also in Mexico:

> Hendrix [sic—Hedrick] asked me if I wanted to organize a poetry reading at the Six, and I didn't several months ago, not knowing of any poetry around worth hearing, but changed my fucking mind, and so you will be glad to know the tradition continues with a gala evening sometime in a month or so or shorter

In later years, Ginsberg himself was quite unclear on the precise order of events and suggested that Rexroth had asked him—perhaps on behalf of Hedrick—but the contemporary sources are the most likely to be true. After all, they are clear, consistent, and Ginsberg had no reason to lie or exaggerate at that time, for there was no way to predict that this would become one of the most important literary events of the century. Later sources are very obviously misremembered, sometimes altered for egotistical reasons, and occasionally influenced by fictional or exaggerated accounts. It is possible that Hedrick asked McClure first but certainly from an analysis of all extant explanations of how the 6 Gallery reading came about, it seems by far the likeliest that Wally Hedrick asked Allen Ginsberg to organize the event.

As for *when* he was asked, we know it occurred prior to the Kerouac letter of August 10 to 13, but in the Ryan letter he says he had been asked "several months" earlier, which suggests June or July.[27] At a stretch, it could even have been May. The fact that Ginsberg had turned down this opportunity makes sense given that in May and June he had been very depressed, so those months seem like likely candidates. July is quite possible because even though he had moved beyond his writer's block and

---

27   Ginsberg mentions Ryan in his journals from late May and Hedrick is named in a July 29 letter to Rexroth, so clearly Ginsberg was familiar with the 6 Gallery group by this time. He had of course also visited the 6 Gallery in January for the *Faust Foutu* performance.

depression, he was not terribly enthusiastic about his own poetry. In that month, he was still uncertain about how to express himself. His journals and letters show a great deal of self-doubt, which explains why he was unwilling to take on the burden of organizing a reading and intimidated by the prospect of performing in front of an audience.

This all changed when he began writing "Howl." We can see from his letter to Kerouac, written soon after producing the first draft of Part I, that he was considering the possibility of a poetry reading, saying "maybe you and I and Neal one night give a program." However, it is telling that as of September 9, by which time he had made great progress on his poem, even drafting Part II, Ginsberg had "changed [his] fucking mind" and seemed incredibly enthusiastic about reading before an audience. Even though he had no experience reading poetry in public, he had crafted "Howl" not as a poem to sit on the page, neatly expressing witty ideas; rather, its long lines aimed to convey real emotion and were intended to rouse an audience. From the beginning, he was obsessed with the "breath" used in this poem and more than likely he wanted to see if he was capable of delivering it as he imagined. Certainly, he felt it had great potential, which is why he sent copies to Kerouac, LaVigne, and his brother. He had even—in spite of various later claims about the poem having been written with no view to publishing it—contacted Bern Porter and Lawrence Ferlinghetti about publishing his poem, even reaching a tentative agreement with the latter to publish it as part of a small collection of his work. This agreement had been reached by the end of August, so clearly Ginsberg understood the importance of his poem and was perhaps eager to find out what an audience would make of it.

When Ginsberg wrote to Ryan on September 9, he was not just enthusiastic about a potential reading; he had already put together the core of the event. In his letter, he told Ryan that the reading would include

> Rexroth as introducer McClure reading new poems [...] Lamantia putting in an appearance to read John Hoffman's work

(which I haven't really seen for years, if it isn't poetry it'll be a great social occasion), myself to read a long poem the first scraps of which I sent to Kerouac, you might look at it if you see him again. [...] and a bearded interesting Berkeley cat name of Snyder, I met him yesterday (via Rexroth suggestion) [...] IF anybody else turns up along the way to read we may add somebody else.

Of the six poets who would perform that night, four had already been confirmed and we can see that it was Ginsberg who, partially advised by Rexroth, had done most of the organizing. Whether or not McClure had ever been asked to organize, he was certainly willing to participate. Ginsberg saw him often around town and probably asked him after bumping into him on the street, which may explain McClure's memories, which were quoted earlier. Allen disliked his poetry but was always willing to help a friend, especially if he was a handsome young man. Then there was Lamantia, one of the best-known young poets in the city and an old friend of Allen's. He did not want to read (for reasons discussed in the next chapter) but was coerced into it by Rexroth and Ginsberg. One relatively consistent point in these versions of events is that Ginsberg sought Rexroth's advice on this matter, which perhaps explains why he misremembered Rexroth asking him several decades later. Most likely, Hedrick asked Ginsberg, who in turn sought Rexroth's advice, and later he believed Rexroth had been the one who originally asked him. As a respected poet, whose living room was a meeting place for the city's literary citizens, Rexroth was the best person to suggest potential participants. Rexroth quickly pointed to Snyder, who was by this point almost a protégé. Amazingly, Ginsberg and Snyder had never met before this, but Ginsberg trusted Rexroth's advice and set off to meet him on September 8.

Part of the reason the two men had not met was that Snyder had spent several months working and traveling in the mountains of the West Coast, arriving back in the

Bay Area on August 28. He had been studying Chinese and Japanese at U.C. Berkeley since 1953, and although he loved the mountains and wondered about working as a logger forever, for now he needed to get back to prepare for the new semester, which began September 19. Conveniently, he lived not far from Ginsberg—in a spartan hut on Hillegass Avenue that was so small Philip Whalen called it "Gary's tiny doghouse." There was no furniture, only climbing equipment. Snyder's obsession with Asia had led him to this Zen-like existence. In *The Dharma Bums*, Kerouac described the little cottage. Here, Japhy is the character based on Snyder:

> Japhy lived in his own shack which was infinitely[28] smaller than ours, about twelve by twelve, with nothing in it but typical Japhy appurtenances that showed his belief in the simple monastic life—no chairs at all, not even one sentimental rocking chair, but just straw mats. In the corner was his famous rucksack with cleaned-up pots and pans all fitting into one another in a compact unit and all tied and put away inside a knotted-up blue bandana. Then his Japanese wooden pata shoes, which he never used, and a pair of black inside-pata socks to pad around softly in over his pretty straw mats, just room for your four toes on one side and your big toe on the other. He had a slew of orange crates all filled with beautiful scholarly books, some of them in Oriental languages, all the great sutras, comments on sutras, the complete works of D. T. Suzuki and a fine quadruple-volume edition of Japanese haikus. He also had an immense collection of valuable general poetry. In fact if a thief should have broken in there the

---

28 Whilst this may seem like careless phrasing, it is in fact a deliberate reference to an old sutra about a small house possessing "infinitely expandable space."

only things of real value were the books. [...] A few orange crates made his table, on which, one late sunny afternoon as I arrived, was steaming a peaceful cup of tea at his side as he bent his serious head to the Chinese signs of the poet Han Shan.

Interestingly, Kerouac omitted one of the more interesting items in the room: a cougar skin Snyder used as his bed. He would roll this up and hide it during the day and then sleep under it at night. "At that time," Snyder said, "it seemed extremely strange to people, but it seemed very nice to me because I was used to sleeping on the ground."

A little younger than the East Coast Beats, Snyder was born in San Francisco (just eight blocks south of the 6 Gallery) in 1930.[29] The Depression had pushed his family to move to Washington and later to Oregon and so he grew up in the Pacific Northwest, meaning that even though he had been born not far from the 6 Gallery, he was not exactly a local poet. It was in the Pacific Northwest that he developed a passion for the outdoors. His "early heroes [were] Indians & frontiersmen, asceticism of the frontier," and this was a view he maintained well into adulthood. A childhood accident also saw him bedridden for months, where he read extensively, particularly on Native American cultures. As a boy, he not only spent time outdoors but began to develop practical skills in the forest, often with his father. "I did a lot of forest work," he said, "starting young... handling two-man saws, helping split shingles and shakes, splitting firewood, handline axes, that sort of thing... and I started going out camping and fishing in the woods really young and picked up a lot of woods skills." At around the age of ten, he began spending one or two nights camping alone and at thirteen he attended a Y.M.C.A. camp at Mount St. Helens, where he was "half camper, half worker," doing work such as clearing trails. He developed a passion for mountain climbing and

---

29   Kerouac was born in 1922, Ginsberg in 1926, and Burroughs—the oldest of the core Beat writers—was born in 1914.

pursued this almost obsessively, but is keen to stress that this was not for the same egotistic triumph-over-nature reasons as most men. Rather, Snyder found that in the mountains he gained a better understanding of himself and the world.

Thus, from an early age he was a mixture of bookish and outdoorsy, with an interest in other cultures—traits that would define him in adulthood. In 1947, Snyder enrolled at Reed College, where he met Philip Whalen and Lew Welch, two more writers who would be considered part of the Beat Generation. He studied anthropology and literature, whilst at the same time beginning his personal inquiries into Chinese poetry.

In 1951, Snyder had several important experiences. He began working as a logger, an occupation that perhaps seems incongruous with his later environmentalist poetics, but he maintains that forest preservation was the main aim of the U.S. Forest Service at this point rather than selling lumber, which he feels became its later focus. He would do various jobs of this nature over the next five years, using his time—mostly spent in isolation—to work on his "religious practices and austerities" as well as poetry and calligraphy. That same year, he ventured down from the mountains to visit Philip Whalen, who was temporarily living in San Francisco. Here, at a "metaphysical bookshop near Union Square," he found books by D.T. Suzuki. He knew quite a bit about Buddhism already but these books would prove to be a revelation, for they dealt with the practical he did not know rather than the theoretical that he had already learned. Snyder had signed up to study in the Department of Linguistics at the University of Indiana and he set off across the country, but en route he read the Suzuki books. "What I really should be doing is going to Japan to study this stuff first hand," he thought. In Indiana, he stayed one semester before "head[ing] back to the West Coast, to make connections with the Zen world." For five years, he would live mostly in the Bay Area as he prepared for life in Japan.

In 1952, he returned to the Bay Area, living with Whalen at 1207 Montgomery Street, not far from where Ginsberg would begin writing "Howl" two years later. They enjoyed the North Beach arts scene and frequented many of the bars and restaurants mentioned by the 6 Gallery founders. He met Robert Duncan that year and was in the city when King Ubu opened, so it is possible he visited 3119 Fillmore, though no record of this exists. Snyder enrolled at U.C. Berkeley in late 1953 to pursue a degree in Asian languages—first focusing on Chinese, then later on Japanese—in the hopes of moving to Japan to study Zen and became a member of the Berkeley Young Buddhist Association, where he practiced meditation and in whose journal he published several poems. However, he grew unhappy with how "square" the organization became. He lived in the area for several years, spending the semesters in Berkeley but then traveling throughout the American West during the holidays, picking up various jobs or attempting to climb the region's biggest mountains. He worked in logging camps, for the U.S. Forest Service, and for the National Parks Service, although he was blacklisted as a potential communist for several years, which hampered his ability to find jobs.

When Ginsberg arrived at Snyder's Hillegass *hojo*,[30] Gary was sitting in his backyard underneath a loquat tree, fixing his bicycle. He was a practical young man, who believed in the concept of self-sufficiency and thus was proudly capable of building and fixing things. This, coupled with his good looks, immediately endeared him to Allen and they quickly became friends. For his part, Snyder was impressed by how forthright Ginsberg was. He immediately said, "Kenneth Rexroth tells me you write poetry. Can you show me some?" and they went inside to have some tea and share their poetry. After seeing what Snyder was working on—which was most likely *Myths & Texts*—Ginsberg said, "Oh, you know what you're doing."

In his letter to Ryan, written the next day, Ginsberg noted that Snyder was a scholar of Asian languages and literature, and was training to be a Zen monk. He also

---

30   Snyder referred to several of his homes as "hojos," which he took from *Hojoki*, a 1212 Japanese literary work, whose title is often translated as *An Account of My Hut* or *The Ten Foot Square Hut*. Snyder probably first encountered this work in Rexroth's 1949 translation. He wrote in his journal in December 1955 that he "could write a HOJOKI simply of this place & how I lived here."

wrote, "He's a head, peyotlist, laconist, but warmhearted, nice looking with a little beard, thin, blond, rides a bicycle in Berkeley in red corduroy and levis[31] and hungup on Indians (ex anthropology student from some Indian hometown) and writes well." To Ginsberg, Snyder's knowledge of and enthusiasm for Asian and indigenous American cultures was especially impressive, with his peyote experiences also a positive sign.[32] Having grown up learning about the Western canon, Ginsberg was fascinated by those with knowledge of more "exotic" cultures. His respect for Snyder was immediate and lasted for the rest of his life. According to McClure, "Allen had respect for Gary in a way that he didn't for some other people. He wanted to learn from Gary."

Interestingly, what first attracted Ginsberg to Snyder was also what captivated Kerouac, who turned him into Japhy Ryder for his 1958 novel, *The Dharma Bums*:

> Japhy Ryder was a kid from eastern Oregon brought up in a log cabin deep in the woods with his father and mother and sister, from the beginning a woods boy, an axman, farmer, interested in animals and Indian lore so that when he finally got to college by hook or crook he was already well equipped for his early studies in

---

31   Ginsberg notes Snyder's clothes here and elsewhere, highlighting how hip he was. In contrast, when asked about their first meeting, Snyder says "the first thing I noticed was how middle-class his clothing was," saying that perhaps he wore a shirt and tie.

32   Peyote was somewhat of a connection between the five poets. "All of us were into it," Lamantia said. Snyder had indeed used it and partially credited it for the "stories [and] symbols" in *Myths & Texts*, the work he would read from at the 6 Gallery reading. Ginsberg had written part of "Howl" after a peyote vision, whilst Whalen wrote all three of his 6 Gallery poems after an experience with the drug. Lamantia had used it and would read poems by John Hoffman, who had allegedly died of a peyote overdose, and in 1958 McClure would write "Peyote Poem." Even Kerouac—not enamored of psychedelics—had been experimenting with it in the summer of 1955.

anthropology and later in Indian myth and in the actual texts of Indian mythology. Finally he learned Chinese and Japanese and became an Oriental scholar and discovered the greatest Dharma Bums of them all, the Zen Lunatics of China and Japan.

Clearly, both Ginsberg and Kerouac saw in Snyder a woodsy, capable, exotic, intellectual poet figure who was politically and culturally hip. He was the authentic bohemian—too cool to care about being cool. Although he was younger than either of them and in a sense less worldly, he had real knowledge of the things they wanted to know about and had a devotion to his passions that largely eluded them. He may have been younger, but they both wrote about him as though he were an older brother. Snyder also proved wise like an elder sibling, helping Ginsberg to realize his poetic destiny. When Allen confided in him that he was fearful about embarking on life as a poet—something that couldn't possibly yield financial security—Snyder told him:

> I used to worry about that but I don't worry about it anymore. Last summer I worked on a trail crew up in the Yosemite Park with a guy who was 60 years old and he could still handle a pick and shovel, and he could still handle dynamite. Now, if he can do it, we can. We can be working men till we're 60.

This advice helped Ginsberg realize that he needn't choose between writing and earning money; he could do both if he really had to. Besides, the wilderness was filled with poetic inspiration. Snyder regularly took work in the mountains and wrote about his experiences there, as did his good friend, Philip Whalen. Some of their greatest works would draw upon these experiences, including *Myths & Texts*, which Snyder was working on at the time he met Ginsberg. His journal from this period suggests he was very enthusiastic about it.

During their first meeting, Snyder told Ginsberg about his friend, Philip Whalen, who was soon to arrive in San Francisco. He was another Oregon poet and had grown up in a ranching town filled with cowboys, where his bookish nature set him apart. He was "witty, articulate, engaging, a way cut above the style of Oregon rednecks," Snyder explained. Whalen had been drafted in 1943 and spent three years in the army, working as a radio instructor. He had wanted to live in San Francisco immediately after the war, but he had no money and so he enrolled at Reed on the G.I. Bill, earning $65 a month. He had gotten into writing around the age of sixteen and continued to write poetry and fiction whilst in the army, but it was at Reed that he became more serious about this. After becoming friends with Snyder and Welch, the latter of whom called Whalen the "portly poet laureate of the school," Whalen was part of a small literary circle. Although Whalen was much older than his peers, they learned from each other and the flow of knowledge ran both ways in their relationship. "It was always very educational talking to Philip," Snyder said. They engaged in poetic games and shared their interests. Snyder attempted to turn Whalen on to Buddhism and Welch talked endlessly about the brilliance of Gertrude Stein. However, surprisingly for someone who would later become a Zen monk, Whalen was not all that interested in the former, with his interests then lying more in Asian art and philosophy. Outside of this friend group, Whalen felt there was little in the way of culture at Reed, but he learned from Lloyd Reynolds, a "great teacher" who gave instruction in the graphic arts, calligraphy, and creative writing. Unlike Snyder, Whalen had no interest in the great outdoors. "He's not physical," Snyder said, "although he can be very strong [...] and he doesn't like to do things, he doesn't like to work hard, except when it's really his own choice." Yet Snyder's influence would soon push Whalen beyond his comfort zone and into the wilderness.

After graduation, Snyder and Whalen stayed friends as Welch went off to temporarily live a conventional life in Chicago. Whalen visited San Francisco several times in the early fifties and clearly found it a stimulating town. He and Snyder lived there for about a year between 1952 and 1953 but Whalen found that his financial situation was such that he could not settle permanently. He took a job in Santa Monica, working in an airplane factory and ended up working as a fire lookout with the Forest Service, something Snyder pushed him into partly because Whalen owed his friend quite a lot of money. "It's not too hard to get there," Snyder said, as a means of coercing him. "Once you're there, you don't have to do much. You'll have plenty of time to read, and they pay you... and the view is lovely." The bookish and unfit Whalen thus found himself spending the summer of 1955 atop Sourdough Mountain, and this is where he was when Snyder wrote to tell him about the upcoming reading at the 6 Gallery. In his journal, Snyder noted: "This town and these new people will do Philip much good." He was right.

Whalen spent nine weeks on Sourdough Mountain, in Washington's Skagit Valley, and he did so mostly without human contact. His stay extended into September whereas Snyder had already finished for the season and was in San Francisco. This was because the lightning storms around Sourdough Mountain were running late that year and it was very dry, so the risk of fire was elevated. In mid-September, he hiked down the trail to Diablo to find a letter from Snyder. "[Y]ou must come as soon as possible," his friend had written, "because you are scheduled to read some of your own poetry at a reading to be given at the Six Gallery on the first Friday in October." Ginsberg had not mentioned Whalen in his September 9 letter, but clearly Snyder had lobbied for his inclusion soon after that first meeting. Snyder explained to Whalen that he was allowed to participate because of three poems Snyder had shared—"The Martyrdom of Two Pagans," "For K.W. Senex," and "If You're So Smart, Why Ain't You Rich?"—which he claimed had "achieved a certain subterranean celebration via Rexroth & others."[33] This likely meant that

---

33   These are the poems Snyder mentioned sharing in a letter to Whalen. In Kenneth Rexroth's archives, however, there are five Whalen poems that Snyder had sent him. There is an untitled work that begins "Kreee! / Cries the eagle" and also "Marigolds."

Snyder had read them aloud at one of Rexroth's Fridaynight salons. Whalen quickly made his way down the West Coast toward Berkeley, enthusiastic about what Snyder promised would be "a poetickal bombshell." He arrived late on September 21, having sent a large box of books ahead of him. His letters to Snyder were short and said little, but they hinted at a desire to settle in San Francisco for the foreseeable future.

Whalen was perhaps an odd choice for the lineup as not only was he older than the others but he was also less well known.[34] Although it is often said that the 6 Gallery reading was the first time each poet read their work in public, this was only true of McClure. However, McClure, Ginsberg, and Snyder all had local reputations, at least among the sorts of people who generally attended literary salons or who socialized in the hippest cafés and bars. McClure was also known among the community of painters in the city, whilst Ginsberg and Snyder had some publication credits and Ginsberg had won some minor awards for his poetry. He was also seen as a protégé of William Carlos Williams, which gave him a degree of respect among the city's poets (and earned some envy from both Snyder and Whalen). Meanwhile, Lamantia had been a highly regarded poet since his teens, championed by André Breton, Henry Miller, and Rexroth. Whalen, on the other hand, had no reputation in the city, having only ever given one small reading at Reed.

That year, Whalen underwent a huge personal and poetic change, coming to reject much of his previous work. "[F]rom about 1949 until early 1955 I had been just down, turned off, and I had written very little," he said, "but in the summer of 1955 I was staying with some friends at Seattle and got turned on to peyote for the first time and that acted on my spirit and mind and body and everything else as a great cure." Before that, he doubted himself and even the power of poetry, occasionally shouting "Poetry is shit!" and "Let it all die and rot and stink." Peyote, however, opened his mind to the world and

---

34   Born in 1923, Whalen was seven years older than Snyder, nine years older than McClure, four years older than Lamantia, and three years older than Ginsberg.

to new concepts in poetry. Previously, his work had been short and Imagist-inspired but now, like Ginsberg and "Howl," his poetry became freer as he realized he need not be constrained by length and form. This effect was compounded when, in San Francisco, he met Kerouac and Ginsberg. They were, he said, "the first people I thought of as being really literary, not literary literary, but then they were doing the same kind of thing I was, living and writing and picking it up out of the air, out of books, out of other people." It was a pivotal moment for him and he connected with his poetic peers immediately. He also saw a kindred spirit in McClure, who like Whalen was an "antipoet" interested in witty, satirical works of social criticism rather than more conventional lyrical poetry.

As Whalen headed down the coast, Jack Kerouac was traveling up it. For almost a year, he had promised to visit Ginsberg in San Francisco but his cross-country meandering had been interrupted by a visit to Mexico, where he had overindulged in marijuana, peyote, codeine, morphine, and of course copious amounts of alcohol. All of this had taken a disastrous toll on his health because they seem to have impaired the medicine he had been taking for phlebitis, but they had helped him to write "150 bloody poetic masterpieces." These would later be published as *Mexico City Blues*. As we saw in the previous chapter, they were written according to his concept of "spontaneous prose," and he had sent a few of them to Ginsberg, who was deeply impressed. He later called them "about the closest you have to subtle recording of consciousness, subtle recording of ordinary mind consciousness—the kind of quirks, day-dreams, interruptions, abruptnesses, gaps, associations, and after-thoughts that come into American mind-tongue." McClure said "nothing is as great as *Mexico City Blues*, except maybe D.H. Lawrence's poetry." Snyder recalled the manuscript being passed around and deeply impressing the poets of San Francisco, especially those schooled in Buddhism.

Kerouac at this point only had one book published: *The Town and the City* (1950). It was not a reflection of his current writing style or indeed how he wanted to be viewed as an artist, but he had another six books written (plus several minor efforts), and one of these he had sold in July 1955. That was *On the Road*, which would be released two years later, in 1957. Kerouac was not as enthusiastic about its publication as one might expect. This was partly because he had written the book in 1951 and so it "had become old to him; he'd moved on from there, written many other books," according to one of his girlfriends, who added that "Jack didn't seem especially excited about the forthcoming publication of *On the Road* [...] It seemed as if he'd waited too long." Kerouac also felt that *On the Road* was a watered-down, commercially viable alternative to his real art. Since writing it, he had moved on to more challenging, experimental works like *Doctor Sax* and *Visions of Cody*. He hoped that *On the Road* would lead to the publication of these, which would turn America on to his concept of spontaneous prose, but he was constantly frustrated by compromises, such as inventing pseudonyms to disguise people's real identities. He felt the publication of his book was being pushed back and that already it described events from the late forties, making it old news. It was time, he felt, for America to experience the immediacy of his newest prose and poetry.

Kerouac's journey north from Mexico City was one of great adventure, parts of which he described in the opening chapters of *The Dharma Bums*. The book begins:

> Hopping a freight out of Los Angeles at high noon one day in late September 1955 I got on a gondola and lay down with my duffel bag under my head and my knees crossed and contemplated the clouds as we rolled north to Santa Barbara. It was a local and I intended to sleep on the beach at Santa Barbara that night and catch either another local to San Luis Obispo the next morning or the first class freight all the way to San Francisco at seven p.m. Somewhere near Camarillo where Charlie Parker'd been mad and relaxed back to normal health, a thin old little bum climbed into my gondola as we headed

into a siding to give a train right of way and looked surprised to see me there. He established himself at the other end of the gondola and lay down, facing me, with his head on his own miserably small pack and said nothing. By and by they blew the highball whistle after the eastbound freight had smashed through on the main line and we pulled out as the air got colder and fog began to blow from the sea over the warm valleys of the coast. Both the little bum and I, after unsuccessful attempts to huddle on the cold steel in wraparounds, got up and paced back and forth and jumped and flapped arms at each our end of the gon. Pretty soon we headed into another siding at a small railroad town and I figured I needed a poorboy of Tokay wine to complete the cold dusk run to Santa Barbara.

After hopping the train and sleeping on a beach, he hitchhiked and was quickly picked up by a gorgeous blonde in a convertible. This is mentioned in *The Dharma Bums* but more extensively recounted in his short story, "The Good Blonde." She took him to San Francisco, where he stayed over in a skid row hotel. The next day, he jumped on another train and rode to Berkeley to find his old friend, but Ginsberg was out. Kerouac let himself in and availed himself of Allen's books and records, playing Bach on the Webcor Hi-Fi and reading Céline. In *The Dharma Bums*, he wrote:

> The old rotten porch slanted forward to the ground, among vines, with a nice old rocking chair that I sat in every morning to read my Diamond Sutra. The yard was full of tomato plants about to ripen, and mint, mint, everything smelling of mint, and one fine old tree that I loved to sit under and meditate on those cool perfect starry

California October nights unmatched anywhere in the world. We had a perfect little kitchen with a gas stove, but no icebox, but no matter. We also had a perfect little bathroom with a tub and hot water, and one main room, covered with pillows and floor mats of straw and mattresses to sleep on, and books, books, hundreds of books everything from Catullus to Pound to Blyth to albums of Bach and Beethoven (and even one swinging Ella Fitzgerald album with Clark Terry very interesting on trumpet) and a good three-speed Webcor phonograph that played loud enough to blast the roof off: and the roof nothing but plywood [...]

Like Ginsberg, he loved the beautiful little house and its tranquil garden. "Someday I'll buy that cottage at 1624 Milvia," he wrote in his journal.

When Ginsberg returned, he told Kerouac about recent developments—namely, meeting Snyder and planning the 6 Gallery reading. A few days later, on September 23, Ginsberg and Kerouac headed into San Francisco on the F train from Berkeley. When they arrived at Key System Terminal, they found Snyder and Whalen waiting for them.[35] It was the first time Kerouac had met the two poets from Oregon but they became fast friends. "Jack was wearing a red windbreaker jacket, smoking a cigarette, looking very James Dean, handsome and gloomy," Whalen recalled. He and Ginsberg had their arms around each other "like Tweedledum and Tweedledee" and were "giggling and bopping." Snyder, meanwhile, liked Kerouac's "affable clarity, and funny little phrasings" that showed him to be "smart and an original." Kerouac, for his part, thought Snyder and Whalen were "the two

---

35   Again, we have contradictory sources for this. Whalen vividly recalled both that he and Snyder arrived to find Ginsberg and Kerouac waiting for them and also the opposite: that they waited for Ginsberg and Kerouac. Ginsberg claimed they all met "by accident," but this seems highly unlikely.

Assembling Another Six

best men [he] ever met." Snyder would become the focus of *The Dharma Bums*, in the same way Neal Cassady had been the focus of *On the Road*.

The four poets walked from the train station via Chinatown to North Beach, where they stopped in at The Place for beers. It was the hippest bar in town at the time, populated by artists and writers, who could just about afford the ten-cent drinks that were served in big fishbowl glasses. Regulars were also allowed up to a two-dollar-per-month bar tab and it had exhibitions, light shows, live music, and open-mic events called "Blabbermouth nights," at which people could say whatever they wanted, speaking from a sort of pulpit. Heckling was encouraged and lewd language tended to get a cheer. Earlier in the year, it was where Ginsberg and Orlovsky had met Duncan and been invited to *Faust Foutu*. Kerouac said it was "the favorite bar of the hepcats around the Beach" and McClure called it "the Deux Magots of Frisco," referring to the Parisian café frequented by the likes of Jean-Paul Sartre, Ernest Hemingway, Albert Camus, Pablo Picasso, and James Joyce. It had been founded in 1953 by Knute Stiles and Leo Krikorian, who bought it from a Sicilian man for $3,000. Called "The Place" mostly because the owners couldn't decide on a name. It was, Stiles said,

> a freak joint, poets of all the sizes and ages, some painters, some photographers, some merchant seamen, some radicals, some conservatives. [...] We arranged it in such a way that there wouldn't be any single-tabled people, that people would be all kind of together. The smallness of The Place ensured the continuity of the dialogue—it was very hard for anybody to get lost.

John Allen Ryan, who started tending bar there in 1956, said, "The Place was like a cultural center, poetry in fourteen languages in the toilet, pasted, written, painted on the wall. We had art shows, Blabbermouth Night, poetry readings, jazz." Its first event had been a reading by Jack

Spicer and they regularly showed artworks by 6 Gallery regulars such as Remington, Barletta, Eichel, DeFeo, and Hedrick. They hosted poetry competitions that included the likes of Joanne Kyger and Jack Spicer, who would stand on a yellow box and read, prefiguring the slam poetry events begun in the 1980s. Kerouac described it in *Desolation Angels* as "a brown lovely bar made of wood, with sawdust, barrel beer in glass mugs, an old piano for anybody to bang on, and an upstairs balcony with little wood tables." At some point probably in 1956 LaVigne had a show there called "The Dangerous Garden" that featured several poems by Ginsberg in among the paintings.

Jack Goodwin suggested that the poet scene surrounding The Place had "more than a whiff of the anti-intellectual to it," lamenting the fact that the poets there could not speak any foreign language, considered Gertrude Stein "classic literature," and pretty much only read each other's work. He suggested that this was because they were mostly painters who had graduated and could no longer afford paints and canvases and were primarily interested in poetry as part of "a big sexual ploy." He noted that some of the old Berkeley poets migrated to The Place as it became the de facto poetic hangout, with Thomas Parkinson and William Everson frequently present, as well as "Allen Ginsberg and his chorus of howling boys [who would] stamp up and down the street, yelling 'Karra-wack! Karra-wack!'"

It was Friday night, so after chatting over their cheap beers, Ginsberg, Kerouac, Snyder, and Whalen set off for Rexroth's home. Snyder had read some of Whalen's work earlier that year and Ginsberg had shared Kerouac's work, so their names and styles were not unknown, but neither man had attended until now. That evening, Kerouac read from "October in the Railroad Earth." The rhythms of it reminded Snyder of something he'd read earlier that year—"Jazz of the Beat Generation," which had been published in the seventh issue of *New World Writing* under the name "Jean-Louis."[36] As Jack spoke, Gary came to

---

36   This was just "Jean-Louis," not "Jean-Louis Kerouac" or any of the other variations of his name that Jack sometimes used.

realize that it was indeed the same writer. "I flashed that he was Jean-Louis," Snyder recalled. "And then I knew he was a truly gifted writer with a new kind of language sense that would change how we wrote prose." For the four poets, it was an exhilarating evening of "good talking" made all the more enjoyable when "some chicks showed up" and they all found themselves quickly enmeshed in an intense intellectual union.

Rexroth, however, was less impressed. Although he adored Snyder and seems to have been quite positive about Ginsberg and Whalen, and despite having previously admired Kerouac's work—even reviewing "Jazz of the Beat Generation" positively on his K.P.F.A. radio station, supposedly[37] comparing Kerouac to Genet and Céline—in person he found Kerouac little more than an irritating poseur. When Kerouac referred to the *Pure Land Sutra* and was surprised when numerous people immediately knew what he was talking about, Rexroth quipped, "Everybody in San Francisco is a Buddhist, Kerouac! Didn't you know that?" Moreover, almost everyone in the room except Kerouac spoke one or more Asian languages, which Rexroth took as a sign of Kerouac's superficial interest in the East. It was to prove the beginning of a difficult relationship. In the words of Kerouac biographer, Gerald Nicosia, "Jack scorned Rexroth's ego-centric 'blabbing' [and c]hafed by this disrespect, Rexroth may also have felt the need to demean Jack because the others thought so

---

He wrote to various people saying that he wanted anonymity in order to write freely but he may also have been trying to avoid paying child support to Joan Haverty for a child he claimed was not his. "Jazz of the Beat Generation" was mostly an excerpt from *On the Road* (then titled *The Beat Generation*) but he had "sneaked in" parts of *Visions of Neal*. Interestingly, this edition of *New World Writing* contained not only fragments of the as-yet-unpublished *On the Road*, but also a piece called "The Texan," which was the first (and then only) chapter of Joseph Heller's *Catch-22*, published in 1961. At the time, he called it *Catch-18*.

37   Evidence of this comes from a letter Ginsberg sent to Kerouac. In the letter, he admits having not actually listened to the radio program but says he "heard about it." It is impossible now to verify what Rexroth said as there are no recordings from that period.

highly of his ability; Rexroth was always edgy of anyone who seemed to be moving too close to his eminence."

Kerouac was not only a gifted writer; he could read beautifully as well. This was due to the fact that his writing was inspired by jazz and so it was written to be read aloud. When he spoke, his prose sounded like poetry. The strange punctuation and unusual—sometimes made-up—lexis contributed to a musicality that captivated readers. However, Kerouac declined to read at the upcoming 6 Gallery reading that Ginsberg was planning. To his editor, Malcolm Cowley, Kerouac explained:

> Allen Ginsberg has arranged for me to read before an audience but I won't do it because I'm too bashful. Poet ain't court jester, I say. He, tho, gets up on stage and howls his poems.

Indeed, for all Kerouac could be boisterous when drunk, he was often painfully shy. The prospect of reading in front of an audience, even from works in which he had a great deal of pride, was frightening for him. "With a small gathering of writers," Snyder explained, "he was quite happy to" read his work aloud, but doing it in public terrified him and he had to get so drunk that he would read badly or get angry with his audience. In 1957, when asked to read aloud to promote *On the Road*, he said, "No, not me. I can't do that. I get stage fright. Wait till Allen comes back—he's great. He loves that." Kerouac agreed to attend the 6 Gallery reading for the purpose of supporting his friends, but there was no chance of him getting up on stage and participating, no matter how much Ginsberg and others cajoled him.

With Whalen in town and Kerouac determined not to participate, the line-up was now finalized. Ginsberg, Snyder, Whalen, McClure, and Lamantia would all read, with Rexroth as the "introducer." There would be six poets on stage at the 6 Gallery, a happy coincidence that Ginsberg would play up in his promotional materials for the event. Drawing upon his experience in advertising, he—and possibly Gary Snyder[38]—wrote the text for a postcard and then mimeographed several hundred copies. It read exactly as follows (including layout):

<u>6 POETS AT 6 GALLERY</u>

Philip Lamantia reading mss. of late John Hoffman-- Mike McClure, Allen Ginsberg, Gary Snyder & Phil Whalen--all sharp new straightforward writing-- remarkable coll- ection of angels on one stage reading their poetry. No charge, small collection for wine and postcards. Charming event.

Kenneth Rexroth, M.C.

8 PM Friday Night October 7, 1955

6 Gallery 3119 Fillmore St.

San Fran[39]

---

38   Snyder says, "we typed up a postcard that I wrote most of." It's a claim he's made in several interviews but only many decades after the event. However, he is almost certainly thinking of the postcard for the second reading, for which he did indeed write most of the text. John Suiter points out that the phrase "a remarkable collection" had been used by Snyder in 1949, which is hardly definitive evidence but it does suggest he may have had some involvement. It should be noted that in these same interviews, he makes a number of claims that are very easy to disprove with contemporary documents, so it's unlikely he's correct about the postcard.

39   There is an alternate version of this text that refers to "dancing girls" and "free satori." This first appeared in Ann Charters' biography, *Kerouac* (1973). It is possible that she quoted Ginsberg or Snyder, who were merely relying on their memory of a postcard from more than a decade earlier. She told me she bought the postcard from Bob Wilson at Phoenix Bookshop in NYC in the mid-to-late-sixties, so it is not clear why the version in her book is incorrect unless she is misremembering the date of purchase. Charters sent her copy to Ginsberg in the mid-eighties and since then the original text of the postcard has been publicly viewable in the book *Howl: Original Facsimile Draft*, but the incorrect version is still commonly re-used in books, essays, and online articles.

Several hundred postcards were mailed to poetry aficionados and people on the 6 Gallery and Poetry Center mailing lists, with another hundred placed in the sorts of locations artists, intellectuals, and bohemians assembled: City Lights, Miss Smith's Tea Room, The Place, Vesuvio's, Gino and Carlo's, and the Co-Existence Bagel Shop. Peter Forakis, a painter and sculptor who became involved with the 6 Gallery shortly before it opened, made a large, red poster for the event, copies of which were put up around town, including on the C.S.F.A. campus. The posters played on the "6" in the name of the gallery and the number of poets on stage. Whalen had the finest handwriting and so he addressed most of the envelopes, estimating that they sent about "seven million" of them. Ginsberg addressed the rest.

Each of the participants did their best to spread the word and it's hard to imagine Rexroth would not have used his radio show to mention the upcoming event. Even so, there were no notices in the media as was the case with art shows at the 6 Gallery, and so the poets had little reason to expect that their reading would have anything close to the impact it did. Snyder, however, seemed confident. Just a few weeks before the event, he wrote in his journal, "Poetry will get a kick in the arse around this town." Ginsberg, in his own journal, wrote something equally prophetic: "I suppose I'll wake up to find myself famous."

Part Three
The 6 Gallery Reading

A Subterranean Celebration

The reading was set to begin at 8 p.m. At his Milvia cottage, Allen Ginsberg shaved and dressed in his finest clothes. By most accounts, this comprised a charcoal suit, white shirt, and tie, but McClure doubts this was true and said he was almost certainly wearing a sports jacket and jeans, which does seem more likely. Then, he and Kerouac hopped on a bus into San Francisco, where they headed for City Lights. Some sources claim they had dinner with Snyder, Whalen, and Lamantia at New Pisa, a cheap Italian restaurant not far from the bookshop. From there, Ferlinghetti drove them in his beat-up old Austin, along with his wife, Kirby, to the 6 Gallery. The "tiny little car" was "weighted down to the axle," he recalled.[1]

They met Michael McClure at the 6 Gallery. McClure, who had been busy with work and family, knew only Ginsberg, Rexroth, and Lamantia, having met each of them at literary events in 1954 and having gotten to know them better at Rexroth's Friday salons throughout 1955. This was the first time he'd met the two Oregon poets—Snyder and Whalen—though they would soon become good friends. It was also his introduction to Kerouac. There were other introductions made that night, including Lamantia and Snyder and Snyder and Ferlinghetti. This all seems particularly surprising given their overlapping social circles and interests, and the fact that they all socialized in the same places. It is certainly possible that they had sat next to each other without realizing in the past, or

---

1   Ferlinghetti says that Gregory Corso was in the car, but Corso did not go to San Francisco until 1956 and was certainly not at the 6 Gallery reading. It is possible that he has misremembered the other presence in the car, which may have been Orlovsky. This would mean a total of six men in the vehicle, which would account for it being "weighted down to the axle."

walked past each other on the street, but it was only at the 6 Gallery that many of these soon-to-be-important poets first got to know one another.

The 6 Gallery was packed that night. Estimates of the attendance vary widely, from Ferlinghetti claiming there were only about 30 people to Rexroth suggesting a figure of roughly 250. Of the various attendees who later spoke about the reading, most agreed it was more than 100 and the average guess was around 125. Given that the theater group that had occupied the space before King Ubu claimed the capacity was 250 people, Rexroth's guess (a figure also suggested by Whalen) is not entirely out of the question. Indeed, a very rudimentary calculation, determining floor space and occupancy, says that the venue could have held about 265 people if they were standing and 200 if seated. Of course, there was no way that the entire length of the 100-meter-long building was used and certain quirks of design meant that the floor space was significantly smaller than the 100x24 dimensions. A revised calculation of occupancy, taking into consideration these factors and the also the fact that some people used chairs and others stood, suggests that the crowd could certainly have numbered between 100 and 150. However, it was not a ticketed event and no one was counting, so there is no way of knowing for certain how many people attended.

The one thing that everyone could agree upon (aside from Ferlinghetti) is that the place was packed, and as was the case with the exhibitions of paintings and sculptures that were regularly held at the 6 Gallery, the reading was attended mostly by members of the city's artistic and literary community. Gary Snyder noted that there had been other interests besides poetry: "A surprisingly large number of people had showed up. Far more than we had expected, and the mood was excellent, so it turned into a real social event as well as an artistic event." Whilst the reading resembled the sort of wine-fueled socio-artistic events that marked the opening of each new show at the 6 Gallery, it seems that this time there were more people and from a wider range of backgrounds. Kerouac wrote later that "[e]veryone was there," calling them "a hundred eager Raskolniks [sic] in glasses crowding in from the rear of the

A Subterranean Celebration

reading hall." McClure added: "The Six Gallery reading was open to the world and the world was welcome. There were poets and Anarchists and Stalinists and professors and painters and bohemians and visionaries and idealists and grinning cynics." Elsewhere, he elaborated:

> There were elderly women in fur coats who were radical social leaders of the time, and there were college professors there, young anarchist carpenter idealists, artists, poets, painters associated with the gallery. So it was a broad spectrum, intensely radical, and intensely hoping for a change to take place. We all saw this not just as a change in poetry but as a change in consciousness.

In the audience were the poets' friends and lovers. Peter Orlovsky was there to cheer on Allen, and so was Neal Cassady, who stood throughout the performance with his arms wrapped around Natalie Jackson, his female companion of that year. Kerouac's half-Japanese ex-girlfriend, Jinny Baker, was in attendance, and so was his drinking buddy, Bob Donlin. Baker was with her husband, Walter Lehrman, who would take many famous photos of the poets in the coming months, but sadly he did not have a camera that night. Michael McClure's wife, Joanna, who was not a poet at the time but would later become one, was present, as were Ruth Witt-Diamant and publisher Bern Porter. Mark Linenthal, a professor from San Francisco State College and later a director of the Poetry Center, brought some of his writing students with him. Painters Inez Storer and Ronald Bladen were present, as were musicians Charles "Red" Richards (a jazz pianist) and Jack Goodwin, among many other artists, patrons of the art, bohemians, and poets. Most of them were sitting on the floor as the gallery was only able to provide something like thirty folding metal chairs.

In describing the event, many of the participants make it sound as though the entire San Francisco arts scene was in attendance, but there were notable absences. The three King Ubu founders (Duncan, Jess, and Jacobus) were in Spain, so they weren't present. Most of the 6 Gallery founders were also elsewhere that night. David Simpson was sleeping because he had to work the midnight shift at a Standard Oil gas station, Hayward King had left for the University of Paris on a Fullbright Scholarship a few weeks earlier, John Allen Ryan was temporarily enrolled at Mexico City College, and Jack Spicer had gotten stuck on the opposite side of the country.[2] Of the six founders, then, only Hedrick and Remington were present that night. Spicer's friend Robin Blaser was also on the East Coast, and so, with Duncan, Spicer, and Blaser all absent, three of the Bay Area's most renowned poets missed out on its most important poetic event. Rather than dooming the reading to failure, however, their absence had the unexpected outcome of helping the newcomers quickly supplant the old guard as the city's preeminent poets. This prompted McClure to comment, much later: "If Spicer had been there; and Robert Duncan had been there, they might have been in the reading also, and we would not have had an event that was 'the beginning of the Beat Generation' as much as an enlargement of the San Francisco Renaissance."[3] He noted, however, that Duncan "may not have agreed to, but he certainly would have been asked."

The six poets soon proceeded to the back of the building and sat on folding chairs arranged in a semi-circle on the dais. A photo from the gallery's opening eleven months earlier shows the dais was probably not much more than six feet deep, so they must have been relatively cramped. It was also only about ten inches high at most, meaning that the poets were probably not easily visible

---

2   Many accounts of the 6 Gallery reading state that Michael McClure read a letter from Spicer, begging for help getting back out West, but this occurred on March 18, 1956, at a repeat performance in Berkeley. Quite a few mistakes about the 6 Gallery reading can be traced back to people conflating the two events.

3   Defining these movements is notoriously difficult but generally it is said that the San Francisco Renaissance began that night, so perhaps McClure is referring to the Berkeley Renaissance, a semi-serious movement started in the forties by Duncan, Spicer, and Blaser.

to those further back in the audience. Fittingly, the poets were also surrounded by experimental works of art by Fred Martin, which had been on display at the 6 Gallery throughout September. His show had technically ended on October 3, but the next exhibition (work by Sonia Gechtoff) did not begin until October 11, and it seems that at least some of Martin's work remained for the October 7 poetry reading. His one-month show had included various nude self-portraits, some of which were absurdly tiny and others very large, and there were also interesting sculptures, apparently made from "the detritus of an Oakland dwelling he was repairing." Alfred Frankenstein, reviewing it for the *Chronicle* in late September, called it a:

> curious and haunting series of constructions, many of them banged together in an apparently haphazard fashion out of odds and ends of discarded lumber, and placed with great care on the little stage at the 6 Gallery. Most of these constructions are smeared with suggestions of barbaric design in black and red, and at one point hangs something vaguely like a bloody shirt.

He also noted a "considerable number of paintings, all on pieces of wrapping paper identical in size, and all like the work of a sophisticated savage bent of rediscovering art from the bottom up with nature as his guide." This is probably what Jack Goodwin referred to when he wrote that there were also "a lot of insulting black blotches painted on large triangles of butcher paper that kept getting torn off the walls." Martin worked in a variety of styles and forms but a quick glance at his output from the 1950s through the 2010s shows that he often used thick black paint in his work and these could well be viewed as "insulting [...] blotches" if one were being unkind.

Martin's work was quite divisive and received some fairly unkind remarks in the local press, but McClure was enthusiastic about what was on display at the 6 Gallery that night:

The 6 Gallery Reading

The October show at the Six Gallery was *Crate Sculpture* by Fred Martin. The pieces looked as if Martin had taken wooden fruit crates, broken them, and swathed them in muslin or some other light cloth then dipped them in plaster. The sculptures probably were exactly right and appropriate to be the setting for the six of us at the Six Gallery.

Specifically, they were orange crates, a fitting choice for this particular poetry reading given their popularity as bohemian furniture. Both Snyder and Rexroth used these as bookshelves in their homes, and Ginsberg even referred to being "surrounded by orange crates of theology" in "Howl."

One of the orange-crate sculptures sat on the little stage, in front of the poets, and this would function as their lectern, although it was absurdly small for the purpose. Rexroth, acting as master of ceremonies, made a witty remark about this when he first stepped up to it. There are a dozen versions of this, but a representative one is: "This is a lectern for a midget who is going to recite the Iliad in haiku form." He was in a "jovial mood," according to Jack Goodwin, and "immediately strove to dissociated [sic] himself from the ceremonies of which he was master, by remarking that he was so used to turning square tricks that now he felt out of place here among all these beards and velvet jackets." For all his faults, Rexroth was experienced and knew how to command his audience's attention, and these remarks broke the ice. After all, this was not to be your typical, stuffy poetry reading. Ginsberg had planned it to be the very opposite of what people expected. He wanted a night that was raucous, rebellious, and fun. Just as the 6 Gallery's art shows flew in the face of convention, this poetry reading was meant, in Ginsberg's words, "to defy the system of academic poetry, official reviews, New York publishing machinery, national sobriety and generally accepted standards to good taste." All five poets, and many of the audience members, were interested in the fusion of Eastern and Western thought, too, so beginning

A Subterranean Celebration

the event with a joke that drew upon classics of Asian and European literature was a fitting start.

Rexroth was wearing a cutaway pinstripe suit that he had found in a second-hand shop, along with a bowtie. Just two months shy of his fiftieth birthday, he was old enough to be the father of any of the five readers. His hair was messy and far longer than usual, but his signature moustache was cropped short. Surrounded by writers and artists, and in a position of authority, he was truly in his element. He was a proud man with a massive ego, certain of his own importance, yet he was hurting badly at this moment due to complex domestic problems involving a divorce.[4] There was little chance of him withdrawing from the event, however, for no matter how much he hurt inside, his literary reputation meant more to Rexroth than almost anything. His internal strife did not cause him to become withdrawn in any way; rather, it increased his bravado, giving him yet more determination to remind San Francisco that he was the city's leading literary figure. He was a passionate supporter of the arts and particularly young artists, but he also wanted everyone to know that he was the patriarch of the emerging scene.

With his usual bohemian swagger, he addressed the audience, keen to impress upon them the importance of the evening and the significance of the San Francisco arts scene, of which he had been a part for several decades now. It was like Barcelona, he said, in the thirties. The rest of the country had no idea yet, but San Francisco was rapidly becoming a cultural hub—the countercultural cousin of establishment New York. Rexroth had long been a vocal proponent of the city he called home and as he stood to address a room jam-packed the city's best minds, he surely felt that it was all coming together. He had been a mentor to two of the five readers and held some influence

---

4   He was living essentially a married life with a woman called Marthe but was still legally married to his ex-wife Marie, who lived across the street and whom he still loved and relied upon. In August, Marthe—with whom he had a one-year-old child—decided to leave him and Marie attempted to fix the situation by finally insisting upon a divorce, which was granted on September 13. For a while, it felt like he was losing two wives at the same time.

over the other three, and no doubt a substantial number of audience members knew and respected him, many having attended his salons, read his books, and listened to his radio show. Later, when reflecting on the seemingly sudden rise of San Francisco as a literary hub, Rexroth said that the 6 Gallery reading was "the culmination of twenty years of the oral presentation of poetry in San Francisco." That was about the length of time Rexroth had been hosting his various salons, workshops, and other forums for poetry.

Although Rexroth was keen to command the attention of the room, and of course the five poets were meant to be the main focus, it was Jack Kerouac—who ironically had refused to participate out of bashfulness—whom most people seem to recall as the center of attention, at least prior to Ginsberg's famous reading. Before it all began, he took responsibility for plying people with booze. In *The Dharma Bums*, he wrote, "I was the one who got things jumping by going around collecting dimes and quarters from the rather stiff audience standing around in the gallery and coming back with three huge gallon jugs of California Burgundy." He walked several blocks with Bob Donlin and bought homemade wine from an elderly Italian man. The reading was delayed until they returned, whereupon they passed the booze around and Kerouac took his place beneath stage, lying on his side, continually slugging from a bottle he kept for himself. The wine continued to circulate until the poets "got drunk [and] the audience got drunk," according to Ginsberg.

Philip Lamantia and John Hoffman

The first poet to read was Philip Lamantia, the most experienced of the five. Although many people, including Ginsberg, have claimed that the reading was the debut of all five poets, this was untrue and especially so for Lamantia, who was reasonably well known in literary circles. He had gained some measure of poetic success as a teenager, with Henry Miller predicting that he would "probably be our greatest living poet since Whitman." Carl Solomon claimed that Lamantia's poems were "highly regarded by avant-garde connoisseurs," which certainly seems to have been true. He was also one of Rexroth's earliest protégés and therefore well known throughout San Francisco, at least in literary and artistic circles. Jay DeFeo was so impressed by his poem, "The Eyes," that she drew a vast picture inspired by it and inscribed it with a stanza from his work: "Tell him I have eyes only for Heaven as I look to you Queen Mirror of the Heavenly Court." However, Lamantia, now twenty-eight years old, was not interested in fame and his own mythology. Poet and artist Gerd Stern, who had been at New York State Psychiatric Institute with Ginsberg and Solomon, said of him, "He didn't harp on his background, the mythology of his connection to Breton. He was not impressed. Others were."

Despite being the best-known of the younger poets that night, Lamantia chose not to read his own work but rather that of his deceased friend, John Hoffman. Surprisingly little is known about Hoffman except that he was a friend of various people associated with the Beat Generation, including Lamantia, Ginsberg, Corso, and Solomon. He was mentioned in *Junkie*, *The Subterraneans*, *The Dharma Bums*, *Visions of Cody*, and he is referenced at least once in "Howl."[5] Carl Solomon was so impressed by him that he wrote a short piece of prose called "The Legend of John Hoffman." Jack Goodwin said in the early eighties that he wrote music for Hoffman and other poets, including Duncan, suggesting that perhaps they had performed live together although he gave no more detail. Ginsberg remembered him being intelligent, poetic, and quiet. He was an intense individual who would often stay silent—the perfect counterpoint to Lamantia, who talked continuously. Although Hoffman never met Snyder, the two shared many interests: anarchism, pacifism, peyote, Indians, anthropology, nature. He was thin and wore glasses, and—pre-figuring the beatnik stereotype of the late fifties—he was also very hip, spaced out, and easygoing. In the forties, Lamantia and Hoffman had been extremely close, remaining friends until Hoffman's death on January 20, 1952. It was "the deepest friendship I've ever had with another male in my life," Lamantia said later. They were hip, literary, and into the same drugs (heroin, peyote, cocaine). Like Ginsberg, they experimented with drugs at least partially for spiritual reasons and were passionate about learning from foreign cultures.

According to Lamantia, Hoffman "was a very religious person," something that became true of Lamantia about six months before the 6 Gallery reading. He had been raised in a non-religious (and perhaps even anti-religious) household and by the age of fourteen was a confirmed atheist. "I hated the Church," he said, blaming that position on Nietzsche and surrealism. He seems to have gone through cycles of mystical belief and explored various religions and belief systems with zeal, something that annoyed his mentor, Rexroth. "Lamantia's poetry is illuminated, ecstatic, with the mystic's intense autonomy," Rexroth said. "Unfortunately, since his surrealist days, although he has written a great deal, he has published practically nothing. Poems he has read locally have been deeply moving, but each in turn he has put by and gone

---

5   Ginsberg also mentions him more directly in "Fragment: The Names II." The first part of "The Names" was originally conceived of being part of "Howl" and seems to have been written between drafts #3 and #4 of Part I.

on, dissatisfied, to something else." Rexroth blamed this on his "mystic temperament," suggesting as others have that Lamantia oscillated between beliefs and interests. Even Ginsberg, who liked Lamantia and had bonded with him over visionary and mystical experiences, felt it was a bit much. In 1952, he had complained to Neal Cassady that Lamantia was "all hung up on being a cabalistic type mystic" and that this made his writing weak. When considering starting his own literary journal, he expressly stated it would not include any "Lamantia bullshit." Unlike many mid-century hipsters, though, Lamantia's beliefs tended to be intense and sincere. In 1953, when reading the Koran, he experienced a powerful vision that he remembered vividly for decades. He felt he transcended this world and visited a place he called the "Ineffable Blissful Realm." Although the vision occurred in San Francisco, Ginsberg transposed it onto New York for this line in "Howl":

> who bared their brains to Heaven under
> the El and saw Mohammedan
> angels staggering on tenement roofs
> illuminated

Here "the El" refers to a section of Manhattan's subway system that was demolished in the 1950s. Just as Ginsberg had moved Carl Solomon's incarceration from New York State Psychiatric Institute to Rockland, he transported Lamantia's vision from the West Coast to the East.

Lamantia's conversion to Catholicism came not long before the 6 Gallery reading, when he was in Mexico. This was likely early in the spring of 1955. His explanations were frequently evasive but in one long, detailed interview he seems to have been eager to articulate what happened. Unfortunately, he was quite old at this point and rambled and digressed so often that even though he talked for a long time, he never really got his point across. However, combining fragments of this interview with others he gave, it is clear that he was stung by a scorpion and put into a state of paralysis, during which time he thought he was going to die. "I was paralyzed for about twelve hours at least, and couldn't move and I vomited constantly," he said. He recalled screaming, "Madonna! Madonna, save me!" and "that is why [he] returned to the Church." There appear to have been other factors, including a priest he met in Mexico, the anthropological brilliance of the religious missionaries, and certain experiences with the native peoples of that region, but mostly he stressed the near-death experience that he believed resulted in divine intervention. When he returned to the U.S., he went to stay at the Trappist Monastery in Oregon and when Ginsberg and Rexroth tried to get him involved in the 6 Gallery reading, he initially refused. This is how he later put it:

> Okay now, the reason I didn't read my own stuff, and read John Hoffman, is simply that I was going through a crisis of conversion and I couldn't write and what I wrote... I didn't want to read my old poems because even though Rexroth said, "Oh you mustn't, you must, you should get out and start... All the poems that you wrote before, you can't go on thinking that they were all mortal sins!" But indeed, I was sort of thinking that they... I didn't want to publish my old poems, I ceased to publish, I wanted to withdraw, I thought I might have a... well I found out that I did not have a vocation at the Trappist monastery.

His accounts are frustratingly hard to follow, probably due to his advanced age when finally speaking at length, but clearly he had lost faith in his earlier work due to this religious conversion. He seems to have viewed them as blasphemous, and it was only through the "persistent urging of Rexroth and Ginsberg" that he agreed to read anything at all.

Various accounts of the 6 Gallery reading mention Hoffman's death and imply that it happened just before the reading, suggesting that Lamantia's choice was a tribute to a recently deceased friend. Few seem to realize that Hoffman had died three years earlier. His death was likely the result of tuberculosis or polio rather than a peyote overdose, which again many accounts have suggested even though such a thing is impossible. A clue to his cause of death lies in the fact that he was cremated, which was impossible in Mexico at that time except in cases of infectious disease. The peyote myth seems to have begun with Jack Kerouac, who noted in *The Dharma Bums* that Hoffman had "eaten too much peyote in Chihuahua (or died of polio, one)." In *Junkie*, Burroughs observed: "He was using [peyote] all the time in large quantities: up to twelve buttons in one dose. He died of a condition that was diagnosed as polio. I understand, however, that the symptoms of peyote poisoning and polio are identical." Lamantia believes he had been picked to do medical experiments that went wrong because he was a junkie and desperate for cash.

Unlike his Beat peers, Lamantia was not forthcoming about his own life and work and so he, like Hoffman, is shrouded in some mystery but it does seem that his near-death experience had distanced him from his own earlier poetry and no doubt the religious conversion brought him closer to the memory of his religious friend. Garrett Caples, writing an introduction to a 2008 City Lights book that included poems by both Lamantia and Hoffman, explained:

> Lamantia thought nothing of condemning a whole body of his own work whenever he underwent a major life change. [...] Lamantia's desire to suppress his own writing was in many ways more typical than his desire to publish it, which accounts for his somewhat slender body of work. [...] Lamantia always strove to do what he thought was the right thing to do, which, on October 7, 1955, at the Six Gallery, meant reading the poems of John Hoffman instead of his own.

Hoffman published no poems in his lifetime but he left behind a number of works, both poetry and prose. These were collected by Lamantia and others in *Journey to the End*, a collection of 29 poems that was meant to be published by Bern Porter. In fact, the reading was prefaced by a remark—it is unclear whether this was Rexroth or Lamantia—about "how Berne [sic] Porter still hasn't gotten around to publishing" a collection of Hoffman's work. As of October, the book was slated for a 1956 release but Lamantia seems to have pulled it and also a proposed book of his own poetry due to his dissatisfaction with Porter's handling of *Graffiti*, by Goldian "Gogo" Nesbit, Lamantia's wife.

Kerouac wrote that Lamantia, resembling "a young priest," was an "out-of-this-world genteel-looking Renaissance Italian" who "read, from delicate onionskin, yellow pages, or pink, which he kept flipping carefully with long white fingers." He said it was "a charming elegy in itself to the memory of the dead young poet" but he was dismissive of Lamantia's "delicate Englishy voice," which made him want to laugh.[6] Kerouac, however, was rather unkind in describing all of the readers that night except Snyder, so this account should not be taken as a reflection of the audience's response. Goodwin said that Lamantia "certainly is a work of art, a persona accomplished. The English accent gets thicker every year," comparing his voice to Edith Sitwell's. Unlike Kerouac, though, he felt that Lamantia read "very well [...] and without a trace of the fashionable Auden-Eliot monotone."

Hoffman's poems have been described as impersonal, austere, and with occult references, as well as laconic, metaphorical, and surreal like Lamantia's own work, but it is unclear which poems he read except that they came from *Journey to the End*. McClure said that they were "beautiful prose poems that left orange stripes and colored visions in the air," but this part of the reading is omitted by almost everyone else who recalled the event. From what little can be found, it seems it was a good performance of

---

6   There are few recordings of Lamantia, but those that do exist show that he indeed had an odd, and strangely English, voice.

impressive poems, but they did not have the same impact that the other four poets' work would have. Various people, in writing about the 6 Gallery, talk about "Phil" or "Philip," clearly referring to Whalen, forgetting that there had been another Philip there that night.[7] In 1955, though, it seems Lamantia was happy to be forgotten.

Jack Goodwin wrote a few paragraphs the next day but they said little about what Lamantia actually read. He wrote:

> I had never heard any of the Hoffman poems, and now that I did I was appalled for a special reason. There seemed to be a mental climate peculiar to the ones he wrote in Mexico, suddenly as familiar as a recurrent nightmare. Shortly after the 1951-52 Holiday Season, Jorge Goya[8] stopped here on his way back from Ajijic, and he spent several days spreading that feeling around my apartment, in the forms of words, ideas, bits of pottery, cigarettes, imaginary pictures, reported conversations and parties with Karen, John, Sue, pot, stench, heat, naked light bulbs, tequila, the new Hoffman incredibly noisy and laughing on peyote. From these cues a certain mood was distilled, only to be transmuted and transfixed in mind a few days later when John acceded to the past tense.
>
> And here he is trotting out that mood just as if it were something as objective as the City Hall, rather than some morbid series of reactions compounded by chance in my own separate skull. Maybe there is

---

7   Whilst Whalen went by both "Phil" and "Philip," Lamantia was only known as "Philip." According to Snyder, he was more commonly referred to as "La Mancha" or simply "Lamantia."

8   Goya was a member of Metart and appeared in a dual exhibition called "Paintings and Prints" at the King Ubu alongside Deborah Remington.

some possibility of communication on a non-symbolic level after all. Such, at least, was the illusion. The uncanny thing is that H seemed aware of what he was up to and up against.

The one time Lamantia was asked about what he read that night, he replied that he could remember reading "the first one," presumably referring to the first poem in *Journey to the Night*. He seems to have been gesturing to a manuscript that neither he nor the interviewer named. He says, "Other than that…" implying that he cannot recall what else he read, which is hardly a surprise given that the reading had taken place 45 years earlier.

"Between poets," Kerouac explained, Rexroth, "in his bow tie and shabby old coat, would get up and make a little funny speech in his snide funny voice and introduce the next reader." Kerouac was trying to be insulting here, writing in 1957 after a big fallout with Rexroth, but he was also fairly accurate. Rexroth did have a rather unfortunate voice, which he disliked and knew was a liability in terms of his radio show. "I play back tapes and shudder," he confessed to a friend. McClure said to an interviewer years later, "Everybody had a Kenneth Rexroth imitation," before giving his own adenoidal impression. Rexroth was also liberal with his humor, attempting to impress the audience with various witty remarks. Recordings of other poetry readings from this period show him making off-the-cuff remarks that got the whole audience laughing.

Michael McClure

"The next poet was one Mike McClure, an unwhiskered ingenu with tremendous aplomb," wrote Goodwin. He was the only poet for whom this was truly the first public reading and he was also by some measure the youngest of the five. He claimed later to have felt "very nervous" but this did not come across during his reading. As he read, he stalked back and forth across the front of the small stage, bringing an uncommon physicality to his work, making it a performance as much as a reading. He had "a more formal style than the others [and was] given to the use of frequent refrain," said Goodwin. He read six of his poems that night: "Point Lobos: Animism," "Night Words: The Ravishing," "Poem," "The Mystery of the Hunt," "The Breech," and "For the Death of 100 Whales." These were all nature poems and they would be collected and published as McClure's first book, *Passage*, in 1956. His love of the natural world had started soon after he arrived in California. It was then that he met naturalist Sterling Bunnell, who showed him the stunning physical beauty of the landscape and introduced him to its flora and fauna. McClure was almost overwhelmed by the majesty of nature and from that point on, the natural world drastically shaped his poetic development. "I had fallen into the rich art and nature of Northern California and was blossoming with poems," he reflected.

"Point Lobos: Animism" was a response to Antonin Artaud, who had died in Paris just seven years earlier after years of incarceration in insane asylums. Artaud had said, "It is not possible that in the end the miracle will not occur," and McClure wrote his poem as a reply to this, claiming, "It is possible that the absence of pain / May be so great / That the possibility of care / May be impossible." He explained in *Scratching the Beat Surface* that

The 6 Gallery Reading

> *Point Lobos: Animism* has a tight, small sound—not entirely different from the sound of a Romantic sonnet. Its intent is personal and specific. I hoped to alter the lyric form into a new shape and to allow a subject to create the exterior shape as well as the sound and music. I wanted to tell of my feelings of hunger, of emptiness, and of epiphany. I hoped to state the sharpness of a demonic joy that I found in a place of incredible beauty on the coast of Northern California. I wanted to say how I was overwhelmed by the sense of animism—and how everything (breath, spot, rock, ripple in the tidepool, cloud, and stone) was alive and spirited.

"Night Words: The Ravishing" is a poem about perception, about how beauty and importance and other judgments are subjective. It is about the interconnectedness of the universe and how even in a room in the middle of a city one is still part of nature, part of a living, breathing world. To see this, one need only open one's mind.

Allen Ginsberg had told the poets to each prepare their wildest, most original work and so McClure brought a poem named only "Poem." "There was no further title," he said, "because it was as far as I had been able to go in poetry." He explained:

> In high school I had written cadenced, imagistic, and even pictographic free verse through the inspiration of Pound, Yeats, cummings, Kenneth Patchen, and William Carlos Williams. Later, I went through experiments in formal genres: sonnets, ballads, villanelles. Now I wished to express the intensity and vividness of my own perceptions and the *manner* in which impressions linked themselves in the exciting swirl that I called my consciousness. I believed the consciousness was physical

and physiological and athletic—and that it rode, and moved, and strode, and had the capacity for laughter and song.

It is indeed a highly experimental, challenging work. Near the end, there are four lines of seven dots except for the final line, which is six dots and an exclamation mark. He explained that he was trying to make a poem into a physical object and that he was utilizing concepts from Asian art in order to effectively employ negative space, providing the poem with a unique shape as he wrote. Explaining why he read such challenging work, he said:

> I did not fear obscurity in my poetry because I had come to believe that the way to be universal was by means of the most intensely personal. I believed that what we truly share with others lies in the deepest, most personal, even physiological core—and not in the outer social world of speech that is used for grooming and transactions.

In this statement, we can see that even though McClure was younger than the others and also from a very different part of the country, poetically he embodied one of the few unifying philosophies of the Beat Generation—the concept of the personal as the universal, something frequently espoused by Ginsberg and evident in the work of most Beat writers. Interestingly, though, Ginsberg claimed McClure was "representative of the Black Mountain School" and falsely recalled him reading various Black Mountain poems.[9] In private, he said

---

9   Black Mountain was a school in North Carolina that produced many poets who would later move to San Francisco and become identified with the San Francisco Renaissance. These include Robert Creeley and John Wieners. Robert Duncan also taught briefly at Black Mountain and The Place was run by two former Black Mountain students: Knute Stiles and Leo Krikorian. It became a hangout for many former students after they arrived on the West Coast. "They are all broke and stay high all the time," Ryan told Ginsberg in 1957.

McClure's poetry "sounds a little tightassed to me" and in an article about the 6 Gallery reading, he said McClure wrote "relatively sober mystical poetry," which is not entirely true and seems rather unfair.

"The Mystery of the Hunt" and "The Breech" are far more accessible poems. For these, McClure used comparatively common language and straightforward imagery. They are passionate yet speak of everyday life. "The Mystery of the Hunt" is thematically similar to "Night Words: The Ravishing." It too is a poem about finding meaning in small, apparently insignificant things, such as "[t]he smell of a shrub, a cloud, the action of animals." "The Breech," meanwhile, seems to speak of the desire for purpose in life. In a sense, it is similar to Ginsberg's "Howl" in that it concerns rebellion against an oppressive force (capitalist society) but it extends McClure's concern with nature by juxtaposing the city and the wilderness. He called it a "very intense poem about working in the produce market [at] three o'clock in the morning [and a] hallucinated nature poem, à la Rimbaud."

The most memorable of the poems he read at 6 Gallery was undoubtedly the final one, "For the Death of 100 Whales," written in response to a *Time* article from October 4, 1954,[10] entitled "Killing the Killers." Calling the animals "[s]avage sea cannibals up to 30 ft. long and with teeth like bayonets," the writer reported:

> This year the largest packs of killer whales in living memory terrorized the seas off Iceland. They destroyed thousands of dollars worth of fishing tackle, forced dozens of Icelanders out of work for lack of gear. Last week the Icelandic government appealed to the U.S., which has thousands of men stationed at a lonely NATO airbase on the subarctic island. Seventy-nine bored G.I.s responded with enthusiasm.

---

10 In the introduction to his poem, McClure states that the article was from April 1954 but he was mistaken. He repeated this mistake many times in the future when explaining his poem.

Michael McClure

> Armed with rifles and machine guns, one posse of Americans climbed into four small boats, put to sea and in one morning wiped out a pack of 100 killers.

McClure had been "horrified and angry" by the senseless slaughter and the ease with which the author joked about their deaths. "I read a poem [...] of outrage and anguish," he said, "that called upon Goya to be the tutelary witness of this mass murder, and that closed with a call to D.H. Lawrence to witness the mindless assassination of these great erotic beings." It had begun as a fairly conventional poem but had morphed into a Cubist-inspired effort, highly opaque but visceral. In one interview, he termed it a "broken ballad." Although challenging in terms of its individual lines, it conveys a clear sense of rage. "Communication was not as important to me as expression," McClure said of his poetry, and this was apparent from the works he read that night.

The audience had been quiet through Lamantia's reading but with McClure they began to feel energized. Perhaps it was the wine; perhaps it was McClure's passion, his theatrical manner, or the subject matter of his poems; or perhaps it was because Kerouac was coming alive below and sometimes on the edge of the small stage. From the second reader on, he began beating on the bottom of a wine jug, moaning, cheering, and scat-singing between the poets' lines. He was likely tipsy when he arrived but became increasingly drunk as the night went on. This irked some, including Rexroth, who told him to stop the "fourth-dimensional counterpoint," but the poets generally appreciated his encouragement and participation. After all, they had planned on an unconventional, jazz-concert-like performance that was intended as the very antithesis of the average stuffy poetry reading. The audience, meanwhile, seemed to approve of his antics, with one of them saying that "he kept a kind of chanted, revival-meeting rhythm going."

Jack Goodwin, who was sitting closest to Kerouac but had never met or heard of him before, recalled him as a "friendly drunk [...] sitting on the floor to my left, leaning against the wall, and he passed me the gallon of Burgundy now and then. He stayed there for the entire reading, quietly crooning responses." At times, it seemed to people that Kerouac had drunkenly nodded off, but in those moments he had merely closed his eyes and was listening intently. "Sometimes Kerouac would flake out," said Ferlinghetti, "and people would think he was passed out or something, but he was taking everything down in his head." Mark Linenthal recalled Kerouac lying down but periodically getting up to shout "Go! Go! Go!" and take a swig from his wine jug. He found Kerouac to be the main spectacle, often louder and commanding more attention than the poets on stage, something Ginsberg seemed to agree with:

> Perhaps the most strange poet in the room was not on the platform—he sat on the edge of it, back to the poets, eyes closed, nodding at good lines, swigging a bottle of California red wine—at times shouting encouragement or responding with spontaneous images—jazz style—to the long zig-zag rhythms chanted in Howl. This was Jack Kerouac, then unknown also […]

Kerouac himself recalled:

> Meanwhile scores of people stood around in the darkened gallery straining to hear every word of the amazing poetry reading as I wandered from group to group, facing them and facing away from the stage, urging them to glug a slug from the jug, or wandered back and sat on the right side of the stage giving out little wows and yesses of approval and even whole sentences of comment with nobody's invitation but in the general gaiety nobody's disapproval either.

Snyder also attested to Kerouac's drunkenness and enthusiasm, saying that he sat "over in the corner, beating time with that jug, with a fork in his hand, or something. He enjoyed that a whole lot."

Philip Whalen

Next to read was Philip Whalen, who many remarked upon as appearing very shy. One might think that this was due to his lack of experience reading poetry but he had appeared on stage many times as an amateur actor in Oregon.[11] Whether he was shy or not, he likely appeared that way coming after Lamantia and McClure, and doubly so considering the confidence oozing from Rexroth and the boisterousness of Kerouac. Whalen was just down from a solitary nine-week stint in the mountains and, unlike the others, he did not know many people in San Francisco. Now, he found himself standing in front of a packed room and about to read three very challenging poems, written in a brand-new style, with little reason to think anyone would understand them. He may also have been self-conscious about his weight, for almost every first-hand account presents him in a rather unflattering light. Kerouac called him a "big fat bespectacled quiet booboo [...] a hundred and eighty pounds of poet meat" and Ginsberg said he was "a strange fat young man." Looking back on the 6 Gallery reading, Whalen's corpulence was the first thing McClure mentioned about him, too. Gary Snyder said, "he's almost always been overweight, sometimes seriously overweight in his life," but David Schneider, Whalen's biographer, denied that he was overweight in 1955 and indeed photos show him to have been trim, but he conceded that Whalen had an unfortunate shape due to his weight being "distributed in an unflattering way." He described him as "a large, strange, openly hedonistic man." McClure recalled Whalen as

---

11   It is seldom noted in books that reference him, but Whalen was a gifted actor. The first time Gary Snyder saw him, Whalen was performing on stage. This was in the fall of 1947, and they met backstage after the play.

looking awkward and reading a bizarre but brilliant form of poetry:

> Standing there on the low wooden dais with his stomach forward and a slight arch to his back, he held his pages up to his eyes as he read. Whalen showed such an insouciance and near-pedagogical indifference to the genius of his own deep scholarship that the poems seemed to break off in the air in hunks as they were spoken and hang there like visionary American cartoons. These poems he was reading, and that I was hearing for the first time, seemed to owe as much to Krazy Kat and Smokey Stover as they did to the Patriarchs of Zen and William Carlos Williams.

Between his appearance and his personality, Whalen did not always make an impressive first impression. Kerouac quoted Snyder, Whalen's best friend, as saying, "At first you think he's slow and stupid but actually he's a shining diamond."

Whalen may have appeared to lack confidence but, like McClure, he "did not fear obscurity in [his] poetry" and trusted that the audience would appreciate it, which it seems some of them did. He told Anne Waldman several decades later:

> It was interesting and exciting because you would read a little bit, and people were actually listening. If they would hear something funny they would laugh. They were a very live audience and they really seemed interested in what we were saying. This was extremely important to me, extremely exciting that people would respond to what I had written. You know, for many years I had been writing things and showing them to people but the people

were all friends of mine and it's one thing to have friends of yours say something is all right rather than to have a stranger, sort of like an audience pick up on what you're doing—it adds another dimension that wasn't there before it, cheers you up in a certain way.

To Steve Silberman, he emphasized his surprise at the audience's reaction:

I was surprised that people would laugh when it was in the funny parts and seemed to be listening and seemed to be having a good time. The audience was extremely receptive and pleasant. So it was a surprise because I didn't expect anybody to pick up much on the kind of stuff I was doing, for sure.

The erudite and insightful Jack Goodwin got the humor in these poems, calling Whalen "a funny man from the northwest," but said nothing else about his performance in an otherwise descriptive letter about the reading. Snyder said Whalen was "[f]unny and dry, his usual style. His wit and learning both came across," and McClure recalled that "the little audience, 150 or so, would suck in their breath with delight and sometimes laugh out loud with surprised pleasure." That's not how Kerouac remembered it, though, calling Whalen "too incomprehensible to understand." Even Whalen in later years looked back with a little regret at what he had read. "None of it [was] terribly sensational," he said.

We do not have any recordings from the 6 Gallery reading, but a "repeat performance" on March 18, 1956[12] shows both a reader and his listeners approaching each

---

12 A follow-up reading was held in Berkeley on this date. It is often called a "repeat performance" of the 6 Gallery reading although this is a bit misleading. See Chapter 4.2 for more details about this event.

other with a degree of uncertainty. He comes across as shy and awkward and, whilst the audience applauded, it is clear that they did not fully understand him—at least to begin with. The first poem fell flat and after the second the crowd did not know whether or not to applaud. However, with each poem Whalen gained confidence and the audience came to understand his deadpan wit, and by the third poem they were laughing hard at certain lines and gave a hearty applause. It is possible that the same thing happened at the 6 Gallery, but here he read only three or four poems whereas in March of the next year he read seven, giving his listeners that vital chance to understand his style and content. He was also very inexperienced at the first reading but much more experienced just five months later, and of course by the second reading many in the audience would have had some idea of what to expect from him.

Whalen sought to be funny but subtly so, through dry, somewhat intellectual humor. Kerouac had attempted, prior to the 6 Gallery reading, to coach him into reading his poems more effectively in order to make clear the humorous aspect, and he recommended that Whalen read a piece of prose by their mutual friend, Lew Welch, in order to break up his own rather difficult poetry. He called Whalen's poems "aridly unemotional" and after the reading he wrote to Whalen, saying, "Damn you [...] Listen to me next time, to break the monotony of serious verse you should read that amusing prose." Kerouac was a good friend of Whalen's by then but in matters poetic he was not one for insincere flattery.

Like Lamantia, Whalen had gone through substantial changes in 1955, partially connected to a series of peyote trips, and he now viewed most of his earlier work as juvenilia. Coupled with the solitude he found as a fire lookout, he came to abandon his earlier approaches to poetry, which were heavily influenced by the Imagists. He began to experiment more, writing longer works that he said took their own forms, not guided by any literary templates. What he brought to the 6 Gallery on October 7 were witty, original, but ultimately difficult poems. Most sources say there were three: "If You're So Smart, Why

Philip Whalen

Ain't You Rich?" "Plus Ça Change," and "The Martyrdom of Two Pagans," but it is likely that he read more as these were short works and it seems all of the poets read for similar lengths of time. One possibility for an additional poem is "Marigolds," which McClure quotes in relation to the 6 Gallery without stating that it was actually read there. The poem was written in 1955 and Snyder had sent it to Rexroth shortly before the 6 Gallery reading along with the poems we know Whalen read that night. It is the longest and most serious-sounding of them, which might explain Kerouac's criticisms.

He read his work, McClure said, "with a mock seriousness that was at once biting, casual, and good natured." Ginsberg said that they were "a series of very personal relaxed, learned mystical-anarchic poems […] written in rare post-Poundian assemblages of blocks of hard images set in juxtapositions, like haikus." Literary critic Paul Christiansen wrote:

> The base of Whalen's poetry is not so much the perception or even the object itself, the historic grounds of Imagist esthetics, but the phrase in which a sensation enters the language function of mind. That point of impact marks a transformation of outer to inner realm, a cross-over into the yielding human imagination which doesn't seek to translate or manipulate the experience, but enjoy it in a felicitous wording of the encounter. That can only be by flashes and intuitive leaps, so the phrase is necessarily like its antecedent, the image, a discrete entity lacking in emotional or psychological connections to anything else. The phrase or sentence in Whalen is in itself a complete occasion, bounded by the input of an experience which the words embed in a lucid perception. And Whalen's poems are lattices of momentary flashes of insight or joyful response.

In other words, understanding and appreciating Whalen's poems required the audience to realize that the words stand by themselves.

The first poem, "If You're So Smart, Why Ain't You Rich?" is, as its title suggests, a witty satire of contemporary American society. This was closest to his earlier style in that it is incredibly short—just thirty words long—but he considered it "[a] new poetickall effusion." Its title is clearly a joke and the poem itself adds only a little more, culminating in the idea that being present and mindful is something money cannot buy. Whalen, who would later become a Zen monk, wrote this after hearing William Carlos Williams read at the University of Washington in May. This was something that McClure picked up on, saying, "When Philip started reading his poetry, I was delighted because I could see it was coming out of Williams." A reverence for Williams was something that united all five of the poets that night.

Next came "Plus Ça Change," an even more challenging work and one that people would either find hilarious or—to use Kerouac's term—incomprehensible. Whalen had begun the poem in 1953 but then in 1955, after changing his views on poetry, he revised and completed this work, which became one of his most famous poems. It is about a married couple that are turning into birds (possibly parrots or parakeets due to the bright colors of the feathers) and the poem recounts their conversation as this happens. Loaded with puns and abstract remarks, it functioned as a sort of play, with Whalen "comically and crankily read[ing] both voices." As the poem proceeds, it should become clear to the reader from little clues—feathers, cuttlefish, sunflower seeds—that the couple are becoming birds and perhaps that this is a satire of the institution of marriage, with their union taking the shape of a cage. McClure, who was hearing Whalen for the first time, said, "As I watched him read, the meaning of his metamorphic poem gradually began to sink in. We laughed as the poem's intent clarified." He also called it "concise, powerful, and humorous," which is a fair assessment. Biographer David Schneider, however, said, "For all its wit and elegance, the poem remains more or less on its surface, where it can serve as a crowd pleaser," which is also a reasonable criticism. John Suiter, author of *Poets on the Peaks*, said it was "wicked sarcasm wrapped in deceptive casualness."

Whalen then read "The Martyrdom of Two Pagans," a far more cryptic poem that is hard to interpret even when read on the page. It is another short poem at just thirty-six lines and again it is playful and silly at times, in spite of its serious subject matter. It begins with people who are presumably tree surgeons cutting a branch as they stand upon it but it is unclear whether the branch will fall or the tree. It is filled with obscure allusions and, as with so much Beat poetry, it brings together Eastern and Western ideas. Ultimately, it ends with a near-rhyme ditty that repeats the lines "Love is better than hate."

When Whalen finished reading, it was 10:30 p.m. and time for a thirty-minute intermission.

Allen Ginsberg

After a short break, Allen Ginsberg stepped up to the miniature lectern at 11 p.m. This would be his second public poetry reading and the first reading of "Howl." The night had been a reasonable success, but no one could have expected what was coming. Even those who had read "Howl"—and that comprised only a tiny group of close friends—could never have imagined the impact it would have. He had shown parts of it to Kerouac, Ferlinghetti, and others, but on paper—particularly in that inchoate form, with dozens of corrections—it did not have the same impact as it would do when read aloud.

He seems to have read a number of other poems first. No one mentions this in their accounts of that night but Jack Goodwin, writing an account of the reading the next day, said that he spoke for more than a half hour with "Howl" coming at the end. He had been extremely productive over the previous weeks and months and had completed versions of several important works, and he may have read some of these. He quite possibly read "A Supermarket in California," which had been positively received three weeks prior at the San Francisco Arts Festival, and he may have performed "Strange New Cottage in Berkeley" and other works of a local flavor. Alas, it seems unlikely that we will ever know.

Whatever he read first was very obviously overshadowed by what he read last: "Howl." Reading from a typed manuscript, he began quietly, carefully, even flatly. McClure said it was "a small and intensely lucid voice." It was "precise, intense, perfectly cadenced... maybe even slightly monotonous." Read before an audience for the very first time, these lines would go on to become some of the most recognizable in all of English literature:

The 6 Gallery Reading

> I saw the best minds of my generation
> destroyed by madness, starving
> hysterical naked,
> dragging themselves through the negro streets
> at dawn looking for an angry fix,
> angelheaded hipsters burning for the ancient
> heavenly connection to the starry
> dynamo in the machinery of night

From those famous opening lines, he moved into his great list of relative clauses, which Goodwin described as "a long descriptive roster of out-group, pessimistic dionysian young bohemians and their peculiar and horrible feats":

> who poverty and tatters and hollow-eyed
> and high sat up smoking in the
> supernatural darkness of cold-water
> flats floating across the tops of cities
> contemplating jazz,
> who bared their brains to Heaven under
> the El and saw Mohammedan
> angels staggering on tenement roofs
> illuminated,
> who passed through universities with radiant
> cool eyes hallucinating Arkansas and
> Blake-light tragedy among the scholars
> of war,
> who were expelled from the academies for
> crazy & publishing obscene odes on
> the windows of the skull

It is worth observing that the above lines are likely not the exact words he read that night for we cannot be entirely certain which draft of "Howl" he was reading from. These are from the published version but his poem changed a great deal between its inception in August 1955 and its publication a little over one year later. There are five known typed drafts of the first part of the poem but these are undated.[13] We can say with confidence that they were written between August 1955 and February 1956 but beyond that it is hard to know for sure and there were certainly other drafts that have been lost to time. There are clues in the manuscripts and in his correspondence, however, that give us some idea of what he read on October 7. Ginsberg had definitely written what we now consider draft #2 of Part I by late August, which is significant because in later versions the changes became increasingly minor, involving mostly word choice and line order. A close examination of his letters and typed manuscripts shows that by the end of August he had also written another draft that is closer to #3 than #2 and that draft #3 was what he sent to William Carlos Williams in early December, indicating that whatever he read in October—halfway between those two points in time—was probably very similar to the version of "Howl" that appears as draft #3 in *Howl: Original Draft Facsimile*.

That said, Goodwin commented on a "Greek chorus by the name of Carrowac (sp?)" in his October 8 letter and the first known draft of "Howl" contained the line "with a greek chorus of visible madman doom." Whilst this could be a coincidence, it does seem more likely that Goodwin was subtly referencing a line he had remembered and so Ginsberg may have read an early draft rather than a later in-progress one. It is also possible that he re-used a line that had appeared in draft #1 and had been subsequently removed. He certainly did this with other lines, so it is not impossible.

At some point during his performance, he read this line:

> who disappeared into the volcanoes of Mexico
> leaving behind nothing but the shadow
> of dungarees and the lava and ash of
> poetry scattered in fireplace Chicago

---

13 These can be viewed online through Stanford University's digitized archives and they are collected and annotated in *Howl: Original Draft Facsimile*.

The 6 Gallery Reading

It appeared in all known copies of "Howl" albeit in different parts of the poem as he continually changed the line order. This line refers to John Hoffman, and Goodwin remembers Ginsberg choosing to make this explicit at the 6 Gallery, saying "who disappeared into the volcanoes of Mexico… like John Hoffman… leaving behind nothing…"

It is worth considering the possibility that Ginsberg even read a version of Part II. A clue to this is the length of his reading coupled with comments from Goodwin and Rexroth saying that Ginsberg had read a "jeremiad," a word more benefitting the "Moloch" section of "Howl" than the first part. Specifically, Goodwin wrote that the "long descriptive roster" part (which quite obviously refers to Part I) of "Howl" led "up to a thrilling jeremiad at the end, that seemed to pick up the ponderous main body of the poem and float it along stately overhead as if it were a kite." He viewed "Howl" as having two distinct parts, with the second being a "jeremiad," or list of complaints, that complemented the initial list of bohemian characters. Again, it is hard to say what version of Part II would have existed around October 7 but the likeliest drafts could all be viewed as "jeremiads." In draft #3 of Part II, for example, Ginsberg wrote:

> What sphinx of cement and aluminum bashed in their skulls and ate up their brains and imagination?
> Moloch! Solitude! Filth! Ugliness! Ashcans and unobtainable dollars! Garbage heap of eyebrows and brains! Children screaming under the stairways! Old men weeping in the parks!
> Moloch! Moloch! Breaking their backs lifting Moloch to Heaven! Pavements, trees, radios, tons! lifting the city to Heaven which exists and is everywhere!

Every account of the 6 Gallery reading either says Ginsberg read "Howl" (presumably meaning the whole poem) or that he just read Part I. However, no one wrote or spoke in any detail about this until decades later and that begs the question of how anyone could possibly have remembered the specifics of his reading, particularly when they heard or read the poem so many times in the intervening years. Goodwin's and Rexroth's accounts are the only contemporary ones and my interpretation of their comments, coupled with the details later remembered, is that Ginsberg read much more than just the first part of his poem. Goodwin wrote less than 24 hours later that the poet had read for "upwards of a half hour" and that the "descriptive roster" (presumably Part I of "Howl") was his "main number," strongly implying that it was only one of several works read over a period much longer than the twelve to fourteen minutes it typically took him to read Part I. This led "up to a thrilling jeremiad at the end" that was clearly distinct from and yet linked to "the ponderous main body of the poem." Considering this and the length of time that Ginsberg read for, I feel relatively confident in saying that he started with several shorter works, then read "Howl" Parts I and II.

Whatever version of "Howl" Ginsberg read that night, his audience was rapt from the very start, and as he read his poem he gained confidence in himself and his work. As he got into it, so too did the crowd, and he began to feed off their enthusiasm, and off Kerouac's shouts and moans, which served not as distractions but as welcome encouragement and approval. It wasn't only Kerouac; the audience participated. "They weren't rowdy," Remington recalled, but the people watching "felt that they could participate by [...] verbally acknowledging and yelling. And there was a lot of that howling and yelling, whistling, and hooting."

This may sound at odds with his slow, quiet start but by all accounts Ginsberg was soon shouting his poem. McClure recalled the transformation:

> Bespectacled, vulnerable and almost willowy in stature, Allen began his poem in a clear, precise and measured voice, "I saw the best minds of my generation destroyed by madness..." And as he entered the

sweep of his new master work he moved into the realm of the bardic. But more than anything else, in my memory is the growing awareness, of first one person and then another that a challenge was being thrown out to the grim, fearful and war-obsessed fifties. [...] This poem was not only a condemnation of society in a prophetic mode; it also kindly offered a helping hand.

Elsewhere, he said he watched his friend metamorphose from "quiet brilliant burning bohemian scholar, trapped by his flames and repressions, to epic vocal bard," comparing him to Percy Bysshe Shelley. "It was like a hot bop scene," he said. "Ginsberg was real drunk and he swayed back and forth. You could feel the momentum building up." Writing about himself in the third person for a Dutch magazine two years later, Ginsberg wrote:

> The reading was delivered by the poet, rather surprised at his own power, drunk on the platform, becoming increasingly sober as he read, driving forward with a strange ecstatic intensity, delivering a spiritual confession to an astounded audience.

Goodwin's account also mentions Ginsberg being drunk but fails to note the transformation that others observed:

> Ginsberg was pretty drunk by this time, and as soon as he began reading everyone knew that this was it, the mccoy and the high point of the evening. No more of the restraint he featured at the Art Festival; this time he came on like a hissing, wide-grinned gargoyle. He shouted at the top of his voice for upwards of a half hour,

and he had the common touch and the audience was with him all the way, he actually whipped them up into hysteria. The scene was set for it anyway---it had become very hot and sweaty, all had tucked away a good deal of wine, and felt crowded in and aching for some kind of release.

Various people remember Ginsberg raising his arms in the air and proclaiming his lines like a prophet, openly weeping as he read particularly emotional lines. The poet himself recalled:

> I was *very* drunk and I gave a very wild, funny, tearful reading of the first part of "Howl."[14] Like I really felt shame and power reading it, and every time I'd finish a long line Kerouac would shout, "Yeah!" or "So there!" or "Correct!!" or some little phrase, which added a kind of extra note of bop humor to the whole thing. It was like a jam session, and I was very astounded because "Howl" was a big, long poem and yet everybody seemed to understand and at the same time to sympathize with it. Like this was the end of the McCarthy scene, and here I was talking about super-Communist pamphlets on Union Square and the national Golgotha and the Fascists and all the things that turned out to be implicit in a sort of social community revolution that was actually going on.

There was indeed laughter and shock from the audience, as well as a recognition of the truth in what Ginsberg was saying. For all his veiled references and

---

14   Ginsberg says here and elsewhere that he read Part I but it is important to remember that he was speaking years after the fact. In an account just two years after the reading, he strongly implied having read the whole poem, so I would caution against putting too much faith in later recollections.

personal mythology, his depiction of a hostile world crushing a disaffected generation was familiar to all. It was not only familiar, nor was it merely an eloquent, passionate statement, but rather the poem and its public reading was an act of tremendous bravery and this is something that struck most of the people listening as Ginsberg read. Goodwin wrote:

> Ginsberg's main number was a long descriptive roster of out-group, pessimistic dionysian young bohemians and their peculiar and horrible feats, leading up to a thrilling jeremiad at the end, that seemed to pick up the ponderous main body of the poem and float it along stately overhead as if it were a kite. There was a lot of sex, sailors and language of the cocksuckingmotherfucker variety in it; the people gasped and laughed and swayed, they were psychologically had, it was an orgiastic occasion.

Certainly, there were many rude words and shocking images—precisely the content that would make the poem so notorious in the coming decades. Professor Ruth Witt-Diamant was supposedly appalled by the language and signaled to Rexroth that she wanted Ginsberg to tone it down, but Rexroth had no intention of interrupting what he already recognized as a landmark moment in American poetry.[15]

It was not only the language that shocked but the content. According to McClure:

> The reading of Howl was like a series of awakening shocks—each one a bit harsh in its sudden newness but also exhilarating in the unveiling of the unspoken—

---

15   It is possible that Witt-Diamant pretended to be more upset than she was. Ida Hodes, who worked for her at the Poetry Center in 1956, said, "Ruth in some ways liked to behave like a person who is really very proper but keeps breaking the rules."

or the secretly spoken—obvious. The homosexual, the pothead, the artist, the gagged professor, the downtrodden aging failure, the aspiring bright spirit, the soul in growth in the automobile graveyard, the victimized boy and girl, the politically suspect, the fearful idealist, the budding voice of revolt against brutal mechanized greed, the crazed neurotic caught in the pinchers of mindless social conformity, the older woman with secret dreams of freedom, the conscientious objector [...] everyone, heard a humane voice that was greeting them with a new sounding *hello*.

McClure wrote and spoke more of the 6 Gallery reading than anyone else and whilst he has gotten a number of details wrong due to flawed memory, and whilst he can descend into hyperbole from time to time, he has always stressed that during the reading of "Howl," he could see Ginsberg change whilst simultaneously feeling a change in the audience that signaled a wider shift in consciousness. In *Scratching the Beat Surface*, he talked about the "bitter, gray" world of 1955, where poets "were oppressed and indeed the people of the nation were oppressed," and "the art of poetry was essentially dead—killed by war, by academies, by neglect, by lack of love, and by disinterest. We knew we could bring it back to life." He talked about how that all changed as Ginsberg first read "Howl":

> In all of our memories no one had been so outspoken in poetry before—we had gone beyond a point of no return—and we were ready for it, for a point of no return. None of us wanted to go back to the gray, chill, militaristic silence, to the intellective voice—to the land without poetry—to the spiritual drabness. We wanted to make it new and we wanted to invent it and the process of it as we went into it. We wanted voice and we wanted vision.

> [Howl] left us standing in wonder, or cheering and wondering, but knowing at the deepest level that a barrier had been broken, that a human voice and body had been hurled against the harsh wall of America and its supporting armies and navies and academies and institutions and ownership systems and power-support bases.

Whalen concurred:

> It was a breakthrough for everybody, actually, I think, because nobody had come out and said all the kinds of things that he was saying—a mixture of terrifically inventive and wild language, and what had hitherto been forbidden subject matter, and just general power, was quite impressive.

Deborah Remington, one of the few painters to comment upon the reading, noted that the poem resonated with the audience and connected it to the visual art that was taking place in the city at that time:

> It wasn't an obtuse thing. I think everybody felt that the whole poem was like an epic poem that really captured, or that encapsulated, what we were doing. "Howl" really talks a lot about the kind of turmoil, the social turmoil, that we were in, and how that fed everybody's art and everybody's thinking. It was wonderful to hear someone actualize that and put it into words. Because paintings are not words. Although we were doing it abstractly—even in the funk sculptures, which were abstract—we didn't have people doing words about it, which really kind of summed it up, and

that's what moved everybody. But it was so overwhelming. It was really, as I remember and as everybody else remembers, I guess, or people who remember that night, we were overwhelmed that this thing was so accurate and so poetically accurate, that somebody could put into words everything that we were doing and thinking and being and trying to create. It was an astonishing feat.

The audience knew it and the poet knew it as he read each line with authority, building toward an emotional crescendo. Lamantia recalled that the effect on the audience was "like bringing two ends of an electric wire together." By the time he had finished, Ginsberg was in tears, and he was far from the only one. Old curmudgeonly Kenneth Rexroth sat behind him, weeping too. He wept for the truth Ginsberg had spoken and the clarity and beauty with which he had said it, and he wept for the possibilities Ginsberg had created with this reading. "I've never seen him unbend that way before," Goodwin wrote the next day. Rexroth was far older and more experienced than the others, yet in all his years he had never witnessed such a powerful, emotional, and cathartic poetry reading. "My only regret is that I am too old to have been included in Allen's poem," he told the audience.

By all accounts, Ginsberg's performance received a terrific applause. Writing just a few days later, Rexroth said that everyone there "clapped & cheered and wept." McClure said, "At the end of the reading, the audience was on their feet with the realization that a new limit of individual expression had been reached. Almost everyone there, from anarchist carpenter to society lady, was willing to put their toe on that new line and to refuse to be made to step back without a struggle." They had just heard the first public reading of the most important poem of its era, a poem that would inspire countless readers and shape the world in the second half of the twentieth century.

When he had finished reading, Ginsberg was congratulated by friends and strangers. Neal Cassady, standing with Orlovsky and dressed in his railroad brakeman's outfit, said, "Allen, m'boy, I'm proud of you!" Of all the praise Ginsberg received—and there was a tremendous amount—he felt that was the nicest. Kerouac said, "Ginsberg, this poem 'Howl' will make you famous in San Francisco," but Rexroth corrected him: "No, this poem will make you famous from bridge to bridge." It sounded like hyperbole, but in fact Rexroth's prophecy fell short of the mark—"Howl" would make Ginsberg famous around the world. Later, Rexroth commented on the accuracy of his prophecy that night, saying that "it just blew things up completely."

Gary Snyder

It is tempting to think of "Howl" as the final poem of the night, with everything before it leading up to that incredible moment, the poets and audience thereafter spilling out into the night to spread the word... and in fact that's how Ginsberg himself sometimes remembered it. When looking back on the 6 Gallery reading, he often reported himself as having read last. Even Jack Goodwin, who had his own letters to look back on as evidence, remembered several decades later that Ginsberg's reading had been "the grand finale." It makes for a neat story, particularly given the publication of his poem the following year and everything that led to it. However, as important as this first reading of "Howl" was, its final lines did not end the evening. Gary Snyder was left with the unenviable task of following this epochal performance. "My first thought," he said later, "was that it was going to be a hard thing to hold the audience after Ginsberg."

When Snyder stood up to read, the audience settled and gave him their full attention. As electrifying as Ginsberg's reading had been, they were eager to see what would come next. The poets thus far had already read thoroughly different work, and from the moment Snyder stood up the difference between him and Ginsberg became clear. Whereas Allen had worn his finest clothes (which admittedly were not that fine), Snyder stood on the dais in his mountain attire—jeans, a flannel shirt, and hiking boots. The difference between them likely helped the audience appreciate Snyder's reading as something entirely new and distinct from what had come before it. John Suiter remarked that "it was the unlikely blending of their styles on the same platform that was one of the most potent aspects of the Six Gallery reading, signifying as it did a joining of East and West Coast energies on such an unprecedented cultural level." Indeed, as many have observed, Ginsberg and Kerouac (though he did not read) represented the East Coast and Snyder and Whalen represented the West, with McClure much closer to the West and Lamantia somewhat bicoastal. The 6 Gallery reading was a synthesis of these views, styles, and attitudes, ultimately forming what would become known as the Beat Generation.

In *The Dharma Bums*, Kerouac was oddly dismissive of the four other poets, but perhaps he was merely repeating what he had done in *On the Road* by denigrating most of his friends in order to more exuberantly celebrate one. In that case, it had been Cassady, but by 1957, when Kerouac sat down to write *The Dharma Bums*, Snyder had replaced Neal as Kerouac's muse:

> The other poets were either horn-rimmed intellectual hep cats with wild black hair like [Ginsberg],[16] or delicate pale handsome poets like [McClure] (in a suit), or out-of-this-world genteel-looking Renaissance Italians like [Lamantia] (who looks like a young priest), or bow-tied wild-haired old anarchist fuds like [Rexroth], or big fat bespectacled quiet booboos like [Whalen]. And all the other hopeful poets were standing around, in various costumes, worn-at-the-sleeves corduroy jackets, scuffly shoes, books sticking out of their pockets. But [Snyder] was in rough workingman's clothes he'd bought secondhand in Goodwill stores to serve him on mountain climbs and hikes and for sitting in the open at night, for campfires, for hitchhiking up and down the Coast. In fact in his little knapsack he also had a funny green alpine cap that he wore when he got to the foot of a mountain, usually with a yodel, before starting to tromp up

---

16   Kerouac used pseudonyms in his novel. I have changed them to the real names of the people on whom these characters were based.

a few thousand feet. He wore mountain-climbing boots, expensive ones, his pride and joy, Italian make, in which he clomped around over the sawdust floor of the bar[17] like an old-time lumberjack.

In his self-congratulatory article about the 6 Gallery reading, Ginsberg may have devoted more space to his own accomplishments than anyone else's, but he reserved more flattery for Snyder than Lamantia, Whalen, or McClure. Like Kerouac, Ginsberg was taken by the exotic, handsome, worldly young man from Oregon:

> The last poet to appear on the platform was perhaps more remarkable than any of the others. Gary Snyder, a bearded youth of 26 [sic—he was 25 at the time of the reading], also from the Northwest, formerly a lumberjack and seaman, student of literature and anthropology who had lived with American Indians and taken the religious drug peyote with them, and who is now occupied in the study of Chinese and Japanese preparatory for the drunken silence of a Zen monastery in Japan. He read parts of a hundred page poem he had been composing for 5 years,[18] *Myths & Texts*—composition of fragments of all his experiences forming an anarchic and mystical pattern of individual revelation.

This is how Kerouac recalled it:

> Then [Snyder] showed his sudden barroom humor with lines about Coyote bringing

---

17   In this passage, Kerouac is talking about The Place, not the 6 Gallery. It is perhaps this reference that gave rise to the claim that the 6 Gallery had a dirt or sawdust floor.
18   This is an exaggeration. Snyder had possibly begun work on early versions of these poems four years prior to the 6 Gallery reading but more likely he had started three years earlier.

goodies. And his anarchistic ideas about how Americans don't know how to live, with lines about commuters being trapped in living rooms that come from poor trees felled by chainsaws (showing here, also, his background as a logger up north). His voice was deep and resonant and somehow brave, like the voice of old-time American heroes and orators. Something earnest and strong and humanly hopeful I liked about him, while the other poets were either too dainty in their aestheticism, or too hysterically cynical to hope for anything, or too abstract and indoorsy, or too political, or like [Whalen] too incomprehensible to understand.

Snyder had indeed been working on a project called *Myths & Texts* and this would be published in 1960, after his debut *Riprap and Cold Mountain Poems* in 1959. He had begun work on this in his poetry notebooks in 1952 and very slowly developed his ideas and writing style over the next few years. "I didn't know at that time that it was going to take me a couple of years," he later reflected. "You know, when you're working on something you're not sure what it's going to do. I was just following my bliss and see what happened, see where it went. That's all you can do." He took lots of notes and worked on them during his free time, pulling from different sources to add parts and making changes whenever his sensibilities changed. His journals show he had been "dabbling in" it in late September, feeling it was "propitious," and seemed to have a version that he was positive about by October 2, which he arranged on the floor of either his *hojo* or Ginsberg's cottage as a semi-collaborative effort alongside the other poets. He wrote in his journal: "my feeling is very simple, anybody who doesn't dig it needn't trouble me with their opinions."

Indeed, he read some of the first part of *Myths & Texts* (the book is divided into three sections) at the 6 Gallery as well as "A Berry Feast," a poem written mostly in 1952 and based on his experiences the previous summer on the Warm Springs Indian Reservation. In *Understanding Gary Snyder*, Patrick D. Murphy explains that "A Berry Feast" was originally intended as part of *Myths & Texts* but did not ultimately get published in that collection. It was included in *Evergreen Review #2* in 1957 and was published as part of *The Back Country* in 1967. Murphy explains its inclusion in this later collection as due to it being "one of Snyder's very early mature poems." Whether or not it was ever really intended for inclusion in *Myths & Texts* is unclear but certainly it is possible, and the fact that Snyder read both at the 6 Gallery lends credence to Murphy's theory. Also, when asked many years later what he had read that night, he replied, "All I know is that I read selections from *Myths & Texts*." Others recall him reading "A Berry Feast," which raises the possibility that in his mind he had only read *Myths & Texts*, which at the time had included "A Berry Feast." Later, of course, he did not think of them as the same work but rather viewed "A Berry Feast" as a "warm-up for *Myths & Texts*." He also admitted that "in 'A Berry Feast' there are some passages which could go right into *Myths & Texts*." With "A Berry Feast" written in 1951 and 1952, and *Myths & Texts* mostly composed between 1952 and 1956, it is quite conceivable then to view them as not just similar works but part of a longer poetic sequence.

Snyder's primary literary theme at this point and indeed throughout his whole career has been nature. As Kerouac and Ginsberg so readily pointed out, he was an accomplished outdoorsman, experienced in hiking and climbing, with a great knowledge of native plants. He was also interested in what would later be known as "Deep Ecology." McClure, who'd read poems connected to nature but viewed through the lens of humanity, said Snyder's readings that night were "the first poems that [he'd] heard that presented Nature in a way that was wholly devoid of urban man and without a trace of the sentiment that until that time accompanied nearly all poems of nature." He called "A Berry Feast" a "scholarly and ebullient nature poem" and commended not only its depiction of a world away from Western man and its perceptiveness, but its good humor: "there was no pouty literariness."

At its core, the poem compares the natural state of the world with the destruction caused by modern Western life, weaving Native American stories about the mythological characters Coyote and Bear with his own experiences berry-picking. Snyder, who at that time was enamored with Asian culture, included pastoral scenes of ancient China and indigenous Americans as models of humans living in peaceful co-existence with nature. This is juxtaposed against the wanton destruction Snyder saw in contemporary Western civilization:

> The Chainsaw falls for boards of pine,
> Suburban bedrooms, block on block
> Will waver with this grain and knot,
> The maddening shapes will start and fade
> Each morning when commuters wake—
> Joined boards hung on frames
>   a box to catch the biped in.

The message was rather optimistic: humans ought to return to earlier values and simpler habits, abandoning their destructive consumerist lifestyles. This idea seemed to resonate with the audience, who admittedly were not a representative sample of American citizens.

"A Berry Feast" was not only a powerful poem; Snyder's performance was also masterful. He focused on individual words rather than the overall presentation. McClure said that his "presence on stage and his words had the effect of catalyzing some of those who heard into a more definite orientation towards wild nature, and it caused some there to make immediate re-evaluations of their nature experiences." He claimed that Snyder was as "[e]qually well received" as Ginsberg.

Snyder's poetry differed from that of the other four poets in various ways, including its reliance upon simple language. It was unadorned and sought to present concrete images depicting scenes of the natural world. That is not to say it is necessarily simpler than McClure's, for example, but certainly he relied more upon workingman's language, the kind that might be heard at a forest ranger outpost. His poems were often non-grammatical, using words in unconventional structures to elicit sounds and form ideas, but one would only need a dictionary if one were unfamiliar with the name of a species of plant or geological feature. In terms of imagery, it is similarly straightforward: a rattlesnake rests in the "groin" of a boulder, for example. A year earlier, when introducing himself to Kenneth Rexroth and sending along "A Berry Feast" as an example of his work, he wrote: "I have been brought back to the old-fashioned idea that intelligible and coherent philosophies are distinctly needed in good writing."

Patrick D. Murphy explains that Snyder's poems are often challenging not because of their language, as is sometimes the case with other Beat writers, but rather because he draws upon systems of belief and concepts that are unfamiliar to his readers:

> What makes Snyder's poetry difficult for many readers is not any single aspect of it. True, in some poems he is highly allusive, referring to Japanese folklore, Hindu mythology, or Buddhist philosophical tenets and terms not known by the average American reader. All of this, of course, makes it difficult to capture the full range of meaning through a single poem, and particularly through his two sequences, *Myths & Texts* and *Mountains and Rivers without End*. But sometimes, his very simple, brief lyric poems seem just as difficult because Snyder draws on such a range of knowledge and experience. He has so synthesized and integrated diverse cultural materials that the context in which the poem is written and the context most suitable for its reading are often not evident.
>
> [...] He also puts material together in unfamiliar ways, altering or questioning common points of view and traditional

perceptions of relationships in order to get his reader to rethink American culture's most basic assumptions and presumptions.

Murphy identifies three major areas of interest in Snyder's life and work: "the cultures of inhibitory or primitive peoples, particularly the Native American tribes of the Pacific West"; "the Asian cultures of China, Japan, and to a lesser extent, India and Tibet"; and "ecology, a concern of Snyder's throughout his life." He mixes these in his poems, often moving rapidly between or blending ideas, tying alien concepts to or contrasting them with familiar elements of modern life. In "A Berry Feast," he borrows Coyote, an anthropomorphic, tutelary spirit creature that appears in the mythological systems of many indigenous American cultures. In those belief systems, Coyote varies greatly but tends to be mischievous and this is a quality Snyder highlights, with the cheeky being representing a rebellious spirit, perhaps akin to the bohemian poets themselves. In this poem, he shouts either "Fuck you!" or "Up yours!" depending on the version one reads. (Kerouac's account in *The Dharma Bums* attests that Snyder used "Fuck you!" at the 6 Gallery. It made "the distinguished audience [...] howl with joy, it was so pure, fuck being a dirty word that comes out clean.")

Murphy notes that Snyder used "field composition," a development of free verse poetry that saw the page as a canvas on which words are painted. This could also make his poetry appear difficult to a reader but perhaps this made it easier for listeners:

> Snyder sees written poetry as arising from and continuing to be based on oral performance. Field composition, then, is a way of "scoring" the poem, as in musical composition, for the way in which it ought to be performed when read or sung aloud.

"A Berry Feast" then can be seen as a song and indeed it appears almost like musical notation in its written form. It includes speech, not necessarily with a speaker given, and most spoken parts are given an opening quotation mark but not a closing one. Snyder was a gifted performer who charmed his audience with wit before reading his poems—even the ones with grim subject matter, such as ecological destruction—and he read with a confident, engaging voice. "A Berry Feast" looks on paper almost like a short play to be performed, and there are playful exclamations like "K'ak, k'ak, k'ak!" (the sound of a coyote) and "Cats at dawn / derry derry down." Though he was young, Snyder was a confident and skilled poet unafraid of experimenting.

Murphy finally notes two more aspects of Snyder's poetry that are of relevance here, which both stem from his extensive studies in Asian literature. Firstly, he has taken from the Chinese the idea of emotion arising from "the juxtaposition of two images rather than through metaphor or simile" and from Japanese haiku he has "learned to write poems that have no stated moral or authorial observation." These quotes are again from Murphy, who says that "Snyder often depicts the thing in itself, in its moment of being rather than in its serving a metaphorical purpose for the intellectualizing mind or individual emotions." These qualities provide Snyder's poetry a unique aesthetic that is pleasantly challenging, which is to say it does not insult or repel its audience but rather invites them to contemplate perhaps in the same way a koan does.

Both of these poetic concepts are utilized in the first part of *Myths & Texts*, although he does at times come close to a "stated moral or authorial observation" when sometimes the imagery is so unsubtle as to leave the reader little option but to feel a mixture of sadness and anger at the destruction of natural beauty. Snyder writes:

> San Francisco 2x4s
>   were the woods around Seattle:
> Someone killed and someone built, a house,
>   a forest, wrecked or raised
> All America hung on a hook
>   & burned by men, in their own praise

When reading this aloud, Snyder uses a cheerful voice and the playful semi-rhyming lines, slightly offbeat, detract from the obvious message of man's destructive habits and the end of grand forests that had existed since before humanity. He is not telling us to be sad but the message is clear.

This is sandwiched between a scene of deforestation in ancient China and a fleeting glimpse of unspoiled nature, before turning to Snyder's own experiences as a logger. Here, we see that in spite of his veneration of all things Asian, he is aware that ecological destruction is not entirely a modern Western phenomenon (although he does sometimes suggest this elsewhere in his work). Rather, it is a problem with all so-called advanced civilizations and perhaps with the human race itself. That section of his book is prefaced with a Biblical quote that warns against the worship of false idols and advocates the destruction of wooded areas as a punitive measure.[19] Snyder believed that most ecological devastation could be traced back to the monotheistic religions' concept of man having dominion over nature and much of his poetry, including the works read at the 6 Gallery, critiqued this whilst proposing apparently primitive worldviews that acknowledge humans' role as a single species within a greater ecosystem, with no more right to dominion over it than any other animal.

The first third of *Myths & Texts* was titled "Logging" and that is the theme uniting the various poems collected here. There are fifteen sections in part one[20] and they

---

19   The text says "But ye shall destroy their altars, break their images, and cut down their groves. —Exodus 34:13." Admittedly, the meaning of "groves" is unclear and could refer to a place of worship. However, the context implies a link between Biblical commands, idolatry, and the needless felling of trees. His journal from this time suggests he was not sure himself, writing "what of Groves?" He was reading the Bible throughout much of 1955 and wrote in August: "The Bible […] is outrageously irrelevant [in the mountains] or elsewhere. Our culture need have no more dealings with this neurotic, barbarian silliness."
20   This refers to the published version but of course it is impossible to know exactly what the poem looked like when Snyder read it in October 1955. In a recording from several

vary a great deal in terms of their references and ideas. Some present stories from the past; others are glimpses of the contemporary world. Parts seem almost like journal records but others are clearly imagined. Some of it is political, some anthropological, some philosophical. Asian and Native American scenes and philosophies mix as well as visions of nature, with the idea of deforestation threaded throughout. As we can see, then, there is no single narrative voice here, and that is a common trait in Snyder's poems. Critic Tim Dean says that "the characteristically Snyderian voice is one in which many voices can be heard." In an unpublished interview from 2000, Snyder noted that parts of the poem were his observations and experiences and other parts came from other people he met in the mountains, with all of these fragments jumbled up. He also said in that same interview that he drew from Japanese Noh drama the idea of the mountains and trees themselves having a perspective, and indeed it seems at times the narrative voice comes from natural and geological features.

As in "A Berry Feast," the language in these poems is plain and the images are of the natural world, sometimes with modern Western man added for the purpose of showing his destructive habits (but never as the center of attention or the reason for the depiction of nature). Unlike "A Berry Feast," though, there are more obscure references but these are mostly contextualized so that an audience could have a good chance of comprehending. Whalen and McClure were content to be obscure but Snyder was more interested in spreading a message clearly and concisely with his poetry. That is why he enunciated his poems carefully on stage, speaking without haste, using intonation to engage his reader.

Just as Allen Ginsberg had done, Gary Snyder presented his audience with a masterful poetic dissection of modern problems but did not come over as whiny or hyperbolic. Rather, he artfully articulated something that many were already partially aware of, thereby connecting

---

months later, the poem is quite different from what was printed in 1960. As with Ginsberg and "Howl," Snyder was constantly working on his poems to bring them closer to completion.

with the people in the room that night, whilst gently—if rather optimistically—suggesting the possibility of change.

McClure, much later, made an unusual observation about the impact of Snyder's reading that night, emphasizing how well it had been received:

> Let me tell you, it moved people so goddamned much that they said "I don't have to write poetry anymore because somebody is now writing what I wanted to do. I can now concentrate on my painting!" This is what people said—Johnny Ryan is the one who springs to mind, and other people took that position, too—like, "Maybe I don't have to write poetry anymore. This is what I've been wanting to have said." And there's this huge contingent... I mean, everybody's saying that about Allen, and a lot of people are a little nervous about it all. But there's this very special group, and it's a sizable one, saying [about Snyder's reading] *"That's* it!"

After the Reading

Snyder finished at around 11:30 p.m., concluding the event. Even before the audience dispersed, they were aware that they had witnessed something of great significance. No one could have predicted just how significant, but certainly they understood that this had been no ordinary poetry reading. To his friend, a lithographer called Will Petersen, who would design the calligraphic cover for *Myths & Texts* some years later, Snyder said, "Save the invitation. Some day it will be worth something."

Later, Snyder reflected that "[i]t succeeded beyond our wildest thoughts. In fact, we weren't even thinking of success; we were just trying to invite some friends and potential friends... Poetry suddenly seemed useful in 1955 San Francisco. From that day to this, there has never been a week without a reading in the Bay area." He said that prior to the 6 Gallery reading, there had been "no sense of community of poets and even less of an audience," but that the reading had been a "curious kind of turning point in American poetry." Elsewhere, he remembered "walking away [and saying] 'Poetry will never be the same. This is going to change everything.' It was the beginning of the Beat Generation and, in a sense, the defining moment in all of our literary careers." Almost everyone agreed. McClure said, "It was very immediately a revelation." Ginsberg, admittedly writing during the peak of Beat hysteria and attempting to further promote his and his friends' careers, wrote that "the poets were left with the realization that they were fated to make a permanent change in the literary firmament of the States." Much later, he called that night the Beat Generation's "breakthrough to public consciousness."

Most importantly, it had been a concerted effort to move poetry away from the dull, academic mode that had dominated American literature for decades. Instead of a crowd of stuffy professors quietly trying to outsmart each other, these young, hip poets had read "with abandon and delight," according to Ginsberg, and both he and Kerouac used the word "gaiety" to describe the atmosphere. The 6 Gallery reading, Snyder said, "reminded everybody that the excitement of poetry is a communal, social, human thing, and that poems aren't meant to be read in the quiet of your little room all by yourself with a dictionary at hand, but are something to be excitedly enjoyed in a group, and be turned on by." Ginsberg agreed, saying that the 6 Gallery reading and a repeat performance the following year "inaugurated the new wave of poetry vocalized, before an audience, rather than read just on the page, carrying out Whitman's instructions for a poetry that was out loud and not just for scholars and not just imitating the older literary style." McClure expanded on this: "All of us were interested in bringing poetry to life with voice, in a heroic and visionary tradition that we associated with Mayakovsky or with Blake."

Ginsberg emphasized the reading's unconventional and anti-establishment nature, calling the participants "unknown," stressing that it had been in a run-down gallery in the city's "Negro section," and highlighting the fact that everyone had been drunk. He explained, writing in the third person:

> Their approach was purely amateur and goofy, but it should be noted that they represented a remarkable lineup of experience and character—it was an assemblage of really good poets who knew what they were writing and didn't care about anything else. [...] This was no ordinary poetry reading. Indeed, it resembled anything but a poetry reading. The reading was such a violent and beautiful expression of their revolutionary individuality (a quality bypassed in American poetry since the formulations of Whitman), conducted with such surprising abandon and delight by the

poets themselves, and presenting such a high mass of beautiful unanticipated poetry, that the audience, expecting some Bohemian stupidity, was left stunned.

Many who were there or who were active at that period commented upon a feeling of disappointment in how poetry had developed in twentieth-century America. It "had been deflated, sunk, in disarray," McClure said, "The academy, with its tinkly-page poetry and know-nothing poets, and the brutal-minded jingoist crew cuts of the time, had essentially done away with poetry through lack of attention, lack of love, and active dislike." He and his Beat peers were looking "for a poetics that would go beyond the unloved art of poetry, which was at that moment the bastard stepchild of twittery academics." In San Francisco, they found and expanded upon a poetic movement of exactly that notion. Jack Goodwin explained:

> That year [1955] everyone was desperately in love with everyone else, and acted like it, and went around foaming at the mouth and bursting into tears and spouting poetry which everyone else understood perfectly because they were going through the same thing themselves.

The reading was, Snyder said, a "subterranean celebration," and McClure claimed that it gave a "voice to a constituency that didn't realize it existed before that night." In a sense, these poets had found their perfect audience. They had gone to the 6 Gallery to share their personal poems, yet those poems had resonated with more than a hundred listeners in an unimaginably impactful way. "We did not dream that we were speaking for anybody but ourselves until that night," McClure said, but as it turned out, the people in the room that night "were hungry for what we had to say." That is fitting for a movement that had emerged in the odd confines of the 6 Gallery, a place of radical, experimental art, performed by unknown poets and attended by the disparate fragments of a bohemian culture on the far edge of the country—a place long overlooked and too often condescended to by the East Coast literary establishment. Rexroth and others had been trying to foster a scene of national note for decades and almost by accident it had happened, and it had done so thanks largely to these ragtag outsiders—Ginsberg from New Jersey; Whalen and Snyder from Oregon (although admittedly Snyder had been born just a few blocks away); McClure from Kansas; and Lamantia, a floating free spirit channeling a friend who'd died in Mexico. The other figures remembered for their participation or attendance were also from the East—Rexroth from Chicago, Kerouac from Massachusetts, and Ferlinghetti from New York.

"[T]here was something about the city that encouraged poets and novelists to draw creative work from their innermost depths," Jonah Raskin observed. In San Francisco, these five quite different poets had read some of their best and most daring work, with no good reason to think the audience would understand or appreciate it, and they had been met with rapturous applause. They were, to varying degrees, spiritual seekers willing to experiment in life and in art. They were united also by a rejection of militarism and materialism and unafraid of announcing this before the world. Unlike the overwhelming majority of Americans, they were not willing to hide their true selves in order to attain the accepted trappings of success. Instead, and like the other artists who had utilized that odd space at 3119 Fillmore, the poets expressed themselves in their own ways for the sheer joy—and perhaps even the necessity—of creation in its purest form. This time, however, the response was overwhelmingly positive. Intersecting local and national poetry movements were born that night. Or if not born, they developed into a coherent form. Beat historian Bill Morgan wrote:

> That night the Beat Generation was made whole. This extended family would grow over the next few years to accommodate a few other names, but the group's original nucleus of Kerouac, Ginsberg, and

After the Reading

Burroughs was forever united with the San Francisco poets by this reading. In the eyes of the outside world, those links would never be erased. To many who witnessed the event at the Six Gallery, it appeared as if a movement had been born. No matter that every one of the writers had his own individual style and his own unique voice, they were bracketed together forever as the Beat Generation. From that moment on, they would be connected by this pivotal reading and by the magnetic nature of Allen Ginsberg, who had the ability to find common ground among diverse people and bring them together.

When it was all over, the poets left the 6 Gallery in a fleet of old cars, headed for Chinatown and Sam Wo's restaurant at 813 Washington Street, a fixture of the Chinatown scene since its founding about a half century earlier, possibly in the aftermath of the 1906 earthquake. There is little information about its origins but by the fifties it was popular yet paradoxically famous for its atrocious service, being the workplace of Edsel Ford Fong, who many—including Herb Caen—believed was "the world's rudest waiter." Practicing what was likely a form of performance art, Fong would verbally abuse customers, calling them "fat" and "retarded" and would deliberately spill hot soup on them.

The narrow restaurant had three levels, with customers entering through the kitchen on the ground floor and then sitting upstairs wherever Fong felt like putting them, which often meant seating random customers together and telling them to "shut up" if they were unhappy about it. The food was cheap but somewhat edible, and of course its being Chinese made it appealing to the writers and artists so enamored of Asian culture. It also had the appeal of being open until three in the morning, perfect for semi-nocturnal hipsters. The fact that customers were often permitted to bring their own booze didn't hurt either. Here, Snyder taught Kerouac to use chopsticks,

The 6 Gallery Reading

forks being banned by Fong. Sam Wo's was Snyder's favorite restaurant in the city and he taught Kerouac how to read the menu, which was entirely in Chinese. It was "a big fabulous dinner," Kerouac recalled in *The Dharma Bums*.[21] After Sam Wo's, the gang proceeded to The Place for libations. Ginsberg later said there had been "big happy orgies of poets" but he did not mean this in the literal sense. Many accounts of the night, however, have taken him seriously and suggested that from The Place the poets proceeded to someone's pad for group sex.

One person who did not attend these various afterparties was Lawrence Ferlinghetti, who headed home to 339 Chestnut Street immediately after the reading. "I wasn't one of [Ginsberg's] gang," he later explained. "I wasn't one of his group at all. He sort of considered me a square bookshop owner [...] I was not invited to read at the 'Howl' reading because I wasn't known as a poet." In his own words:

> I was leading a perfectly conventional life, married on Potrero Hill, San Francisco. I went home by myself, or with my wife at the time, to Potrero Hill and I sent a Western Union telegram—this before there was any Internet or fax, and the way people communicated in emergencies was Western Union. I copied what I had heard Emerson had written to Walt Whitman upon reading the first copy of his Leaves of Grass. So, I wrote to Allen, "I greet you at the beginning of a great career dot dot dot dot when do I get the manuscript?" That's how that went.

---

21   A cautionary tale regarding Beat mythologies: Kerouac tells an amusing anecdote in *The Dharma Bums* about an interaction with a Chinese chef at Sam Wo's but this occurred in May 1956. He included it and revised the real event to involve Snyder (who was then in Japan) because he felt it enhanced the story. While most writers do this to varying degrees, it does serve as a warning for those who rely too heavily on books like *The Dharma Bums* when attempting to uncover real events.

Part Four
Aftermath

The Beginning of a Great Career

Ferlinghetti quoting Emerson to Ginsberg after the 6 Gallery reading is one of the great stories of the Beat Generation. Not only does it frame the Beats as the Transcendentalists of their era—the next step in a great literary lineage—but looking back it is easy to see that Ginsberg *did* become the Whitman of his era in more ways than one, and Ferlinghetti's various cultural roles (defender of free speech, spokesperson, publisher, critic, poet laureate) could well be seen as making him a twentieth-century Emerson, so there was a prophetic aspect to the event.[1] The fact that the original letter had been sent in 1855, one hundred years earlier, provided even more significance. Both men would have seen that telegram message as signaling Ferlinghetti's understanding that "Howl" was the era's answer to *Leaves of Grass*—a long, groundbreaking poem of tremendous significance and bravery.

It is not clear, however, that the telegram was ever sent. Many have searched for evidence of it but to no avail. Ferlinghetti and Ginsberg both repeated this story, the former adamant in the face of suggestions that it was not entirely true. Ginsberg, on the other hand, admitted to his Italian translator in 1964 that perhaps it had never been sent at all. Bill Morgan, Ginsberg's archivist and biographer, and a good friend of Ferlinghetti, spent decades looking for it and concluded that "it seems unlikely [that it ever existed], since even short telegrams were expensive." A rough calculation, adjusting for inflation, shows that the roughly sixteen-word message would have cost almost $19 in today's money compared to the price of a letter, which would have cost only about $0.34 when adjusted for inflation, meaning that the telegram would have been

---

1   Further evidence that Ferlinghetti saw this parallel comes from his observation that Snyder was "the Thoreau of the Beat Generation."

about fifty-five times the cost of a letter, and in those days City Lights was popular but unprofitable, so Ferlinghetti did not have money to throw around so carelessly. Additionally, this was hardly a message that required such a means of communication given that the two men lived just a short distance from one another and saw each other regularly. In fact, they lived so close and saw each other so often that they did not communicate by letter until mid-1956, when Ginsberg left the Bay Area to earn money at sea in the Merchant Marine. Ferlinghetti did, however, regularly send letters and postcards to friends around the Bay Area, but he simply paid for a stamp and posted it. Given how quickly letters were delivered, the idea of him sending a telegram is a little absurd.

Ferlinghetti's story is also called into question by the fact that Ginsberg's letters to others show that he and Ferlinghetti had come to a loose agreement about publishing "Howl" some months earlier. Even though Ginsberg later spoke of "Howl" as an intensely private poem not intended for public consumption, he had shown it to Ferlinghetti with a view to publishing it just a few weeks after beginning work on it. On August 25, Ginsberg wrote Kerouac that "Bern Porter or City Lights bookstore here will publish a book of poems for me," but it was unclear from that message which poems were intended for publication. He had wanted some of his earlier work published and he had shown Ferlinghetti and others a sequence of poems called *Empty Mirror*, but no one was interested.[2] By the end of the month, though, they had agreed upon "Howl" being part of the upcoming Pocket Poets series. On August 30, Ginsberg told Kerouac that "City Lights bookstore [...] will put out *Howl* (under that title) next year, one booklet for that poem, nothing else—it will fill a booklet."

We have already seen that August 1955 was a terribly important month for Ginsberg, during which he started and then made huge progress on "Howl," even sending it to a number of friends for their approval. He did not

---

2   *Empty Mirror* was dismissed by Rexroth, Duncan, and Ferlinghetti, but was published in 1961 by LeRoi Jones' Totem Press after Ginsberg had achieved much notoriety. The collection was subtitled "Early Poems by Allen Ginsberg."

The Beginning of a Great Career

send a copy to Ferlinghetti due to their living so close to one another, instead bringing a typed manuscript to the bookshop for his friend to read. Ferlinghetti often suggested that he and Ginsberg were not close friends at this stage and that Ginsberg had little respect for him as a poet, but this was untrue. Whilst their friendship and mutual admiration certainly grew over time, it was clear that by August Ginsberg already saw Ferlinghetti as someone he might trust to publish this daring new poem. This was probably due to the advent of City Lights' Pocket Poet series—a collection of short, roughly square-shaped books with simple covers sold at affordable prices as a means of making avant-garde poetry more accessible. On August 10, City Lights had issued the first of this series, Ferlinghetti's own *Pictures of the Gone World*. It was well received in the local press and most reviews highlighted the fact that City Lights had already lined up future publications for this "much needed" series, including e.e. cummings, Kenneth Patchen, Kenneth Rexroth, William Carlos Williams, "as well as significant younger writers." Did that include Allen Ginsberg? This review, in the *San Francisco Examiner*, was published on August 29 and Ferlinghetti had agreed to publish "Howl" by that point, so it is possible but neither Ginsberg nor his poem are mentioned.

Ginsberg had been a regular visitor to City Lights since arriving in San Francisco and he was surely aware of its various quirks and controversies, and it is highly likely that in Ferlinghetti he saw someone whose values were mostly aligned with his own. The fact that the shop specialized in paperbacks drew great criticism and gave it an outsider charm whilst the very low prices of its books flew in the face of literary pretensions. Ferlinghetti, who wrote for a number of publications in the mid-fifties, was an outspoken defender of civil liberties and free speech, something Ginsberg recognized would be needed if his poem were to be published without censorship. Just a month after the 6 Gallery reading, Ferlinghetti toyed with the authorities by promoting a 25-cent edition of a legally published Henry Miller book (*Nights of Love and Laughter*) by putting copies of the banned *Tropic of Cancer* and *Tropic of Capricorn* in the window of the shop. These were not for sale and were French translations, meaning he had

241

technically not broken the law, but it was an amusing act of defiance nonetheless. In December, he held an exhibition of Miller's non-banned works but again made much of the evils of censorship by displaying foreign editions of the banned ones, which had been lent to him by the author. He was intent on showing the arbitrariness of censorship and the fact that these books were perfectly legal in other, more progressive parts of the world. To Ginsberg and others, Ferlinghetti appeared like someone who was unafraid of provoking and mocking the authorities. Of course, a great many artists were willing to do the same, but how many of them had businesses they might lose if they pushed too far? Ferlinghetti's courage was obvious from an early stage.

All this is to say that despite Ferlinghetti claiming that Ginsberg considered him a "square bookshop owner" and therefore not hip enough to hang out with the Beat poets, this was untrue and Ginsberg had held Ferlinghetti in a position of respect since meeting him. Almost as soon as the idea of publishing "Howl" entered his mind, he went to Ferlinghetti and showed him the book and thereafter they worked toward its publication, with Ferlinghetti's advice proving indispensable in turning the poem into a successful collection. The alternative, as he mentioned in a letter to Kerouac, was Bern Porter. Like Ferlinghetti, Porter supported controversial artists and sought to publish worthy poets through his small press, Bern Porter Books, but his plan for "Howl" was to print it on expensive paper in a limited edition sold for $30 (the equivalent of $350 in 2025). There was no way Ginsberg's friends could have afforded this, nor the people he felt would relate to the book, and so City Lights was by far the best option. In fact, even Porter seemed to agree with this, claiming years later that he'd offered Ginsberg a deal but at the same time suggested he publish with Ferlinghetti for wider distribution.

If Ginsberg and Ferlinghetti had already agreed to release "Howl" through City Lights, then why did both men thereafter claim that the decision had been made following the 6 Gallery reading? Ferlinghetti had read many of Ginsberg's poems and seen little of real value

The Beginning of a Great Career

until "Howl," which itself did not strike him as particularly brilliant. Messy, disorganized, and incomplete, the poem seemed to Ferlinghetti to be good but not great. He saw its potential, however, and he knew that Ginsberg was continuing to work on it, so he agreed to publish it with the assumption that it would end up being more polished, but when he heard it read aloud at the 6 Gallery on October 7, everything changed. Ferlinghetti recalled:

> Bespectacled, intense, streetwise, Ginsberg showed me "Howl" with some hesitation, as if wondering whether I would know what to do with it. Later [...] when I heard him read it at the Six Gallery, I knew the world had been waiting for this poem, for this apocalyptic message to be articulated.

It is quite possible that Ferlinghetti heard the poem read aloud and changed his mind, or perhaps that the reaction of the audience convinced him of its potential, and that this drastically improved his opinion of the poem. This may sound far-fetched, but in fact—as we shall see later—he had a similar reaction after sitting in the audience for a reading of another Ginsberg poem, "America," so it is far from impossible. Although he was an astute critic who knew what he liked, he was also a savvy businessman who saw opportunities and could make choices based upon what he saw the public react to. All of those who had seen the poem written down, including its own author, were surprised by the performance at the 6 Gallery. Its effect when read aloud in front of just the right audience was something no one could have predicted. Of course, as Gregory Corso once remarked, "Howl is essentially a poem to be read aloud." On paper, it is striking but the experience of reading it is nowhere near as powerful as hearing it read by its author, particularly in the perfect setting of the 6 Gallery, on an emotionally charged night in the middle of the 1950s. Perhaps Ferlinghetti heard the poem and feared that another publisher was hidden in the audience, waiting to offer Ginsberg a big fat check for the rights to his poem...

Aftermath

We must also remember that "Howl" in August was very different from "Howl" in October, the poet having worked tirelessly to expand and improve upon his work, which after all was only the first of three parts (four if we include "Footnote to Howl"). Whilst many of the ideas and phrasings that appeared in the published version were present in the manuscript that existed in August, it was also missing a lot and Ginsberg was very uncertain over which parts worked and which did not. Despite Kerouac's admonishment about wanting "lingual spontaneity or nothing" from his friend, Ginsberg rewrote his poem until it was vastly improved. This was often ironically due to Kerouac, who would sit and listen at the Milvia cottage and then help him to revise it. Whalen, too, would listen and offer suggestions.

If Ferlinghetti did send Ginsberg a telegram, then it was likely to show his renewed enthusiasm in a project they had tentatively agreed to two months prior, possibly reminding Ginsberg of their agreement. He mentioned later that telegrams were "the way people communicated in emergencies" and perhaps this is how he viewed that night. Perhaps he felt the success of the reading was so great that the expense of a telegram was justified. Regardless of when their agreement came about, Ginsberg stuck with Ferlinghetti and did not seek a more lucrative offer elsewhere. He could have done, for telegram or no, the two men never even signed a contract. Incredibly, for a book that would go on to sell more than a million copies, their deal was never put on paper, nor even sealed with a handshake. It was just a verbal agreement. Such was the state of affairs in San Francisco in the mid-fifties. It was a time and place when art transcended business. Ginsberg liked this informality and had seen up close the soulless New York publishing environment when acting as literary agent for his friends. He was happy for City Lights, then with just a single book in its catalog, to put out his first collection and he trusted that Ferlinghetti would do his best to get it into as many hands as possible.

He made the right choice. Even though he did not always agree with Ferlinghetti's input, and later felt aggrieved when his publisher unilaterally made changes to

The Beginning of a Great Career

his book, he always recognized the role his friend played in helping make *Howl and Other Poems* one of the most successful collections of poetry in American history. For his part, Ginsberg continued to support City Lights after becoming a world-famous poet even though he sometimes went elsewhere for large publishing projects.

Despite the surprise success of the 6 Gallery reading, it was not immediately obvious in the following days that some of the poets would go on to become world famous or that "Howl" was one of the most important poems of the century. There were no news reports about it, which makes sense considering there were no reporters present, but given how significant the reading proved in retrospect, one might expect to look through the archives and see mention of it in the city's cultural pages. After all, San Francisco had a few relatively hip columnists with an interest in avant-garde art and literature and these men often highlighted the small-scale successes of the city's poets and painters in their columns. However, in the days after the event not a single newspaper mentioned that the literary world had been shaken by a small group of unknown poets in a strange art gallery. Letters by those who were there testify to its immediate importance and it was talked about a great deal in the cafés and bars of San Francisco, but outside of the hip world, no one had any idea what had taken place. Many people later spoke of it as a revolution, giving the impression that everything changed overnight, but whilst there is some truth in that, it took time for the effects to be realized.

Even if it took a few months for the poets to really gain local fame, word started to spread immediately. Unfortunately, not a lot of letters survive but those that do often mention others that have been lost and all of them seem to state or hint at the success of the reading. As I've mentioned many times, Jack Goodwin wrote about it on October 8, telling John Allen Ryan that it had been "an orgiastic occasion." Even though Ryan was in Mexico and missed the reading, he wrote to Spicer in Boston to pass along the news. "It was a success," he said, adding that "Ginsberg is handling poetry for the gallery now." It

Aftermath

seems unlikely that Ginsberg was really "handling poetry for the gallery" but this remark shows Ginsberg had indeed done most of the work organizing the 6 Gallery reading and it highlights the success of his reading, thrusting him suddenly into a position of authority in the artistic community. Ginsberg wrote an account for Ryan, too, but this letter was lost. A reply from Ryan was saved and in it he says that Ginsberg's account "fits well with Goodwin's," which adds further validity to Goodwin's description. Kerouac wrote a long, descriptive letter to Burroughs in Tangier, but sadly it was destroyed when the paranoid Burroughs burned his correspondence. To John Clellon Holmes, he began an exuberant description but then wrote, "I just wrote a huge letter to Burroughs about it... so have no more energy to tell it." Meanwhile, Rexroth wrote to a friend several days after the reading, saying:

> Allen Ginsberg read a terrific poem—a real jeremiad of unbelievable volume—"This is what you have done to my generation." When he finished the audience of 250 stood and clapped & cheered and wept...

Certainly, Rexroth was never a reliable reporter of his own or his friends' lives, but aside from perhaps exaggerating the audience size, his account is very much in keeping with everyone else's reports both at the time and in later years. Allen Joyce, a friend and sexual partner of both Ryan and Spicer, also wrote about the reading, his letter coming about a week later:

> Rexroth lead [sic] a party howling at "6" last week, a few new cats from up north I don't really dig, plus McClure + Ginsberg. Ginsberg's was the best—a long rambling diatribe, completely disaffiliated, and superficially reminiscent of Duncan's "A [sic] Faust Foutu." Will send you a copy.

It is quite surprising to see a negative reaction to Snyder and Whalen but it is purely a personal opinion and does not necessarily speak for the audience's response. His comparison of "Howl" and *Faust Foutu* is certainly interesting but what is more tantalizing is the line, "Will send you a copy." Whilst copies of *Faust Foutu* had been circulating for two years prior to this letter, and so it is tempting to think Joyce referred to that mimeographed publication, Spicer had of course been part of the January reading and already had a copy, which Joyce knew. Thus, he could only be referring to "a copy" of "Howl."

In any case, from these limited accounts written in the days after the event, we can conclude that the 6 Gallery reading was as exhilarating as most later accounts suggest even if it is tempting to view it as something that was exaggerated or propagandized into existence. It was not as though the poets woke up on October 8 and found themselves famous, as Ginsberg had predicted in a journal entry not long before the reading, but certainly they found themselves en route to fame. Ginsberg was particularly affected. Just four days later, he stopped going to his therapist. There could have been various reasons for this decision but it is quite likely that his sudden success as a poet convinced him that he no longer needed professional help. Jonah Raskin, who interviewed Ginsberg's therapist, Dr. Hicks, and scrutinized his medical records, said that "[t]he reading at the Six Gallery on October 7, 1955, seemed to be all the proof he needed that his therapy was an unmitigated success." Of course, there were also financial considerations. It was now five months that he had been unemployed and despite his poetic breakthroughs, there was little chance of any real income from literature in the immediate future.[3] Therapists were not cheap and sometimes Ginsberg looked for work largely as a means of paying his psychiatrists.

On November 23, Ginsberg was given an "indefinite leave of absence" from his master's course at U.C. Berkeley. According to the university's documentation, the

---

3   As of late September, he was making $20–30 per week as a busboy at a hipster canteen called Robbie's and marking English papers. It was "sufficient" to scrape by without eating up too much of his time. In December, he would start work as a baggage handler for Greyhound in order to bring in extra cash.

leave of absence was given due to his "good standing" and on the assumption that he "expects to resume his studies at Berkeley at the beginning of some future session," but Ginsberg had no intention of returning. He had come to realize that his intelligence was primarily creative and that devoting his life to academia was a poor choice. He struggled to sit through dull bibliography lessons and preferred to be at home in his cottage, scribbling or typing new poems. He was not cut out for the structures and strictures of academic life, with its emphasis on memorization and its discouraging of various qualities important to him. "I didn't have the brains or the mind for that kind of scholarly study," he said. "I was reading and studying from the point of view of producing, creating something, rather than writing studies of older texts."

Fame and fortune did not arrive immediately but from late 1955 onwards, Ginsberg began to receive opportunities to read his poetry around San Francisco. With the advent of the San Francisco Poetry Center and then the success of the 6 Gallery reading, as well as another regular poetry occurrence called Poet's Follies,[4] there were now regular readings and these seemed to increase in number each month, popping up almost like franchises. Goodwin said:

> During the following year, this Dionysian, public confessional, Howl-type reading caught on like the plague. It blew so loud that the public actually discovered

---

[4] This was a series of jazz-and-poetry nights begun in January 1955 and running until May 1958 that combined poetry with music, dance, and other art forms. It was described by the *San Francisco Examiner* as a "giddy literary-theatrical show." It catered more to native San Franciscan poets than the East Coast Beat contingent and encouraged poets to "come down from their towers to poke soft and serious fun at their art." The idea came from Weldon Kees, who had been bored by the events held at the San Francisco Poetry Center and wanted to make poetry readings fun. The first show occurred on January 22 and included Lawrence Ferlinghetti, who had reverted to "Ferling" (a name he'd abandoned a year earlier) to perform "POEMS & TRANSLATIONS from the French." The poets read whilst jazz musicians played and dancers performed. Pretty soon, they added a stripper to the bill.

The Beginning of a Great Career

poetry. The show moved out of the small conference room into the gymnasium. People brought gallons of wine and responded, cruised and fought.

Snyder, looking back perhaps somewhat fancifully, said, "After the Six Gallery, poetry readings became regular cultural events not only in this country but all over the world."

Word spread around town that Ginsberg's "Howl" was a passionate, incendiary poem that any self-respecting hipster just *had* to hear, and so he was in demand. Publishing opportunities would come later, but for now the interest was in the spoken word, the spectacle of oral poetry in a hip environment. Ferlinghetti explained it as a major shift in American poetics:

> The printing press has made poetry so silent that we've forgotten the power of the oral message. [...] Up to the Beat poets, or up to the poets of the late 1950s, poetry was a great big mumble. Poets were contemplating their navels or talking to themselves in a low mumble and no one was listening because they weren't saying anything relevant to the average person in the streets. Allen Ginsberg comes along with "Howl" and he's saying something very important to everybody.

Recordkeeping was poor and most events were not advertised, so it is hard to know how often Ginsberg read in the weeks after the 6 Gallery reading, but it seems he did so quite frequently. The audiences' responses to his readings helped shape his in-progress poem. He continued to revise Part I and did substantial work on Parts II and III, the latter specifically about Carl Solomon, to whom the poem was dedicated. He wrote these lines at his Milvia Street cottage and whilst they make up the most joyful and playful part of the poem, they are also the ones that are the most contentious, for he divulged and also fictionalized his friend's personal and medical history, something that upset Solomon. The poem had originally been called "Howl for Carl Solomon" but Ginsberg eventually changed it to "Howl" and made "for Carl Solomon" a dedicatory line. Still, Solomon spent much of his life the subject of unwanted attention due to his friend's poetic tribute. Ginsberg also added his "Holy" coda, which ended up becoming "Footnote to Howl" rather than "Howl" Part IV as he initially intended.[5] He wrote this on the Kearney Street bus in ballpoint pen and made relatively few changes to it before it was published.

As he continued to work on his poem, Ginsberg delved into Whitman's work, reading everything he could find and attempting to meld this with his other influences, including Kerouac and Corso, whose *The Vestal Lady on Brattle and Other Poems* had come out earlier that year and had inspired Ginsberg. He noted down his main areas of poetic interest: "1) a spontaneous method of composition, 2) a long imaginative line, 3) using the immediate consciousness of the transcriber (or writer) as the subject of a poem." Surrounded by supportive friends and spurred on by the responses to his public reading, he continued to produce important works through this unprecedented period of creativity. During this time, he wrote "Sunflower Sutra" (a spontaneous composition made while Kerouac rather ironically watched with impatience) and "America." In an early version of the latter, he announced himself as the new Whitman: "I Allen Ginsberg bard out of New Jersey take up the laurel tree cudgel from Whitman." Ginsberg was for a time embarrassed by the poem but eventually grew to like it as a comedic work. Corso and Kerouac, however, thought it was childish and trivial.

Ruth Witt-Diamant may have been unhappy about Ginsberg's swearing at the 6 Gallery reading, but she was

---

5   Ginsberg wanted a positive ending for a poem that had contained much negative sentiment and he liked the idea of a joyful, enthusiastic counterpoint to grim Moloch, but Rexroth said, "No, no, that's enough," and oddly he took the elder poet's advice, making this a separate but related poem. "Footnote to Howl" would appear directly after it in *Howl and Other Poems* but was considered a distinct work.

smart enough to see the value in his work, as well as the other poets who had appeared there. The San Francisco Poetry Center was already an important local institution, established just a year earlier, and several major poets had read there, including Theodore Roethke. Witt-Diamant had also been associated with Dylan Thomas, T.S. Eliot, and William Carlos Williams, meaning that an invitation to read for her was a major endorsement of a poet's ability or potential, and following the 6 Gallery reading everyone except Lamantia was invited to read there. According to Whalen, this was largely due to Rexroth's efforts, but Goodwin claims Witt-Diamant, "who made all the readings [and] digs the scene," had seen Ginsberg read at the Arts Festival and had been very impressed. "He traumatized [her] with his reading at the 6 Gallery, and so she had to put him on the Poetry Center program."

While the others were invited on the strength of their 6 Gallery performances, Snyder had in fact been offered a reading *prior* to that event thanks to Rexroth. He had written in his journal on September 16 that it was "Rexroth's doings, no doubt; amiable monster." Invited before the others, Snyder was first on the roster, his reading taking place on October 30. It appears to have been a success, for he wrote in his journal, "SUNDAY I had a poetry reading & many people came." A few weeks later, he may even have been offered a position at the Poetry Center, as he noted in another journal entry that he had been offered "a square trick" by Witt-Diamant. He was, however, not interested in anything "square" and was awaiting the issuance of a passport so that he could leave the country in 1956. He had been monitored by the F.B.I. since 1948 due to suspicions that he was a communist, resulting in his being blacklisted from various positions and prohibited from obtaining a passport. However, on December 5, after much effort, he finally received his passport and was ecstatic about finally being able to visit Asia.

Ginsberg's reading followed on November 20 and in December Whalen and Ferlinghetti had a joint reading. Rexroth also read that month (his second of the year) and McClure read there in March 1956. These events were announced in the San Francisco press, helping to push the poets' names into the public consciousness. They all took place at the Telegraph Hill Neighborhood Association, at 555 Chestnut Street, and like the 6 Gallery reading they began at 8 p.m. and were social as well as literary events. It is worth noting, however, that the Poetry Center held two kinds of readings—major poets were invited to read at the Little Theater at San Francisco State College, where crowds routinely numbered between 200 and 300, while local poets of less renown read at the 555 Chestnut Street address. The latter was a fortnightly event and usually attracted much smaller numbers. The stated purpose was "to encourage young poets by providing a sympathetic and informed audience." Thus, although it was an honor to be invited, the young Beat poets were not yet being lauded as modern greats even if their personal letters and books about the Beats make it seem that way. That said, some of them were extremely successful. Ida Hodes reported in mid-December that "[t]he Poetry Center readings at the Telegraph Hill Community House have been tremendously attended. Rexroth read last Sunday to an overflow crowd—much over a hundred people, and sold books too." Media reports also tended not to distinguish between these types of reading. The former U.S. Poet Laureate Louise Bogan read on November 4, and later the *Chronicle* wrote that "such talents as Louise Bogan, Gary Snyder, Allen Ginsberg, Philip Whalen and Kenneth Rexroth" had performed there in the past few months. Bogan's name came first, yet no distinction was made between her status as one of the country's leading poets and the three Beat newcomers.

On November 20, when it was Ginsberg's turn to read before a small room of listeners, he once again got drunk in order to loosen up. This time he did his drinking beforehand because Witt-Diamant, annoyed at all the drunken revelry, had banned alcohol from her events. She may also have understandably found it distasteful to have so much drunkenness in a building that also housed Alcoholics Anonymous meetings. Ginsberg recalled that just before the reading began, Witt-Diamant "asked [him] not to say any of the 'dirty words,' 'cause she was afraid she'd get busted or it would create a scandal for the Poetry Center." One might have expected him to refuse, but

The Beginning of a Great Career

he acquiesced out of respect for Witt-Diamant and her organization. Instead of swearing, then, he used the word "censored" to replace every word that might offend his audience.

Ginsberg said that it was "a terrible reading," but that was only partly because of his self-censorship. The small crowd—which included painter Ronald Bladen as well as poets Helen Adams and Philip Whalen— was reportedly rather stiff and sedate, which is what he had successfully tried to avoid at the 6 Gallery. Annotating a photo from the Poetry Center reading, Ginsberg wrote that it was "a small school-sponsored affair, not one of our wilder nites." He was used to performing his poem with the feedback of an enthusiastic audience. Oddly, Gary Snyder wrote the following day of "Allen's huge bawling evening," which seems to imply a much more successful event. One wonders if he was perhaps talking about a second reading at The Place, located quite near the 555 Chestnut Street venue. After most Sunday-night readings, the poets and audience would walk to the bar for drinks, and certainly around this time Ginsberg gave a handful of readings at The Place, so it's possible that he did a sedate, censored reading in front of a quiet crowd followed by a raucous drunken reading. Around this time, Goodwin wrote:

> These Sunday nights after the readings are swinging occasions. All the poets and people pour out the doors of the building and virtually march in formation over to the Place---Witt-D., Rexroth, Ferlinghetti, Dreykus, McClure, Ginsberg and his chorus of howling boys--there to get down to the really serious issues of drinking, ego-building and fornication. All these poets look so much like poets, bless their hearts.

However, Goodwin seemed to agree with Snyder's assessment reading as on December 3 he wrote to John Allen Ryan about the Poetry Center readings and then in a new paragraph wrote:

253

> Ginsberg really gave them their money's worth. Inspired fellow. When at his best as a reader, he can prolong and atmosphere of hysteria almost indefinitely, and effect such a point of concentration in the audience that a poem seems like one long moment, as if time had stopped. It's electrifying. Wow—talent, integrity and the common touch. Formidable, formidable.

The fall and winter were a time not just of poetic success but of great fun and socializing. With the exception of Lamantia, the 6 Gallery poets became great friends.[6] At first, they mostly spent their time in the two close pairs—Kerouac and Ginsberg; Snyder and Whalen—but before long they were all hanging out together. It was a boozy but joyful time filled with heart-to-heart conversations and extemporaneous poetic compositions. Reading their notebooks and letters, as well as comments made much later in interviews, one gets the feeling that these were not friends so much as soulmates or even lovers, and that meeting each other permanently changed them. Ginsberg and Kerouac were both utterly infatuated with Snyder, practically worshipping him for his wisdom and self-determination, and later McClure would also become very close, eventually becoming an atheist Buddhist under Snyder's influence. Snyder, too, had tremendous respect for Kerouac and in November, just a month and a half after their first meeting, he seemed to suggest in a journal entry that his life had been empty before Kerouac entered it:

> Between 1948 (leaving the Marine Cooks and Stewards Hiring Hall) & the day I talked to Kerouac, what? My life like

---

6   Lamantia did spend a small amount of time with the others at Snyder's house in the weeks after the reading but he was never particularly close with any of them except for Ginsberg. Although there was no animosity, he had limited contact with the other poets in the fifty years between the reading and his death.

a Chinese Box or a Japanese sentence, living several alternately & picking up the dropped clauses; the VERB (what will it be?) is at the end.

Snyder felt that both Cassady and Ginsberg talked too much even though he did like them, but in Kerouac he saw someone he truly could learn from. He called their relationship "mutually instructive," saying:

> I felt I learned a lot from him—about his particular prose style and raconteurship, his storytelling style, and his sense of having the courage to make your language be right there with the moment totally all the time as a mode of writing—and a real freshness [...] in his way of seeing people and things, which I really benefitted a lot from. There was for me a really mutual sense of value in our relationship.

One day, Ginsberg brought Kerouac to spend time with Michael and Joanna, and they brought a matchbox filled with marijuana. McClure was taken aback at how shy and awkward Kerouac was, particularly after his drunken boisterousness at the 6 Gallery. "At last," McClure thought. "I've seen somebody [...] who's more self-conscious than I am!" As we have seen with other participants in this story, there was a sudden and intense bond formed. "I liked Jack immediately," McClure said. "I felt very close to Jack. I felt like we were the same species." They had an argument over jazz but it was amicable. Soon, the McClures were part of the scene as well, even if they were closer to the painter clique. The friends traveled together and spent time in Allen's cottage, writing haiku and listening to music, as well as discussing Buddhism. There were other houses around Berkeley, too, where these poets and their friends gathered to drink wine and brandy and smoke pot. Ginsberg now stayed in the city a lot because of his job at Greyhound, so he lent his cottage to Whalen and it became a sort of communal space. Lamantia largely disappeared from both the poetic and social scenes after the reading, returning to the Trappist retreat in Oregon. Even when he was in San Francisco, the poets rarely saw him again. Snyder, despite being younger than Ginsberg and Kerouac, taught his new friends much about Asian culture and the American wilderness. "I became the old man telling tales & I told it all," he wrote in his journal. He sat patiently for hours as Kerouac asked him questions about logging camps and mountaintops and then took Ginsberg to see Japanese movies. Snyder instructed them all in meditation and other Buddhist practices, including something he may have invented just to screw with them—"running meditation," which involved running around at night.

Kerouac was inspired not only by Snyder's talk of the mountains but by Whalen's "Sourdough Mountain Lookout." He said, "I want to see what this mountain stuff is that you guys are talking about," and so Snyder took Kerouac to climb the Matterhorn, a trip that became the basis for *The Dharma Bums* and which kickstarted the "rucksack revolution" of the late fifties and early sixties. This phrase comes from Kerouac's novel and a passionate speech he attributes to Snyder:

> see the whole thing is a world full of rucksack wanderers, Dharma Bums refusing to subscribe to the general demand that they consume production and therefore have to work for the privilege of consuming, all that crap they didn't really want anyway such as refrigerators, TV sets, cars, at least new fancy cars, certain hair oils and deodorants and general junk you finally always see a week later in the garbage anyway, all of them imprisoned in a system of work, produce, consume, work, produce, consume, I see a vision of a great rucksack revolution thousands or even millions of young Americans wandering around with rucksacks, going up to mountains to pray, making children laugh and old men glad, making young

girls happy and old girls happier, all of 'em Zen Lunatics who go about writing poems that happen to appear in their heads for no reason and also by being kind and also by strange unexpected acts keep giving visions of eternal freedom to everybody and to all living creatures, that's what I like about you [Ginsberg] and [Kerouac], you two guys from the East Coast which I thought was dead.

The two men—and at times Whalen, too—had big but mostly amicable disagreements over Buddhism, mainly debating the merits of Mahayana and Hinayana. Snyder tried to teach Kerouac and Ginsberg meditation, but Kerouac's bad legs made it hard for him to sit for extended periods. There was a lot of drinking, too, and some recreational drug use, as well as nudity and sex. Ginsberg said:

We'd have parties at the cottage at night and run around naked in the backyard, looking like fauns, and all the girls in the neighborhood would come over. During the day, though, it was like a very funny little Buddhist hermits' retreat. We'd garden and carve poems on trees and sit and talk and meditate like a bunch of slightly crazy Japanese mountain monks.

Ginsberg and Orlovsky came to enjoy threesomes and orgies due to Peter being primarily heterosexual, and Snyder taught Kerouac about "yabyum," a Tibetan sexual practice. He also taught his friends about orgies, which he called "a discipline in generosity and non-attachment." In the liberal atmosphere of artistic San Francisco, fueled by cheap red wine and occasionally marijuana, the new local celebrities found it easy to get laid. Handsome, smooth-talking Gary Snyder, with his enchanting knowledge of foreign languages and cultures, certainly had no problems. His journal from that year shows a man nearly obsessed with screwing, even writing a short essay that seemed to justify his seemingly insatiable sexual appetite as part of a religious quest while decrying the Puritan American values that caused so much guilt for people like Kerouac. "The fruit of the tree of knowledge was cunt!" he explained, noting that certain Buddhist paths were unlikely to work out for him due to his lack of "restraint from cunt & drink." He seemed to genuinely believe that this was not merely a physical urge, though, and in the middle of December he appeared worried that perhaps he had given the wrong message when teaching his friends. In his journal, he said he needed to explain to "Ginsberg that you mean love, not promiscuity; generosity, freedom to & with oneself."

Snyder's journals were pretty light in terms of detail and heavy on philosophical and theological justification, whereas Ginsberg's were the opposite. He didn't mind admitting it was all about experience. His journals recount nights listening to jazz and drinking, then bringing home various men and one or two women, everyone drunk and high and naked. They were also practicing non-sexual nudity. Whalen claimed that Ginsberg frequently disrobed at parties in order to shock academics, many of whom of course pretended not to have been shocked. "He would remove his clothes," he recalled, "and everyone would say, 'How interesting,' or 'My goodness,' and some would leave. Very funny reactions. It happened a lot."

The new poetic heroes of the city were not beloved by all, though. Even the man who had introduced them at the 6 Gallery, Kenneth Rexroth, would soon turn against them, although that was to no small extent as a result of his own personal issues. He had always been a difficult and sometimes extremely unpleasant man, and the divorce he went through just prior to the 6 Gallery reading had made him increasingly vulnerable and erratic. Perhaps it was inevitable that he would resent the young newcomers who threatened to supplant him as the city's most famous poet, leading to animosity that threatened what Ginsberg hoped was the beginning of a poetic movement.

There were various issues over several years that put distance between Rexroth and the Beats, and to his credit Rexroth mostly supported them in spite of his own personal feelings, but the first major falling out occurred shortly after the 6 Gallery reading. There are dozens of accounts, perhaps conflating multiple incidents or maybe stemming once again from poor memories and mythologizing, but it seems that not long after the reading, Rexroth invited his young poet friends for dinner. They had been drinking all day and "misbehaved [...] very badly," in Ginsberg's own words. Rexroth already disliked Kerouac, feeling that his interest in Asian culture was "very superficial and largely factitious," and he had clearly been annoyed by Kerouac's drunken ad-libbing at the 6 Gallery, but while the first visit Kerouac paid to Rexroth's house had shown Rexroth that Kerouac was insincere, the second was far worse. Rexroth, who at this point and in the next year or two was undergoing a major mental breakdown, made various claims about Kerouac's behavior that night, ranging from his asking for a drink to laughing too loudly and on to the highly improbable claim that Kerouac took out a needle and injected drugs in front of Rexroth's children. Whatever happened, Rexroth felt gravely insulted and responded by calling Kerouac a "son of a bitch" and demanding that he leave the house. This caused Kerouac to shout that Rexroth was a "boche"[7] or "dirty German." Meanwhile, Ginsberg—hyped up on his recent poetic successes—told Rexroth that "Thou Shalt Not Kill" was inferior to "Howl" and that at just twenty-nine years old, he was already a far better poet.

Rexroth was understandably aggrieved. From his perspective, these young invaders had come onto his poetic territory and used him to gain an audience, then

---

7   "Boche" is a pejorative term for Germans that was commonly used by people in Allied countries during World War II. Some genealogical research allowed me to find out that Rexroth's great-grandfather had been born in Germany, but it is unclear why exactly Kerouac shouted this slur, as he is unlikely to have known that about a man he'd met only a handful of times. In *The Dharma Bums*, Kerouac called him Rheinhold Cacoethes. The first name is clearly Germanic and the surname could be interpreted in various negative senses, with Latin and Greek roots relating to "malignant" and "malicious." Some have inferred a more scatological meaning.

quickly received the sort of adulation he had always wanted. Now they had come into his home—not only his private residence but the place where he held court before the city's literati—and insulted him. Rexroth "took it very badly," Ginsberg said two decades later. Duncan recalled that "Rexroth had wanted to be a popular poet, and here was a popular poetry, a popular writing, that was taking the town—his town—as a matter of fact, his territory." Several years later, Rexroth wrote a furious letter to Ginsberg accusing him of "stealing San Francisco" from him.

The falling out did not end there. In 1956, Marthe Rexroth helped Ginsberg to mimeograph copies of "Howl" for a reading, and in doing so she worked alongside poet Robert Creeley. She and Creeley soon began an affair and Marthe decided yet again to leave her husband. Creeley was Kerouac's drinking buddy—as well as a friend of Ginsberg and McClure—and Rexroth became obsessed with the idea that there was a Beat conspiracy afoot, greatly worsening the resentment he already felt toward these young interlopers. His biographer wrote:

> The envy Rexroth must have felt for the rising popularity of these younger poets was now exacerbated by Marthe's falling in love with one of them [...] His eminence as a creative artist was threatened. His machismo was under siege. He became paranoid and would accuse the McClures or Ginsberg of harboring Creeley and Marthe.

He had by this point developed a reputation for outrageous outbursts and his mental deterioration was public knowledge. He was often seen ranting or screaming in public and would turn up at McClure's house "three times a day to talk to us about how the FBI was after them. [...] He got pretty loony about it." One night, when Ginsberg called Rexroth to ask him a question, the older poet screamed into the phone, "You sons of bitches! I know what you're doing. I feel as if I walked into a candystore

The Beginning of a Great Career

and got beaten up by a bunch of juvenile delinquents." He later said "I heard that you and your friends—Kerouac and all—are having orgies with Marthe in your cottage in Berkeley—you, Creeley and Kerouac." He truly believed this and for a long time it seemed the humiliation and jealousy had driven him mad. His writing about the Beats over the next few years tended to be shaped by his personal life and so sometimes he would acknowledge them as an exciting and gifted new movement, defending them passionately against conservative attacks, playing up his role as the trailblazing elder who had welcomed and introduced them to the San Francisco artistic community, but other times he would disparage them and call them worthless.[8] While he quickly came to forgive Ginsberg and even to some extent Creeley, he retained a burning hatred for Kerouac and never passed up the chance to write brutal reviews of his books. One particularly notable attack came in the *New York Book Review* in 1959. Writing about *Mexico City Blues*, Rexroth said:

> In the last three years Jack Kerouac has favored us with his observations about hitchhiking, riding freights and driving other people's fast cars across country. It would seem he did these things poorly and that doing them frightened him severely. Next he gave us his ideas about jazz and Negroes, two subjects about which he knew less than nothing; in fact he knew them in reverse. In this reader's opinion, his opinions about Negroes are shared only by members of the Ku Klux Klan. Jazz, he seems to believe, is throbbing drums and screaming horns, pandemonium in the jungle night over a pot of missionary fricassee. Now, in this book of poems, he has turned to Buddhism and dope with

---

8   Rexroth acted this way toward many of his friends and associates. His letters to James Laughlin, his closest friend, show a deeply disturbed man who would routinely lash out at the people closest to him with almost no provocation.

similar results. [...] The naive effrontery of this book is more pitiful than ridiculous.

Rexroth was not the only local poet to be annoyed at the Beat writers. Whalen said that in 1955 "[w]e were all carpetbaggers, which did not sit well with the locals." Robert Duncan had been in Spain when the 6 Gallery reading happened and returned in September 1956 to find that these outsiders had overtaken the whole poetry scene. Soon after arriving, he wrote to a friend saying, "I am indeed in Ginsbergenlandt," a term used by several other San Francisco poets around that time. Years later, he reflected that it had been "like an invasion." Ginsberg was well aware of this:

> It was really like a mess, trying to keep everything together. First Rexroth, and then Duncan, who was a little suspicious of us at the time because we were like invaders, who had made some sort of overrated local success, and he felt that the seriousness of the community already established in San Francisco wasn't being properly attended to.

Such resentment is understandable. It is sometimes suggested that the 6 Gallery reading was the birth of the San Francisco poetry scene but whilst it was certainly the most important event of that era, there had been a vibrant scene before it. Poets like Duncan, Rexroth, and Spicer had worked for decades to achieve recognition and these Beat "invaders" had shown up and almost immediately become celebrities. Duncan recalled:

> Returning to the City after these events, we were in a sense objects of nostalgia from before. By the time we came back in '56, it was really Allen Ginsberg's city—Allen Ginsberg's and Lawrence Ferlinghetti's city.

The Beginning of a Great Career

More than anything, he hated that he became associated with the Beats and was dismissed as a beatnik poet by ignorant East-Coast critics who lazily categorized West-Coast writers and writers of a certain age without even considering the vast diversity of writing styles and attitudes. Many other local poets were annoyed that an already vibrant poetry scene had been co-opted and possibly destroyed by these "pretentious ignoramuses." One local artist noted the influence of Ginsberg on the scene, saying that "Dionysian homosexual 4-letter-word poetry [was] all the rage." Jack Spicer was even less impressed than most, quickly coming to despise Ginsberg and the Beat writers and frequently criticizing them in public. His biographer said that "[t]o some extent the remainder of Spicer's career can be seen as a reaction to the behemoth that the event gave birth to." Even Ferlinghetti, who supported and profited from the Beats, and was often identified as one (although he vociferously denied the link) quickly grew to detest the movement he had helped birth. After reading Rexroth's vicious attacks on Kerouac and others, Ferlinghetti commended him and offered to publish "a real broadside attack on the Beat" in book or pamphlet form, and later complained to Rexroth about the lack of real politics in Beat poetry, confiding that he felt Ginsberg looked down on him as a "naïve" and "unfashionable" poet who wrote "propaganda poems."

To be fair, Ginsberg and his Beat friends had not deliberately excluded the San Francisco poets. They had invited Rexroth to share the stage with them and could hardly be blamed for the fact that Duncan, Spicer, and Blaser had all temporarily left the area. They had also wanted the event to be about young poets, so that largely excluded the older local contingent. Besides, it was not entirely Ginsberg who organized the event; it had been Rexroth's idea to invite Snyder and Rexroth was *the* San Francisco poet at that time, familiar with all the local talent. Ginsberg genuinely wanted a "united front" of poets in the city and even nationwide, a movement that would benefit him but also further the cause of poetry itself. He felt that if the various poetic factions had been able to put aside their differences, they could have made a bigger impact early on:

had there been a united front at that point—the older poets plus us from the East Coast—we would have been much more clear and impregnable in literary terms. And it would have helped in, like, high-teacup literary circles like *Encounter* and *Partisan Review*, where a good reception would have eased the whole intellectual torment. It would have made the younger professors of the fifties start reading real American poetry and appreciating Williams then and there [...] All they saw was a bunch of rebels who didn't know how to write, who didn't have any tradition, who didn't have any real learning, going out and bleeding and bleating about their so-called free verse [...] The whole literary establishment just goofed. Completely.

Ginsberg could certainly be egocentric at times (although he became aware of this and invested great efforts into overcoming it) but he was always eager to support his friends and other gifted poets, and he hoped for a world where poetry was widely respected. Duncan, Spicer, and others may have felt aggrieved, and that is certainly an understandable reaction, but Ginsberg had not wronged them—not in any major sense and certainly not in a deliberate one.

The sense of resentment among the local poets probably stemmed as much from Ginsberg's apparent efforts at promoting himself as it did from the sudden fame and respect gained from his various readings of "Howl." Perhaps due to his background in marketing, he was more aware than most poets of how to influence people and communicate via the media. He understood the power of words beyond their use for artistic expression and he knew how easy it was to manipulate people even with subtle syntactical changes. In a 1970 interview, he spoke of his time in the advertising world as an education in "brainwashing technology" and while he denied this had almost any effect on his poetry, it probably impacted

The Beginning of a Great Career

how he promoted himself and his peers. Ginsberg wanted to be a famous poet and he wanted the world to recognize the genius of Kerouac, Corso, and Burroughs, and he was willing to make use of his various skills and contacts in order to make this happen.

Reading "Howl" at the 6 Gallery had shown Ginsberg that he now possessed a literary property with genuine potential for national acclaim (or notoriety), but whilst living in San Francisco was beneficial in a creative sense, it made the leap from local to national consciousness more challenging. Rexroth once explained that being on the West Coast made it "harder to get things, if not published, at least nationally distributed." Understanding this, Ginsberg quickly set about trying to position himself as an exciting young literary sensation whose poem was the voice of a generation. It was in his own words "a blitzkrieg" of publicity. This did not go unnoticed by other writers. Denise Levertov, a poet sometimes associated with the Beats and at the time living in Mexico, said that Ginsberg was "conducting a regular propaganda campaign." In a book otherwise about Jack Kerouac, the writer James Jones remarked that "Ginsberg was probably the first poet in America since Walt Whitman to create a full-blown media campaign on his own behalf." He even managed to get *Howl* (then a single-poem book rather than a collection) mentioned in the *Chronicle* eleven months before it was published, and indeed before the poem was even completed. In a sense, this campaign would last for several decades as he tirelessly promoted Beat poetry, acting as a spokesman for an amorphous literary movement comprised of people who created wildly original art but were not very good at promoting themselves.

It is true that he did less for the San Francisco poets he had essentially replaced than for his Beat friends, but he truly wanted to unite the poetic factions of San Francisco for everyone's benefit, and he wanted to bring together the various elements of the Beat Generation, scattered around the world at this point. From his perspective, the hostility and resentment emanating from certain factions in San Francisco merely impeded this progress. Rexroth understood this and despite his antipathy toward the Beat writers, he was usually supportive of them in public, particularly during that crucial time when they were first entering the public consciousness and desperately in need of intellectual support. As we will soon see, it was arguably his efforts—made during a period of profound personal pain and marked by a raw hatred of these younger poets— that pushed them onto the national stage. It is to his everlasting credit that in spite of his belief that the Beats had stolen his wife and insulted him in his own home, Rexroth still publicly vouched for them on any number of occasions and even in private made great efforts to help them. He could be egotistical, but like Ginsberg he believed in poetry more than anything and was willing to do whatever it took to foster a vibrant poetic culture. He would continue to use his influence to ensure that the Beats were given a public platform even though at times his support damaged his own reputation.

After three happy months in San Francisco, Kerouac left the city in early December 1955. He had fallen out with Ginsberg, calling him a "lecher" due to his relationship with Orlovsky. The two would make up and Kerouac would soon return, but for now Kerouac had left the scene and others were soon to follow. The San Francisco Renaissance had only just come into existence and yet its progenitors were already departing.

It was not long after Kerouac's departure that Ginsberg and Snyder went on a trip of their own, only instead of climbing the Sierra, they spent several weeks hitchhiking around the Pacific Northwest. For Snyder, it was a farewell trip as he would soon leave for Japan, where he would live for the next decade. Ginsberg, who was starting to feel the pressures of being a local celebrity, happily tagged along. He was eager to escape San Francisco for a while and explore a new part of the country, but he also wanted to learn about the natural world that many of his San Francisco peers seemed so obsessed with. Talking about the influence that Snyder had over both Kerouac and Ginsberg, McClure said, "These Eastern boys finally got out here and finally got past North Beach, and discovered that there were forests and mountains and deserts and wildflowers, and they didn't have to be on

The Beginning of a Great Career

the side of the highway in Colorado as Neal Cassady is babbling and driving through it."

Even though he was growing tired of public readings, Ginsberg also knew that Reed College, Snyder's *alma mater*, would provide a new audience for his work. He had never read outside of the Bay Area before and wanted to see how an audience would react—particularly one with no preconceptions about his poetry. The two men hitchhiked, camped, and walked across the Pacific Northwest over a period of three weeks, briefly venturing into Canada. Ginsberg found the trip inspiring and wrote various poems, including "Afternoon Seattle," but his sexual attraction to Snyder caused friction between them. They were given a reading at the University of Washington, where Ginsberg read all three parts of "Howl" possibly for the first time. A few old ladies were offended by the language and walked out, something Ginsberg played up for his friends, telling Neal Cassady that "5 old ladies ran out screaming."

They moved on toward Portland, where at Reed College they met calligrapher Lloyd Reynolds and poet Lew Welch and then gave two readings—one on February 13 and another the following evening. They read at Anna Mann Cottage and because they were virtually unknown there, they were not named in the announcement. A listing in the campus magazine simply said, "Poetry Reading, 8 p.m." and on the first night only twenty people showed up. The second night seems to have been an unplanned repeat performance, perhaps due to the success of the first. It is significant because in 2007 John Suiter discovered a wonderfully preserved recording of that reading, the earliest known audio of Allen Ginsberg.[9] It was released in 2021 by Omnivore Recordings.

He began the Valentine's Day reading with "Epithalamion" (later retitled "Love Poem on Theme by Whitman"). There were no opening remarks; he just launched into this highly erotic poem. This was followed by "Wild Orphan," "Over Kansas," "Dream Record:

---

9   There is a comment in a December 1955 journal entry from Gary Snyder that notes the existence of "Ginsberg's tape." It is not clear what exactly this refers to but by then Ginsberg had done many readings and clearly one of these had been taped.

June 8, 1955," "Blessed Be the Muses," "Supermarket in California," and "The Trembling of the Lamb" (later retitled "Transcription of Organ Music"). His reading of "Dream Record" is interesting because he began several times, each time saying only part of the first line—"A drunken night in my house"—before restarting. At one point, he said "shhh" and then described the punctuation. He joked about not wanting to "corrupt the youth," which the audience presumably thought was a reference to being drunk, but when he finally read the line he censored it to remove the fact that he was lying next to "a boy" (John Allen Ryan). Each attempt prior to that had stopped short of "with a boy" and eventually he read with those words omitted. Given that homosexual sex was illegal at this time, it is perhaps unsurprising, yet he would go on to read "Howl," which was far more provocative.

But maybe he had not planned on the latter poem. On the recording, we can hear someone ask, "Do you want to read 'Howl'?" and Ginsberg replied, wearily, "I don't know if I have the energy." Even by this point—before the poem had been published or even finalized—he had become tired of reading it in public. It was emotionally draining for him. He read the first part reasonably well although he began very flatly—something various people had noted regarding his 6 Gallery performance. One listener recalled that "he started out like he was kind of drunk, and I wasn't sure he was going to be able to carry it off, but he gained power as he went on. He had me both laughing and in tears some of the time." This sounds very similar to what audience members at the 6 Gallery had witnessed four months earlier, and indeed it is a fitting description of his early renditions of this poem. Ginsberg himself said, "I still hadn't broken out of the classical Dylan Thomas monotone [...] The divine machine revs up over and over until it takes off."

It is interesting, however, that despite the progress he had made in writing "Howl," he only read Part I. He began Part II but managed only four lines before stopping. He said, "I don't really feel like reading anymore," and then muttered something like "I just sorta haven't got any kind of steam, so I'd like to cut, do you mind?" There was no emotion when he said "Moloch." Perhaps he would have started flatly and then found confidence later, as he had done with Part I, but it is possible that he simply had no faith in either his work or himself. A careful comparison of what he read on tape and what he had written (or at least what was saved and later collected) shows that he was on draft nine of eighteen versions of Part II that would be written before the book was published. Importantly, the fourth line that he read was changed slightly in the next few drafts before being entirely removed, so it seems that he simply lacked confidence in what he was about to read and decided to stop. Another clue about his attitude comes from a letter Snyder sent to Whalen, who was staying at Ginsberg's Milvia Street cottage. It said that Allen was "reconsidering rhetorical poetry, sez it makes him feel foolish to shout MOLOCH! at fir trees." It seems, though, that he had managed to read Part II the previous evening because Alice Moss, with whom they were staying at Reed, recalled audience members asking him, "Was Moloch the embodiment of ravenous capitalism? Was it a metaphor for some broader spiritual decay of the West? A cultural monolith? What?" She went on: "Everybody wanted to know what he meant [...] And Allen said, 'It's all of those things—and more.'"

A Repeat Performance

The poets returned from the Pacific Northwest and quickly began preparing for another reading. Organized by University of Berkeley professor Thomas Parkinson, this event was billed as a repeat performance of the 6 Gallery reading even though it would differ in many ways. First of all, it would not be held at the 6 Gallery. In fact, it was not even in San Francisco. It was held at the short-lived Berkeley Town Hall Theater at 2797 Shattuck Avenue on March 18.

The Berkeley Town Hall Theater existed only for a short period of time. It was the home of the Berkeley Drama Guild from its inception in August 1954 to its demise in December 1958. According to a local newspaper, the group "specialize[d] in in the performances of first productions or generally best plays in dramatic literature." They took over the Town Hall Theater and immediately renovated the building. "The theater has been completely redecorated, rewired and generally made more comfortable for audiences," the director of their first plays told the *Oakland Times*. The Berkeley Drama Guild seems to have been quite popular and their performances were well received. In December 1957, however, a seven-car accident outside the theater resulted in a vehicle flying through the back wall during rehearsals, causing one reporter to quip that their next show would be a "smash hit." None of the actors were hurt but the building was badly damaged. It was repaired for an estimated $500 but a year later the Guild disbanded due to a combination of financial difficulties and creative differences between the producers, Robert Ross and Herbert Eaton.

It is not clear how or why this venue was chosen for the March 18 reading, but it was likely due to Parkinson, who was a professor at U.C. Berkeley. As he was partially responsible for organizing the event, he probably chose the venue, which was located not too far from the university

Aftermath

campus. It is also possible that they wanted a bigger venue than the 6 Gallery had provided but also one that would be more affordable than large options in San Francisco. The Berkeley Town Hall Theater also happened to be just a half hour's walk or a five-minute drive from Ginsberg's Milvia Street cottage. Although he often slept in San Francisco at this point due to his work at Greyhound, his cottage was sometimes used by Snyder, Kerouac, and Whalen.

Snyder, who was now living in Mill Valley with author Locke McCorkle in order to prepare for his upcoming trip to Japan, wrote a letter to Ginsberg on February 24. Although he did not explicitly state it, he appears to have been suggesting the text for a new postcard to promote the event:

> Good-time poetry / Nobody goes home sad / Ginsberg blowing hot / Snyder blowing cool / Whalen on a long riff / McClure blowing high notes / everybody invited free / free wine / Rexroth on the big bass drum.

He went on to suggest the inclusion of Japanese music by ethnomusicology professor Robert Garfias and proposed a number of other poets for the lineup. However, they would keep the original six poets from the 6 Gallery reading, minus Lamantia, who was in Oregon.

This time around, publicizing the event was hardly a problem. The first one had been so popular that all the organizers needed to do was let it be known there was a repeat performance. They didn't even bother putting an announcement in the newspapers. Almost the entire artistic and bohemian community was eager to attend. The reading was also recorded, so unlike the first one in October, there is little mystery surrounding this event. The only uncertainties come from the usual sources: poor memory and conflation of multiple similar events.

Although word of mouth was enough to inform most of the community that there would be a poetry reading, they also put together another postcard, which drew upon Snyder's suggested text:

A Repeat Performance

<u>CELEBRATED GOOD TIME POETRY NIGHT</u>
Either you go home bugged or completely enlightened.
> Ginsberg blowing hot,
> Snyder blowing cool,
> Whalen puffing the laconic tuba,
> McClure his hip high notes,
> Rexroth on the big bass drum.

Small collection for wines and postcards.
Drunkenness, abandon, noise, strange pictures on walls.
Oriental music, lurid poetry.
Extremely serious. Free satori.
> Sunday, March 18 --- beginning 8 p.m.
> Town Hall Theatre – Stuart and

Shattuck, Berkeley
One and only final West Coast farewell appearance of this apocalypse. Admission free.[10]

On March 18, Ginsberg held a big spaghetti dinner prior to the reading. He enjoyed cooking for his friends and was pretty good at providing large quantities of food for very small sums of money. Many people stopped by because Ginsberg's cottage was near the Cedar-Shattuck Avenue F-train station, making it convenient for those coming from San Francisco. The guests occupied the single room of his little cottage, and one visitor recalled

---

10 This is the text for the postcard as sent from Allen Ginsberg to Kenneth Rexroth five days before the reading. However, as with the 6 Gallery postcard, a seemingly incorrect version has circulated. This stems from Richard Eberhart's "West Coast Rhythms" article and Lawrence Lipton's *The Holy Barbarians* (1959), both of which provide a text similar to but different from the above. That version was shortened, perhaps due to space constraints. Of most interest is the omission of the words "final West Coast farewell appearance," which referred to Snyder's imminent departure.

it being "lit mostly by candles." There was wine, too—specifically "cheap red California wine poured from a gallon bottle"—and just as they had done at the 6 Gallery, both performers and audience members began drinking to get in the right state of mind. The atmosphere was jovial, as evidenced by a photograph from that day which shows Ginsberg in a tree with Robert LaVigne and an unknown woman. They are all laughing and LaVigne is completely nude. Beat historian Ann Charters (then Ann Danberg) arrived with her date for the evening, Peter Orlovsky. Primarily straight, Orlovsky often dated or slept with women and Ginsberg was fine with this. The couple arrived too late for food but stood around drinking wine with the others at the cottage.

They all piled into a handful of cars and drove the short distance to the Town Hall Theater. This was to be a multimedia event, and LaVigne had decorated the place with seven-foot-tall paintings that reminded Ginsberg of Henri de Toulouse-Lautrec. Whalen remembers one of them featuring "a naked lady throwing her arms about." There were also drawings of Ginsberg having sex with another man. Charters recalls the drawings depicting Ginsberg and Orlovsky, but LaVigne denied this, saying the other man was someone else.[11] Ginsberg referred to the venue as being "festooned with Chinese brush orgy drawings."

Neal Cassady was in the audience once again but his date from the first reading, Natalie Jackson, was not present this time. She had killed herself in November partly due to Neal's sociopathic behavior. Her death had devastated Kerouac and Ginsberg, who felt no small degree of guilt for her tragic fate. Several of Kerouac's biographers report that he was sitting at the back of the room, quietly listening and "cheering modestly," but letters show that he only left North Carolina the day before the reading and did not make it to the West Coast until March 23 or 24. Whalen recalls Alan Watts being in

---

11   LaVigne certainly did draw Ginsberg and Orlovsky nude together on at least a few occasions, so perhaps Charters has mixed up her memories of this event with LaVigne illustrations that she saw elsewhere.

A Repeat Performance

the audience, which is certainly possible as he had been a friend of Snyder since 1952, worked alongside Rexroth at K.P.F.A., and at some point around this time had a cordial dinner with Ginsberg and Kerouac. Musician Samuel Charters was there, too. He would soon begin dating Ann Danberg and they would marry in 1959. Will Petersen, a friend of Kerouac and Snyder, who had been present at the 6 Gallery reading, showed up again. He later wrote a poem about Snyder called "September Ridge," in which he seems to describe the first reading but unfortunately confused the two events. His poem refers directly to the 6 Gallery and October 1955, but he mentions several things that happened at the second one. Even the first lines make it clear that he is remembering the Town Hall Theater reading:

> You need a goddam passport, Rexroth complained,[12]
> but nonetheless crossed over from The City, served
> as MC, as coach bringing on the rookies.

Rexroth, who was then only somewhat contemptuous of the Beat poets, reprised his role as M.C. Now wearing a white turtleneck rather than his Goodwill suit and bowtie, he began the event by getting the audience laughing. The audio recording is unclear but he stammered and made various incomplete statements to great laughter. This was partially because both he and the audience were extremely drunk. He seemed to poke fun at either Ginsberg or Snyder (or perhaps Beat poets in general) by referring to a "poet who objects to everything," which also got a big understanding laugh. He was jovial but boastful, wanting his audience to know that whilst the poets were the stars of this show, he was the city's leading literary voice and he

---

12   It's unclear whether Rexroth said this or Petersen was quoting his "letter" from *Evergreen Review #2*, in which Rexroth said: "I always feel like I ought to get a passport every time I cross the Bay to Oakland or Berkeley." Possibly, he made the remark at the reading and then again in print. Rexroth quite often re-used what he considered witty or poignant remarks.

had lived the bohemian life long before they showed up. When talking about Snyder and Whalen, he said that "one of the reasons I like these two cats is that they've lived very much the same kind of life that I have except I've done more of it." Even when issuing compliments, he had to present a positive picture of himself.

In stark contrast to the small dais at the 6 Gallery with its little semi-circle of folding chairs, the poets sat on "elaborate throne-like wooden chairs" at the Berkeley Town Hall Theater, a nod perhaps to their vastly inflated status. A photo shows at least one of these chairs having an armrest carved in the shape of a snarling lion. The audience, meanwhile, sat in old chairs taken from a cinema. Above the poets was "a small row of lights that could be turned on in wild flashes of color," Charters remembered. With its larger audience, the recording equipment, several photographers, the fancy chairs, and dramatic lighting, this reading may have been marketed as a repetition of the one at the 6 Gallery, but it was in many ways the very opposite of that humble event.

In addition to the change in venue, the lineup of poets was different. Lamantia was out of town, so the six had become five, but Rexroth was no longer merely the M.C. or "introducer," as Ginsberg had called him. He was now one of the performing poets and he would read one of his more unusual works. The order of speakers also changed. Whereas Snyder had gone last in October, he was now first on the bill, possibly because he was by far the most confident of them.

For the reading, Snyder had his hair cropped extremely short and wore a dark coat over a sweater. He was only twenty-five but looked even younger. For the first reading, he had dressed in his lumberjack clothes but now he resembled an urban hipster. Sitting next to the smartly dressed McClure and the dorky Ginsberg, drawing casually on his cigarette, he looked more like a rock star than a poet.

All the poets read different poems this time around and Snyder chose "For a Far-Out Friend," "Song and Dance for a Lecherous Muse," and the latest version of Part I of *Myths & Texts*. After his first poem, he received a big applause and responded by shouting "I suspect dishonesty!" which caused the audience to erupt in laughter. His poems were on serious topics but he infused them with humor and knew how to work a room. Before reading from *Myths & Texts*, he told the audience, "After I read at the San Francisco Poetry Center, Rexroth said to me, 'Your animals have got the loosest bowels!'" and yet more laughter filled the hall. Indeed, his poems sometimes referenced feces, prompting Ferlinghetti to later refer to his style as "Bearshit-on-the-trail poetry." It wasn't only his witty asides that amused his listeners; certain lines in his poems elicited laughter even when he was making a serious point. When talking about deforestation, he tied it to religion and remarked that Christians "would steal Christ from the cross if he wasn't nailed on." Occasionally, someone would shout out in response to a line, and the quick-witted poet was able to respond with yet more humor, bringing an interactive, participatory dynamic to the reading.

Whalen followed up with a well-received reading, performing "For K.W. Senex," "The Martyrdom of Two Pagans," "Plus Ça Change,"[13] "Three Variations, All About Love," a short section of "Sourdough Mountain Lookout," "Static," parts of "The Slop Barrel: Slices of the Paideuma for All Sentient Beings," and "Denunciation, or Unfrock'd Again." The poems he read were very different from the published versions and he did not always give the title when reading. He read "Denunciation" as though it were a section of "Slop Barrel," suggesting that at the time these were indeed intended to be one poem. "Sourdough Mountain Lookout" was very much a work in progress, and its composition had been inspired by watching Ginsberg work on "Howl."

He started nervously and the audience did not seem to immediately understand him, with his first poem ending suddenly, leaving the room silent. The second poem also appears to have caused confusion, earning only a hesitant applause. However, "Plus Ça Change / The More It

---

13   This time, he called it "The More It Changes, the More It's The Same Thing" perhaps due to his 6 Gallery audience having not fully understood the humor.

Changes, the More It's The Same Thing" elicited a lot of wild laughter and once his audience understood his style and humor, Whalen became a confident reader, deftly able to lead listeners toward important realizations. He also began to throw himself into his performance with the last poem, doing accents, acting out various roles, and varying his reading speed for comic effect, then switching to a deadpan style for certain lines. His jazzy performance of Part III of "Three Variations" was also extremely popular. The audience loved it, with some people crying with laughter, and he ended his reading to a long and rapturous applause.

"It is being debated whether we should have an intermission or keep going," Rexroth said before pointing out that there was nowhere for people to go. Indeed, the "theater" was a converted refrigerated warehouse that had briefly been a gym. There was a lobby of sorts but the theater was quite small and rather makeshift, so if there was an intermission the audience would have spilled out onto the street, and someone would have had the unfortunate task of herding dozens of drunk bohemians back inside. Realizing this, Rexroth then introduced Michael McClure, who had read at the Poetry Center the week before. "I understand that he had a sudden burst of creativity of a very high-class nature," Rexroth said.

McClure stood up from his wooden chair and addressed his audience in a smart grey coat over a plaid shirt. Before he started his reading, he read a letter from Jack Spicer, who was stuck in Boston and begging for help getting back to San Francisco. Spicer had moved to the East Coast in July in an effort to improve his literary prospects, which was more than a little ironic given that the San Francisco Renaissance began just a few months later, but he hated everything about it. He wrote to John Allen Ryan in desperation and Ryan passed the letter to McClure, who read it to the crowd.

When Spicer's name was read out, there was much cheering. Someone (the voice sounds very much like Gary Snyder's) shouted, "Jack Spicer turns tricks on Mars!" This was a reference to Spicer's obsession with the made-up "Martian" language that he used with his lovers. The letter was well-written even though McClure struggled to decipher the handwriting. Clearly the work of a poet, it sounded good when read aloud, so it was an oddly memorable part of the evening in spite of it being a sincere and desperate cry for help. Spicer said he was "lonely as a kangaroo in an aquarium" and that he "would leave for San Francisco tomorrow if it were not for the horror of unemployment." He begged for help finding a job and said he would consider "anything from nightwatchman at a museum to towel boy at a Turkish bath." "San Francisco has a chance to regain its second poet," he said. Although the letter entertained the crowd, no one helped him and Spicer remained stuck on the East Coast, depressed by his surroundings and resentful that San Francisco's poetry scene was blossoming in his absence. "I hate this town," he wrote to Ryan in another letter. "Nobody speaks Martian."

McClure had with him an almost comically large binder full of poetry, from which he selected his readings for the night, apparently unprepared. His choices, however, were quite similar to what he had read in October. He read "Poem," "Mystery of the Hunt," "Point Lobos: Animism," an unnamed poem about whales, and "The Feeling." After the high-energy performances of Snyder and Whalen, McClure's reading was conspicuously sedate. He read in a flat tone and the audience was silent throughout, usually unaware when he finished a work, leaving an awkward silence. They only responded with interest when he picked up his large binder and struggled to find a poem. When he selected his fourth poem, he introduced it as "another poem about whales" but did not give it a title. It does not appear in any of his books, either. It is clearly based on the same event that "For the Death of 100 Whales" addressed but it is an entirely different work, repeating the line, "the whales in your chest." This poem seems to suggest that modern American life was killing whales rather than bullets. They were being killed by retirement funds and creature comforts even if "the army is mowing them down."

At the end of his performance, there was no applause. Perhaps it was for this reason that in "September Ridge," Will Petersen wrote that McClure was "almost booed off."

Aftermath

Certainly, no booing can be heard on the recordings of that night, but it was not a successful performance. Petersen's poem, rather cryptic, says "Expressionists impatient / wanting wantonness, long before minimalism." He seems to be saying McClure was too subtle for them and that they wanted something funny or rude, and indeed the only real snicker came when he said "clitoris," so Petersen might be right. The audience that night was drunk and tittering, looking for fun and laughter rather than serious contemplation, and before McClure they had gotten a mix of intelligent poetry and silly humor. McClure, however, had only brought the former.

Next, in a big change from the 6 Gallery reading, Allen Ginsberg introduced Kenneth Rexroth. He joked that Rexroth was "a very famous writer of nursery rhymes" and Rexroth drunkenly repeated that idea but then clarified that "actually, these are *parodies* of nursery rhymes." At one point during the reading, providing commentary on his own work, he claimed at least part of it was a translation from French, but the origins of the poem are unclear. He started by reading the first three stanzas of his poem, "Mother Goose":

> Do not pick my rosemary.
> Do not pick my rue.
> I'm saving up my sorrow,
> And I have none for you.

After these oddly conventional stanzas, he paused to joke about reading "old-fashioned poetry that rhymes." It was a carefully calculated insertion because the next lines are about a masturbating ogre and women's urine, all linked together with childish rhymes. The audience was suitably amused. He continued with his poem, sometimes explaining parts between stanzas.

Next, it was Ginsberg's turn. Rexroth introduced him in his usual joking style: "And now, for better and worse…" but Ginsberg was not in the mood for joking as he planned to begin with "Howl." The audience had been laughing and goofing around, heckling the speakers in a playful way, but when Ginsberg stood up to read, someone made a noise and the whole crowd laughed, clearly annoying him. He tolerated it for a while but then became audibly irritated and said, "I won't put up... cut out all the bullshit now." He told them he wanted to "read without sound effects [...] without hip static." The audience quietened for a while but would punctuate his reading with shouts and laughs, mostly enthusiastic but also distracting and inappropriate. Ann Charters did not care for it either. She recalled being impressed by the poets but "unnerved by the drunken wildness of their friends in the audience."

Ginsberg, who was not drunk but was drinking during his reading, appealed to his listeners by explaining that this was a different sort of poem to the ones that had been read before it. In one recording of the event, it is just possible to catch the following remarks:

> The difficulty is to read straightforward through without laughter, y'know, for a moment. The difficulty is to read straightforward through intelligently to arrive at some kind of emotional conclusion with everybody, which I feel pretty strongly having read the poem several times and feeling a certain amount of insincerity in reading it over and over and over again. [...] What I've done is revise the poem, so I'm reading it in a sense afresh with revisions in it which I'm testing out still [...] so in a sense I'm reading you an old poem with revisions. A lot of you have heard a lot of it already.

It is interesting if not wholly surprising that he admits feeling "insincerity in reading it over and over and over again." As we have seen, even by February he had become tired of reading it, for it was a long, emotionally exhausting work. It took a substantial amount of focus and energy and no doubt brought to mind dark moments from his personal life. If he did not invest enough effort and become emotionally involved, then he felt it was a hollow performance that did not do the work justice.

The audience more or less knew what to expect. By now, "Howl" was relatively well known and so was the poet. Rexroth had introduced Ginsberg by saying that he needed no introduction and someone in the audience even asked, "Is this the Ferlinghetti poem?" to which Ginsberg replied, "Yeah. Same poem. Same poem." By March it was already common knowledge that he had an exciting work that would be published by City Lights, yet he was keen to stress the fact that this was a work in progress and that it had changed a great deal, so listeners should not expect exactly the same work he had read at previous events.

Although a much-cited account of the reading given by an eyewitness described Ginsberg "wearing a ragged sweater," photos show him wearing a dark-colored sports coat over a shirt and tie. His clothes are several sizes too large and his jacket and trousers do not match. He looks rather goofy, especially compared to the painfully hip Snyder and the achingly handsome McClure. Yet in a famous photo of him from that night, his hand is nonchalantly in his pocket and he is confidently and happily addressing his audience. He is beneath stark white lights, a thick pile of papers open in his right hand. He seems very much at ease. It is astonishing that just six months earlier he had given his first-ever poetry reading.

This time around, Ginsberg read the whole of "Howl." It was not exactly the same as the published version, but it was getting closer.[14] He read the dedicatory page for the book, which mentioned Lucien Carr, something that would appear in the first edition but would subsequently be removed due to Carr's desire for anonymity. Kerouac's various unpublished books were listed and he was credited with naming "Howl" and contributing "several phrases." The title of *Naked Lunch*, not published for another three years, got a big laugh.

Once again, he read very slowly, focused on individual words or small groups of words rather than whole lines:

---

14 We saw that he read from something similar to draft #9 of Part II at Reed and here he read from a version very close to #17 out of a total eighteen known drafts.

A Repeat Performance

"I saw the best minds of *my* generation... starving... hysterical... naked... dragging themselves through the negro streets... at dawn... looking for an angry fix..." It is extremely slow and the pauses are odd, but they allow his listener the chance to contemplate each line rather than merely consume it. Once again, the poem gave him courage and with each line and with each passing minute that he spoke he grew in volume and power. Within five minutes he was chanting his great poem as though he were delivering a religious message, gesturing and shouting in certain emotional parts. "It was, in a way, sort of scary," Whalen recalled. The audience began to signal its enthusiasm, laughing at the line "who reappeared on the West Coast investigating the FBI." Sometimes the laughter and applause caused him to stall and pause longer than he wanted, but he continued and gave a fine reading (although in his own opinion it was not sufficient). In total, the first part of his poem took about twenty minutes to read, much longer than the twelve or fourteen minutes it had reportedly taken him at the 6 Gallery and the thirteen minutes it took him at Reed College.

This time, he did not end after Part I. After a short pause, he slowly began Part II and then quickly proceeded with a deeply emotional, almost disturbing reading of "Moloch! Moloch!" By now, the audience was silent. There was nothing to laugh at here. They listened intently as Ginsberg delivered his terrifying sermon. They were captivated. A small ripple of applause followed Part II and then he began Part III: "Carl Solomon! I'm with you in Rockland / where you're madder than I am." He continued his passionate reading, now thoroughly in control. It was a powerful performance. Charters recalled the end of "Howl":

> When Ginsberg finished with the last shouts of "Moloch, Moloch" someone backstage began turning the overhead stage lighting on and off, bathing the stage in shades of yellow, red, and blue. The other poets, who were sitting on the stage behind him, stood up and solemnly shook his hand.

Aftermath

However, Ginsberg did not finish by shouting "Moloch, Moloch" because this time he read the whole of the poem, ending with Part III, which finishes "in my dreams you walk dripping from a sea-journey on the highway across America in tears to the door of my cottage in the Western night," receiving a loud applause for his efforts. It was a great success but certainly the audience that night had been primed for Snyder and Whalen. They were drunk and rowdy, looking for something to laugh at rather than the emotionally charged masterpiece Ginsberg had brought. Ginsberg, whilst a gifted reader, lacked the force of personality Snyder had and even the shy Whalen had transformed into an outgoing speaker once he knew the audience understood him. Their playful works entertained the masses more than Ginsberg's emotional oration.

Charters wrote: "I remember Kerouac drunkenly embracing his friends on the stage as the house lights were turned on and the audience jammed into the aisles" after Ginsberg finished "Howl," but apart from forgetting that he read Part III, she also overlooked the fact that Ginsberg went on to read several other poems. There was no invasion of the stage. No dramatic lightshow. No wild applause. No audience surging into the aisles. (In fact, there was no Kerouac, for he was not yet on the West Coast.) Instead, after finishing "Howl," Ginsberg read "Sunflower Sutra," "A Supermarket in California," and "America." He did not, as some have claimed, read "Footnote to Howl." Once again, memory has resulted in a distortion of reality and even though it is minor, mythology has supplanted factual history in spite of the existence of several recordings.

What is most surprising about this reading is that "Howl" was by far the least well-received of these four poems. The audience enjoyed it, but they were far more enthusiastic in their responses to the others. Certain lines from "A Supermarket in California" produced big laughs but the highlight of the reading was "America," which was very different from the version published later that year. Ginsberg started it with a notable lack of enthusiasm, speaking flatly and sounding eager to get through it as quickly as possible, yet again and again the audience

A Repeat Performance

reacted to parts they liked and he got into the swing of it, feeding off their energy. Lines like "America I used to be a communist when I was a kid I'm not sorry" and "I smoke marijuana every chance I get" received some of the biggest laughs of the night and when he finished the first section of the poem there was nearly thirty seconds of rapturous applause. It took a long time to read because the crowd kept laughing and clapping, meaning that once again Ginsberg had to add more pauses than he otherwise would have. The response was so positive, in fact, that Ferlinghetti—who was sitting in the audience—decided that Ginsberg's book should include more than just "Howl"; he now wanted it to be "a book full of representative work not just the one poem." Ginsberg was uncertain about "America," sometimes loving and sometimes hating the poem (an apt feeling given his attitude toward his own country) but Ferlinghetti felt now that it had to be a part of *Howl and Other Poems*. It remains one of his most popular poems.

When the reading finished, there was of course an afterparty, but Ginsberg did not attend. Unlike in October, he had a job and needed to get up early. He was rapidly moving toward fame but not quite there yet, so for now he had to slog away in the Greyhound baggage room, writing and performing his poetry only in his spare time. But fame was just around the corner…

Infamy, Infamy!

Soon after the Berkeley reading, Ginsberg explained to his father just how successful it had been:

> The reading was pretty great, we had traveling photographers, who appeared on the scene from Vancouver to photograph it, a couple of amateur electronics experts who appeared with tape machines to record,[15] request from State college for a complete recording for the night, requests for copies of the recordings, even finally organizations of bop musicians who want to write music and give big west coast traveling tours of Howl as a sort of Jazz Mass, recorded for a west coast company called Fantasy records that issues a lot of national bop, etc. No kidding. You have no idea what a storm of lunatic-fringe activity I have stirred up.

The 6 Gallery had been the first sign of a major poetic movement, but it was the follow-up reading that really grabbed people's attention and pushed the movement toward a wider audience. In that same letter, Ginsberg said "there appears to be, according to Rexroth, a semi

---

15   Ginsberg's portion of the reading was released in Canada by Pinewood Soundtracks in July 1956. It was credited to "Allen Ginsburg." There were actually several people in the audience recording the performance, including Walter Lehrman. Lehrman had been at the 6 Gallery reading and soon after bought a camera. Over the coming months, he took numerous photos of Ginsberg, Snyder, and the other Beat poets, including one of Ginsberg reading at the Poetry Center in November 1955, which is almost certainly the first photo of Ginsberg reading his poem.

major renaissance around the west coast due to Jack and my presence—and Rexroth's wife said he'd been waiting all his life hoping for a situation like this to develop." The use of the word "renaissance" was prophetic for that is precisely what the local poetry scene would become known as—the San Francisco Renaissance. Many disliked or disagreed with the name. Duncan complained that "[t]he term [...] shows that someone didn't know what a renaissance was at all. What did it mean? That we revived the Yukon poets or something?" Ann Charters called it "a later journalist's term" and said, "Poetry had no need to be reborn in San Francisco since it had always been alive there." Some people preferred the term "revolution" and others thought "renaissance" was fine, but whatever the terminology, there can be little arguing with the fact that there was a vast enlargement of interest in poetry at this time and that it stemmed to no small degree from the poetic and promotional efforts of Ginsberg and his Beat peers.

Certainly, the local poetry scene was buzzing and it was not only Ginsberg and the others from the 6 Gallery who were performing. Across the city, new poetry nights sprang up. The Cellar launched a series of jazz and poetry evenings, with Rexroth, Ferlinghetti, and others reading poems in front of a jazz band. According to Rexroth, on the first night four hundred disappointed fans were left outside due to the venue being packed. "Just as a show it was a wowser," he said. "The audience every night thinks it is wonderful." Others have noted that they were wildly popular but that the poetry and music tended to be awful. For one thing, no one could ever hear the poet over the music. John Allen Ryan, who was in attendance, agreed with Rexroth, saying that the older poet—whom he terms "Rexwrath," which in another letter he seems to suggest was coined by Jack Spicer—"came on like Elvis" and that "the police came and made half of the people go away because of fire regulations and only one exit." Miss Smith's Tea Room had similar events and even included live painting shows set against live jazz performances.

Before the 6 Gallery reading, Ginsberg had given serious thought to a career in academia but had later realized that his brain was wired for creating poetry instead of merely analyzing and contextualizing it. In a sense, though, reading "Howl" fast-tracked him into teaching, for shortly after the March 18 reading, he was asked to lead a poetry workshop. To his father, he explained that he was "now the local poet-hero" and thus had been asked to teach "one class a week at S.F. State College." He made it seem as though he was a part-time professor when in fact it was merely a weekly workshop run by the San Francisco Poetry Center, which was affiliated with San Francisco State College. The class was "half old ladies and half hip young kids who have been attracted by all the recent activity." He took his teaching duties seriously but at the same time taught a wildly unconventional class. To his father, Louis, who was a high-school teacher as well as a poet, Allen explained:

> My teaching technique could shock you undoubtedly and certainly get me kicked out of anywhere else or not be countenanced, I bring in bums from North Beach and talk about marijuana and Whitman, precipitate great emotional outbreaks and howls of protest over irrational spontaneous behavior—but it does actually succeed in communicating some of the electricity & fire of poetry and cuts through the miasmic quibbling about form vs. content etc. and does this phrase "work" and is that line "successful" and are all those "p & f" sounds too intense, etc. [...] The thing I do in class is get them personally involved in what they're writing and lambaste anything which sounds at all like they're writing "literature" and try to get them to actually express secret life in whatever form it comes out. I practically take off my clothes in class myself to do it. The students all dig it and understand and the class is now grown weekly to where it's too big to handle, starting with 8 and ending with 25.

Aftermath

If this sounds revolutionary, it is worth remembering the efforts of Douglas MacAgy at C.S.F.A. and the atmosphere of creativity and free expression he fostered. Consider David Park, for example, who was a tremendously influential teacher during the time that the 6 Gallery founders were at C.S.F.A., and who showed his paintings at both King Ubu and the 6 Gallery. In a poster advertising his advanced painting class, he outlined three aims:

> 1. That the students should develop their originality and independence.
> 2. That they should constantly look for what is meaningful to themselves, and to try to present this meaningfulness to others.
> 3. To try to make working habits as genuinely simple, unselfconscious and vital as any process of nature.

He went on to explain that there would be no assignments and indeed "[n]o specific course of studies."

Teachers like Jack Spicer and later Bruce Conner were no less controversial in their lessons, the latter using his class budget to hire fourteen naked women, who came in and drew the art students instead of acting as life models. Ginsberg was certainly not the only artist attempting to subvert norms and question traditional practices in art and education.

Put in charge of his own workshops, Ginsberg seized the opportunity to present his own views and set about spreading the concept of what would later be known as Beat poetry rather than broadly teaching poetry with a subtle push toward his own literary inspirations. He even used "Howl" in his class. Robert Creeley, who worked for the Poetry Center, typed it up and Marthe Rexroth mimeographed and stapled it together, making it "Allen's first 'book,'" in the words of Bill Morgan. Explaining it for his students and having them discuss it surely helped as he worked to finish the poem and collect the others that were intended for inclusion in *Howl and Other Poems*.

Infamy, Infamy!

The closer "Howl" came to finality, the more confident in it he was, but at the same time he was uncertain of some other poems in the collection. He and Ferlinghetti had disagreements over what poems should be included. Ginsberg wanted "The Green Automobile" and "Dream Record: June 8, 1955" but Ferlinghetti didn't; Ferlinghetti wanted "America" and "In the Baggage Room at Greyhound" but Ginsberg didn't. Ultimately, the publisher got his way, and Ginsberg complained that the book itself was "sloppy and egocentric." He was unhappy with how the printer had indented his poems, too. In some ways, his reaction differed little from that of most writers as their book moves toward publication—a mixture of euphoria, confidence, frustration, and self-doubt.

In spite of the concerns he had about his poetry and his first book, Ginsberg persevered with his promotional drive. The Berkeley reading had drawn a small amount of media attention and around the country rumors were spreading of a poetic movement birthed in the Bay Area. This awareness would rapidly grow thanks to Rexroth, who got in contact with his old friend Richard Eberhart and also the editors of *The New York Times*, proposing an article on the West Coast poetry scene. By 1956, Rexroth and Eberhart, a successful poet, had been friends for more than a decade and their families often spent time together. They admired each other's work and helped promote each other. Eberhart, however, was far more successful than Rexroth and so he was constantly involved in schemes to get his friend grants, publication opportunities, and reading or lecturing gigs. In 1953, Eberhart wrote "Kenneth Rexroth: The Man and the Works," which he said in a letter to his friend was "an article I knocked off in love of you." Rexroth seems to have been embarrassed by the overly exuberant first draft and so Eberhart toned it down before publication. Months later, he offered to put a Rexroth poem in *New World Writing*, a prestigious publication for which Eberhart was acting as guest editor. He did not ask for any particular poem; he simply told Rexroth to send him anything new that he wanted published.

Eberhart had visited Rexroth in San Francisco in early 1956 as part of a lecture tour, during which he gave a reading at the Poetry Center on April 3, and so he was not entirely ignorant of the developing poetry scene. He had met with Ginsberg and even heard "Howl," although only on tape because Ginsberg out "of sheer temperament" refused to read it for him. In fact, Eberhart had spoken publicly about his enthusiasm for San Francisco's young poets before Rexroth had even contacted him about the article. A *San Francisco Examiner* article from April quoted him as saying:

> It's the nearest thing to a group movement I've seen. I've met more poets here than anywhere else on my present trip. Back East they are more individualistic; they don't go around in packs. Here you get two or three hundred together to hear a reading. It's very vigorous, and most promising.

Soon after this visit, Rexroth proposed the *New York Times* article and Eberhart readily agreed. Over the next months, Eberhart put together his article but what is most interesting from their correspondence is the degree to which Eberhart leaned on Rexroth, essentially writing what his friend wanted him to write. Eberhart wrote, "I get the aura but I want the accuracy," and asked his friend to "give [him] a precise, thum-nail [sic] sketch of each of the young poets [including] where from, age, education, marital or other status, how long on the Coast if not native there, all that." Over the course of several letters, he pushed Rexroth to contribute as much detail as possible and later, after he had written drafts that were largely based on Rexroth's notes, he asked his friend for edits and insertions. Rexroth wrote so much of it, in fact, that Eberhart gave him half of his payment. This is all the more fascinating because several years later Rexroth seemed to plagiarize Eberhart's article when in fact he was probably just reusing his old notes to write a new work.

It was not only Rexroth who influenced Eberhart in the writing of his article. Eberhart hoped for input from the poets themselves and unsurprisingly Allen

Infamy, Infamy!

Ginsberg obliged. He had already taken Eberhart around San Francisco and informed him about Beat poetry and explained "Howl," but now he wrote "a long explanatory letter" about his poem. At thirty-four pages, this vast defense of "Howl" was such an interesting document that it was not only collected in Ginsberg's published correspondence but was printed as a stand-alone book in 1976. He wrote it because he felt that Eberhart had not quite understood "Howl." He didn't want to be seen as an angry young man, launching an incoherent tirade. He wanted his poem viewed as an intelligent dissection of problems in contemporary America and an expression of solidarity with the downtrodden. As well as explaining "Howl" from a technical standpoint, he called it a "religious" poem and said that it espoused not just sympathy for people like Carl Solomon but acceptance of them. It also, he claimed, preached "self acceptance." He explained that it was therefore an optimistic poem that encouraged love and aimed to bring about a sense of compassion for the self and for others. "You heard or saw Howl as a negative howl of protest," he wrote, but "[t]he title notwithstanding, the poem itself is an act of sympathy not rejection." He also made sure to promote his other poet friends, such as Burroughs, Snyder, and Kerouac, whom he called "the Colossus unknown of U.S. Prose who taught me to write and has written more and better than anybody of my generation that I've ever heard of."

Eberhart's article, agreed to in April and with its deadline in June, was finally published in September 1956. It informed the country of an exciting new literary form growing out of bohemian San Francisco. It was titled "West Coast Rhythms" and it began with astonishing enthusiasm:

> The West Coast is the liveliest spot in the country in poetry today. It is only here that there is a radical group movement of young poets. San Francisco teems with young poets.

Aftermath

He went on to praise Witt-Diamant and the Poetry Center, as well as Rexroth and Patchen, before turning to what really inspired him—the participation of young people. He said, "Poetry here has become a tangible social force," and called the regular readings "an authentic, free-wheeling celebration of poetry." Importantly, he turned to focus on Ginsberg:

> The most remarkable poem of the young group, written during the past year, is "Howl," by Allen Ginsberg, a 29-year-old poet who is the son of Louis Ginsberg, a poet known to newspaper readers in the East. [...] This poem has created a furor of praise or abuse whenever read or heard. It is a powerful work, cutting through to dynamic meaning. Ginsberg thinks he is going forward by going back to the methods of Whitman.

He then went on to briefly describe several other Ginsberg poems before praising Ferlinghetti (both as publisher and poet) and offering a few kind words for Snyder, Whalen, and McClure. He also spoke highly of Jim Harmon, an "anarchist, Rexrothian poet" who lived with McClure. He concluded:

> It is certain that there is a new, vital group consciousness now among young poets in the Bay region. However unpublished they may be, many of these young poets have a numerous and enthusiastic audience. They acquire this audience by their own efforts. Through their many readings they have in some cases a larger audience than more cautiously presented poets in the East.
>
> They are finely alive, they believe something new can be done with the art of poetry, they are hostile to gloomy critics, and the reader is invited to look into and enjoy their work as it appears. They have

exuberance and a young will to kick down the doors of older consciousness and established practice in favor of what they think is vital and new.

Clearly, Eberhart had been impressed by what he had seen in San Francisco, and his article did much to promote the area and its artists, but one can hardly fail to note that he totally overlooked the local poets (Blaser, Duncan, Spicer) and focused instead on the "invaders" (Ferlinghetti, Ginsberg, Snyder, Whalen, McClure). Perhaps this was Rexroth's fault... or Ginsberg's... or perhaps it was simply because, when Eberhart had visited, the local poets were temporarily absent.

In September, Michael Grieg[16] wrote an article about the San Francisco poetry scene for *Mademoiselle*, a popular women's magazine that largely focused on fashion but also published high-brow literature. His article would appear in February 1957 as "The Lively Arts in San Francisco," but even by the time Eberhart's article was published it was known that Grieg would produce a glowing report. Luther Nichols, a columnist for the *Examiner*, had very obviously read the article months before it was published and summarized it when sharing the news of Eberhart's endorsement of San Francisco. He compared the two reports and concluded that San Francisco was the most exciting literary town in America, with Rexroth and Witt-Diamant as its champions and Kerouac and Ginsberg as its leading voices (even though by this point Ginsberg no longer lived in San Francisco and Kerouac had only ever been in the city for short stints). "The Lively Arts in San Francisco" mentioned various local writers, including Robert Duncan, but Duncan refused to pose for a photograph, unhappy about being publicly associated with Kerouac and Ginsberg. McClure also refused, feeling that he was distinct from the Beat poets. The Beat Generation was on the cusp of national recognition, and already a number of the most prominent poets associated with it wanted to distance themselves.

---

16   Along with Weldon Kees, Greig was the founder of Poets' Follies. He was a reporter, playwright, poet, sportswriter, and film scenarist.

Aftermath

With articles about them in two nationally distributed publications, the Beats were about ready to go mainstream. By the time this happened, however, their days in San Francisco were coming to an end. In retrospect, this was hardly surprising. Although San Francisco was an unusually open and pleasant environment, allowing these young writers the freedom to create and to find a receptive audience, one of the few qualities the Beat writers shared was a sense of restlessness, a yearning to move on to the next place no matter how wonderful the present one was. Kerouac's novel, *On the Road*, most famously captured this spirit and particularly in the oft-quoted line, "the road is life," but all of the most famous writers associated with the Beat Generation suffered this affliction. If they found a place they particularly liked, they might settle for a few years or use it as a base from which to set out on their various voyages, but they were not ones to stay in a place too long.

Gary Snyder adored the American West and had some of the best experiences of his life in the Bay Area in the months before and after the 6 Gallery reading, but he still felt the need to move on. In the first half of December, he wrote:

> Must quit school, so as to leave this country right—no scholar hounded from one library to another—but Saigyo-ing it,[17] full of visions, of wandering men, mad poets, American people and land, uneducated sanity, simple self-known wisdom.

On May 6, 1956, he took off for Japan, where he would live for the next decade. Soon after, Kerouac headed north to spend the summer working as a fire lookout on Desolation Peak. "It was [Snyder] who had advised me to come here," he wrote on the penultimate page of

---

17   Saigyō was a traveling Buddhist priest-poet in twelfth-century Japan. His *waka* poetry and commitment to living in nature rather than among other people influenced Snyder, and his life of wandering started around the same age that Snyder was in 1955.

The Dharma Bums. He imagines Snyder standing "by the gnarled old rocky trees certifying and justifying all that was here," and he says, "I don't know when we'll meet again or what'll happen in the future, but Desolation, Desolation, I owe so much to Desolation, thank you forever for guiding me to the place where I learned all." However, despite the intensity of their friendship, Snyder and Kerouac never saw each other again. Even on his returns to the U.S. Snyder did not meet with his old friend. They kept in touch by letter and occasionally on the phone, but as Kerouac became more drunk, incoherent, and right-wing, he was increasingly difficult to communicate with. Snyder returned to the U.S. permanently in 1966 and Kerouac died just three years later.

In May, Ginsberg also left the Bay Area, albeit temporarily. He rejoined the Merchant Marine, setting off on the U.S.N.S. Sgt. Jack J. Pendleton for Alaska. This trip, however, was made largely to fund a longer one. By going to sea, he knew he could—in a relatively short period of time—save the money necessary for a long-awaited trip to Europe. On June 9, he received the crushing news that his mother, Naomi, had passed away. Profoundly mentally ill, she had lived a tortured life and in a sense her death was a release from severe emotional pain, but naturally it hurt her son, who had helplessly watched her suffering and now learned of her death from afar, unable even to attend her funeral. In fact, so few people did attend that they were unable to read the Mourner's Kaddish, the Jewish funeral rites. Ginsberg vowed to write his own one and several years later he did. Although "Howl" is undoubtedly better known, "Kaddish," published in 1961, is considered by many to be his greatest poem. Several days after his mother's death, he received a letter she had sent shortly before the stroke that killed her. It worsened an already excruciating pain.

During all this, *Howl and Other Poems* was going through the final stages of publication. In May, the book was sent to Villiers, a small vanity press in England that Ferlinghetti believed would be willing to publish controversial material for a reasonable price. They said they would print *Howl and Other Poems* but required certain words to be replaced by asterisks. Ferlinghetti and Ginsberg were unhappy but they felt that it was the only option, and so they reluctantly agreed and City Lights contracted Villiers to print 1,500 saddle-stitched copies of the book. These arrived in San Francisco in June and in August Ginsberg received the finalized version at sea.

Both the poet and publisher were aware of the potential for trouble. In March, Ferlinghetti had contacted the American Civil Liberties Union, asking for their support if the U.S. government were to prevent *Howl* from being sold. With the controversial words censored, any attempt to censor the poem would be an attack on the ideas behind it rather than the language it contained, and that meant the suppression of free speech.[18] The A.C.L.U. agreed to support the publisher. Some have suggested that Ferlinghetti wanted the fight to happen, but this is mere conjecture. Whilst obviously an attack by the government would have been wonderful publicity for the book—perhaps a better advertisement than any amount of money could buy—there is no good evidence that he hoped for this. Some have suggested that he connived to have copies sent from England with the word "cocksucker" visible on the outside, but this defies logic and overlooks the fact that such words had been censored.

Ginsberg, on the other hand, seemed to relish a fight. To his father, he wrote:

> Civil Liberties Union here was consulted and said they'd defend it if it gets into trouble, which I almost hope it does. I am almost ready to tackle the U.S. government out of sheer self delight. There is really a great stupid conspiracy of unconscious

---

18 Most very strong swearwords were removed but other words like "snatches" and "lays," as well as obvious references to sexual acts (oddly heterosexual rather than homosexual ones), drew criticism from the prosecution. Bizarrely, the word "fuck" had not been deleted in "America," perhaps because the poet and publisher had mostly worked together to censor "Howl." [This observation was made by Kurt Hemmer in a forthcoming essay, "6 Gallery and the Breakthrough of 'Howl.'"]

negative inertia to keep people from "expressing" themselves. I was reading Henry Miller's banned book *Tropic of Cancer*, which actually is a great classic—I never heard of it at Columbia with anything but deprecatory dismissal comments—he and Genet are such frank hip writers that the open expression of their perceptions and real beliefs are a threat to society. The wonder is that literature does have such power.

He cared deeply about his poem and its presentation and did not merely want fame through controversy, and so he complained when he found that the printers had not faithfully reproduced his work, the censored words notwithstanding. The problem was that he had used very long lines, which the printers had taken as a sign that he did not care about how they were divided and indented. They believed they could place line breaks wherever they wanted, and when Ginsberg saw this he was devastated. He begged Ferlinghetti to fix it, offering to pay for the mistake himself, up to a limit of $200. "I mean you can't tell *what* I am doing," he wrote, "it looks like just primitive random scribbling in pages. I had not intended the prosody to be *that* arbitrary." Thankfully, it was fixed for just $20. "Everything worked out fine with the typography—it looks much better this way and it seems to have been real cheap to do—$20 is nuthin," he said. However, between this and Ferlinghetti's sneaky removal of certain poems Ginsberg had wanted included, he felt regretful about leaving so much to his publisher. "Next time will take my time and not be so eager to finish a book," he wrote to Kerouac.

The book went on sale October 1, 1956—one week short of one year after its public debut at the 6 Gallery. Priced at $0.75, it sold well in San Francisco but was hard to find outside of the city. Ginsberg embarked on another publicity blitz, sending copies to every major writer and influential contact he knew or could find contact information for: Auden, cummings, Eliot, Miller, Patchen,

Pound, and a great many magazine editors. He even sent books to Marlon Brando and Charlie Chaplin. City Lights placed advertisements in *The Nation* but no doubt the articles in the *New York Times* and *Mademoiselle* did more to move copies. The initial run of 1,500 copies sold out in six months and in March 1957 a second printing was ordered. By then, however, Ginsberg had left San Francisco for good.

In October 1956, Ginsberg ended his two-year stay in the city. It was not that he disliked it but rather that he was keen to move on to new experiences. With money from his mother and more saved from his time at sea, he set out for New York on a rather circuitous route via Hollywood and Mexico City. It began with a "rally of poetry" at the Poetry Center with Corso on October 21. Here, he made the odd choice to *not* read his signature poem and instead went with "Many Loves," which he had written on board a ship that summer. The poem was "not printed till [1984] for reasons of prudence and modesty," and was even more explicit than "Howl," so one can only wonder how it was received by Witt-Diamant. The event was Corso's first ever public reading but he would not stick around to join the poetry renaissance because soon after this they headed down the coast and in Hollywood, on October 30, they gave a private reading sponsored by a magazine called *Coastlines*. It was "a square audience," according to Lawrence Lipton but Ginsberg reflected that they were "receptive." Anaïs Nin was meant to be in the audience but showed up late and Ginsberg refused to read until she arrived, which annoyed his "dull" hosts. Once she was present, he gave what was in his opinion a wonderful reading of "Howl." He explained in a letter to Rexroth: "I got my howl machine all worked up to a pitch I haven't had since 6 gallery."

However, it was not his reading that caused controversy in this case. It was a poetic gesture. "I took off all my clothes finally at a reading for real," he excitedly reported about a month later. It seems to have been something he'd wanted to do since witnessing Robert Duncan do it at the 6 Gallery. Years later, he recalled:

a red-haired lush from Hollywood interrupted poet Gregory Corso in the middle of his long poem, "Power," and shouted, "Whatter you guys tryana prove?" and I spontaneously shouted back, "Nakedness!" and he shouted back, "Whadya mean nakedness?" and so, thinking over my own language, I silently disrobed, and then clothed myself again, and then Corso continued the reading of "Power."

Lawrence Lipton tells it a little differently in *Holy Barbarians* but the essence of the story is the same. Ginsberg and Corso had been challenged by a heckler and rather than meet him with aggression, Ginsberg proceeded to take off all his clothes and demonstrate the poet's willingness to bare everything—his soul, his mind, his body. The audience seemed generally impressed but the event organizers were unhappy. Ginsberg only cared what one audience member felt, though: Anaïs Nin. She said it reminded her of "Artaud's mad conference at the Sorbonne" and gave Ginsberg and Corso five dollars to help with their onward travels. Word of the event spread and helped provide Ginsberg further infamy, which combined with the events of the following year would secure his place among America's literary *enfants terribles*.

In New York, Ginsberg found himself much less famous and noted that *Howl and Other Poems*, easily available in San Francisco, was hard to find and selling poorly on the other side of the country. On the West Coast, Ginsberg had felt on the cusp of genuine poetic success but now he felt like an unknown poet once again. Nonetheless, he persevered with his efforts to contact the media and was interviewed by Harvey Breit of *The New York Times* after he showed up uninvited to show them his book. He was interviewed for the *Village Voice*, too, and photographed for *Life* and *Esquire*. He then toured the city's publishing houses and magazines to recommend they publish Kerouac, Burroughs, Corso, Whalen, Snyder, and other Beat writers. He visited William Carlos

Aftermath

Williams and shared with him poems by his West Coast friends, and at parties he accosted influential people and informed them about the poetry of the Beat Generation. He complained that "[p]eople are generally negative," but still he was determined to use his own growing fame to bring attention to the work of his closest friends. He even contemplated using the money his mother had left him to start a press, printing Burroughs' books in Japan and shipping them to the U.S. for distribution.

Although he seemed determined to make himself and his peers famous, Ginsberg was also feeling a certain amount of unpleasant pressure from his growing infamy, and he prepared to leave the country. His destinations were North Africa and Europe, which he envisioned as good places to live and write. William Burroughs had been writing positively about Tangier, where one could easily procure hashish, opium, and any number of other drugs, and male prostitution made sex cheap and easy. He yearned to explore the cities of Europe, too, following in the footsteps of his favorite writers and painters. As he made his preparations for departure, Ginsberg received a letter from Ferlinghetti about being photographed for *Life* magazine at one of Rexroth's Friday-night soirées. "I am sick of these con operations," the publisher wrote. At another party, Spicer threatened the photographers with a $100,000 lawsuit if they took a single photo of him. The horrors of media scrutiny were only just beginning.

It could well be argued that Ginsberg created the San Francisco Renaissance and Beat Generation phenomena through his poetry and his promotional efforts, and it is consequently of note that he managed to get out of San Francisco just before the media hysteria and tour buses descended, as well as the police crackdowns that made life difficult for the once carefree artist communities. He also managed to leave the country a fortnight before legal action was brought against his book. On March 25, U.S. Customs intercepted 520 copies of *Howl and Other Poems* on the grounds of obscenity. It was the government's first move in a seven-month-long battle. Ferlinghetti, leveraging his status in the city and utilizing his media contacts, was given a platform in the *San Francisco Chronicle*, where he thanked the Collector of Customs, Chester MacPhee, for making "Howl" famous. He went on to make an eloquent defense of the poem and indeed the necessity for socially critical art: "it is not the poet but what he observes which is revealed as obscene," he wrote. Other columnists in the city supported him in attacking MacPhee, who had justified the confiscation of the book by saying, "The words and the sense of the writing is obscene. You wouldn't want your children to come across it." *Chronicle* columnist Abe Mellinkoff responded: "the collector has no duty to protect my children [...] If he is going to pick up everything that is a menace to them, he is going to be confiscating night and day."

Ferlinghetti summoned the A.C.L.U., which in turn told MacPhee of their intent to challenge the confiscation of books. At the same time, Ferlinghetti rather shrewdly found an American printer to produce another 2,500 copies, thereby removing the legal authority of the Customs Department while at the same time using their actions to generate publicity for the book. It was a brilliant move, leaving MacPhee looking like a fool and causing a huge number of orders for the now infamous publication. When the U.S. Attorney's Office in San Francisco declared that it would not prosecute, MacPhee was forced to give up and on May 29, 1957, the 520 copies of *Howl* were sent on to City Lights, which now had plenty of eager customers clamoring for copies.

Success was short-lived, however. William Hanrahan of the Juvenile Department of the San Francisco Police sent two undercover officers to City Lights on June 3 to buy copies of *Howl* and also a journal called *Miscellaneous Man*.[19] They returned later in the day with an arrest

---

19   *Miscellaneous Man* was published by William Margolis and also printed by Villiers. This issue of the journal was devoted to poet Gil Orlovitz, and certain poems in it were judged to be obscene. Ferlinghetti defended Ginsberg's poem but not Olovitz's, which convinced the latter poet that there was a conspiracy against him. In fact, Ferlinghetti had merely chosen to defend the publication that he had edited and published, knowing that the court case would be good for business. It was also a matter of simply choosing one fight and winning rather than taking on multiple fights and risking loss.

Aftermath

warrant for Shig Murao and Ferlinghetti, who were to be charged with selling "obscene and indecent" materials. The arrests began a short but stunningly important legal trial. Between August and October of 1957, City Lights was defended in court by the A.C.L.U. Again, the *Chronicle* was on Ferlinghetti's side, publishing an editorial called "Making a Clown of San Francisco." It warned that "the raiding of bookstores on such a slim pre-text is dangerous, to say nothing of a stupid, precedent." Another column was titled "Orwell's 'Big Brother' Is Watching over Us." Twenty-one of the city's bookstores also united to petition the mayor to do something about this pathetic act of censorship.

After the charges against Murao were dropped on the basis that no one could prove he had read the book, Ferlinghetti stood as the defendant. But of course the outcome would decide whether or not *Howl and Other Poems* was to be legally defined as obscene, and so the case was largely seen as *the U.S. vs Howl*. By this time, Ginsberg was in Tangier and would soon travel to Europe, leaving his publisher to fight the case. For all he had supposedly relished a fight, he was happy to let Ferlinghetti do the actual fighting and never once appeared in court to defend his work.

On one of his trips to the city, Kerouac visited City Lights and saw that *Howl* was no longer on sale. He wrote to Ginsberg:

> It's disgusting—what's worse is even some intellectuals are saying it's too dirty, I have a hunch the intelligentsia of America is really so gutless they might knuckle under the dumb fat Irish cops in time and it'll be like Germany, a police state. I'm really worried and Bill [Burroughs] was always right. However Rexroth is burning and there are some who won't be gutless so Allen do not worry.

Kerouac was right. In spite of their differences and his personal problems, Rexroth stood by Ginsberg and his poem and would defend it in court as an expert witness. In total, nine such witnesses were assembled, including college professors and book reviewers. These witnesses attested to its social value and artistic merit. The prosecution, meanwhile, argued that their testimony was irrelevant. Ultimately, Judge Clayton Horn had to decide whether or not the poem had social value. If it did, it was art; if it did not, it was pornography. Ferlinghetti, Rexroth, and others understood that this was not only about "Howl." Victory here would mean other writers and publishers could claim their works had redeeming social value and should not be censored. Ginsberg wondered whether it would be possible to not only win but to carry the fight further, "freeing Miller, Lawrence, and maybe Genet."

On October 3, Judge Horn found Ferlinghetti not guilty and declared that the poem was not obscene. He explained:

> I do not believe that *Howl* is without redeeming social importance. The first part of "Howl" presents a picture of a nightmare world; the second part is an indictment of those elements in modern society destructive of the best qualities of human nature; such elements are predominantly identified as materialism, conformity, and mechanization leading toward war. The third part presents a picture of an individual who is a specific representation of what the author conceives as a general condition. [...]
>
> The people state that it is not necessary to use such words and that others would be more palatable to good taste. The answer is that life is not encased in one formula whereby everyone acts the same or conforms to a particular pattern. No two persons think alike. We are all made from the same mould, but in different patterns. Would there be any

freedom of press or speech if one must reduce his vocabulary to vapid innocuous euphemism? An author should be real in treating his subject and be allowed to express his thoughts and ideas in his own words.

The obscenity trial made "Howl" nationally renowned and so immediately after the trial Ferlinghetti printed another 5,000 copies—this time with the "dirty" words included. That added to the 10,000 copies already in print. The book has remained in print ever since and has gone through numerous reprints and translations, becoming one of the most famous poems of the twentieth century. There have been many attempts—some of which were successful—to ban the book in different jurisdictions or to forbid it from being read during certain hours on radio or TV, but this landmark trial meant that the book could legally be printed and distributed in the United States.

The "Howl" verdict more or less coincided with the release of Jack Kerouac's landmark novel, *On the Road*, which was positively reviewed in the *New York Times*. That same year, the *Evergreen Review* put out its second issue, devoted to the San Francisco Renaissance. It featured work by all the 6 Gallery reading participants except Lamantia, as well as Lawrence Ferlinghetti, Henry Miller, Brother Antoninus, Jack Spicer, Ralph J. Gleason, Robert Duncan, and James Broughton. In his introductory letter for this issue, Rexroth offered unusually high praise for Ginsberg (although he did so after first introducing the poets he preferred: Lamantia and Duncan). He wrote:

purely technically, Ginsberg is one of the most remarkable versifiers in American. He is almost alone in his generation in his ability to make powerful poetry of the inherent rhythms of our speech, to push forward the conquests of a few of the earliest poems of Sandburg and of William Carlos Williams. This is more skillful verse than all the cornbelt Donnes laid end to end. It is my modest prophecy, that, if he keeps going, Ginsberg will be the first genuinely popular, genuine poet in over a generation— and he is already considerably the superior of predecessors like Lindsay and Sandburg.

It is often claimed that Ginsberg convinced Donald Allen to devote *Evergreen Review #2* to the San Francisco poetry scene and this view is supported by Ferlinghetti, who said the editor "went heavily by what Allen Ginsberg told him to publish," overlooking the likes of Bob Kaufman and Diane di Prima and including various poets who weren't even from San Francisco. However, despite Ferlinghetti's claim, one must admit that the list of writers looks more like Rexroth's choice than Ginsberg's, and a letter Ginsberg sent in December 1956 claimed the whole thing was Donald Allen's idea. Another letter from the following year shows that Ginsberg was not impressed by the poets or poems included in *Evergreen Review #2*. He did not like Duncan, Broughten, or Spicer's work, and in spite of his love for Snyder, Whalen, and McClure, he felt their contributions were poor.

Suddenly, the Beat Generation writers were practically household names, their faces appearing in mainstream news outlets and major journals. Ginsberg was in Europe, ostensibly to ignore it all, yet constantly bugged to record his poems for record labels, write articles and introductions, and do interviews. He was becoming the spokesman for a literary movement and perhaps even for a generation. On the streets of Paris, he was stopped by people who had seen his photo and back in San Francisco, at the Arts Festival where in 1954 the 6 Gallery had irked their neighbors with avant-garde poetry and in 1955 Ginsberg had given his first public reading, now there was a puppet show gently mocking the Beats. A movement that had begun in New York in 1944 had exploded into the public consciousness on the other side of the country some thirteen years later and was quickly going global.

Over the coming few years, this literary movement would become a national hysteria, with a plethora of hyperbolic articles about the Beats, silly Hollywood Beatsploitation movies, and the dreaded beatnik phenomenon—a horde of talentless pseudobohemians who flocked to North Beach with berets and bongos but no discernible talent, determined to join the exciting new countercultural movement. By then, of course, the Beat writers—which is to say the creatives rather than the poseurs—had long since moved on, and those who hadn't already fled were being driven out of the parts of town they had made their own. Eventually, even the beatniks would give it up, replaced by the hippies. Ginsberg and McClure and Snyder would make that transition, staying relevant and contributing to events like the Human Be-In, but the hippie movement too would be co-opted and commodified. Such is human nature. Ginsberg and Snyder would become semi-respectable college professors, accepted into the academy that had once feared and rejected them, attempting to change it from the inside.

Of the writers who spoke at the 6 Gallery reading, Allen Ginsberg would go on to enjoy the most fame, largely evolving beyond the infamy of the late fifties and sixties, becoming America's most famous living poet and traveling the world to read his work. "Howl" was the most famous poem not only of its era but of the whole of the second half of the twentieth century, with only a handful of poems exceeding it in terms of renown when it comes to American literature. Gary Snyder became one of the country's most successful poets, winning a Pulitzer Prize and becoming a member of the American Academy of Arts and Letters. McClure thrived in the sixties as a radical poet and playwright, and later worked with Ray Manzarek of the Doors, one of many efforts to bring the Beats into the world of rock music. Whalen achieved less fame than those three but was a respected poet and Zen monk, while Lamantia shunned the spotlight and published relatively little during the remainder of his life. Each of the five poets, however, had a significant influence over subsequent countercultural movements and together the Beat Generation paved the way for the hippies and the punks. Their experimental poetry and prose, their commitment to art over profit, and their battles against censorship meant that regardless of whether you enjoyed

Infamy, Infamy!

their work or not, it was hard to deny their tremendous importance in American letters. Even outside of the United States, Ginsberg and Snyder have been hugely influential, spawning literary movements in Europe and Asia. Their work is taught and their names are known around the world. And that was to no small extent the result of a single reading in a small art gallery in a run-down part of San Francisco, far away from the centers of publishing.

The End of the 6

As Ginsberg's fame waxed, the 6 Gallery's waned. The venue that had birthed the Beat Generation closed just two months after "Howl" was deemed not obscene and three months after *On the Road* was published, marking the beginning of a period of nationwide obsession with all things Beat. Had it kept its doors open just a little longer, it might have become a tourist landmark, finally proving profitable for the artists who ran the cooperative. But it is doubtful they would have wanted anything to do with the hordes of squares soon to descend upon San Francisco, hoping to jam their cameras in the faces of any artistic types they encountered.

For the artists in and around Fillmore-Union, the 6 Gallery's demise came as no surprise. It was not only the Beat poets who had moved on; the gallery's founders eventually lost interest in their own creation. Opening the gallery each day had become a chore and they no longer needed it to exhibit their own work. Other artists largely took responsibility for the cooperative and it still showed interesting, experimental art in a range of styles and forms. They collaborated with the Poetry Center to put on group readings of plays but soon there were other venues in town and the 6 Gallery was no longer the de facto artistic hangout. With no money coming in, with the six founders pursuing their individual careers, and with a host of alternative gallery spaces opening around the city, it was only a matter of time before it shut its doors.

Despite its short life, and seemingly against all odds, the 6 Gallery had been a tremendous success, inspiring artists, fostering a community, and launching careers. One month after Ginsberg read "Howl" there, Alfred Frankenstein wrote about it once again, this time even more positive than ever:

Aftermath

> The 6 Gallery, at 3119 Fillmore Street, is a place where ideas are given their fling. If, in the process, some reputations can be made or started, so much the better, but the young artists who manage this institution seem to be much more concerned with the present than the future, and they exhibit complete indifference to the horse-trading and mutual back-scratching whereby reputations are cooked up. They run their own independent show, without eccentricity or fanfare, and they stand sponsor to more ideas in a week than most private galleries would dare to underwrite in a decade.

Perhaps this was the most fitting description of the 6 Gallery written during its short lifetime. With a few changed verb tenses, this passage could have served as the perfect epitaph.

From October 1954 to December 1957, the 6 Gallery continued in more or less the same spirit, showing experimental work by interesting young artists and sometimes more famous names—usually teachers from C.S.F.A. Financially, it scraped by, with the number of dues-paying members rising from about a dozen in late 1954 to around forty in 1956, allowing it to pay its modest rent and bills. It hosted enough hip opening nights and exhibited enough daring art to achieve a sense of local infamy, but just a year after its founding the 6 Gallery reached its zenith with the poetry reading that ensured its place in the history books. It had served its purpose and thereafter coasted toward inevitable closure.

Throughout 1955 and 1956, the six founders began to move on to other projects. David Simpson seems to have lost interest first and was replaced by photographer Sandra Carlson, an old friend of Remington's. Hayward King moved to France in mid-1955 on a Fulbright Scholarship to study printmaking at the Sorbonne and Remington moved to Japan to work and study from 1956

The End of the 6

to 1958.[20] Spicer was on the East Coast during much of 1955 and 1956, and after he returned he became more interested in the former Black Mountain poets hanging out at The Place, so he had little interest in going back to the 6 Gallery. Ryan moved between San Francisco and Mexico City, but then had a massive mental breakdown after his lover died, pushing him into alcoholism. Like Spicer, who helped him recover from his grief, Ryan gravitated toward The Place and seems to have had no further involvement with the 6 Gallery. Hedrick stuck around but increasingly devoted himself to his art and engaged in other artistic organizations. The art newsletters of the era are filled with mention of his various prizes and projects.

The six artists had started their gallery partly out of community interest but largely for their own benefit and now they no longer needed it. They were talented young men and women and so they succeeded as artists and found places to show their work in other parts of the city and other cities around the country. Although none of them became world famous in the sense that Ginsberg and Snyder did, they all achieved a degree of recognition. Hayward King held a number of prestigious roles as director and curator of leading galleries. Hedrick also became a respected artist, but it was his wife, Jay DeFeo, who gained the most renown and certainly produced the most iconic artwork of that scene: "The Rose," a 2,500-pound painting that took nearly a decade to complete.

New artists came and the gallery continued to show interesting work and operated as a meeting place, but those newcomers found a 6 Gallery with a diminished purpose. The sense of enthusiasm that had once kept everyone's spirits high in spite of a perpetual lack of funds was rapidly fading. Artists began looking for venues that might actually sell their work rather than merely display it for a short time before it ended up in the trash. Bruce Conner, who moved to San Francisco in 1957 and became a close friend of McClure, said:

---

20   Remington's time in Japan overlapped with Snyder's time there. She said later that she spoke with him about the trip prior to his departure in early 1956 but that they never met during her time in Asia.

there wasn't anything to do with the work once we did it. Nobody was going to buy it. And probably there wasn't going to be a gallery that would show it. The only gallery that might show it would be a co-op gallery like the Six Gallery, or some other gallery run by artists. And invariably what would happen is that at the opening everybody would come and have a party, Wally's band would play, everybody would get drunk, and after the opening the guy who ran the gallery would get tired of coming in. You'd never get into the place unless he'd open the door for you. So it seemed ludicrous to have a gallery and do all this other stuff if all you were going to do was have a party.

For those who remained nearby, running the place became less enjoyable and ultimately it was a chore that brought few rewards. Hedrick recalled that "towards the end, sitting got to be a drag. The whole thing was an effort at times. Sometimes people didn't even show up. But it didn't matter—by that time, our function had ceased […] There was no reason for the '6' Gallery to continue." Most of the people who were around the 6 Gallery at that time have made similar comments. Sitting the gallery became intolerably dull and eventually the sitters stopped showing up. Conner said later that "by the time I got there, the artists didn't like to sit around the gallery. They'd have an opening and lots of people would come […] and after that, you wouldn't see anybody again until the next opening."

Other galleries began to appear or to grow more appealing for artists who wanted to display and sell their work rather than simply put on an opening-night party. East and West was located across the street from the 6 Gallery and had opened shortly after, in early 1956. Being located so close to one another, they would hold joint openings to share publicity. Its founder, Ethel Gechtoff, knew ahead of time that the 6 was closing and suggested to Dimitri Grachis, a young artist who had shown at and hung around the 6, that he open his own place, and so he

The End of the 6

founded Spatsa around the time that the 6 Gallery closed. "At the end," he said, "the Six was never open. You had to get the key from Mrs. Gechtoff to get in. I thought that if I could keep a gallery open all the time, more people would come out to see it." He said that "it definitely was an extension of the Six," but his gallery was not a cooperative and it did not have poetry readings. It was more of a typical art gallery and was more professionally run. "The thing was to have regular hours and stick to them," he said. "The Six was like a festival of artists. They had all these great ideas and nobody really saw them except other artists and their friends." Musician, art curator, and TV producer Jim Neuman opened Dilexi a few months after the 6 Gallery closed. It also emphasized a mixture of artistic forms but it offered "a commercial space [...] a fabulous place to show" where paintings sold for around $500, an amount that dwarfed anything sold at the 6 Gallery. Then Batman Gallery, another iconic but short-lived venture that mixed poetry, drama, and the visual arts, opened in 1960. These were all located within a short walk from 3119 Fillmore and were very much inspired by the art galleries that had existed there.

By 1957, Wally Hedrick had moved on to other projects and Manuel Neri had taken over as the director of the 6 Gallery. He had done several shows there in 1956 and 1957 and eventually took the reins. His approach to art sounds rather like Kerouac's approach to writing, which had of course been passed along to Ginsberg. Neri believed that creation was about "immediacy. You'd jump into something without stopping to think, just to see what the results would be." As director of the 6, he pushed his peers to do the same, encouraging artists to paint their works the night before a show. Neri himself would sometimes be seen finishing a painting as the gallery opened and his canvases would remain wet throughout the opening night.

Toward the end of 1957, the whole scene was changing. The old faces had vanished and new ones appeared. Not only had most of the founders left the 6 Gallery, and even the city, but four of the five poets who had read in October 1955 had departed San Francisco.

Aftermath

Whalen had left the city earlier in the year when the Milvia cottage he took over from Ginsberg was razed, and Kerouac was back East, beginning to settle down to life with his mother. Only McClure was left of the five original poets, and he had been the one who refused to be photographed with the others, initially reluctant to be seen as a Beat poet. It was still a creative environment, and with the arrival of Bruce Conner and Wallace Berman, as well as the Black Mountain poets, the Beat-bohemian world got an infusion of new creative energy, but even so the milieu that had spawned the 6 Gallery was fading into memory. The new scene was darker in part due to the more cynical attitude of the Los Angeles artists who migrated north, while pot and peyote were replaced by harder drugs such as heroin.

The San Francisco art scene had arguably attained its unusual level of vibrance and innovation because of the apparent unlikelihood of success. The seemingly provincial, detached world of the Bay Area allowed artists to create for the sake of pure expression. They made art for themselves and for their peers and gave little thought to selling it or cozying up to gallery owners in the hopes of an exhibition. Yet the success they did achieve ironically helped change all that. Once upon a time, poets would go to Rexroth's house to share their latest work or read poems in smoky cafés, whilst artists would gather to show their efforts in places like King Ubu and the 6 Gallery. Following the 6 Gallery reading, however, and the meteoric rise of Allen Ginsberg, this no longer seemed enough. Perhaps there were other contributing factors, but even by 1957 these artists wanted more. Poets wanted to read before larger audiences and painters no longer wanted dank little galleries where their work would sell for barely more than the cost of a canvas. As other venues opened with more resources, larger numbers of visitors, and the possibility of more profitable sales, exhibiting at the 6 Gallery seemed less appealing.

The 6 Gallery finally closed on December 1, 1957. Unsurprisingly, this is also shrouded in myth and nonsense. Some books state that the closing party featured a reading by Ginsberg, Kerouac, and other Beat poets, during which

The End of the 6

a piano was smashed to bits with axes, a sledgehammer, and a blowtorch, and that Bob Kaufman spiked the punch with Benzedrine. The event was not wholly imagined but as with so much in Beat history it seems the people who have written about it felt at liberty to bring together multiple stories and then invent elements to make it coherent, with each successive account adding a new layer of bullshit upon the previous one so that ultimately the story bears only a passing resemblance to the original truth.

There was in fact a poetry reading at which a piano was destroyed but this happened on November 8 and no Beat poets were present (at least no one we would today classify as Beat). The day after the event, Peter Forakis explained that the 6 Gallery had been turned over to a group of poets that wanted to hold a reading. Three poets called Jamie Perpinan, James Dunne, and Chester Hardy Jr read their work before pianist Edward Silverstone Taylor attacked the gallery's forty-year-old piano with an axe. A news report from a week later said that he had "expressed his violent disinterest in any combination of poetry and jazz." The audience of about one hundred and fifty were inspired by this performance art and began smashing the gallery's chairs.[21] Some passing teenage boys were attracted by the commotion and came in to help, then ripped artworks from the wall and destroyed them.

Starting on November 10, the 6 Gallery held a group show entitled "Drawings by Local Artists." It featured a number of regulars, including Bruce Conner, Julius Wasserstein, Manuel Neri, Fred Martin, and Joan Brown. It would be the last show. On December 1, gallery secretary Beverly Pabst sent out a letter announcing its closure:

> Dear Six Gallery members:
> I am very sorry to have to tell you that as of December 1st the Six Gallery is permanently closed. Towards the last of November our

---

21   Note that the figure given is the same as the average of the audience size given for the October 7, 1955, reading. This tells us that the gallery could hold at least that number of people, which suggests that lower estimates for the supposedly packed 1955 reading are unlikely.

landlord, Art Barney, informed us that he wanted to take over the gallery space for his own use. During the last four years the gallery has been a very valuable impetus to many individuals and groups concerned not only with painting, but with music, dance, experimental photography and sound, and poetry. It has afforded all of us the space and freedom to experiment not usually offered by other galleries or the museums. As such the gallery has always been open to resounding defeats as well as moments of excitement and inspiration. Both kinds of experience were valuable to the gallery, or for that matter to any individual or group of individuals vitally concerned with creative activity and human growth. Because the gallery was founded and maintained to perpetuate and encourage experimentation, and because it was therefore prone to both failure and success, it was considered by some to be a very risky venture; the established institutions offer a much more appealing security. Support, moral or financial, was hard to come by at times. I personally would like to thank everyone who in any way felt the gallery important enough to themselves, to other artists, and to the community to help the gallery with their time, money or any other kind of support or help. Without this help the gallery would have remained merely an idea.

The 6 Gallery was the sort of venture tried a thousand times throughout the world and these efforts seldom have had much impact except in the lives of a few optimistic artists, but the 6 Gallery was different. Despite never making much money or attracting national attention, it was home to a number of artists who went on to become successful, including its founders. The 6 Gallery was a perfect example of the creative atmosphere of San Francisco in the fifties—a place of tremendous excitement, which remains in popular memory an almost utopian space that produced some of the most important art and fashion of the twentieth century and was responsible for the development of many of that century's progressive ideals. It was a product of its era but it also helped to shape that era and had an almost absurdly outsized influence on subsequent ones. It came quietly into existence, flew below the radar, and then slipped out of existence just three years later. Yet the environment it fostered and was fostered by, and the social and creative connections it allowed, helped the likes of Jay DeFeo and Wally Hedrick to become artists worthy of national attention. Inspired by King Ubu, the 6 Gallery itself became an inspiration to others including the aforementioned Spatsa and Dilexi, and later the Batman Gallery.

The 6 Gallery is mostly remembered for launching the careers of several poets, which is an odd accolade for an art gallery, but as we have seen the 6 was always interested in *the arts* rather than just *art*. When it opened in 1954, Allen Ginsberg was an unknown poet, but when it closed in 1957, he was a household name, the author of the most celebrated poetry collection in recent memory, and that fame stemmed from the poem he first read on the little dais at the back of the oddly shaped building. "Howl" changed American literature and indeed has influenced poets in dozens of countries around the world. Ginsberg sits alongside Whitman, Eliot, and Poe as among the most important American poets, and he is perhaps more imitated than any of them. There is surely no line in all of American literature more iconic, more plagiarized, or more parodied than the words he first uttered at 3119 Fillmore Street: *I saw the best minds of my generation destroyed by madness...*

In December 1957, as the gallery shut its doors, Ginsberg had not just left San Francisco but had fled the United States and was living in the Beat Hotel in Paris' *Quartier latin*. He missed the fallout from his poetic efforts, temporarily avoiding the trap of fame. He had arrived in San Francisco, borrowed from its creative energy to produce a masterpiece, and then skipped out just before that masterpiece brought down upon the city the sort of attention that would doom it, bringing to an end a very special era.

Aftermath

As is so often the case, the scene was co-opted. Mainstream culture quickly created the image of the lazy beatnik and soon North Beach was teeming with tour buses promising a glimpse of real live poets in action. To quote Jack Goodwin one last time: "Suddenly everyone was a poet." Wally Hedrick took a job beating bongos in a café window. Others painted tourists' portraits. But the scene was basically over, a victim of its own success and proof as ever that true art and innovation will eventually be commodified. Subcultures of real merit will eventually attract the masses, cease to be subcultures, and lose precisely what made them appealing in the first place. Some of the true bohemians stayed on and others left, but the little world they had created no longer existed. Bruce Nixon, in *Beat Galleries and Beyond*, wrote:

> Bay Area bohemia [...] suddenly found itself in a national spotlight; people who had lived and worked and partied together, merrily undisturbed in their pursuit of rebellion, were now the subjects of local Grey Line tours. The scene was devastated by this unexpected and often unwelcome tidal wave of publicity.

Thankfully, the tour buses mostly took the gawking squares around North Beach, leaving the Fillmore-Union area to the real artists, but that wouldn't last long either. Mainstream culture has more than one way of crushing dissent, and soon the authorities began to crack down on the bohemian artists whose way of life was at odds with American social norms. Both The Place and the Co-Existence Bagel Shop closed in 1960, their owners tired of being hassled by cops and generally depressed by the end of the scene. A few years later, the hippies would start a new community in the Haight-Asbury district. They would also have an outsized influence on the culture, but their scene would suffer a similar fate. By 1971, Hunter S. Thompson had already written a eulogy for that particular movement:

The End of the 6

> San Francisco in the middle sixties was a very special time and place to be a part of. Maybe it *meant something*. Maybe not, in the long run ... but no explanation, no mix of words or music or memories can touch that sense of knowing that you were there and alive in that corner of time and the world. Whatever it meant....
>
> [...] You could strike sparks anywhere. There was a fantastic universal sense that whatever we were doing was *right*, that we were winning....
>
> And that, I think, was the handle—that sense of inevitable victory over the forces of Old and Evil. Not in any mean or military sense; we didn't need that. Our energy would simply *prevail*. There was no point in fighting—on our side or theirs. We had all the momentum; we were riding the crest of a high and beautiful wave....
>
> So now, less than five years later, you can go up on a steep hill in Las Vegas and look West, and with the right kind of eyes you can almost *see* the high-water mark—that place where the wave finally broke and rolled back.

Thompson had been a latecomer to San Francisco, arriving about ten years after the 6 Gallery opened, but he was there for the peak of the hippie movement and got out before it too was commodified. In his short time there, he witnessed the special atmosphere of creativity and anti-authoritarianism that gave him hope and which he saw transforming briefly into a nationwide movement before it was forever stamped out, in his mind resulting in "the Death of the American Dream." Local poets and painters may well have pointed out that the city's artistic peak had come well before the mid-sixties, and it is hard to disagree with Ferlinghetti's rather brutal assessment of the era as "a nonliterate age" dominated by a "childlike cult" that failed to produce "important writers." However, up until around 1967 or '68, San Francisco continued to possess an atmosphere unusually conducive to creation and remained a place where people could live lifestyles at odds with national norms. It also of course fostered the new art form of rock music, which arguably drew attention from other forms. Ferlinghetti also overlooked a few writers, such as Ken Kesey and Richard Brautigan, both of whom were drawn to the Bay Area as one of the few places in the United States at that time where outsider artists could live comfortably.

As is the case in many a city, it was gentrification that drove out the artists and put an end to the vibrant culture of the Fillmore-Union. In 1956, a program of urban renewal began that many saw and continue to see as racist in its origins. But whether due to racism or greed, or born of a genuine interest in improving living conditions, it resulted in the familiar pattern of the poor being replaced by the rich, with an original culture displaced and dispersed, replaced by the soulless and the uniform.

In spite of numerous buildings in the area having been torn down, the one then known as 3119 Fillmore still stands today. It seems to have been empty for several years after the 6 Gallery closed its doors, with the gallery still listed in phone directories as late as 1959. The contact name was Peter Forakis (misspelled in various ways). Forakis had been a supporter of the gallery since before it opened in 1954 and helped out in various ways during its short existence. The space was taken over in the late sixties by Moby Dick's Carpentry Service, then for most of the seventies it was the quirky Museum Shop, which tended to be listed as an art gallery when it advertised in local newspapers. It sold a range of artwork, trinkets, handicrafts, maps, and allegedly ancient objects. It was such an unusual shop that guidebooks recommended tourists add it to their itinerary, with one in 1984 describing it thusly:

> Even if you have no intention of buying, this intriguing locale is worth a browse-through. You're bound to find pre-Columbian pillows handwoven in Peru, old Peking glass beads, spectacular masks

The End of the 6

from West Africa, Moroccan rugs, batik scarves from India, Haitian voodoo crafts, Mexican ceramics and Coptic crosses.

Its focus seemed to change from year to year and in 1979 it hosted a "multi-media show by Bay Area artists," which sounds rather appropriate given the building's history.

In the middle of the 1980s, Abdul Ibrahimi, fleeing Afghanistan after the Soviet invasion, started Silkroute International, a shop selling carpets and rugs from all along the old Silk Road. He took over the property and found it to be a perfect building for a rug emporium, its odd length and shape allowing plenty of display space. One visitor in the 1990s reported that the building was still dimly lit, with bare rafters, just as it had been in 1955. He even reported that the stage remained in place at the back of the shop. Ibrahimi operated out of the 3119 address for twenty-five years, selling for more than $1.2 million in 2004. Reverting back to its earlier address of 3115 Fillmore, the space became Liv Furniture, then Kasa Indian Restaurant, and as of 2025 it is occupied by an up-market eatery called Tacko, where two tacos and two beers would cost you the same as the 6 Gallery paid for a month's rent back in 1955.

Myth and Legacy

In writing this book, I have done my best to present a thorough and accurate history of the 6 Gallery reading. To do this as effectively as possible, I began the story long before the reading by tracing the origins of the building in which it took place and showing why San Francisco provided the right audience for the groundbreaking poetry that was read on October 7, 1955. In order to effectively explain the success of that poetry and why it proved so important, I have discussed events stretching from 1846 to 1958. It has been a long tale and establishing even the most basic of facts has been a huge challenge for various reasons.

As I said at the start of this book, it is strange that this is the case, for the reading happened within living memory. As I write these words, one of the poets who read that night, one of the founders of the gallery, and at least one of the audience members are still alive. The mid-fifties may seem like ancient history to some people but it was well within the modern era and various means of recording existed. We have photos, video, and audio records of other important events from that period. Of course, there are a great many paper records that survive, and letters, journals, and news reports from the mid-fifties can be found with a bit of effort.[22] However, in spite of all that no one has ever been able to say honestly and accurately what happened that night, why it happened, or what had happened in that building before the reading took place. Even the events immediately after it are somewhat unclear despite the easily available letters and journals of Ginsberg, Snyder, and others.

---

22   A little over a decade ago, for example, the Joan Anderson letter—the Holy Grail of Beat artifacts, believed lost for more than a half century—was discovered in a stack of old letters.

Aftermath

Not only did the 6 Gallery reading occur within living memory and within an era when the recording and sharing of information was relatively easy, but it was also an event of extraordinary importance. The first thing I did when researching this book was read all prior accounts, and that involved finding several hundred books because the 6 Gallery reading was famous enough to have been mentioned that many times. I doubt any poetry reading in history has been considered so important, which makes it even stranger that we knew so little about it. This has led to a strange situation wherein no one really knew anything about the reading, yet everyone realized that they needed to write *something* about it. In this final chapter of the book, I will briefly outline the process by which the 6 Gallery reading was historicized. This should serve two purposes. Firstly, I believe it is important to question the extent to which the reading may have been a deliberate creation of Allen Ginsberg and Jack Kerouac, two young writers eager to achieve literary immortality not only through the creation of original works but through their association with a wider movement. I do not mean to say that it never happened or that they completely exaggerated it out of all proportion, but rather we ought to examine the extent to which they took a single event and designated it one of the most important literary events of the century. Secondly, understanding how and why the 6 Gallery reading came to enter the historical record can partially explain why there is so much myth surrounding the event.

More than almost anyone else, Ginsberg was responsible for the historicization of the Beat Generation because he was a tireless campaigner for his own writing and the writing of his friends. Most people familiar with the Beat Generation are aware that he acted as a literary agent for Burroughs and Kerouac and that he actively promoted the work of Corso, Snyder, Whalen, and others whom he liked. However, less has been said about his later role in writing Beat history. Even after he and his peers had achieved much success, he continued to speak publicly of the Beat group, partly to counter what he saw as inaccurate media representation and partly to draw the attention of the academy. He made himself available to scholars, historians, and journalists who were interested in the Beat Generation, and by giving them his memories and opinions, and sometimes access to his personal documents, he was able to exert a tremendous influence over the process of writing the Beats into literary history. Naturally, this meant Ginsberg had a substantial role in positioning the 6 Gallery reading as a foundational moment in Beat history and, given all the myth that surrounds it, it is important to investigate the extent to which he created the idea of the 6 Gallery reading as the beginning of the Beat phenomenon.

Particularly in those early years of fame, when he was eager to raise his own profile, and to elevate the stature of his friends and of poetry in general, Ginsberg made efforts to create a coherent and appealing narrative that included those tantalizing, fortuitous, auspicious moments that elevate an artistic movement above mere value judgments and create a sense of history that lends it additional credibility. These include the early antics and late-night discussions of the Columbia circle, with emphasis placed on their hip literary influences; their travels and interior exploration; dramatic events such as violent deaths and incarcerations; accounts of unusual approaches to literary composition, including the early drafts of *On the Road*, "Howl," and *Naked Lunch*; visions and other mystical phenomena; and countless other unusual, coincidental, or consequential events. Again, I do not wish to suggest that most of Beat history was invented or exaggerated beyond reason, but rather that Ginsberg—the primary source for most of this history—imbued certain events with significance through repeated acknowledgement of their existence, and in doing so created a sort of mythology that fed into the generation he portrayed so dramatically in "Howl." These events took on legendary significance, becoming almost as well-known as the literary works created by the people involved.

In terms of the 6 Gallery reading, we have by now seen that there were multiple sources but that not many of them were very reliable. The most frequently cited ones are Kerouac's account in *The Dharma Bums*, which is of course a novel; Ginsberg's account in a Dutch literary journal, which was a quite shameless exercise in self-promotion; and a number of interviews and memoirs mostly coming

Aftermath

in the seventies and eighties, which all suffer from big mistakes due to the flaws of human memory and ego. It is important that Ginsberg and Kerouac's accounts were the first to reach the public and it is even more important to note that almost all other accounts came after a gap of more than fifteen years, meaning that the vast bulk of what we really know of the 6 Gallery reading is drawn from fiction, self-promotion, and poor memory. Understanding all this helps us to know how to approach these sources, so let's now look more closely at how the 6 Gallery reading entered the historical record.

As I have noted, there are a handful of early accounts of the 6 Gallery that attest to its power and impact, so we can say with certainty that it was an event of at least some importance and that it had a degree of local influence, either beginning the San Francisco Renaissance or triggering a series of events that led to it. What is suspicious, though, is how little it was mentioned in contemporary documents. Even after an exhaustive search of countless archives, I found hardly any reference to it aside from a handful of enthusiastic letters in the days immediately following the reading. It certainly seems to have caused Ferlinghetti to move forward with his plans to release a book version of "Howl," and may have pushed Witt-Diamant to offer Poetry Center reading slots to some of the poets, including Ginsberg; however, as we have seen, Ferlinghetti had already agreed to this and Rexroth had connived for Snyder to be offered a reading. Coupled with the unlikeliness of the telegram ever having been sent, it does seem then that the reading may not have had the impact we like to think of it having. It is truly surprising that the journals and letters of certain people (especially Ginsberg, Snyder, and Kerouac) were not filled with details of this most stunning of triumphs, particularly given that these young men loved to document the minutiae of their lives and to describe with nearly religious fervor the most exhilarating of their experiences.

Certainly, there are explanations for this. For one thing, we know that the participants were so busy writing poems and goofing around with booze and pot and sex that their journals were largely forgotten. We know too

Myth and Legacy

that certain key documents were sadly destroyed a few years later, which robs us of that valuable insight, leaving us only with teasing replies from the recipients of those letters. Yet more documents have probably been lost to time. Surely at least a few of the hundred-plus audience members wrote something of it and then, over the next decades, lost or forgot those notebooks or letters. Still, it is odd that so little exists and this is worth exploring further if we are to be as honest as possible in discussing this event.

By far the hardest part of this story to explain is the fact that Ginsberg did not write about the reading in the days, weeks, or months following it. Given that it supposedly changed his life and set him on course for being the world-famous poet he had always wanted to become, you would expect journal entries and letters and poems. After all, that was how he responded to most events of far less significance. He mentioned the reading a few times in letters beforehand but said nothing in his journals or letters from after the event. This supports the theory that it was a minor occurrence that he later rewrote as part of his personal mythology. I should note that this is in keeping with a view proposed by Stevan M. Weine, who in the recently published *Best Minds: How Allen Ginsberg Made Revolutionary Poetry from Madness* claimed that Ginsberg only spoke of his 1948 vision of Blake after 1958, suggesting that he essentially invented it, and that he did so because it gave him more legitimacy as a poet and countercultural ambassador. Weine noted that Ginsberg spoke often of a vision (using language such as "Vision of Eternity") and that sometimes he did mention it in relation to Blake but that he never publicly said until 1958 that he had heard Blake's voice, and that by this point Ginsberg was fully in the role of Beat spokesperson and making a concerted effort to position himself and his peers as the poet heroes of their day replete with underground credentials that included the mystical and the mad. Weine suggests that Ginsberg did not deliberately distort his personal history but rather came to genuinely believe this vision had occurred.

Considering this, it is possible that Ginsberg only began to push the 6 Gallery reading into the position of

Beat creation myth in late 1957, around the time Weine says he started speaking of a vision of Blake. It was only then—two years after the fact—that he first wrote about the reading. He did so in a short essay entitled "The Literary Revolution in America" whilst he was on a European trip with Corso and Orlovsky. The article was credited to Corso until Ginsberg admitted partial authorship in 1986, and that is likely because Ginsberg wrote it to promote himself and did not want to have "Allen Ginsberg" as a byline for an article that included the line, "The most brilliant shock of the evening was the declamation of the now-famous rhapsody, *Howl*, by Allen Ginsberg." The article points to the 6 Gallery reading as the event that launched both the Beat movement and the San Francisco Renaissance, and this part at least was written by Allen Ginsberg. Although it is credited to Corso and written in the third person, it is very clearly in Ginsberg's voice and presents his opinions. It also provides facts that only Ginsberg knew, so I feel confident in calling this section of it Ginsberg's work even if the rest of the article was more collaborative.

It is unclear when exactly Ginsberg and Corso wrote "The Literary Revolution in America" but it was published in November 1957 in a Dutch journal called *Litterair Paspoort*.[23] The two men were in Amsterdam for parts of September and October of that year, and the essay refers to the Little Rock incident in early September of that year, so it was likely written in September or October. The section of the article that focused on the 6 Gallery reading is clearly intended to convince readers of the hip, bohemian, anti-establishment nature of the event. It begins by highlighting such elements: it was "a moment of drunken enthusiasm" and intended to "defy the system of academic poetry"; it was "free" and "in the Negro section of San Francisco." It goes on to emphasize the poets' more bohemian qualities, such as their life experiences, mystical visions, and esoteric interests, and it repeatedly mentions

---

23   Founded in 1946, this was an ambitious journal that lasted for almost three decades. It celebrated its 100th issue a year prior to Ginsberg and Corso's article. It was written in Dutch but included much French poetry and reviews of foreign literature.

their youth. Oddly, Ginsberg was dismissive of the gallery itself, not bothering to mention its name and calling it "a run down second rate experimental art gallery." He attempted to present the poets as inexperienced, offbeat, and unconventional, yet at the same time serious and intellectual. He placed them in the lineage of Whitman and as the American answer to Rimbaud, Artaud, and Genet. He wrote that "the poets were left with the realization that they were fated to make a permanent change in the literary firmament of the States."

Ginsberg briefly outlined the event, focusing on his own effort as "[t]he most brilliant shock of the evening" and then explaining it carefully, again positioning himself as the next Walt Whitman and also the new Hart Crane. He went on to credit Kerouac as "the most celebrated novelist in America" (*On the Road* having been released just two months prior to the publication of this article) and lauded William Carlos Williams, Lawrence Ferlinghetti, and William S. Burroughs. Altogether, it was a quite shameless attempt at self-promotion but it was very much in line with Ginsberg's efforts at that time. In February 1957, he had given a joint interview to the *Village Voice* with Corso and Kerouac in which they attempted to play up their Zen-lunatic credentials, goofing around and saying strange and provocative things to stir up interest. Ginsberg flat-out lied when he told readers he "was thrown into jail for vagrancy the first week [he was in San Francisco]" and that "[t]he cops apologized after the poetry readings." Corso went on to say that the 6 Gallery reading had been a "series of readings in a big art gallery" and that he had participated, when in fact he had not arrived in San Francisco until many months later.[24] Obviously, then, they were more interested in presenting an image than providing a factual account.

The *Litterair Paspoort* article was an odd and egotistical piece of writing. Published in English in a Dutch journal, it helped to spread word of the Beat

---

24   I wonder if perhaps the interviewer had confused statements made by Corso and Ginsberg, crediting the former. Corso was of course not at the original reading and never did perform there.

movement in Europe but it would have had little impact back in the United States, where public awareness of the Beat Generation was growing at an astounding rate but was mostly filtered through mainstream media accounts that misrepresented them in order to provide a more entertaining viewpoint. This would drastically worsen with the beatnik phenomenon of the next few years, at which point newspapers would attempt to tie beatniks to various murders and would invent bizarre stories about the real Beat writers, while TV and movie producers began pushing the beatnik stereotype, with Bob Denver's Maynard G. Krebs character standing as the most memorable of these. The Beats, when they consented to media interviews, did their best to portray themselves as different from the criminal hoodlums and poseurs. They tried to present themselves as serious artists, but then sometimes they undermined that same message with the sort of antics as displayed in the aforementioned interview.

Importantly, although its impact was limited, Ginsberg's Dutch article was his first effort to position the 6 Gallery reading as the birth of the Beat movement, or at least the beginning of its sudden ascent. He would refer often to it in later years but the fact that he had not done so prior to this suggests that perhaps it was a deliberate effort at contextualizing the literary movement for which he was now a spokesman. Preston Whaley, in *Blows Like a Horn*, suggested that "Kerouac may have read the article and used it as a source for his account of 6 readings." This may initially seem plausible, for Kerouac wrote the first draft of *The Dharma Bums* between November 26 and December 7, 1957, but there is no evidence that he read Ginsberg's article and in fact it seems very unlikely. Their correspondence around this time does not mention it and Kerouac's account goes into much more detail, so even if he was inspired in some way by Ginsberg finally writing about the 6 Gallery reading, Kerouac almost certainly did not draw upon his version.

Kerouac's account of that night, which again I have cited many times in this book, can be found in the second chapter of his 1958 novel, *The Dharma Bums*. It is sometimes suggested that it was a major part of the book or that it comprised the whole of that chapter but in fact it makes up slightly more than three pages. In the absence of detailed contemporary accounts of the 6 Gallery reading, most scholars and biographers have relied heavily on his depiction of it, with almost all of them taking his description at face value. Whilst this is obviously problematic, it is somewhat understandable because Kerouac famously recorded his own life in his novels, which are generally considered to be "thinly veiled" works of autobiography. Yet relying upon his version of events presupposes two things: firstly, that he intended to tell the whole truth; and secondly, that he had a good enough memory to accomplish this two years after the fact.

Few doubt the power of Kerouac's memory—indeed, he was sometimes referred to as "Memory Babe" for his astonishing powers of recall—but can we trust what he said about the 6 Gallery reading? I have mentioned one instance from his account of that night that was in fact borrowed from a later event, but it was a very minor thing taking place in the restaurant after the reading. He merely brought an event forward in time to include it because it helped him to better explain Snyder's character. However, Snyder has frequently remarked that Kerouac's depiction of him as Japhy Ryder was largely fictionalized and has warned readers not to take it as the literal truth. To pick but one example, he said in 2011, "Japhy Ryder is not me. The novel is fiction. It's not journalism." Ginsberg, too, has noted that Kerouac sometimes gave the impression of writing truth but in fact engaged in fiction. He said:

> Kerouac's characters are modeled on real people, but Kerouac is a novelist and a fiction maker, so the anecdotes are embellished and exaggerated for dramatic charm. What he did was fictionalize people, or fictionalize reality, so that there's not a one-to-one correlation. The quotations are invented by Kerouac, paraphrasing or imitating the rhythms or diction of the people talking, sometimes a little crudely and sometimes very, very wittily. [...] For

the most part, while he was typing, he had to make up speeches that sounded like the people or as he remembered it sounding. He took from real characters but he's fictionalizing them. Biographers tend to assume that the incidents and speeches are one-to-one reality and construct biographies out of his novels. They're all awry, the facts are not accurate, because he's invented scenes and invented confrontations and exciting conversations.

Kerouac's biographer, Gerald Nicosia, went further, saying that "even by 1956 he was a highly unreliable reporter of his own life, becoming unable to distinguish between fact and fancy."

So, does this negate his account of the 6 Gallery? I do not think so. For one thing, many people, including Snyder and Ginsberg, have acknowledged that although Kerouac fictionalized, he was excellent at recalling details, capturing people's characters and speech patterns, and generally perceiving and recording the world around him. In other words, if he wanted to do so, he could have provided a very accurate account of the reading even if he perhaps placed more importance on himself than others or chose to elevate Snyder's stature, making him the archetype of fifties cool. Philip Whalen, speaking in 1971, said that Kerouac had selected scenes and parts of people's characters very carefully and that although the book was not factually true, it was "fairly accurate." He explained, quite rightly, that Kerouac could not have made a novel out of an exact reproduction of events, but that his method of writing captured scenes and people quite faithfully in spite of his being very selective. Snyder called the novel a "sloppy [...] really second-rate book" but never denied the accuracy of Kerouac's depiction of the 6 Gallery reading, only really taking issue with how Kerouac made him into a "cartoonish" character. Echoing Whalen's comment above, Snyder said for example of *The Dharma Bums* depiction of his mountain-climbing trip with Kerouac: "it's pretty accurate," with the only real "novelistic" exaggeration being his own fear of the mountain. "Jack always does that. [...] That's the way he makes good stories."

Indeed, if one compares Kerouac's accounts with those given by others, or accounts otherwise possible to verify, one indeed sees that he has condensed or highlighted parts of his story for dramatic or illustrative effect. For example, he says in chapter two that Ray Smith (Kerouac) first saw Japhy Ryder (Snyder) on the street and that he was on the way to the 6 Gallery reading. In fact, he most likely did see Snyder on the street but their meeting seems to have been pre-arranged and it took place a few weeks before. Kerouac's book was a novel and for storytelling purposes, he compressed events so that the narrative flowed more effectively.

Most importantly, Kerouac's account has never been questioned by any of the other participants. Whilst it is certainly possible that they read his book and perhaps internalized it, later repeating his version as a sort of implanted memory, clearly his account was close enough to reality that they could not distinguish even a few years after the fact. Of all the people who were present that night and later read Kerouac's account of it, none publicly questioned his version. Also, there was little in his recounting of the reading that seems unrealistic. Whereas Ginsberg wanted to show himself and his peers as mad poet geniuses changing the world, Kerouac simply depicted a fun night. Although its inclusion in his book obviously positions the reading as being of importance, Kerouac does not exaggerate it in any obvious way. In fact, the opposite is true: He is rather critical of all the poets except for Snyder. Ginsberg heaped praise on his fellow poets and Kerouac played down their achievements. Thus, whilst one should not rely entirely on Kerouac's account, when held alongside other accounts it seems as valid as any journal or letter, and possibly more reliable than an interview answer given many years after the fact.

By the time *The Dharma Bums* was published in late 1958, there had been two written accounts of the 6 Gallery reading, the first of which suggested it was part of a "revolution" and the latter called it the start of a "renaissance." Now immortalized in a popular novel, released at the height of Beat and beatnik hysteria, it seemed to become an accepted part of the Beat origin story. But this raises another problem, which is that the 6 Gallery reading is curiously absent from texts related to the Beat writers for the next fifteen years, after which it was constantly mentioned as part of the history of the movement.

In 1957, for example, Kenneth Rexroth wrote "Disengagement: The Art of the Beat Generation" for *New World Writing*, a major avant-garde publication. As one would expect from him, it was long-winded, filled with bragging (he name-drops the famous people he knew and flat-out says "I am one of the country's most successful poets"), and was written both as a defense of the Beat Generation and as a means of showing how hip and knowledgeable its author was. Rexroth talked about jazz and literature, arguing that the best writing comes from the "disaffiliated." He was keen to dispel the idea that subversive and exciting literature had died in the 1920s and explained that it was very much alive and well in the 1950s, particularly in San Francisco, and that this was evidenced in the assortment of little publications and poetry readings found there. Interestingly, although it was framed as a defense of the Beats, he only briefly mentioned Kerouac[25] and provided one line about Ginsberg, Ferlinghetti, and Snyder toward the end of his essay. Here, he simply admitted that their reputations were sort of deserved. Given that it was a prestigious publication, this meant a certain degree of validation but one feels Rexroth had perhaps seized the opportunity to write about literature and show himself to be a hip and erudite figure, and that he had mentioned the Beats only as an afterthought. Yet I

---

25 Rexroth repeatedly revised and re-published his essay, later removing the one mildly flattering reference to Kerouac and replacing it with a scathing one. After reading the first version, in which he is mentioned favorably, Kerouac wrote to Ginsberg to complain about "that dumb Rexroth article." His opinion of Kerouac seemed to worsen with each passing year, and some of his reviews of Kerouac's books are embarrassing hatchet jobs. Ginsberg wrote him in 1959 to beg for reason after Rexroth called *Mexico City Blues* an "evil parody" of Buddhism.

note this here because while he wrote about the explosion of interest in poetry in the Bay Area and about the Poetry Center and the proliferation of poetry readings, he did so without ever mentioning the 6 Gallery reading, the event that had supposedly kick-started it all. He also failed to make reference to it in his introduction to *Evergreen Review #2* that same year even though he fawned over Ginsberg and Lamantia and spoke of the culture of poetry in the city.

Looking back, this seems incredibly odd. It is not as though Rexroth was unaware of the event or its significance. He had been there, after all, and he had even mentioned it in a letter just a few days later, testifying to its importance. So why did he not write about it in "Disengagement"? The event perfectly fit the impression he wanted to give—that San Francisco was a hip town with wild poetry readings in underground art galleries and that he was at the center of it all. When this essay was collected in the landmark *A Casebook on the Beat* in 1961, a collection of various early writings about the Beat movement, edited by Thomas Parkinson, who had organized the repeat performance in Berkeley in March 1956, there was not a single reference to the 6 Gallery reading. Even Ginsberg's own account of writing and recording "Howl" omitted it. In fact, in almost every book and essay about the Beats between 1958 and 1971, this supposedly integral part of history is conspicuously absent.[26] There were a few references to it in an article about a San Francisco reading in 1968, Jack Goodwin briefly referred to it in an essay published that same year, Ginsberg commented briefly on it in Jane Kramer's *Allen Ginsberg in America* in 1969, but nothing else. Even the texts one would assume would have discussed it at length fail to mention it.

In 1971, two years after Jack Kerouac's death,

---

26   In Seymour Krim's 1960 collection *The Beats*, there is arguably one veiled reference to it in a short fiction piece by Herbert Gold but to say that it really refers to the 6 Gallery reading requires quite a leap of imagination. He simply alludes to a San Francisco poetry reading and a poet screaming "C____ S_____!" which one assumes refers to "Howl." [p.155] However, there are other interpretations and it is far from a clear reference to the 6 Gallery reading.

newspapers began noting that the Beat Generation and the San Francisco Renaissance had come out of the famed 6 Gallery reading of 1955, with one article about Michael McClure stating that it "later became recognized as a historical literary occasion," but it is odd that these same newspapers had failed to mention that event in the sixteen years since it occurred. Perhaps those reporters had finally picked up copies of *The Dharma Bums* and become curious about this overlooked part of Beat history, but then even the few pioneering Beat scholars seemed to ignore it and as we have seen, Kenneth Rexroth, who considered himself an expert on the subject and uniquely qualified to write about it, had omitted the reading in everything he wrote about the Beats between 1955 and 1971, at which point he suddenly changed his tune:

> As in painting and music the change was in the medium. In fact it was change of medium—poetry as voice not as printing. The climacteric was not the publication of a book, it was the famous Six Gallery reading, the culmination of twenty years of the oral presentation of poetry in San Francisco.

This essay was an incoherent account filled with appalling errors but it is interesting that Rexroth now openly claimed the 6 Gallery reading was a critical moment.

Two years after Rexroth finally made reference to the 6 Gallery reading, Ann Charters published *Kerouac: A Biography*, one of the first major texts on the Beat Generation. Here, she would put the first critical seal of approval on the story, describing the event by drawing from *The Dharma Bums*, as well as interviews with Ginsberg and Snyder (mostly conducted in 1969). As we have seen in earlier chapters, however, this book gave rise to a number of falsehoods about the reading, so although it was the first real acknowledgement of it by a scholar, it began a long series of inaccurate accounts.

In 1978, Barry Gifford and Lawrence Lee put out *Jack's Book: An Oral Biography*. This is particularly interesting for it only adds to the confusion, but it does so in a way that highlights the frailties of memory. From even the briefest look at the testimony provided here, which is given by people who were present at the 6 Gallery reading, it is immediately obvious that none of them could agree on what happened. Ferlinghetti even recalled driving Corso to the 6 Gallery, despite Corso being several thousand miles away and only coming to San Francisco for the first time in the middle of 1956. McClure said he read a letter from Spicer, but in fact that happened at the March 1956 reading. Ginsberg said Rexroth had asked him to organize the reading when in fact letters from 1955 show that Hedrick had asked Ginsberg. The book therefore helped confirm the status of that event but at the same time presented an array of falsehoods about it.

Those two books were groundbreaking texts that helped establish the field of Beat Studies, and so they are rightfully respected for their role in the history of this literary discipline, but unfortunately they have both contributed to major misunderstandings about the 6 Gallery reading. Instead of building upon these works by identifying and correcting their mistakes, biographers and scholars have merely picked their preferred version of events and then created narratives around the parts of the story they found most appealing, often adding dubious details or drawing upon interviews that came later, by which point memories were even more flawed, with subsequent generations of writers then repeating and expanding upon these misinterpretations, leading to a state of utter confusion.

Two books about Kerouac—a man who didn't even read that night—helped cement the 6 Gallery reading in Beat history and began the long process of mythologization. It certainly makes sense that there was a sudden flurry of interest in Kerouac following his death.[27] This is normal with experimental artists. But the question remains: Why was it only then, and in books

---

27   John Suiter notes in *Poets on the Peak* that just one year after Kerouac's death, "pilgrims" began showing up on Desolation Peak. Clearly, his death caused a great deal of interest in his life.

about Kerouac, that the 6 Gallery reading was suddenly of interest? Why had there been silence for so long, and why all of a sudden was there a tremendous focus on one night that was disappearing into the fog of time?

Perhaps it was because by the 1970s the Beat poets were borderline respectable. Prior to this, almost everything written about them (excluding works by Parkinson and Rexroth) had been sensationalist nonsense playing up their drug use and general immorality, or decrying their ungrammatical writings. To look into their origins could have been perceived as giving them undue consideration, which most academics and journalists wanted to avoid. However, with Kerouac and Cassady dead, and the beatniks and hippies consigned to history, the Beat writers and Ginsberg especially were no longer frightening specters for much of the American public. In various ways, they had shaped the culture even for those who knew nothing of them or hated them. From fashion to music to literature to politics, the influence of the Beats was everywhere and even if Ginsberg and Burroughs seemed weird and silly, they were no longer as threatening as they had once been. They were provocative but their influence had been so great that their work was now somewhat tolerable and even critics could acknowledge it having some degree of merit. Most academics still scoffed at them (something that is arguably true even today) but they had gained enough acceptance that they could not be wholly dismissed. Ginsberg was routinely interviewed on mainstream TV and radio, and was invited to lecture or read poetry at prestigious institutions. He was mocked or criticized for his Asian-inspired chanting, radical honesty, advocacy of psychedelics, political views, and graphic accounts of homosexual intercourse, but by this point there was a growing acceptance that the Beat Generation had been a legitimate literary movement rather than a passing social fad. In 1974, he was inducted into the American Academy of Arts and Letters, received the National Book Award for *Fall of America*, and even helped found the Jack Kerouac School of Disembodied Poetics at the newly created Naropa University. The following year, Gary Snyder won the Pulitzer Prize for poetry.

Myth and Legacy

Almost certainly it was due to this newfound acceptance that people began wondering about the origins of the Beat Generation. It was not simply that Ginsberg (or anyone else) decided to write that history, but rather that it was something that needed to be addressed. A scruffy gang of hoodlums didn't need a backstory, but a group of popular and respected writers who had somehow found their way behind the lecterns of leading universities and into the most sacred of academic institutions did, and so people began asking questions.

Ginsberg, in his capacity as preeminent poet and spokesperson, was given a great many opportunities to explain the Beats and not merely in the soundbite form afforded him in the early days. In long interviews and lectures, he was free to recount his and his friends' histories. He began referring to moments in Beat history that we now know so well, repeatedly discussing them in public. He took pains to explain their literary influences—Rimbaud, Blake, Spengler, Whitman, Shakespeare, Céline, Genet, etc.—and their religiosity and the sincerity of their inquiries into Eastern philosophy and art. And at the heart of it was the 6 Gallery reading of 1955, an event that from his perspective, at least in retrospect, was of monumental importance. That's why, in 1976, in another of the earliest critical examinations of the Beat Generation, *Naked Angels*, John Tytell called it "the germinating public seed of the Beat movement." He had spoken at length to Ginsberg during the research for his book.

Ginsberg understood the power of interviews and viewed them not as a burdensome part of fame, but as "his personal art form," according to one of his former assistants. He was generous with his time and exposed his vulnerabilities readily, essentially taking the same approach with interviews that he did with his poems, which is to say that the personal was the universal. Reading newspaper articles and books about the Beats from this period, one senses Ginsberg's guidance, and time and again one checks the sources and finds that Ginsberg was consulted. Even where he is not directly quoted, it feels as though the writers of these works are taking his version of history and repeating it. And why wouldn't they? He was the authority, of course, and he allowed himself to be easily contacted by journalists, scholars, lecturers, critics, and other interested parties, so that he could provide them with answers unfiltered by what he perceived as a biased and irresponsible media. For the most part, Ginsberg was keen to take control and put forth his own history, for he had felt aggrieved about prior depictions of him. In 1977, he explained to Victor Bockris that

> whatever image of myself or Kerouac or Burroughs or Warhol was spread in the sixties began with a smelly inarticulate image passed through the hands of the CIA and transformed to become a sort of bum kick, originally. [...] So the problem then is to make use of the media for transmissions of the spark of intelligence, of awareness and awakedness. The person who does it has to be very straightforward.

But this brings us back around to that question: Was the 6 Gallery reading something Ginsberg elevated in status, essentially creating it as a defining moment in American literature? I don't think that's entirely accurate. Carefully examining his interviews from this era, it seems he was attempting to provide a sincere account of his and his generation's history. This is particularly true for audio recordings, where there was no later revision, no subsequent attempt to persuade the journalist to stress one thing over another, to omit this and add that. We can see him trying very hard to get the details right rather than to exaggerate or invent, and any mistakes seem genuine. He was happy to be corrected and appeared frustrated when he could not give precise dates, names, or addresses. When his memory failed him, he was disappointed. When he got something wrong, it was seldom a case of exaggeration but instead a confusion of names or dates. Moreover, his version of events seems—at least as far as one can tell through a study of other sources—extremely faithful. If he had invented or exaggerated, it would be possible to compare his account against others and label

Myth and Legacy

it improbable, as I have done throughout this book with claims later made by Snyder, Hedrick, and others. In all likelihood, Ginsberg pushed the 6 Gallery reading as a major part of Beat history because it really *was* such an important event, at least in his mind.

As the years went by, and as the 6 Gallery reading disappeared into the rearview mirror of time, it seemed to grow in importance and no doubt that partially came from the allure of the unknown. Who doesn't love a good mystery? For years, no one could even say when it happened and today, whenever they choose to write about the 6 Gallery reading, people just pick from the smorgasbord of available accounts, adding their own assumptions and flourishes. Many decades after the event, Wally Hedrick—whose own accounts of that period could be wildly inaccurate—said, "it's all gotten kind of myth-like. Everybody remembers what they remember," and whilst that is true of many historical events, it is even more of a problem for the 6 Gallery reading. It has certainly made for a tantalizing myth, one that is all the more alluring because it was so recent, so seemingly important, and yet so mysterious. There were no photos, no videos, no audio recordings. Few letters and journals survived. Nothing appeared in the media about it for several years. None of the people who were there could really keep their records straight. For the Beat writers, it was the perfect story. It marked the start of a paradigm shift, the beginning of a countercultural movement that transformed into yet more countercultural movements, impacting almost every facet of life in the Western world for the next half century. Is it a stretch to say that without the 6 Gallery the Beat Generation would not have broken through and become a public sensation? And if that had not happened, would there have been a hippie movement? What of the related battles for civil rights, the environment, gay rights, and gender equality in the 1960s? What of artists like Bob Dylan, who were so inspired by the Beats? What of Mick Jagger and David Bowie and Jerry Garcia, all of whom were influenced by the Beats? And let's not forget it's the *Beatles*, not the *Beetles*. Skip ahead to metal and grunge and hip-hop and we continually see the direct and indirect influence of the Beat writers. They shaped our world.

343

Aftermath

They made it all possible. Had the 6 Gallery reading never happened, would *On the Road* and *Naked Lunch* have had the same impact, with the same knock-on effects? Would we have had the hippies and the punks? What of the freedom of expression we so readily take for granted all these decades after the "Howl" obscenity trial?

I could go on for a dozen more pages asking questions like these and whilst they are impossible to answer with absolute certainty, my head and my heart both tell me that the 6 Gallery reading made it all possible. That night set in motion a chain of events that shaped our world to an almost unimaginable degree and in most cases it seems that it was for the better. And yet for all its importance, for all it was discussed by the various participants and attendees (some of whom are still alive), we know shockingly little. This book has unpicked much of it and dispelled a great many falsehoods, and it has brought us far closer than ever before to understanding that night, but even so there is no way to know for certain—at least to the extent we would like for such a monumental event—what exactly happened on October 7, 1955, at the 6 Gallery.

Appendices

Appendix #1: Correcting Common Errors

When writing this book I had to balance the dual goals of providing a readable narrative and also being as honest as possible about how certain we can really be about what happened before, during, and after the reading. In some places, I mentioned mistakes that others have made, leading to commonly held beliefs about the event. However, I did not want to address these too extensively or else the text would have been even more bogged down by digressions than it already is. For the most part, I was interested in simply presenting what I believe happened based on a common sense reading of the available information, but at the same time I'm aware that many quite influential people writing for reputable publishing houses have made substantial errors in the past which are so commonly believed that perhaps some might have read this book and doubted my account, assuming that I overlooked something simply because I had not addressed it. Thus, in the following pages I will run through some of the most common falsehoods related to the 6 Gallery reading and explain briefly where they came from and why they are incorrect.

Falsehood #1—The 6 Gallery reading happened on October 13.

About half of books that discuss the reading give the wrong date and many, unsure of the real one, just say "early October." The event was definitely scheduled for October 7 and some have tried to justify the very random claim about October 13 as being due to a delay, but several letters written between October 7 and 13 affirm that it happened on the former date. Many who spoke of it, including McClure and Rexroth, failed to get the month or even year correct, so you can see why establishing the exact date was a challenge.

The origins of the October 13 claim are unclear but it seems Dennis McNally's Kerouac biography, *Desolate Angel*, published in 1979, might have been the first to use this date.[1] This was probably a guess because McNally would have known the reading was on a Friday in early October. With a lack of other sources available to verify or dispute his claim, subsequent generations of scholars and biographers merely repeated his assumption, with Ann Charters using it in *Beats & Company* in 1986 and Thomas Merrill claiming the reading had been held on October 13 in his 1988 Ginsberg biography. By the 1990s, almost everyone used October 13, seemingly on the assumption that McNally had some evidence for his guess. By the fiftieth anniversary of the reading (October 7, 2005), the correct date had been fairly well established but major biographies and histories continued to use October 13 for years after that due presumably to relying too heavily on earlier sources.

Jack Goodwin's letter (written October 8) emerged in the early eighties when Goodwin was in contact with Lewis Ellingham in regards the Jack Spicer biography *Poet Be Like God*. It was not mentioned in that book but Rebecca Solnit found the document when researching her 1990 work *Secret Exhibition*. Almost no one else has seen it, so few have been able to confidently say when the reading occurred. They have merely quoted whatever date had been given by earlier biographers, leading to all this confusion.

Falsehood #2—The gallery opening included a toilet in the window beside a draft notice.

This was the sort of controversial statement/artwork that the 6 Gallery artists appreciated, but it did not take place at the 6 Gallery. It's not clear how this became associated with the 6 Gallery, but it is often repeated because it

---

[1] I am grateful to Kurt Hemmer for this insight.

makes for a good story. This event actually occurred at The Place. This was confirmed by John Allen Ryan in his introduction to *Lyrical Vision*.

Falsehood #3—The gallery closing party featured a smashed piano.

This did happen but it was not at the closing party. It was a poetry reading about a month prior to the gallery's closing (when few would have known that closure was imminent). Many accounts say that Kerouac and other Beat poets—including Allen Ginsberg, who was many thousands of miles away at the time—were reading, but in fact it was three local poets who gave a reading and a musician then smashed a piano. This turned into a minor riot when teenage boys passing by came to help rip art from the walls. The event was documented in local newspapers, so it's hard to believe so many people have simply repeated the false version without checking it, and it's disappointing to see how many have simply added random elements. In fact, even otherwise scrupulously researched books such as Rebecca Solnit's *Secret Exhibition* have repeated this story, sometimes expanding the destruction to include blowtorches and sledgehammers.

Falsehood(s) #4—The 6 Gallery reading was attended by Gregory Corso, Lew Welch, and Weldon Kees.

Ferlinghetti misremembered Corso being there but he didn't come to San Francisco until the following year. Welch similarly was not in the city at that time, and Kees had a better excuse: he had died a few months earlier. All of these errors stem from interview responses given many years later. It is understandable that people made these mistakes looking back at an era filled with much revelry but those biographers who have quoted these mistakes ought to have done more fact-checking.

Appendices

Falsehood #5—A letter from Jack Spicer was read aloud at the 6 Gallery.

This is one of the most common mistakes made about the 6 Gallery reading but it is also one of the easiest to disprove. A letter from Jack Spicer was indeed read aloud by Michael McClure but this happened at the March 1956 "repeated performance" in Berkeley. McClure was the one who seems to have started this by conflating the two events. It has been repeated many times probably because Spicer had been an important poet in the area but had gotten stuck on the East Coast and missed the reading. The absence of various San Francisco poets led to the event changing the local poetry scene to put the out-of-town Beat writers at the center, and this is something various writers have wanted to highlight. There are various pieces of evidence proving that the letter was read at the second reading rather than the first. For one thing, the Berkeley reading was recorded and so we can actually hear the letter being read aloud on those tapes. As for the possibility that this was somehow part of a "recreation," with McClure perhaps reading the letter a second time, it was handed to him by John Allen Ryan, who was in Mexico during the first reading.

Falsehood #6—There was an orgy after the event.

Ginsberg mentioned this once as a joke and various people have taken it to be the truth. He meant it in the sense of a group of poets gathering and having fun rather than organized group sex. It is not impossible that an orgy took place and these certainly happened after later poetry readings but there is no evidence that one occurred on October 7. This rumor was repeated in Ed Sanders' poetic biography of Ginsberg, where he confidently asserted "There was an actual orgy after the reading" but then admitted he "forgot / to ask A.G. to describe" it.

Oddly, people often state that Kerouac depicted an orgy taking place after the reading in *The Dharma Bums*, but this does not happen in the book. There are instances of group sex later in the novel but these are not the same night of the 6 Gallery reading. It is possible that people have simply remembered that the book featured the reading and then later there was an orgy and somehow misremembered the orgy occurring immediately after the reading.

Falsehood #7—It was the first public reading for all of the poets.

This is a mistake that the poets themselves have made and which others have repeated because it makes for a better story. In reality, only McClure was making his reading debut that night. The others were inexperienced for sure but they had some practice. Ginsberg had read at the San Francisco Arts Festival in September and Snyder and Whalen had given a few readings in Oregon. Lamantia was the most experienced of the five poets, having read in public many times.

Falsehood #8—There was a makeshift dais and a dirt floor.

The dais/stage can be seen from photos about a year earlier and was possibly built by the theater group that had the building before it became the King Ubu. By some accounts, the raised area that functioned as a stage still existed in the 1990s, so it was not a temporary structure built for that reading.

In Chapter 1.3, I quoted Deborah Remington referring to a movable stage, which was often propped up against the back wall. This was small and moved on wheels, so it was clearly not the same dais that the poets read on and which can be seen in the one existing photo of that part of the gallery. It could have sat only about two poets with one standing and even then it would have been crowded. Remington mentions this existing at the King Ubu but not the 6 Gallery, so perhaps it was converted to make it bigger and permanent, but in any case, the dais the poets read from was not "makeshift."

There are also claims about a sawdust floor, perhaps stemming from Kerouac's account of The Place, which did in fact have sawdust on the ground to soak up spilled beer. It is possible people have mixed up his description of the two venues. Various photos also show a concrete floor rather than a dirt one.

Falsehood #9—The postcard mentioned "dancing girls" and "free satori."

For years, the text of the famous 6 Gallery reading postcard circulated, proclaiming "6 Poets at the 6 Gallery." This seems to originate with Ann Charters' 1973 Kerouac biography. The text was not cited in the notes section and I believe that she put it together based on interviews with Ginsberg and Snyder, who likely pulled the text from their memories. Oddly, the real postcard surfaced in the mid-eighties thanks to the same Ann Charters, who sent it to Ginsberg when he was compiling *Howl: Original Draft Facsimile*. However, the real and fake versions, and several hybrids, all circulate now in about equal measure. Sometimes they include parts of another postcard used to promote the "repeat performance" of March 1956.

On a similar note, Gary Snyder claimed to have written the text for the first postcard but in fact it was his suggested text that ended up on the second one. At least one copy of this second postcard still exists and it differs slightly from the text quoted in early articles and books. It is interesting that it does include a reference to "free satori," adding further evidence to my idea that the text for the first postcard, reported in early Beat histories, was merely pulled from people's memories.

Falsehood #10—Ginsberg began his reading on the toilet.

This story comes from Wally Hedrick, who was recalling the event more than forty years later and at a very advanced age. He said that when it was time for Ginsberg to read, he was sitting on the toilet, then pulled his trousers up after the spotlight hit him. The audience watched him proceed to the stage as he read. This version not only contradicts every other account but it is just absurdly unlikely. Hedrick also claims that Kerouac was outside directing traffic whilst wearing a gas mask. He did not appear to be joking but still his words here should not be taken seriously. Hedrick was a wonderful character but he was a storyteller and his tales sometimes moved beyond the exaggerated and into the ridiculous. There are numerous accounts of Ginsberg starting his reading in a much more conventional way and these are far more plausible.

One should note, however, that there was a small toilet right at the back of the 6 Gallery, located very close to the stage and certainly within view of the audience. It is not impossible that Ginsberg used the restroom shortly before his reading (there had been an intermission, after all) and then proceeded to walk on stage. This is quite different from him starting "Howl" whilst pulling up his trousers, though.

Falsehood #11—Hoffman died just before the reading of a peyote overdose.

Various books state or suggest that John Hoffman, whose poems Philip Lamantia read at the 6 Gallery, had recently died. He had in fact passed away about three and a half years earlier, on January 20, 1952. This mistake seems to stem from a general lack of information about the lives of Hoffman and Lamantia and likely comes from the assumption that Lamantia chose to read Hoffman's work due to the impact of his friend's recent death. As this book has demonstrated, however, his choice was due to doubts about his own poetry. Hoffman's death remains somewhat of a mystery, but a death certificate and newspaper announcements can be found, proving the date. They simply do not list the cause of death.

Appendix #2: The 1955 San Francisco Arts Festival

Throughout this book, I have attempted to explain the story of the 6 Gallery reading as thoroughly and honestly as possible and that has been a challenge because so much of the history of the building and the event held there was hard to verify. As such, I have frequently presented information in terms of probability rather than certainty. Even if this makes for a slightly clunky narrative at times, I believe it is generally a good approach to history as it allows the reader a fuller picture and even provides them with enough data to disagree with the author's own conclusion in certain matters. This is especially important when discussing events as shrouded in uncertainty as this one. However, I am aware that sometimes such discussions can detract from the narrative a little too much and I felt that there was one part of this story that deserved to be discussed at length in a separate section. That was the San Francisco Arts Festival and specifically the claim that Allen Ginsberg read "Howl" there about three weeks prior to the 6 Gallery reading. I felt the claim was untrue but nonetheless quite plausible. I did not want to spend more than seven thousand words discussing it in the context of the preparations for the 6 Gallery reading, where it would only have detracted from the narrative, so I will instead do that here.

I will state right now that I do not think Ginsberg really read "Howl" at the Arts Festival but the purpose of this essay is to acknowledge that it is very hard to say what he read and that there is one extremely convincing source—one of only two sources concerning the poetry portion of this particular event—who wrote several times about Ginsberg reading "Howl" on stage at the Nourse

Appendices

Auditorium on September 16. Personally, even though he was an eyewitness and had a very good memory, I think he was mistaken. However, there are several documents he produced, some shortly after that reading and some in the decades that followed, which need to be addressed if this is to be an honest appraisal. Perhaps my focus on the 6 Gallery reading has blinded me to the possibility of Ginsberg reading his poem a few weeks earlier. After all, if "Howl" was not first read at the 6 Gallery, it largely diminishes that event's importance and thereby minimizes the significance of this book. Evading my own bias on the matter is a major reason why I wanted to discuss this event in more detail and let readers draw their own conclusions. It would be remiss of me not to.

Additionally, a great many people have written about "Howl" and most of them report that the 6 Gallery reading was its first public performance, so if I am wrong and the San Francisco Arts Festival was in fact the first reading, then this information ought to be shared for the benefit of the wider Beat Studies community. The documents to which I refer have only ever been seen by a handful of people and are not cited in any books on the Beat Generation,[1] so hopefully the details shared here will help future generations of scholars to more accurately explore the poem's development.

In the section that follows, I will closely examine a number of documents produced and collected by Jack Goodwin. These documents span a period of nearly thirty years and include a note written shortly after the poetry reading, another written immediately after the 6 Gallery reading, a memoir written thirteen years later, and some letters from the early 1980s. As you might imagine, the date of each piece of evidence is important, so pay close attention. I will run through these and pass comment where necessary before drawing upon another piece of evidence, which is a letter written by Allen Ginsberg ten days after the Arts Festival. Whereas almost no one has ever seen the Goodwin documents, a small number have

---

1   As best I can tell, they have been cited in a book about Richard Brautigan, a book about café culture, and a book about West Coast painters of the mid-twentieth century.

viewed this letter. It does not, however, appear in any published collections in spite of its importance.

The First Reading of "Howl": Considering a Credible Alternative

According to Jack Goodwin, almost certainly the most reliable source of information regarding the 6 Gallery reading and other poetry events of that era, "Howl" was first read at the annual San Francisco Arts Festival on September 16, 1955. This is a date widely recognized by Beat historians as Ginsberg's first public reading but Goodwin, who was in attendance that day and wrote about it less than a week later, distinctly recalled Ginsberg reading "Howl" rather than—as others have suggested—comparatively short and minor works.

The San Francisco Arts Festival[2] was founded in 1946 by the San Francisco Arts Commission, but as a 1953 program mentioned, this was only the *official* beginning and in fact artists had been holding their own large-scale arts festivals in the city since at least 1938. These had been astonishingly popular until they were disrupted by the Second World War. After the war ended, the event was made official and even by 1947 it was attracting nearly a half million visitors. It continued to grow in stature, becoming a celebrated annual event that affirmed the city's enthusiasm for a wide variety of art forms.

In keeping with the city's liberal attitudes and its acceptance of experimental, challenging artworks, the Arts Festival was ostensibly one of openness and free expression. In the event's 1951 program, Harold Zellenbach, the president of the commission, wrote the

---

2   The name alternated between "Arts Festival" and "Art Festival" from one year to the next. In 1955, "Art Festival" was in use but "Arts" was more common across a longer period of time and so I will use that term here for the sake of consistency. Also, given that it was arranged by the "Arts Commission," it seems more logical, and as we have seen in this book, there was a strong belief in "arts" over "art" in San Francisco from the mid-forties onwards.

following about the festival's aims:

> It is not the intention of the Art Commission[3] to establish criterias nor to foster an "official" art. Our purpose here is to offer the artists and craftsmen of the Bay Area, in the most democratic fashion, the means of exhibiting their work and thought. It is our purpose to foster and stimulate the integration of the artist within his community, for only then can he work effectively and creatively. Only then can our citizenry lead vital and enriched lives.
>
> Finally, it is our purpose to bring together and promote the integration of the various arts. The gay informal atmosphere of the municipally sponsored Art Festival, unique in the country, has proven to be the most popular vehicle in accomplishing our purpose. The Art Commission, a municipal body, concerned with the aesthetic needs, desires, the resulting well-being of the people therefore considers this annual municipally sponsored event as an important area of its activities.

The event was held annually in September but for various reasons it tended to change locations. In 1954, it had been held at Aquatic Park, in the north of San Francisco, near Fisherman's Wharf, and generally it was perceived as an outdoor event. This was where the six

---

3 We can see here that although "Arts Commission" was the official term, "Art" was used even by its president, compounding the confusion over names. It may be of some minor interest that one of the members of the Arts Commission tasked with arranging this event was Antonio Sotomayor, who was the first artist whose work was ever shown at 3119 Fillmore. That was in 1952, during its very brief period as headquarters of the San Francisco Community Theater.

The 1955 San Francisco Arts Festival

founders of the 6 Gallery had staged their fundraising event a little over a month prior to opening the gallery. However, in 1955 the venue chosen to host most of the event was Civic Auditorium (now Bill Graham Civic Auditorium) and the performance arts portion of the festival was held a few blocks west at Nourse Auditorium. This Spanish revival building is presently known as the Sydney Goldstein Theater, and it had functioned as a school auditorium until it closed in 1952, after which it was used intermittently for cultural events until 1985 when it became a courtroom and then for several decades a storage facility. It was restored and reopened as a theater in 2013.

In the months leading up to the Arts Festival, the local media questioned the change of venue and many people were critical when it opened. In fact, the Arts Commission had nearly canceled this section of the event at the last moment due to problems with the equipment at the venue, but after considering the preparations made by a great many dancers, musicians, and poets, they instead raised funds to fix certain problems. On the final day, the *San Francisco Examiner* summed it up, saying:

> this year's move indoors has had mixed results. The show is now safe from wind and weather. On the other hand, its attendance, while pretty lively, appears to be considerably smaller than its outdoor crowds have been in Union Square.

They went on to say that the "indoor setting [may have had] something to do with the distinct improvement in this year's fine arts standards" and mentioned other interesting art forms (citing blacksmithing and glassblowing as welcome new additions, alongside landscape design, architecture, and pottery), but noted one particular failure:

> Location of most of the stage programs (ballet, theater, concert and poetry readings) in Nourse Auditorium seems

to have been a flop. The Nourse is three blocks away from the Civic Auditorium. The festive spirit and crowds don't reach that far. Maybe in the future, the local stage arts ought to settle down somewhere for a festival of their own.

In spite of that critical account, the Arts Commission's internal documents showed that they believed the "performance arts" portion of the event had been a success. Over a four-day period, the Nourse Auditorium attracted 6,900 people, and it seems that on at least one of the days (Saturday), the building had been very nearly packed to capacity. However, there exist no detailed reports on the poetry reading and most coverage of the Arts Festival itself tended to focus on the unwelcome change of venue and another controversy that was generated when one artist's work openly criticized Vice-President Richard Nixon. This caused such a storm, in fact, that the Arts Commission removed the work, drawing accusations of hypocrisy. This act of censorship received much condemnation, eventually becoming national news. Even Nixon defended the artist and his right to free expression, saying, "One of the sacred precepts of our legal heritage is the right of the individual to criticize public officials. [...] The people should not be denied full opportunity to hear or see his expression of that opinion." However, the Arts Commission president, Harold Zellenbach, was resolute and repeatedly stated that the Arts Festival was no place for partisan politics. It should be noted that this was the same man who wrote the earlier statement about the importance of allowing artists the freedom to express themselves.

Aside from general commentary about the event and its organization, and various opinion pieces concerning the Arts Commission's regrettable censorship, there was little in the media about the specifics of the 1955 festival and sadly only the programs from 1951 and 1953 have been preserved. However, once again it is Jack Goodwin we can thank for chronicling this little piece of literary history. He saved the page of the program that shows the

The 1955 San Francisco Arts Festival

Nourse Auditorium itinerary for September 15 and 16 and also wrote a letter, less than a week later, describing the event.

Goodwin's latest play *The Pizza Pusher* was performed at Nourse Auditorium on September 15. It had played at the hungry i club a month earlier, where it was stage managed by Zekial Marko,[4] and Marko reprised this role at the Arts Festival. Not long after, Goodwin wrote, "We had an audience of about a thousand for Pizza that night and they loved it and I was drunk with power," noting that Ruth Witt-Diamant had been in the audience and "gave [him] a big rave." Poet and secretary of the Poetry Center Ida Hodes was also in the audience that day. Later that day, Maya Angelou took to the stage with the BooBam Drum Ensemble. Back then, she was a moderately well-known singer and dancer and had not yet begun her career as a poet. She was managed by BooBam Bamboo Drum Company founder Gerd Stern, who by coincidence had been in a mental hospital with Ginsberg and Carl Solomon and knew Bern Porter and others from the Sausalito scene. Stern was also Angelou's boyfriend and they lived together for "some time" until an explosive breakup.

On Friday, September 16, between 6 and 7 p.m., four poets gave a reading: Allen Ginsberg, Jack Gilbert, Jack Nugent, and Guy Wernham. According to Goodwin, the nervous poets received some coaching prior to taking the stage that evening:

> Backstage, while everyone was sweating and waiting for curtain time, Marko horned in and coached the poets as they rehearsed and what Marko saw was that in Ginsberg we had a genuine Old Testament prophet, straight out of DeMille. This was to be the first public reading of "Howl," and Marko made suggestions—about tone, volume, tempo and gesture.

---

4   Marko's real name was Marvin Schmoker. He went by Zekial Marko or just the mononym Marko.

It is important to stress that Goodwin wrote the above words in the 1960s, possibly as late as 1968.[5] This was for an essay titled "Dress Rehearsal: Or, Life Among the Founding Fathers." In this piece, Goodwin claimed that Marko started the San Francisco Renaissance in part by coaching Ginsberg to read "Howl." Although he did not give many details, he recalled the performance and mentioned Ginsberg's poem as being about "Moloch." From this account, then, we seem to learn two quite astonishing facts:

> 1. Allen Ginsberg read "Howl" for the first time three weeks earlier than had been previously thought and did so in front of a much bigger audience than is believed to have been at the 6 Gallery.
> 2. He read not only Part I of "Howl," as we believe was the case at the 6 Gallery, but in fact also Part II, something of which there is no record until 1956.

Whilst this all seems very unlikely, it is far from impossible. Firstly, Goodwin's testimony is compelling and as he's the only eyewitness to have come forward, and as he is generally a very reliable source, it seems wise to believe him. As for Part II of "Howl," Ginsberg had certainly begun work on it by this time. He sent letters quoting the "Moloch" part of his poem at the end of August and mentioned that it would be included in a book version published by City Lights, so there can be little doubt that as of September 16 he had a version of "Howl" in which he had the confidence to go public and which included lines about Moloch.

If we consider time constraints, the early versions of Part II were extremely short and so it is also quite possible that he read "Howl" Part I and Part II on stage that day.

---

5   This was when the quoted essay was published in *Rolling Renaissance: San Francisco Underground Art in Celebration*. I would have assumed the essay was written a little before that date, but in the 1980s Goodwin remembered it being thirteen years after the 6 Gallery reading.

The 1955 San Francisco Arts Festival

With four poets reading for an hour, and Ginsberg taking about twelve to fourteen minutes to read Part I, it is not impossible that he read one of the earliest drafts of Part II, which at a fraction of the length of Part I would only have added a minute or two. Thus, if the time had been divided equally between each of the four poets, Ginsberg could certainly have read whatever text of "Howl" he had confidence in at that time.

I am speculating there but certainly Goodwin—who I will reiterate was in the building before and during the reading—claimed that Ginsberg read "Howl." He even noted this on the schedule although it is likely he wrote this much later. He was not only an eyewitness but, unlike many of the Beat writers, he was a fairly reliable source when drawing upon his memories of the mid-fifties scene. Where others would forget or invent details, Goodwin was able to recall names and places and wrote at length about that era, easily remembering conversations and events with a degree of accuracy most others struggled to achieve. He seems to have done so in part by drawing upon a number of documents he had saved, and in his letters sometimes corrected himself after double- and triple-checking dates and documents. He seemed to have had an interest in historical accuracy, chastised others for lacking that motivation, and seldom pushed himself to the center of a story. Born in 1920, he was older than most of the artists active at the time and he recognized that he was in a special environment, so he wrote short descriptive passages that he saved for decades as a means of preserving those memories, and when he was asked by a biographer for details about Jack Spicer, The Place, Allen Ginsberg, the beatnik phenomenon, and the San Francisco Renaissance, he was able to pull from his own memory but also confirm these against his own saved letters. As such, we should not immediately dismiss his claims about the Arts Festival and "Howl" as based upon flawed memory.

That said, I must note that his memory was not perfect and he sometimes made mistakes when remembering details years later. His memories of the 6 Gallery, for example, raise questions. He spoke of the gallery as being an L-shaped basement but it was neither L-shaped nor a basement. Certainly, it was an unusual shape and I suppose his description could be an odd interpretation of that, but it was not a basement. One might argue over whether it could be called the first or ground floor, but it was not below ground even if it had a subterranean vibe. He remembers Philip Whalen saying "camp, camp, camp," during one of his poems but it is hard to see where that might have come from given that no such line appeared in the poems he read or is likely to have read that night.

Considering this issue of memory, it is important to acknowledge that he only claimed Ginsberg read "Howl" much later and the documents he actually produced at the time only noted that the poet had read something impressive and perhaps a bit daring. The letters Goodwin wrote were mostly to John Allen Ryan, who was in Mexico for almost the whole second half of 1955. On September 21, just five days after the reading at the Nourse Auditorium, Goodwin wrote him:

> One of the poetry-readings I saw at the fiesta de los artes was a most risable gas. At the table on the stage of the Nourse Auditorium was seated a most ill-assorted panel of literati. From right to left: Jack Nugent (the baseball poet), Ginsberg, Jack Gilbert, and Wernham fresh from a fix at the Alcoholics' Clinic and dressed like a poet. Nugent began by informing the audience that sentiment makes the world go round (sic),[6] and then with a just-plain-folks kind of leer, he lit into a couple of Nick Kenny style of things about Isn't it great to have had a great guy like Joe Lewis in there punching for us Americans. Ginsberg and Gilbert sat there biting their lips and shuddering, while I devoted

---

6   This "(sic)" is Goodwin's, not mine. To avoid confusing matters, I have not used "[sic]" in this excerpt. All mistakes here are as Goodwin typed them.

myself to stilling the uncouth mirth of Marko and Harmon on either side of me in the front row. It was a real instance of double-edged poetic justice, because after Nugent finished, he in turn had to sit thru the free-form eroticism of Ginsberg and Gilbert, which to him probably seemed like the most unwholesome thing since Whitman. Actually they were thrilling, both of them G's. I don't know whether you've met Gilbert, but on the stage with his flashing blue eyes he looks the perfect image of the romantic poet. I hadn't dug Ginsberg before, and he really comes on.

Let's take a moment to dissect this. Given that Goodwin later recalled Ginsberg reading "Howl," one might jump to the conclusion from this description that he had indeed read that landmark poem, but he did not specifically name "Howl," nor did he give any detail that strongly indicated that was the poem read. Admittedly, he would also fail to use the poem's name a few weeks later when writing a much lengthier description of the 6 Gallery reading, but in that account he was very clearly referring to Ginsberg's most famous poem. Here, we are left only with a few clues to examine. In fact, we have three pieces of information and none are particularly useful:

1. Ginsberg read something like "free-form eroticism."
2. It may have seemed "like the most unwholesome thing since Whitman."
3. He "really comes on."

His reference to "the free-form eroticism of Ginsberg" certainly makes it seem—at least in hindsight—as though he had read "Howl," and Goodwin mentioned later in that same letter the following conversation, which suggests some good-natured jousting between Ginsberg and Wernham:

Appendices

> They had to call a dirty-word conference before the reading. "Well, I don't know," said Ginsberg, "but I'm going to say 'come.'" "Well," insisted Wernham, "I've got to say Piss." etc. etc. They did. And appeared to be enjoying it.

If it is a reasonably faithful recollection of the conversation (and that is hardly guaranteed), then could Ginsberg have been referring to the following line from "Howl"?

> a vision of ultimate cunt and come eluding
> the last gyzym of consciousness

"Come" is certainly not the rudest word in that line, but then this comes from the published version and Ginsberg was likely reading from something closer to what we now know as draft #2 or #3 of "Howl." Had he read from typed draft #2, it would have read:

> a vision of ultimate jazz eluding the last come
> of consciousness

Still, that would not be the rudest word in the poem unless Ginsberg engaged in some degree of self-censorship (which admittedly he did later in 1955 when reading at the San Francisco Poetry Center). Plus, it is more likely that he was reading from a manuscript closer to draft #3, by which time he had included "cunt" in that line.

In his mid-sixties recollection, "Dress Rehearsal," Goodwin recalled:

> The result was electrifying. Ginsberg shouted, wept, chanted and mopped his brow, with a telling little Marko gesture across the forehead on the word "lobotomy." The message was drearily

familiar but the presentation was hair-raising.

It is specific and therefore believable, but can we trust it? Did Ginsberg really say "lobotomy" or did Goodwin remember that because of later hearing and reading "Howl" at the 6 Gallery and elsewhere? Did he remember hearing "Moloch" for the same reason? In his description of the second reading, written October 8, he mentions Ginsberg shouting and chanting and it being extremely "hot and sweaty." In fact, the above description is rather similar to his account of the 6 Gallery reading and one wonders if he had perhaps combined the two events in the same way that many eyewitnesses mixed together the 6 Gallery reading and the Berkeley Town Hall reading. Goodwin attended many other readings that year, too, and so if he did not conflate the 6 Gallery reading with the Nourse one, perhaps he accidentally borrowed from another event.

Taken together, and given just a cursory reading, Goodwin's two documents seem like conclusive proof that Ginsberg read "Howl" that day, but upon closer inspection we only know that he read "free-form eroticism" that may have included the word "come" and that later, when looking back upon a vibrant scene, he remembered the poem as "Howl," one that he heard a few weeks later and described in very similar terms. Considering how myth-like the 6 Gallery reading was and how many inconsistencies and uncertainties surround the writing of "Howl," it is tempting to believe Goodwin and view this as an essential document upending the official story. In other words, we could choose to believe that Ginsberg forgot about the Arts Festival reading or that he chose the 6 Gallery as part of his personal mythology because it was more befitting his bohemian, outlaw-poet credentials. However, it does not seem very likely. A likelier explanation is that he later transposed his memory of another "Howl" reading onto this reading, where Ginsberg read something less incendiary.

I will return to further dissect Goodwin's testimony but for now it is worth turning to perhaps the only other valuable source regarding the Nourse Auditorium poetry reading, and that is a letter Ginsberg wrote to Robert LaVigne on September 26, ten days after the event. As we have seen in the main text of the book, Ginsberg wrote frustratingly little about these key events, largely due to being carried away by the wild and creative scene and his explosion of poetic output, but he did write to a number of distant friends, including LaVigne, who was at the time staying in Mexico. This letter was not archived alongside the vast bulk of his correspondence but was one of a small number of documents stored at the University of Texas. As a result, it has been generally overlooked by researchers and does not appear in any of his letter collections. In it, Ginsberg quotes the first four lines of "A Supermarket in California" and then tells LaVigne:

> I read this poem (about a full page ending with both of us on Charon's ferry over the Styx) aloud at the Art Festival amid much laughter and applause. Amazed to hear how virile it sounded. I had been afraid it was too much fairy poem.

He says nothing else about the Arts Festival. There had been some news about his friends, updates about the San Francisco literary scene, then the four lines of his poem and this short paragraph. That's all. The way he delivers this news to LaVigne makes it seem as though "A Supermarket in California" was his only poem for that event, unlikely as that may appear. And if you know this poem well, especially if you have heard it read aloud, then it certainly does appear unlikely for it is a very short poem. There are recordings of him performing it in a little over two minutes even going at a slow pace. One biographer claims that Ginsberg "read some of his breezy, funnier poems to that audience" but cites only the above letter and also erroneously claims that the reading took place at Aquatic Park. It is certainly a reasonable assumption that he read more than just a single two-minute poem, but aside from Goodwin's account, there is simply nothing else to go on and so it is impossible to say for certain.

The 1955 San Francisco Arts Festival

How can we reconcile this information with Goodwin's September 21 account that spoke of Ginsberg's "free-form eroticism"? What about the claim that he had boasted about swearing, and in particular the word "come"? After all, even if Goodwin later mixed up two readings or somehow created a false reading of "Howl" in his memory, the letter to Ryan soon after the event can hardly be disputed.

I don't think it's hard to explain the first point, namely the idea of "A Supermarket in California" being considered "free-form eroticism." It is true that one has to look rather closely and make certain inferences. But remember that Goodwin—an educated gay man— was recalling this event almost a week later in a letter to another educated gay man. He had likely been impressed by Ginsberg's poem, which had been literary and witty enough that gay references could have passed over the heads of most audience members. Perhaps he heard the line "I saw you, Walt Whitman, childless, lonely old grubber, poking among the meats in the refrigerator and eyeing the grocery boys," and five days later remembered the suggestive imagery and homosexual references as more daring than they had been. Certain lines that follow could also be said to suggest gay sex. Ginsberg was clearly aware of this as we saw in the above quote about it being perceived as a "fairy poem," but unless he read an early version that differed from the published one, then there are no "dirty words" and certainly not the word "come." (The lines quoted in the letter to LaVigne, however, are nearly identical to the published version, so that does seem unlikely.)

Had he perhaps continued to read "Love Poem on a Theme by Whitman," a work written a year earlier? It is highly erotic and includes the phrase "till the white come flow in the swirling sheets," so it fits Goodwin's descriptions. Whilst highly provocative, it is less so than "Howl," so it might have been something Ginsberg read that evening. He even read this poem first in a reading at Reed College just five months later, one of his first readings outside of San Francisco, again in front of an audience he would not have known or trusted to

369

necessarily understand his work. At that reading, he read both "A Supermarket in California" and "Love Poem on a Theme by Whitman" (albeit under a different title: "Epithalamion") and so it is not out of the question that he did it at the San Francisco Arts Festival. He was certainly going through a Whitman obsession at the time and may have felt that a number of short works connected by this literary titan made for suitable subject matter. If he was truthful about there being "much laughter and applause," then likely the audience appreciated that his "Supermarket" poem inverted lines from Whitman's "Crossing Brooklyn Ferry," published 99 years earlier. Would they have reacted favorably to "Love Poem on a Theme by Whitman"? It is hard to say, but where "Howl" would surely have struck them as pornographic, a handful of works about Walt Whitman, even including references to homosexual intercourse, might have been just literary enough to be deemed acceptable.

This is pure conjecture, of course. It attempts to explain how he might have included explicit language and also used up more than two minutes of his allotted time. However, it is also possible that both Ginsberg and Goodwin were right, and that "A Supermarket in California" and "Howl" were read together. That would have pushed the time to about fifteen minutes and also satisfied the criteria for provocative words, whilst validating Goodwin's later memories. But I also find this quite unlikely as Ginsberg failed to mention it to LaVigne, who was aware of Ginsberg's work on "Howl."

Ginsberg had sent his painter friend an excerpt from "Howl" some weeks earlier, even saying, "I have 5 pages of this to read at the arts festival." One might think that is yet more proof that he read "Howl," but I think it is quite the opposite. Although short, his post-Arts Festival letter was fairly comprehensive and explained for a friend his latest poetic accomplishment and the most important happenings in the San Francisco Beat poetry circle, so if he had read "Howl," he would surely have noted this fact. He would've considered it a great milestone in his poetic life—something to share with a friend whom he kept updated about such matters. LaVigne had been one

The 1955 San Francisco Arts Festival

of the few to learn about "Howl" in August and Ginsberg wanted his respect and approval, so a public reading undoubtedly would have earned at least a sentence or two in this letter. Indeed, his letters at this point often highlighted developments with "Howl," casually bragging about breakthroughs and publishing opportunities. If he'd read it in front of a thousand or more people—even if the reception had been negative or ambivalent—he would not have failed to note this. However, when he writes, "I read this poem aloud at the Art Festival amid much laughter and applause," it strongly implies that he read it and nothing else.

And that brings up the fact that this was a very different reading from the one at the 6 Gallery a few weeks later. The Arts Festival was a public event sponsored by the Arts Commission, which although not exactly a conservative organization was unlikely to approve of the explicit references to gay sex and drug use in "Howl." Goodwin mentioned in his recollection of the conversation between Ginsberg and Wernham that Ginsberg felt he was being daring by saying "come" and Wernham rivaled that with "piss." These hardly rank as rude words when compared with lines from "Howl," such as "who let themselves be fucked in the ass by saintly motorcyclists, and screamed with joy." That is just one of countless examples of language that was risqué for a hipster crowd in an offbeat art gallery, but in front of a crowd that likely numbered 1,500 in a large theater at a tax-funded event, it quite possibly would have resulted in a scandal as great as the one surrounding the artist who had depicted Richard Nixon in an unflattering light and referred to him as "Dick McSmear." The poetry readings would not merely have been dismissed as "a flop" but derided as obscene. Goodwin also noted in his September 21, 1955, letter that Wernham told the audience: "I'm going to read you a few selections from a syerihs of poms I've bean doing concehning DOPE. [...] The first one is called H̲." Goodwin said there were some "heads" in the audience who got these references but quite possibly the average listener did not know what he was talking about. Controversial as this would have been, it hardly ranks alongside the drug-related content of "Howl," which

371

would have been easier for the squares to decipher.

Another consideration is that "Howl" was very much a work in progress at this point whilst "A Supermarket in California" and other short poems had quickly been composed and completed. He had become quite carried away with "Howl" in August, sending lines to some of his friends, but he had soon realized it was not a finalized work and in fact would take a very long time to finish. The more he worked on it, the more he felt that—in spite of Kerouac's advocacy of spontaneous composition—his poem improved with revision. Part I was being changed in many small ways and Part II was still in its infancy, barely more than a concept as of mid-September. It would go through a great many changes, some of which were quite substantial. He felt confident that "Howl" would be published one day, but it was not ready for the public's attention just yet, and even after his early readings he continued to write and edit it over many months.

There is one more piece of "evidence" that I would like to present before drawing some conclusions and that is a comment from the letter Jack Goodwin wrote the day after the 6 Gallery reading. It is a letter that many people writing about the Beats have pretended to have read but perhaps only a handful ever have. (They all suspiciously draw from a few scattered lines that were originally quoted by one of three authors to have actually found it and almost every account repeats the same telling typo and another accidental omission that function as a sort of literary "paper town.") Here, Goodwin said of Ginsberg's performance that there was "[n]o more of the restraint he featured at the Art Festival; this time he came on like a hissing, wide-grinned gargoyle."

To what extent is this evidence? One could argue that he was talking about Ginsberg's tone and his style of reading. Perhaps he had been shy and quiet at the Nourse Auditorium but now he read with great confidence. Indeed, Goodwin said, "He shouted at the top of his voice," which supports this theory. However, I think that by "restraint," he refers more to content. At the Arts Festival, Ginsberg had read a witty poem that snuck sexual content in underneath its literary façade, but now

The 1955 San Francisco Arts Festival

he was bold, brazen, and preaching to *his* people. In this letter, Goodwin describes "Howl" in some detail. He does not name the poem but talks about it in ways that make it very clear what Ginsberg was reading: "Ginsberg's main number was a long descriptive roster of out-group,[7] pessimistic dionysian young bohemians and their peculiar and horrible feats." Could there be any doubt that this refers to "Howl"? Only "The Names" fits this description and whilst it was textually linked to "Howl," likely a part of "Howl" that emerged between drafts #2 and #3, it was a short and unimpressive poem that was only expanded and finished years later.

He goes on to tell Ryan that "[t]here was a lot of sex, sailors and language of the cocksuckingmotherfucker variety in it." Again, this largely confirms that he had heard "Howl" at the 6 Gallery, but it also tells me that this was his first time hearing that poem. If Ginsberg had read it at the Arts Festival, why had Goodwin not mentioned it then? Why had it been merely "free-form eroticism" and why had he only said Ginsberg was daring for using the word "come"? Why was the word "piss" so shocking if he had delivered lines like "with mother finally fucked"? In addition to all that, Goodwin's description shows him to have been surprised and impressed by Ginsberg's reading at the 6 Gallery and gives absolutely no indication that he had heard the poem before. His admiration seems entirely based on the quality of the work and its bold language and content rather than the manner in which it was delivered.

Considering all this, I strongly suspect that Goodwin's accounts are misleading. I think that he heard Ginsberg read "A Supermarket in California" and five days later he slightly overstated the eroticism and risqué language when writing to John Allen Ryan, not out of any intent to mislead but rather as a genuine attempt to recall an exciting

---

7   Yes, this is "out-group" and not "our group." Almost every other account says "our group" because they have—whether they admit it or not—copied this text from Rebecca Solnit's 1990 work, *Secret Exhibition*. She made a tiny error in transcription (an understandable one but one unlikely to be made twice) that people have repeated for thirty-five years rather than find the original letter.

373

poetry reading in the midst of a long arts event featuring many other interesting performances. He was probably not playing up the eroticism (and in fact Goodwin was more likely to do the opposite—he was annoyed by Ryan's propensity for exaggeration) and instead he most likely did his best to remember Ginsberg's reading five days later, as well as the content of his conversation with Werham. In that part of the letter, he did seem uncertain and how could he not? He was quoting a random, overheard conversation from nearly a week before that related to poems he had surely never seen written down and had probably only heard read aloud once.

I suspect that the line about Ginsberg's work "probably [seeming] like the most unwholesome thing since Whitman" to another poet may have been a reference to the fact that "A Supermarket in California" was an homage to the great American bard rather than an indication of Ginsberg having read the twentieth century's equivalent of "Song of Myself." Years later, looking at the letter and remembering Ginsberg's much more famous poem, Goodwin probably misremembered certain details—an honest mistake and not unlike the countless mistakes we've seen from others in interviews and memoirs. Then, in the early 1980s he continued to write about this false version of events by drawing upon his letter and the mid-sixties memoir, doubling down on the idea of a "Howl" reading in September 1955.

I believe that Allen Ginsberg intended as of late August to read "Howl" in front of an audience at the San Francisco Arts Festival but that he changed his mind in the two or three weeks between that letter and the event. Perhaps this was due to a recognition that his poem was incomplete or perhaps it was due to the potential ramifications of reading lines like "who let themselves be fucked in the ass by saintly motorcyclists, and screamed with joy," which was in every draft from the first onwards. Perhaps his decision took into consideration both of these thoughts.

Remember also that by early September he had a new event lined up—the 6 Gallery reading of October 7. I think it is highly probable that he decided to keep working

The 1955 San Francisco Arts Festival

on "Howl" and test it in front of a smaller audience more open to challenging work, which might include people mentioned in the poem or similar enough that they could see themselves as among "the best minds of [his] generation." Reading "Howl" at the Nourse Auditorium might have landed him in jail or put him back in a mental hospital but reading it at the 6 Gallery had the potential to kickstart a literary revolution. I believe Ginsberg recognized this, made a smart choice, and used the Arts Festival as a warm-up for the reading of a lifetime.

Appendix #3: Timeline

The following is a basic timeline of events covered in this book. Such a timeline could easily become a book-length work, so I've had to be quite selective. I've included dates of birth for some of the people involved as a means of providing context and there are various events here from the history of San Francisco that are mentioned in the book.

1846   **July 9.** U.S.S. Portsmouth captures the Mexican town of Yerba Buena.

1847   **January 30.** Yerba Buena is renamed San Francisco.

1848   **January 24.** Gold is discovered at Sutter's Mill, leading to the California Gold Rush, a period of immigration lasting approximately from 1848 to 1855.

         February 2. Treaty of Guadalupe Hidalgo cedes California and other formerly Mexican territory to the United States, ending the 1846–1848 Mexican-American war.

1850   **September.** California gains statehood.

1853   The Montgomery Block is built. It is the tallest building west of the Mississippi at the time. From the late 1800s onwards, it houses many writers and artists. Lawrence Ferlinghetti later calls it "the most famous literary and artistic structure in the West."

1869   Japanese immigration to the United States begins.

1882   Chinese Exclusion Act is passed, banning the immigration of Chinese laborers for a period of ten years. It is renewed in 1892 and 1902.

1903   The Artigues building, which will later house City Lights Bookstore, is built.

Appendices

1905   **December 22.** Kenneth Rexroth is born.

The building known as 3115-3117 Fillmore (later 3119 Fillmore) is constructed. The first owner is Andrea Moni.

1906   **April 18.** San Francisco Earthquake kills more than 3,000 people and destroys 80% of the city. The area surrounding 3115-3117 Fillmore is relatively unscathed.

1908   Dash, a notorious but short-lived gay bar, opens and closes, causing a public scandal.

1919   **January 7.** Robert Duncan is born.

1923   **August 8.** Jess is born.

October 20. Philip Whalen is born.

1925   **January 30.** Jack Spicer in born.

1926   **June 3.** Allen Ginsberg is born.

1927   Kenneth Rexroth arrives in San Francisco, where he will live for most of the rest of his life.

1928   **January 20.** David Simpson is born.

March 28. Hayward King is born.

July 21. Wally Hedrick is born.

September 19. John Allen Ryan is born.

1929   **March 31.** Jay DeFeo is born.

1930   **May 8.** Gary Snyder is born.

June 25. Deborah Remington is born.

1936   Mona's 440 opens. It is allegedly the city's first lesbian bar.

1941   **December 7.** The Empire of Japan attacks the United States at Pearl Harbor, forcing the U.S. into the Second World War.

1942   **February 19.** Executive Order 9066 is signed, requiring the temporary incarceration of many persons of Japanese ancestry in the United States. The historically Japanese parts of San Francisco become predominantly black during this period.

1943   The core Beat group of Allen Ginsberg, William S. Burroughs, and Jack Kerouac meet late in the

Timeline

year in New York City, where the latter two are students at Columbia. Along with Lucien Carr, they begin to form an informal socio-literary group that will later become known as the Beat Generation.

1944 George Leite and Bern Porter found *Circle*, an influential small magazine that publishes work by many important Bay Area writers.

August. Robert Duncan publishes "The Homosexual in Society," a landmark essay in which he admits to being gay.

August 14. Lucien Carr kills David Kammerer, a pivotal moment in Beat history.

1945 **July 1.** Douglas MacAgy becomes director of C.S.F.A. He will remain in this position for five years, during which time he has a massive influence on the direction of art in the city.

1946 The Progressive Art Workers—an informal group—is formed, comprised of Wally Hedrick, Deborah Remington, David Simpson, Hayward King, and John Allen Ryan. They choose the name as a joke and compete together in a competition at Pasadena Museum.

1947 **Fall.** The Progressive Art Workers group moves to Los Angeles and briefly attends the Otis Art Institute. They dislike it and continue looking for a progressive educational institute. A little later, Hedrick drives to San Francisco and is the first of the group to visit the C.S.F.A. campus.

1948 Jess, who had worked on the Manhattan Project as a chemist, has a vision and quits his job, moving to San Francisco for a career in the arts.

Fall. Gary Snyder and Philip Whalen meet at Reed College. They had both enrolled in 1947 and live together in 1949.

1949 **February.** Four of the five painter friends (Remington, King, Simpson, and Ryan) travel to San Francisco and enroll at C.S.F.A. Hedrick cannot afford it but makes frequent visits, dropping in on classes.

Appendices

April 8-9. "Western Round Table on Modern Art" is held at the San Francisco Museum of Modern Art, bringing together experts in different artistic disciplines, including Frank Lloyd Wright and Marcel Duchamp.

April 15. Berkeley radio station K.P.F.A. begins broadcasting. It is funded by the Pacifica Foundation, which grew out of a conscientious objector camp. Kenneth Rexroth claims to be a co-founder and soon has a popular radio show. Jack Spicer is also given a show but is fired less than a year later for using obscene language.

April. Metart opens at 527 Bush Street. It is run by Clyfford Still's students and lasts for a little more than one year. Although not terribly successful, it paves the way for co-operative, artist-run galleries in the 1950s.

December 3. Clay Spohn's "Museum of Unknown and Little Known Objects" shows at C.S.F.A.

Robert Duncan meets Jess.

1950 **July 14.** Metart closes.

Wally Hedrick, Hayward King, and John Allen Ryan are called up for military service.

1951 Duncan and Jess exchange vows, thereafter living as a married couple despite the illegality of homosexuality at the time.

Summer. Gary Snyder graduates from Reed College and works at Warm Springs, where he witnesses the "first-fruits" festival that he would write of in "A Berry Feast."

1952 **January 20.** John Hoffman dies in Mexico, supposedly from a peyote overdose but most likely from an infectious disease.

Spring. Gary Snyder moves to San Francisco and lives with Philip Whalen. He will leave to spend the summer at Crater before returning in the fall. When in San Francisco, he works for Kodak and U.S. Customs. This is also when he meets Alan

Timeline

Watts and Robert Duncan.

June. The first issue of *City Lights* is published by Peter D. Martin.

July. The building at 3119 Fillmore temporarily becomes home to the San Francisco Community Theater, headed by W. Edwin Ver Becke.

December 20. Robert Duncan, Jess, and Harry Jacobus open King Ubu gallery at 3119 Fillmore.

1953 **Spring.** Lawrence Ferlinghetti contributes translations of Jacques Prévert poems to *City Lights* magazine.

June. Peter D. Martin and Lawrence Ferlinghetti open City Lights Bookstore.

Summer. Gary Snyder works on Sourdough Mountain and Philip Whalen works on nearby Sauk. Snyder moves from San Francisco to Berkeley in the fall, enrolling at U.C. Berkeley to study Chinese and Japanese.

September. C.S.F.A. starts its first accredited program.

November 3. Robert Duncan performs *The Five Georges*, a Gertrude Stein play, at King Ubu.

December. Snyder—who had recently become a fan of Kenneth Rexroth's poetry—is invited to dinner and becomes good friends with San Francisco's leading poet.

December. King Ubu closes. The last show begins on December 6 and lasts for several weeks, so the gallery probably closes around December 20, at the end of a one-year lease.

Unknown date. Robert Duncan performs *Faust Foutu* for the first time and prints a run of 100 copies for friends and audience members.

Unknown date. The four painters (Remington, King, Simpson, and Ryan) receive their certificates of completion from C.S.F.A. Hedrick and Ryan temporarily enroll at California School of Arts and Crafts.

Appendices

Unknown date. Knute Stiles and Leo Krikorian open The Place.

1954 **Early in the year.** The San Francisco Poetry Center is founded by Ruth Witt-Diamant and Madeline Gleason.

February. Snyder is blacklisted from the U.S. Forest Service at the height of McCarthyism. He had been watched by the F.B.I. since 1948 as a potential communist.

Summer. Whalen works at Ross Dam and Sourdough Mountain for the U.S. Forest Service. Snyder works as a logger at Warm Springs.

June. The five painter friends start on degree programs at C.S.F.A. That same month, they decide to open a gallery.

June. Allen Ginsberg crosses into California from Mexico after a long stay in the jungles of Oaxaca. He stays with Neal and Carolyn Cassady in San Jose for about two months.

August 19. Carolyn Cassady finds Allen Ginsberg in bed with her husband, bringing to an end Ginsberg's stay in San Jose. A few days later, she drives him to San Francisco and leaves him in North Beach.

August 26. Wally Hedrick and Jay DeFeo are married.

September 13. Ginsberg begins working for Towne-Oller & Associates.

September 23. The five painter friends hold a rummage sale at Aquatic Park to raise funds for the opening of their gallery. They are spotted by Herb Caen, earning them a brief mention in the *San Francisco Chronicle* before the 6 Gallery even opens.

October 4. *Time* magazine reports the death of 100 whales in Iceland. The article inspires McClure to write a poem he reads at the 6 Gallery.

October 7. W.H. Auden reads at the San Francisco Museum of Modern Art in an event

Timeline

sponsored by the San Francisco Poetry Center. At the afterparty, Allen Ginsberg first meets Michael McClure.

Mid-October. Ginsberg has a vision in front of the Sir Francis Drake hotel. This will eventually morph into the idea of Moloch, antagonist of his poem, "Howl."

October 25. Ginsberg begins therapy with Dr. Philip Hicks.

October 26. The 6 Gallery founders host a poetry reading at Opus One in North Beach in order to raise more funds for the gallery opening.

October 31. The 6 Gallery opens.

December. Ginsberg meets Robert LaVigne and then Peter Orlovsky. Orlovsky will become Ginsberg's life partner and LaVigne will prove to be a long-term friend.

1955 **January 14.** Ginsberg reads Kerouac's *Visions of Neal* at Rexroth's house for a Friday-night salon.

January 20. Robert Duncan strips naked during a performance of "Faust Foutu" at the 6 Gallery. Michael McClure, Jack Spicer, and others participate in the reading.

January 22. The first Poets' Follies event takes place. It is arranged by Weldon Kees and Michael Greig, with Lawrence Ferlinghetti performing. It mixes jazz, dance, and poetry.

February. Snyder is refused a passport due to suspicions of being a communist.

April 22. Whalen takes peyote for the first time. He takes it again in June and the two trips deeply affect him. (Snyder also takes it that year and the word "psychedelic" is coined around this time.)

May 1. Ginsberg is made unemployed and devotes himself to writing poetry.

June 8. Ginsberg has a dream of Joan Vollmer. This dream helps break his writer's block and leads to a number of important works, including "Howl."

Appendices

June. Weldon Kees disappears, presumably jumping to his death from the Golden Gate Bridge.

June. Whalen starts work on Sourdough Mountain again. Snyder, now blacklisted, manages to get a job at Yosemite with the National Park Service.

July. Kerouac finally sells the manuscript for *On the Road*. It will be published two years later.

August (likely between 7 and 10). Allen Ginsberg writes Part I of "Howl."

August. Kerouac writes most of *Mexico City Blues*.

August 10. City Lights' Pocket Poets series begins with Lawrence Ferlinghetti's collection, *Pictures of the Gone World*.

August 28. Snyder arrives in the Bay Area after spending the summer in the mountains, working and traveling.

September 1. Ginsberg moves into 1624 Milvia Street in Berkeley, the cottage where he will write many important poems and spend time with Kerouac, Snyder, Whalen, and others.

September 8. Ginsberg meets Snyder. He is advised to visit him by Kenneth Rexroth, who suggests Snyder as a possible poet for the 6 Gallery reading.

September 13. Kenneth and Marie Rexroth divorce.

September 16. Ginsberg gives his first ever public poetry reading at Nourse Auditorium.

September 20. Whalen arrives in San Francisco after spending the summer working for the U.S. Forest Service in the Pacific Northwest.

September 23. Kerouac and Ginsberg meet up with Snyder and Whalen in San Francisco. It is the first time Kerouac meets Snyder and Whalen, and the first time Whalen meets Ginsberg.

October 7. The 6 Gallery reading takes place.

Timeline

October, date unknown. Hedrick and DeFeo move into "Painterland" apartments at 2322 Fillmore. James Weeks, Paul Beattie, Joan Brown, Sonia Gechtoff, Michael and Joanna McClure, Bruce Conner, Manuel Neri, and Robert Duncan all live there at various times during the mid-fifties.

Late October. Snyder takes Kerouac mountain-climbing.

October 30. Snyder reads at the San Francisco Poetry Center.

November 20. Ginsberg reads at the San Francisco Poetry Center.

November 23. Ginsberg quits his studies at U.C. Berkeley.

November 30. Natalie Jackson dies. She had been Neal Cassady's lover and a good friend of Ginsberg and others in the San Francisco poetry scene. Her death shocks and scars many of these people.

December. Ginsberg begins working for Greyhound.

December 4. Philip Whalen and Lawrence Ferlinghetti give a joint reading at the San Francisco Poetry Center.

Mid-December. Kerouac leaves San Francisco and heads to his sister's house on the East Coast. He plans a 1956 fire lookout post like Snyder and Whalen had held in the past.

1956 **January 24.** Ginsberg and Snyder hitch-hike north from Berkeley to the Pacific Northwest, where they give several poetry readings and even cross into Canada. One reading in mid-February is recorded and is the first known audio recording of Ginsberg.

Late February. Snyder moves from Berkeley to Marin County, living with Locke McCorkle.

March 11. Michael McClure reads at the San Francisco Poetry Center.

Appendices

March 18. Ginsberg, Snyder, Whalen, McClure, and Rexroth give a reading at the Berkeley Town Hall Theater. This is recorded and is a huge success.

April 3. Richard Eberhart reads at the San Francisco Poetry Center.

April 20. Eberhart, pushed by Rexroth, begins compiling information for a *New York Times* article on the nascent San Francisco poetry scene.

September 2. Eberhart's article, "West Coast Rhythms," appears in the *New York Times*. It brings a huge amount of attention to the San Francisco poetry scene.

October 1. *Howl and Other Poems* goes on sale.

October 21. Ginsberg and Gregory Corso give a Poetry Center reading.

October 30. Ginsberg strips naked during a poetry reading in Los Angeles.

1957 Jack Spicer's first book, *After Lorca*, is published by White Rabbit Press.

March 25. U.S. Customs seizes 520 copies of *Howl*. It's the first move in a seven-month-long battle over the book's alleged obscenities.

May 29. Defeated, U.S. Customs releases the 520 copies of *Howl and Other Poems*.

June 3. Undercover police officers visit City Lights and buy copies of *Howl*, returning later that day with arrest warrants for Shig Murao and Ferlinghetti.

September 5. *On the Road* is released.

October 3. Judge Clayton Horn rules that *Howl* is not obscene.

November 8. A poetry reading occurs at the 6 Gallery reading and a piano is smashed.

November 10. The 6 Gallery's final show opens, featuring a number of artists who regularly exhibited their work there.

November. "The Literary Revolution in

Timeline

America," an article credited to Gregory Corso but written mostly by Allen Ginsberg, is published in a Dutch journal, *Litterair Paspoort*. It describes the 6 Gallery reading and emphasizes it as starting a poetic revolution in America.

Late November. Kerouac writes *The Dharma Bums*.

December 1. The 6 Gallery closes.

1958 **October 5.** *The Dharma Bums* is published. The 6 Gallery reading is described in chapter two.

1959 The famous Montgomery block is demolished in spite of protests.

1969 **October 21.** Jack Kerouac dies. Following his death, there is a renewed interest in the Beat Generation as a serious literary movement, prompting people to begin discussing the 6 Gallery reading.

1973 Ann Charters' *Kerouac: A Biography* is published. It is the first major book to explicitly mention the 6 Gallery reading.

1974 Allen Ginsberg is inducted into the American Academy of Arts and Letters, receives the National Book Award for *Fall of America*, and helps found the Jack Kerouac School of Disembodied Poetics at the newly created Naropa University.

1975 Gary Snyder wins the Pulitzer Prize for poetry.

1976 John Tytell's *Naked Angels*, another early work of Beat history, calls the 6 Gallery reading "the germinating public seed of the Beat movement."

1978 *Kerouac: An Oral Biography* is published. This is the first book to go into detail about the 6 Gallery reading. However, almost none of the details are correct.

2004 The 3119 Fillmore building is sold for $1.2 million and the address reverts to the original pre-6 Gallery 3115/3117 numbering.

2005 **October 7.** A plaque is installed outside the 3119 Fillmore address to commemorate the reading.

Bibliography

I have divided this section into four parts: books, "other sources," archives, and audio. The "other sources" section mostly refers to webpages and other online materials. Some audio interviews or recordings cited appear under the Allen Ginsberg archives rather that in the separate "audio" section. This is because they are part of his digitalized archives. These are not commercially released audio recordings. Individual newspaper articles are listed in the endnotes by publication, date, and page number. The endnotes follow and refer to the texts listed in the bibliography.

Books

Allen, Donald, *Off the Wall: Interviews with Philip Whalen* (Four Seasons Foundation: Bolinas, 1978)

Allen, Donald, and Barney, Rosset, *Evergreen Review, Volume 1 | Number 2: The San Francisco Scene* (Grove Press: New York, 1957)

Ball, Gordon, *Allen Verbatim: Lectures on Poetry, Politics, Consciousness* (McGraw-Hill Book Company: New York, 1974)

Bartlett, Lee, *Kenneth Rexroth and James Laughlin: Selected Letters* (W.W. Norton: New York, 1991)

Beasley, David, *Douglas MacAgy and the Foundations of Modern Art Curatorship* (Davus Publishing: Buffalo, 1998)

Berry Campbell Gallery, *West Coast Women of Abstract Expressionism* (Berry Campbell: New York, 2023)

Bertholf, Robert J., *Robert Duncan: A Descriptive Bibliography* (Black Sparrow Press: Santa Rosa, 1986)

Bertholf, Robert J., and Smith, Dale M., *The Correspondence of Robert Duncan and Charles Olson* (University of New Mexico Press: Albuquerque, 2017)

Bockris, Victor, *The Burroughs-Warhol Connection* (Beatdom Books: St. Andrews, 2025)

Burroughs, William S., *Junkie*, (Olympia Press: London: 1966)

Burroughs, William S., *The Letters of William S. Burroughs: 1945-1959* (Viking: New York, 1993)

Calonne, David Stephen, *Conversations with Allen Ginsberg* (University of Mississippi Press: Jackson, 2019)

Calonne, David Stephen, *Conversations with Gary Snyder* (University of Mississippi Press: Jackson, 2017)

Campbell, James, *This is the Beat Generation: New York—San Francisco—Paris* (University of California Press: Berkeley, 2001)

Caples, Garrett T, *Retrievals* (Wave Books: Seattle, 2014)

Cassady, Carolyn, *Off the Road: Twenty Years with Cassady, Kerouac, and Ginsberg* (Flamingo: New York, 1991)

Charters, Ann, *Beats & Company: A Portrait of a Literary Generation* (Doubleday: New York, 1986)

Charters, Ann, and Charters, Samuel, *Brother-Souls: John Clellon Holmes, Jack Kerouac, and the Beat Generation* (University Press of Mississippi: Jackson, 2010)

Charters, Ann, *Kerouac: A Biography* (Straight Arrow Books: San Francisco, 1973)

Charters, Ann, *Jack Kerouac: Selected Letters 1940-1956* (Penguin: New York, 1996)

Charters, Ann, *The Portable Beat Reader* (Viking: New York, 1992)

Charters, Ann, *The Portable Jack Kerouac* (Viking: New York, 1995)

Clark, Ewan: *He, Leo: The Life and Poetry of Lew Welch* (Oregon State University Press: Corvalis, 2023)

Collins, Ronald K.L., and Skover, David M., *The People v. Ferlinghetti: The Fight to Publish Allen Ginsberg's Howl* (Rowman & Littlefield Publishers: 2019)

Cook, Bruce, *The Beat Generation: The Tumultuous '50s Movement and Its Impact on Today* (Quill: New York, 1994)

Cook, Ralph, *The City Lights Pocket Poets Series: A Descriptive Bibliography* (Atticus Books: La Jolla, 1982)

Notes

Corcoran Gallery of Art, *Manuel Neri Early Work, 1953-1978* (The Corcoran Gallery of Art: Washington D.C., 1996)

Cornfield, Daniel, *Working People of California* (University of California Press: Berkeley, 1995)

De Vecchi, Walter, *My Memoirs of Cow Hollow* (Self-published, 1966)

Dobie, Charles Caldwell, *San Francisco's Chinatown* (D. Appleton-Century Company: San Francisco, 1936)

Duncan, Robert, *Faust Foutu: A Comic Masque* (Station Hill Press: Barrytown, 1985)

Duncan, Robert, *The H.D. Book* (University of California Press: Berkeley, 2011)

Eberhart, Richard, *Of Poetry and Poets* (University of Illinois Press: Urbana, 1979)

Ellingham, Lewis, and Killian, Kevin, *Poet Be Like God: Jack Spicer and the San Francisco Renaissance* (University Press of New England: Hanover, 1998)

Gifford, Barry (ed.), *As Ever: The Collected Correspondence of Allen Ginsberg & Neal Cassady* (Creative Arts Book Company: Berkeley, 1977)

Gifford, Barry, and Lee, Lawrence, *Jack's Book: Jack Kerouac in the Lives and Words of his Friends* (Hamish Hamilton: London, 1979)

Ginsberg, Allen, *Collected Poems: 1947-1980* (Harper & Row: New York, 1984)

Ginsberg, Allen, *Composed on the Tongue* (Grey Fox Press: Bolinas, 1980)

Ginsberg, Allen, *Deliberate Prose: Selected Essays 1952-1995* (Perennial: New York, 2001)

Ginsberg, Allen, *Howl: Original Draft Facsimile, Transcript & Variant Versions, Fully Annotated by Author, with Contemporaneous Correspondence, Account of First Public Reading, Legal Skirmishes, Precursor Texts & Bibliography* (Harper Perennial Modern Classics: New York, 2006)

Ginsberg, Allen, *Journals Early Fifties Early Sixties* (Grove Press: New York, 1977)

Ginsberg, Allen, *Journals Mid-Fifties: 1954-1958* (Viking: New York, 1995)

Ginsberg, Allen, *Reality Sandwiches* (City Lights: San Francisco, 1963)

Ginsberg, Allen, *The Book of Martyrdom and Artifice: First Journals and Poems 1937-1952* (Da Capo Press: New York, 2006)

Ginsberg, Allen, *Wait Till I'm Dead: Uncollected Poems* (Grove Press: New York, 2016)

Ginsberg, Allen, and Ginsberg, Louis, *Family Business: Selected Letters Between a Father and Son* (Bloomsbury: New York, 2002)

Ginsberg, Allen, and Orlovsky, Peter, *Straight Hearts' Delight: Love Poems and Selected Letters 1947-1980* (Gay Sunshine Press: San Francisco, 1980)

Gray, Timothy, *Gary Snyder and the Pacific Rim: Creating Countercultural Community* (University of Iowa Press: Iowa City, 2006)

Halper, Jon, *Gary Snyder: Dimensions of a Life* (Sierra Club Books: San Francisco, 1991)

Faas, Ekbert, *Young Robert Duncan: Portrait of the Poet as a Homosexual in Society* (Black Sparrow Press: Santa Barbara, 1983)

Ferlinghetti, Lawrence, *San Francisco Poems* (City Lights Press: San Francisco, 2001)

Ferrier, William Warren, *Berkeley, California: The Story of The Evolution of A Hamlet Into A City of Culture and Commerce* (Self-published: Berkeley, 1933)

Hamalian, Linda, *A Life of Kenneth Rexroth* (W.W. Norton & Company: New York, 1991)

Japantown Task Force, *San Francisco's Japantown* (Arcadia Publishing: 2005)

Jarnot, Liza, *Robert Duncan, The Ambassador from Venus* (University of California Press: Berkeley, 2012)

Johnson, Joyce, *Door Wide Open: A Beat Love Affair in Letters, 1957-1958* (Viking: New York, 2000)

Johnson, Mark, *Robert Duncan* (Twayne: Boston, 1988)

Johnson, Ronna C., and Theado, Matt, *Journal of Beat Studies #11* (Pace University Press: New York, 2023)

Notes

Jones, James T., *A Map of Mexico City Blues: Jack Kerouac as Poet* (Southern Illinois University Press: Carbondale, 1992)

Karlstrom, Paul J., *On the Edge of America: California Modernist Art* (University of California Press: Berkeley, 1996)

Kerouac, Jack, *Desolation Angels* (Perigree Books: New York, 1980)

Kerouac, Jack, *On the Road* (Penguin: New York, 1972)

Kerouac, Jack, *The Dharma Bums* (Penguin: New York, 2006)

Kinsey, Alfred C., *Sexual Behavior in the Human Male* (W.B. Saunders Company: Philadelphia, 1949)

Knight, Arthur, and Knight, Kit, *The Beat Vision: A Primary Sourcebook* (Paragon House Publishers: New York, 1987)

Knight, Brenda, *Women of the Beat Generation: The Writers, Artists and Muses at the Heart of a Revolution* (Conari Press: Berkeley, 1996)

Kramer, Jane, *Allen Ginsberg in America* (Random House: New York, 1969)

Krim, Seymour, *The Beats* (Gold Medal Books: Greenwich, 1960)

Lamantia, Philip, *The Collected Poems of Philip Lamantia* (University of California Press: Berkeley, 2013)

Landauer, Susan, *The San Francisco School of Abstract Expressionism* (University of California Press: Berkeley, 1996)

Lotchin, Roger W., *San Francisco, 1846-1856: From Hamlet to City* (University of Illinois Press, 1974)

Maher Jr., Paul (ed.), *Empty Phantoms: Interviews and Encounters with Jack Kerouac* (Thunder's Mouth Press: New York, 2005)

McClure, Michael, *Lighting the Corners: On Nature, Art, & the Visionary: Essays and Interviews* (University of New Mexico College of Arts and Sciences: Albuquerque, 1993)

McClure, Michael, *Scratching the Beat Surface* (Penguin: New York, 1994)

Miles, Barry, *Ginsberg: A Biography* (HarperPerennial: New York, 1990)

Miles, Barry, *Jack Kerouac: King of the Beats* (Virgin Books: London, 1998)

Morgan, Bill, *I Celebrate Myself: The Somewhat Private Life of Allen Ginsberg* (Viking: New York, 2006)

Morgan, Bill, *The Best Minds of my Generation: A Literary History of the Beats* (Grove Press: New York, 2017)

Morgan, Bill, *The Letters of Allen Ginsberg* (Viking: New York, 2008)

Morgan, Bill, *The Selected Letters of Allen Ginsberg and Gary Snyder* (Counterpoint: Berkeley D.C., 2009)

Morgan, Bill, *The Typewriter is Holy: The Complete, Uncensored History of the Beat Generation* (Free Press: New York, 2010)

Morgan, Bill, and Peters, Nancy J., *Howl on Trial: The Battle for Free Expression* (City Lights Books: San Francisco, 2006)

Morgan, Bill, and Stanford, David, *Jack Kerouac and Allen Ginsberg: The Letters* (Viking: New York, 2010)

Murnaghan, Sheila, and Rosen, Ralph M., *Hip Sublime: Beat Writers and the Classical Tradition* (The Ohio State University Press: Columbus, 2018)

Murphy, Patrick D., *Understanding Gary Snyder* (University of South Carolina Press: Columbia, 1992)

Natsoulas, John, *The Beat Generation Galleries and Beyond* (John Natsoulas Press: Davis, 1996)

Natsoulas, John, *Lyrical vision: The 6 Gallery 1954-1957* (John Natsoulas Press: Davis, 1989)

Nicosia, Gerald, *Memory Babe: A Critical Biography of Jack Kerouac: The Kerouac Centennial Edition New & Revised* (Noodlebrain Press: Corte Madre, 2022)

Nin, Anaïs, *The Journals of Anais Nin, Volume 6 1955-1966* (Quartet Books: London, 1979)

Parkinson, Thomas, *Casebook on the Beat* (Crowell: New York, 1961)

Plagens, Peter, *Sunshine Muse: Contemporary Art on the West Coast* (Praeger Publishers, New York, 1974)

Notes

Raskin, Jonah, *American Scream Allen Ginsberg's Howl and the Making of the Beat Generation* (University of California Press: Berkeley, 2004)

Reidel, James, *Vanished Act: The Life and Art of Weldon Kees* (University of Nebraska Press: Lincoln, 2003)

Rexroth, Kenneth, *American Poetry in the Twentieth Century* (Herder and Herder: New York, 1971)

Rexroth, Kenneth, *An Autobiographical Novel* (Whittet Books: Surrey, 1977)

Rexroth, Kenneth, *In Defense of the Earth* (New Directions: New York, 1956)

Rexroth, Kenneth, *The Alternative Society: Essays from the Other World* (Herder and Herder: New York, 1970)

Rosenthal, Bob, *Straight Around Allen: On the Business of Being Allen Ginsberg* (Beatdom Books: St. Andrews, 2017)

Rumaker, Michael, *Robert Duncan in San Francisco* (City Lights: San Francisco, 2013)

Sanders, Edward, *The Poetry and Life of Allen Ginsberg: A Narrative Poem* (Overlook Press: Woodstock, 2000)

Schaffner, Ingrid, *Jess: To and From the Printed Page* (Independent Curators International: New York, 2007)

Schevill, James, *Where To Go, What To Do, When You Are Bern Porter: A Personal Biography* (Tilbury House: Gardiner, Maine, 1992)

Schneider, David, *Crowded by Beauty: The Life and Zen of Poet Philip Whalen* (University of California Press: Oakland, 2015)

Schumacher, Michael, *Dharma Lion: A Biography of Allen Ginsberg* (University of Minnesota Press: Minneapolis, 2016)

Silesky, Barry, *Ferlinghetti: The Artist in his Time* (Warner Books: New York, 1990)

Smart, Christopher, *The Religious Poetry of Christopher Smart* (Carcanet Press: South Hinksey, 1972)

Smith, Richard Cándida, *The Modern Moves West: California Artists and Democratic Culture in the Twentieth Century* (University of Pennsylvania Press: Philadelphia, 2009)

Smith, Richard Cándida, *Utopia and Dissent: Art, Poetry, and Politics in California* (University of California Press: Berkeley, 1995)

Snyder, Gary, *Myths & Texts* (Totem Press: 1970)

Snyder, Gary, *The Back Country* (Fulcrum Press: London, 1967)

Snyder, Gary, *The Gary Snyder Reader: Prose, Poetry, and Translations 1952-1998* (Counterpoint: Washington D.C., 1999)

Snyder, Gary, *The Real Work: Interviews and Talks, 1964-79* (New Directions: New York, 1980)

Solnit, Rebecca, *Hollow City: The Siege of San Francisco and the Crisis of American Urbanism* (Verso: New York, 2000)

Solnit, Rebecca, *Infinite City: A San Francisco Atlas* (University of California Press: Berkeley, 2010)

Solnit, Rebecca, *Secret Exhibition: Six California Artists of the Cold War Era* (City Lights Books: San Francisco, 1990)

Stryker, Susan, *Gay by the Bay: A History of Queer Culture in the San Francisco Bay Area* (Chronicle Books: San Francisco, 1996)

Suiter, John, *Poets on the Peaks: Gary Snyder, Philip Whalen & Jack Kerouac in the North Cascades* (Counterpoint: Washington D.C., 2002)

Thompson, Hunter S., *Fear and Loathing in America: The Brutal Odyssey of an Outlaw Journalist* (Touchstone: New York, 2000)

Thompson, Hunter S., *Fear and Loathing in Las Vegas: A Savage Journey to the Heart of the American Dream* (Warner Books: New York, 1982)

Tytell, John, *Naked Angels: The Lives & Literature of the Beat Generation* (McGraw-Hill: New York, 1976)

Watson, Steven, *The Birth of the Beat Generation: Visionaries, Rebels, and Hipsters, 1944-1960* (Pantheon Books: New York, 1985)

Weidman, Rich, *The Beat Generation FAQ: All That's Left to Know About the Angelheaded Hipsters* (Backbeat Books: Montclair, 2015)

Notes

Weine, Stevan M., *Best Minds: How Allen Ginsberg Made Revolutionary Poetry from Madness* (Fordham University Press: New York, 2023)
Whaley, Preston, *Blows Like a Horn: Beat Writing, Jazz, Style, and Markets in the Transformation of U.S. Culture* (Harvard University Press: Cambridge, 2004)
Wills, David S. (ed.) *Beatdom #24: The West Coast Issue* (Beatdom Books: St. Andrews, 2024)

Other Sources

"1950 Census of Population: Advance Reports," U.S. Department of Commerce Bureau of the Census. URL: https://www2.census.gov/library/publications/decennial/1950/pc-14/pc-14-13.pdf
"5th Annual Art Festival." S.F. Art Commission. 1951. URL: https://archive.org/details/sanfranciscoarts1951sanf/mode/2up
"About the Sydney Goldstein Theater" City Arts & Lectures. URL: https://www.cityarts.net/theater/
"A Conversation with David Simpson," by Dan Golding, Curator. URL: https://curator.site/interviews/2016/12/18/david-simpson
"A History of City Lights. 56 Years in the Life of a Literary Meeting Place," by Maia Ipp, Presses universitaires de Provence. URL: https://books.openedition.org/pup/21649?lang=en
"Allen Ginsberg Interview with Aaron Latham 408 E.10 St," Allen Ginsberg papers, 1937-2017. URL: https://searchworks.stanford.edu/view/bq830cy8469
"An Inglorious Slop-pail of a Play," Dan Piepenbring, Paris Review, September 2015. URL: https://theparisreview.org/blog/2015/09/08/an-inglorious-slop-pail-of-a-play/
"An Interview with Bern Porter, by Mark Bloch, circa 1985." URL: http://www.panmodern.com/berninterview.html
"An Interview with David Simpson," *Charlotte Jackson Fine Art*. URL: https://charlottejacksonfineart.tumblr.com/post/150742010190/an-interview-with-

david-simpson-august-2016

"An Interview with Wally Hedrick," by Mark Van Proyen. URL: https://wallyhedrick.org/pdfs/exposee_1985.pdf

"A selection of paintings, 1955-7. Harrison Street and the landscapes of travel," *The Art of Fred Martin*. URL: http://www.fredmartin.net/Fred_Martin_Art/1955-57_Harrison_Street_1a-img_Landscape_of_Travel.htm

"Beat Generation," John Natsoulas Center for the Arts. URL: https://natsoulas.com/blog/beat-generation/

"Chinese and Japanese in the United States, 1910," Department of Commerce Bureau of the Census, Bulletin 127. URL: https://www2.census.gov/prod2/decennial/documents/03322287no71-80ch6.pdf

"di Rosa Artist Interview Series: Wally Hedrick," WallyHedrick.org. URL: https://www.wallyhedrick.org/pdfs/di_rosa_artist_interview_series.pdf

"Flashback: Allen Ginsberg's 'Strange New Cottage in Berkeley'," by Tom Dalzell, *Berkeleyside*. URL: https://www.berkeleyside.org/2018/03/08/flashback-allen-ginsbergs-strange-new-cottage-berkeley

"Gerd Stern: From Beat Scene Poet to Psychedelic Multimedia Artist in San Francisco and Beyond, 1948-1978," Regional Oral History Office of the University of California, 2001. URL: https://digicoll.lib.berkeley.edu/record/218085?ln=en&v=pdf

"Gerd Stern Remembers Philip Lamantia," American Legends Interviews. URL: https://americanlegends.com/Interviews/gerd-stern-philip-lamantia.html

"Harry Jacobus," by Kevin Killian, *SFMOMA's Open Space*. URL: https://openspace.sfmoma.org/2009/05/harry-jacobus/

"House Work: Domesticity, Belonging, and Salvage in the

Notes

Art of Jess, 1955-1991," by Tara McDowell. URL: https://escholarship.org/uc/item/5mf693nb

"How Beat Happened," by Steve Silberman, Enterzone. URL: http://ezone.org/ez/e2/articles/digaman.html

"Howl," *Witness History*, BBC Sounds. URL: https://www.bbc.co.uk/sounds/play/p0104hly

"ICELAND: Killing the Killers," *Time*. URL: https://content.time.com/time/subscriber/article/0,33009,857557,00.html

"Iconic Beat Generation Bookseller & Poet Lawrence Ferlinghetti Turns 100," Democracy Now! URL: https://www.democracynow.org/2019/3/25/iconic_beat_generation_bookseller_poet_lawrence

"In Conversation: Lawrence Ferlinghetti with John Held Jr.," *SFAQ*. URL: https://www.sfaq.us/2014/12/in-conversation-lawrence-ferlinghetti-with-john-held-jr/

"Interview with Deborah Remington by Carlos Villa," Rehistoricizing.org. URL: https://rehistoricizing.org/wordpress/wp-content/uploads/Deborah-Remington-Interview_-Carlos-Villa.pdf

"It all happened on Fillmore Street," The Fillmore Museum. URL: https://www.amacord.com/fillmore/museum/index.html

"Jay DeFeo | The Eyes," Whitney Museum of American Art. URL: https://whitney.org/collection/works/11066

"Jay DeFeo | The Rose," Whitney Museum of American Art. URL: https://whitney.org/collection/works/10075

"Meditation and Poetics – (Mexico City Blues)," The Allen Ginsberg Project. URL: https://allenginsberg.org/2015/06/meditation-and-poetics-102-mexico-city-blues/

"One Hundred Years of Togetherness," by Jim Van Buskirk, *The Gay & Lesbian Review*. URL: https://glreview.org/article/one-hundred-years-of-togetherness/

"Oral history interview with Bruce Conner, 1974 March 29," Smithsonian Archives of American Art. URL: https://www.aaa.si.edu/collections/interviews/oral-history-interview-bruce-conner-13116

"Oral history interview with Dean Fleming, 2013 August 6 and 7," Smithsonian Archives of American Art. URL: https://www.aaa.si.edu/collections/interviews/oral-history-interview-dean-fleming-16130

"Oral history interview with Deborah Remington, 1973 May 29-July 19," Smithsonian Archives of American Art. URL: https://www.aaa.si.edu/collections/interviews/oral-history-interview-deborah-remington-13319

"Oral history interview with Jay DeFeo, 1975 June 3-1976 January 23," Smithsonian Archives of American Art. URL: https://www.aaa.si.edu/collections/interviews/oral-history-interview-jay-defeo-13246

"Oral history interview with Larry Jordan, 1995 Dec. 19 - 1996 July 30," Smithsonian Archives of American Art. URL: https://www.aaa.si.edu/collections/interviews/oral-history-interview-larry-jordan-12216

"Oral history interview with Wally Hedrick, 1974 June 10-24," Smithsonian Archives of American Art. URL: https://www.aaa.si.edu/collections/interviews/oral-history-interview-wally-hedrick-12869

"Paste-ups," Jess Collins Trust. URL: https://jesscollins.org/paste-ups/

"Phil Nurenberg's Bern Porter Interview," *Panmodern*. URL: http://www.panmodern.com/bern_nurenberg.html

"Philip Whalen talks to Steve Silberman," *Rock and the Beat Generation*. URL: https://simonwarner.substack.com/p/philip-whalen-talks-to-steve-silberman

"Rank of the most populous cities at each census: 1790-1890," Norman B. Leventhal Map & Education Center Collection. URL: https://

Notes

collections.leventhalmap.org/search/commonwealth:gb19h9840

"'Reinvent America and the World': How Lawrence Ferlinghetti and City Lights Books Cultivated an International Literature of Dissent, by Gioia Woods, *European Journal of American Studies,* Summer 2017. URL: https://doi.org/10.4000/ejas.12041

"Remembering Wally Hedrick," by Carlos Villa, *stretcher.* URL: https://www.stretcher.org/features/remembering_wally_hedrick/

"Robert Duncan (1919-1988)," The Allen Ginsberg Project. URL: https://allenginsberg.org/2012/01/robert-duncan-1919-1988/

"'Six at the Six' at 50 -- Return of S.F.'s poetic beat," by Jonah Raskin, *S.F. Gate.* URL: https://www.sfgate.com/opinion/openforum/article/Six-at-the-Six-at-50-Return-of-S-F-s-poetic-2576858.php

"Six Gallery," Literary Kicks. URL: https://www.litkicks.com/Places/SixGallery.html

"Take a Tour of Our Bookstore," City Lights Bookstore. URL: https://citylights.com/our-story/bookstore-tour/

"The art of California counter-culture in the 1950s," by Judith Delfiner, *Perspective.* URL: https://journals.openedition.org/perspective/5976

"The History of the Consulate General of Japan in SF," Consulate-General of Japan in San Francisco. URL: https://www.sf.us.emb-japan.go.jp/itpr_en/e_m01_06.html

"The life and times of North Beach's renowned Beat dive the Place," by Gary Kamiya, San Francisco Chronicle. URL: https://www.sfchronicle.com/bayarea/article/The-life-and-times-of-North-Beach-s-renowned-11010424.php

"The Monkey Block," by Woody LaBounty, San Francisco Story. URL: https://www.sanfranciscostory.com/the-monkey-block/

"The "6" Gallery: Roots & Branches," by John Allen Ryan, Community of Creatives. URL: http://communityofcreatives.com/hayward-king/

"To hunt for words under the stones," by Paul Christensen, *Jacket #11*. URL: http://jacketmagazine.com/11/whalen-christensen.html

"Untitled" [a poetry reading by Allen Ginsberg and Gregory Corso given January 17, 1960 at the Hotel Sherman, Chicago]. URL: https://searchworks.stanford.edu/view/wj640qd7451

"Vision Become: The Artists of the Six Gallery, San Francisco 1954-1957," by David Keaton, *Modern Art West*. URL: https://www.modernartwest.com/six-gallery-essay

"Wally Hedrick Interview - His Place - Bodega - February 4, 1998," by Mary Kerr. URL: https://wallyhedrick.org/pdfs/hedrick-mary%20kerr_interview%201998.pdf

"Was There a San Francisco School?" by Mary Fuller, Artforum. URL: https://www.artforum.com/features/was-there-a-san-francisco-school-213267/

"Western Addition: A Basic History," Found SF. URL: https://www.foundsf.org/index.php?title=Western_Addition:_A_Basic_History

"When The Beats Came Back," by John Suiter, *Reed Magazine*. URL: https://www.reed.edu/reed-magazine/articles/2008/ginsberg-howl-reed.html

Archives

Allen Ginsberg Collection, Manuscript Collection MS-01621, Harry Ransom Center, The University of Texas at Austin.

Allen Ginsberg papers, M0733. Dept. of Special Collections, Stanford University Libraries, Stanford, Calif.

Gary Snyder Papers, D-050, Special Collections, UC Davis Library, University of California, Davis.

John Suiter papers USU_COLL MSS 480. Special Collections and Archives. Utah State University Merrill-Cazier Library. Logan, Utah.

Kenneth Rexroth papers, Collection 175, Department of Special Collections, UCLA

Notes

Lewis Ellingham's Poet Be Like God Research Materials, MSS 126. Special Collections & Archives, UC San Diego.

The Robert Duncan Collection, circa 1900-1996, the Poetry Collection of the University Libraries, University at Buffalo, The State University of New York.

Audio

Ginsberg, Allen, *At Reed College: The First Recorded Reading of Howl & Other Poems* (Omnivore Recordings: 2021)

Endnotes
Introduction

iii	**"The thing that's wonderful..."** "Philip Whalen talks to Steve Silberman," Rock and the Beat Generation
iii	**"San Francisco is the poetry center..."** Empty Phantoms, p.73
v	**"If it wasn't for Kerouac..."** "Interview with Michael McClure," by John Suiter, December 9, 2000
vii	**"Ginsberg's main number..."** Jack Goodwin to John Allen Ryan, October 8, 1955
ix	**"the birth of the San Francisco..."** Dharma Bums, p.9
x	**"nearly as much a part of..."** "'Six at the Six' at 50 -- Return of S.F.'s poetic beat," S.F. Gate
xi	**"wrote a huge letter to Burroughs..."** Jack Kerouac: Selected Letters 1940–1956, p.524
xi	**"The reading sounds really great..."** The Letters of William S. Burroughs, p.293
xi	**"[a] wild week or two"** Journal entry, October 2, 1955, Gary Snyder Archives
xiii-xiv	**"Annie had written to McClure..."** E-mail correspondence

A Countercultural Capital

1	**"moment that the 'Beat Generation' became..."** Beats & Company, p.45
1	**"San Francisco was a very provincial..."** "Iconic Beat Generation Bookseller & Poet Lawrence Ferlinghetti Turns 100," Democracy Now!
2	**"there was a rigidity in the N.Y. literary..."** Composed on the Tongue, p.86
2	**"For instance I took my poetry and..."** Composed on the Tongue, p.87
2	**"from 1950 to 1960 the town..."** Composed on the Tongue, p.86
3	**"the last great city in America"** Empty Phantoms, p.72
3	**"As far as I was concerned..."** "Philip Whalen talks to Steve Silberman," Rock and the Beat Generation
3	**"this city has always been..."** San Francisco Poems, p.9
5	**"Soon after, Mormons arrived en route..."** San Francisco, 1846–1856: From Hamlet to City, p.8

405

5	**"the population increase was as follows…"** San Francisco, 1846–1856: From Hamlet to City, p.102
5	**"its population reaching 300,000 by 1890…"** "Rank of the most populous cities at each census: 1790-1890," Norman B. Leventhal Map & Education Center Collection
6	**"In 1847, about half of the people…"** San Francisco, 1846–1856: From Hamlet to City, p.103
6	**"In 1860, only two cities had higher…"** San Francisco, 1846–1856: From Hamlet to City, p.103
6	**"By 1851, there were already 12,000 Chinese…"** San Francisco's Chinatown, p.41
6	**"In 1860, for example, there were 35,000 Chinese…"** Working People of California, p.57
7	**"indigenous"** American Poetry in the Twentieth Century, p.137
7	**"After all, the Pacific Ocean is just…"** American Poetry in the Twentieth Century, p.138
7-8	**"The following year, Japan opened its first…"** "The History of the Consulate General of Japan in SF," Consulate-General of Japan in San Francisco
8	**"By then, there were 72,000 Japanese…"** "Chinese and Japanese in the United States," p.7; p.13
8	**"At the turn of the century, there were…"** San Francisco's Japantown, p.7
8	**"San Francisco was headquarters for Buddhist churches…"** San Francisco's Japantown, p.7
8	**"the first regular instruction in Zen…"** "It all happened on Fillmore Street," The Fillmore Museum
8	**"One newspaper account from 1902…"** The San Francisco Call and Post, July 20, 1902, p.15
9	**"By 1949, there were only about 100…"** "Western Addition: A Basic History," Found SF
9	**"California still had a Japanese population about eight times…"** "1950 Census of Population: Advance Reports," p.1
10	**"never saw such crazy musicians…"** On the Road, p.168
10	**"population was 89.5% Caucasian…"** "1950 Census of Population: Advance Reports"
10	**"Between the years 1846-56…"** San Francisco, 1846–1856: From Hamlet to City, p.163
11	**"San Francisco is the only major city…"** American poetry in the twentieth century, p.137
11	**"a burning bed of anarchism…"** Howl on Trial, p.xi
11	**"…inhabitants happened to speak American."** American Poetry in the Twentieth Century, p.139
11-12	**"the long honorable San Francisco tradition…"** Allen Ginsberg in America, p.46

Notes

12	**"the West has this enormous tolerance for deviants..."** "Interview with Gary Snyder," by John Suiter, November 12, 1998
12	**"concentration camps"** Kenneth Rexroth and James Laughlin: Selected Letters, p.27
12	**"a majority of these people settled..."** American Poetry in the Twentieth Century, p.138
12	**"Patchen [...] had NO influence..."** The Letters of Allen Ginsberg, p.323
12-13	**"most of the local poets [were] paranoid..."** Jack Goodwin to Lewis Ellingham, May 12, 1982
13	**"This arguably stems from the Gold Rush..."** Chinese and Japanese in the United States," p.8
13	**"There is a fair amount of sexual contact..."** Sexual Behavior in the Human Male, p.457
14	**"one of the vilest saloons and dancehalls..."** The San Francisco Call and Post, Oct 20, 1908, p.1
15	**"where girls can be boys."** "One Hundred Years of Togetherness," by Jim Van Buskirk
15	**"[o]ne of the most publicized police raids..."** LGBTQ America, p.20
15	**"World War II was a transformative event..."** Gay by the Bay, p.29
15	**"As one of the primary departure points..."** Gay by the Bay, p.29–30
15	**"the main neighborhood bar"** Goodwin to Ellingham, February 6, 1983
16	**"Remember that you had a lot of gay men here..."** Journal of Beat Studies 11, p.66
16	**"There was none of that macho bullshit..."** West Coast Women of Abstract Expressionism, p.3
16	**"If they respected you..."** Journal of Beat Studies 11, p.64
16	**"was winning prizes at the museums..."** "Interview with Deborah Remington by Carlos Villa," Rehistoricizing.org
16	**"if you were serious about your work..."** "Oral history interview with Deborah Remington"
17	**"were all held up as goddesses"** Journal of Beat Studies 11, p.65
17-18	**"nobody cared what you did as long as..."** An Autobiographical Novel, p.367
18	**"[T]here was something about the city..."** American Scream, p.9
18	**"Perhaps no other area..."** "A Note on Climate and Culture," p.180
18	**"the most equable..."** "A Note on Climate and Culture," p.179

18	**"I used to make up all these literary reasons…"** Ferlinghetti: The Artist in his Time, p.39–40
19	**"According to Lamantia, Leite founded…"** Philip Lamantia interview with John Suiter, December 11, 2000
19	**"was the first distinguished literary magazine…"** Philip Lamantia interview with John Suiter, December 11, 2000
19	**"I think it was different in San Francisco…"** West Coast Women of Abstract Expressionism, p.3
20	**"I came here because New York…"** San Francisco Examiner, January 19, 1975, p.24
20	**"[n]ot only did local poets develop quite…"** American Poetry in the Twentieth Century, p.137
21	**"The country had the feeling of martial law…"** Scratching the Beat Surface, p.13
22	**"I'm a politician. I'm trying to make…"** "di Rosa Artist Interview Series: Wally Hedrick"
22	**"[c]rabbed, pinched, elliptical, and oblique things…"** The Beat Generation, Bruce Cook, p.117
22	**"total rejection of the official high-brow culture"** The Alternative Society, Kenneth Rexroth, p.15
22	**"was jumping from the end of the war to 1955"** The Beat Generation, Bruce Cook, p.61
23	**"there was a period of stagnation…"** Casebook on the Beat, p.284
23	**"a faculty […] which would emphasize vision over craft…"** Douglas MacAgy and the Foundations of Modern Art Curatorship, p.30
23	**"A biography of an art curator is…"** Douglas MacAgy and the Foundations of Modern Art Curatorship, p.vii
23-24	**"MacAgy was convinced that…"** Uptopia and Dissent, p.92–93
24	**"a sense of rebellion against…"** Douglas MacAgy and the Foundations of Modern Art Curatorship, p.30
24	**"a living creature in flight…"** Douglas MacAgy and the Foundations of Modern Art Curatorship, p.36
24	**"investigate city plans, architecture, sculpture, printing…"** Douglas MacAgy and the Foundations of Modern Art Curatorship, p.31
25	**"Surely one of the more disquieting aspects…"** "A Note on Climate and Culture," p.183
25	**"between 1946 and 1949—the San Francisco Bay Area…"** West Coast Women of Abstract Expressionism, p.3
25	**"Art is not only free of anything that has to do…"** On the Edge of America: California Modernist Art, p.57
25	**"has been cited as an early…"** Douglas MacAgy and the Foundations of Modern Art Curatorship, p.42

Notes

26	**"located mines of meaningful imagery in the refuse…"** Douglas MacAgy and the Foundations of Modern Art Curatorship, p.43
26	**"These veterans—who in 1949 made up a staggering 87%…"** Uptopia and Dissent, p.474
26	**"Most of these men and women were older than…"** "Was There a San Francisco School?"
27	**"MacAgy was going toward the ultimate art school…"** "Oral history interview with Wally Hedrick"
27	**"what distinguishes this period…"** Lyrical vision: The 6 Gallery 1954–1957, p.16
27	**"the one community in the United States…"** The Alternative Society, Kenneth Rexroth, p.99
27	**"its old halls [and] cavernous, friendly studios…"** Sunshine Muse, p.31
28	**"[i]n San Francisco in the late '40s…"** "di Rosa Artist Interview Series: Wally Hedrick"
28	**"Gary Snyder complained that there had…"** The Real Work, p.162
28	**"including Knute Stiles"** San Francisco Art Institute, College Bulletin, Evening and Saturday Classes, Spring 1967, "Faculty" section.
28	**"Bruce McGaw"** San Francisco Art Institute, College Bulletin, Summer Session 1967, "Faculty" section.
28	**"He resigned from C.S.F.A. shortly after…"** San Francisco Art Association Bulletin - 1950–06/1950–07
28	**"A handful of surviving photos…"** San Francisco Art Association Bulletin - 1949–09
29	**"Each member had full control of…"** Beat Galleries and Beyond, p.16
29	**"was an attempt to put on shows without commercial"** Beat Galleries and Beyond, p.16
30	**"pioneers in producing [whose] work is such…"** "An Interview with Bern Porter"
30	**"tried to coax one of the founders…"** Where To Go, What To Do, When You Are Bern Porter, p.117

The Confusing History of a Strange Building

31	**"Name any writer, poet, or painter associated with…"** "The Monkey Block," San Francisco Story
31	**"the most famous literary and artistic structure…"** San Francisco Poems, p.14
32	**"like a reservation in which there…"** Hollow City, p.93
32	**"[A]s in every city in the world…"** Jack Goodwin to Lewis Ellingham, May 12, 1982

32	**"I certainly saw North Beach…"** San Francisco Poems, p.11
33	**"like a core sample"** Infinite City, Rebecca Solnit, p.68
37	**"In 1906, the plot was…"** SF Chronicle, June 25, 1904, p.7
38	**"One man who lived in the Fillmore-Union area…"** My Memoirs of Cow Hollow
39	**"the license Moni obtained was for a 'private garage'"** San Francisco Examiner, November 11, 1917, Automobile Section, p.1
39	**"The closest thing to evidence is…"** San Francisco Examiner, March 30, 1919, p.14W
40-41	**"to stage clean plays with family appeal to please audiences…"** Oakland Tribune, September 21, 1952, p.M-12
41	**"a rather unfavorable reception"** Oakland Tribune, October 19, 1952, p.B-3
41	**"a disappointment […] exceedingly amateurish"** Oakland Tribune, September 26, 1952, p.D-23
41	**"workshop gallery"** Oakland Tribune, Sept 21, 1952, p.M-12
41	**"exhibitions of theater designs"** Oakland Tribune, Sept 21, 1952, p.M-12
41	**"Artist Laureate"** SF Chronicle, February 12, 1985
41	**"exhibitions of theater designs"** Educational Theatre Journal, May 1953, p.137

Arise, King Ubu

43	**"So I was out, just read out…"** Robert Duncan, p.4
44	**"thin and shy, a pallor like someone who stays indoors…"** Robert Duncan in San Francisco, p.18
44	**"which he called 'Paste-Ups,' as a means of differentiating…"** Jess: To and From the Printed Page, p.16
44	**"Visual and verbal puns organize the intricacies…"** "Paste-ups," Jess Collins Trust
45	**"unbearably twee, even trite"** "Harry Jacobus," by Kevin Killian, SFMOMA's Open Space
45	**"MEANWHILE we are starting a critical…"** An Open Map, p.35
45	**"which he called picture-poems'"** "The art of California counter-culture in the 1950s," by Judith Delfiner
45	**"Second only to his love of…"** Young Robert Duncan: Portrait of the Poet as a Homosexual in Society, p.64
45-46	**"always had time to discover and encourage…"** Jess: To and From the Printed Page, p.51
46	**"Metart was an art gallery; King Ubu was…"** Beat Galleries and Beyond, p.19

Notes

46	**"it was Jacobus who came up with the idea of starting..."** Secret Exhibition, p.39
47	**"Duncan originally wanted to call the gallery..."** Beat Galleries and Beyond, p.23
47	**"a play so contentious that its premiere..."** "An Inglorious Slop-pail of a Play" Paris Review
47	**"[s]omeone was always putting on 'Ubu Roi'"** Jack Goodwin to Lewis Ellingham November 24, 1982
47	**"big deep wide very funky space"** "Oral history interview with Jay DeFeo"
48	**"sort of like a bowling alley"** "Oral history interview with Wally Hedrick"
48	**"the 6 Gallery was like a stable"** "Wally Hedrick Interview - His Place - Bodega - February 4, 1998," by Mary Kerr
48	**"There was a narrow opening..."** Journal of Beat Studies 11, p.63
48	**"Jacobus, who had some skill as a handyman"** Secret Exhibition, p.39
48-49	**"a strong social rebellion"** Journal of Beat Studies 11, p.59
49	**"household salon bursting at the seams"** Robert Duncan, The Ambassador from Venus, p126
49	**"We are bourgeois. We like to live in a nice house..."** "Oral history interview with Larry Jordan"
49-50	**"At Baker St. gradually the temper of the old manse..."** "House Work: Domesticity, Belonging, and Salvage in the Art of Jess, 1955-1991," by Tara McDowell
50	**"It had a real funky cement floor..."** Journal of Beat Studies 11, p.64
51	**"Well, the Ubu was primarily a place for 10 poets..."** Journal of Beat Studies 11, p.63
51	**"a place where anything, anything creative..."** Beat Galleries and Beyond, p.24
52	**"introduced a crude and vital Zen-like high taste"** Beat Galleries and Beyond, p.24
53	**"a job that Rexroth helped him to get"** Lawrence Ferlinghetti to Kenneth Rexroth, January 11, 1953
53	**"the most interesting non-objective art of the season..."** Art Digest, June 1953, p.13
53	**"a showplace for artworks and stage for drama"** Jess: To and From the Printed Page, p.51
53	**"It has been described as being like a cabaret..."** The San Francisco School of Abstract Expressionism, p.162
53	**"other yeasty poets"** Art Digest, June, 1953, p.13
53	**"[i]t was very poetry oriented"** "Oral history interview with Jay DeFeo"
53	**"was primarily devoted to..."** Journal of Beat Studies, p.63

53	**"obliterated every possible trace…"** Robert Duncan, The Ambassador from Venus, p.127
54	**"his biographer claims the play was only…"** Robert Duncan, The Ambassador from Venus, p.134
54	**"[i]n 1953 when this play was completed, I rented…"** Descriptive Bibliography, p.34
54	**"It was indeed very different from other galleries…"** Robert Duncan, The Ambassador from Venus, p.127
54	**"Duncan had a $100-per-month inheritance…"** Goodwin to Lewis Ellingham, June 9, 1983
55	**"The gallery also took only ten percent…"** Beat Galleries and Beyond, p.30
55	**"Mailings, and openings, utilities and props eat…"** Robert Duncan, The Ambassador from Venus, p.126
55	**"His esthetic majesty, King Ubu, has vacated his quarters"** Vallejo Times-Herald, November 28, 1954, p.38
55	**"they ran out of money; they were going to lose…"** "An Interview with Wally Hedrick," by Mark Van Proyen
55	**"Jess and Robert did their gallery for one year…"** Journal of Beat Studies 11, p.63
56	**"Is it MONEY or is it ART that Harry is after?"** W. Edwin Ver Becke to Robert Duncan, November 23, 1953
56	**"About the UBU, it is sad that it cannot…"** W. Edwin Ver Becke to Robert Duncan, September 28, 1953
57	**"The King Ubu really set the stage"** Beat Galleries and Beyond, p.110
57	**"That's where we got the idea…"** Lyrical vision, p.35

Five Painters and a Poet

59	**"The only reason we made this little club…"** "Oral history interview with Wally Hedrick"
59	**"We wore black Navy sweaters…"** Beat Galleries and Beyond, p.57
59	**"They were all passionate about art…"** Journal of Beat Studies 11, p.58
59	**"We were always trying to marry the arts…"** Journal of Beat Studies 11, p.58
60	**"I remember Wally Hedrick made a light machine…"** Journal of Beat Studies 11, p.58
60	**"there wasn't any art activity in Pasadena…"** "Oral history interview with Deborah Remington"
60	**"After a couple of months, the instruction was…"** "Oral history interview with Deborah Remington"
60	**"The first thing to do is to get out…"** "Wally Hedrick Interview - His Place - Bodega - February 4, 1998"

Notes

61	**"Here was this really good place..."** "Oral history interview with Wally Hedrick"
61	**"I fell in love with it immediately..."** "Oral history interview with Deborah Remington"
61	**"I looked at all the art hanging on the walls..."** "Oral history interview with Deborah Remington"
62	**"The idea of moving to San Francisco..."** "di Rosa Artist Interview Series: Wally Hedrick"
62	**"by the non-bourgeois atmosphere created..."** "How Beat Happened"
62-63	**"During the first three semesters, we studied..."** Beat Galleries and Beyond, p.58
63	**"In this little community, we didn't have to..."** "Oral history interview with Wally Hedrick"
63	**"this integration with all the arts was taking place..."** Journal of Beat Studies 11, p.58
64	**"became a kind of poetic mentor to"** "The "6" Gallery: Roots & Branches"
64	**"There wasn't a place we could go..."** Beat Galleries and Beyond, p.60
64	**"There was a good melting pot of people and ideas..."** "Oral history interview with Deborah Remington"
64-65	**"a decrepit, cavernous Gothic-Victorian..."** Secret Exhibition, p.34
65	**"We couldn't keep our benefits unless..."** Beat Galleries and Beyond, p.58
65	**"a catastrophe"** "Oral history interview with Wally Hedrick"
65	**"The history, the English, the art history..."** "Oral history interview with Deborah Remington"
66	**"There was nowhere in San Francisco we could show our work..."** "Oral history interview with Wally Hedrick"
66	**"kind of obstreperous kids..."** Lyrical Vision, p.33
66	**"I knew Duncan and Jacobus..."** Lyrical Vision, p.36
66	**"were all part of our group..."** Journal of Beat Studies 11, p.59
67	**"sad poems about his bohemian life"** Goodwin to Ellingham, June 29, 1981
67	**"John Ryan was more of a painter than a poet..."** Interview wth author
67	**"I admire poetry, but poets are a very strange group..."** "An Interview with Wally Hedrick," by Mark Van Proyen
68	**"a faculty advisor"** Interview with author
68	**"head of the new humanities department"** Poet Be Like God, p.49
68	**"Everything."** Poet Be Like God, p.50

68	**"There was a wonderful teacher who showed up…"** "Oral history interview with Deborah Remington"
68-69	**"All of the bartenders thoroughly disliked Spicer…"** Goodwin to Ellingham, January 28, 1983
69	**"Queen of the put-down"** Goodwin to Ellingham, January 28, 1983
69	**"I think he thought that my own method was…"** Poet Be Like God, p.58
69	**"FUCK GINSBERG"** John Allen Ryan to Allen Ginsberg, February 14, 1957
70	**"magical"** Journal of Beat Studies 11, p.72
70	**"He was a wonderful teacher…"** Journal of Beat Studies 11, p.70
70	**"I'm not teaching you what to think…"** Journal of Beat Studies 11, p.73
70	**"when he was teaching classes [a] supportive…"** Goodwin to Ellingham, December 5, 1982
70	**"Your assignment is to write an interpretation…"** Poet Be Like God, p.51
70-71	**"Well, in a three-hour period he taught us…"** Journal of Beat Studies 11, p.73
71	**"He taught Shakespeare but would not let…"** Poet Be Like God, p.51
71	**"he would bring a strobe light into the room…"** Poet Be Like God, p.51
71	**"I plan to be my own best student"** Poet Be Like God, p.51
71	**"he was beaten by Ryan, whose letter appeared…"** Poet Be Like God, p.52
71	**"Remington said everyone thought it…"** Journal of Beat Studies 11, p.73
72	**"According to one regular…"** Goodwin to Ellingham, May 12, 1982
72	**"ongoing epic"** Lighting the Corners, p.116
72	**"they all laughed out loud"** Journal of Beat Studies 11, p.72
72	**"Spicer soon began sleeping with Ryan…"** Poet Be Like God, p.58
72	**"fuck buddy"** Poet Be Like God, p.56
72	**"a love-hate thing going on"** Goodwin to Ellingham, May 12, 1982
72	**"came in as a poet, as a full-fledged member"** Interview with author

Notes

The 6 Gallery

75	**"We sat there one afternoon..."** Journal of Beat Studies 11, p.64
75	**"Hedrick claimed that the man who invented..."** "An Interview with Wally Hedrick," by Mark Van Proyen
76	**"Stopped by booth called 'Six,' sponsored by..."** San Francisco Examiner, September 26, 1954, p.33
76	**"the group raised about $80 for plasterboard"** "An Interview with Wally Hedrick," by Mark Van Proyen
77	**"a well-attended poetry reading"** Lyrical Vision, p.36
77	**"was a big success"** Beat Galleries and Beyond, p.59
77	**"devoted to the reeducation of its audience..."** Rexroth and Laughlin Letters, p.210
77	**"was a total political, social education..."** The People vs Lawrence Ferlinghetti, Kindle edition, no page number
77	**"mature non-fiction, high-brow literature..."** A Life of Kenneth Rexroth, p.221
77	**"outrageous pronouncements on the state of..."** A Life of Kenneth Rexroth, p.221
77	**"he didn't review just literature..."** "Iconic Beat Generation Bookseller & Poet Lawrence Ferlinghetti Turns 100," Democracy Now!
78	**"A new gallery of poetry, painting, sculpture..."** Lyrical Vision, p.80
78	**"Spicer, who knew he had no talent for..."** Poet Be Like God, p.59
78	**"very damp"** "Oral history interview with Jay DeFeo"
78-79	**"The ceiling was open..."** Journal of Beat Studies 11, p.63
80	**"It was exactly what we wanted..."** Beat Galleries and Beyond, p.60
80	**"I was the director of the gallery..."** "An Interview with Wally Hedrick," by Mark Van Proyen
80	**"ringleader"** "A Conversation with David Simpson," by Dan Golding
80	**"chief organizer"** "Remembering Wally Hedrick," by Carlos Villa
80	**"unofficial head"** "An Interview with David Simpson"
81	**"because he was a poet and could write"** "An Interview with Wally Hedrick," by Mark Van Proyen
81	**"would just send penny postcards"** Journal of Beat Studies 11, p.64
81	**"was very supportive..."** Journal of Beat Studies 11, p.65
82	**"[f]ew sold"** Poet Be Like God, p.59
82	**"forced and even sentimental..."** Journal of Beat Studies 11, p.56

82-83	**"A new gallery has opened at 3119 Fillmore Street…"** San Francisco Arts Association Bulletin, Nov–Dec 1954, p.5
83	**"Southland Artists Open S.F. Gallery…"** LA Times, October 31, 1954, part IV, p.6
83	**"[s]ix youthful pioneers, in revolt against…"** Lyrical Vision, p.32
84	**"It was from similar beginnings that Picasso…"** Lyrical Vision, p.32
84	**"When the '6' Gallery opened late this…"** Arts Digest, January 15, 1955, p.13
84	**"One of my favorite art critics was Lawrence Ferlinghetti…"** "An Interview with Wally Hedrick," by Mark Van Proyen
85	**"We commit ourselves to exhibiting…"** Lyrical Vision, p.13
85	**"The spontaneous, unpremeditated action is…"** Journal of Beat Studies 11, p.57
86	**"he was very supportive of what we were doing…"** Journal of Beat Studies 11, p.65
86	**"No self-respecting art community…"** Lyrical Vision, p.45
86	**"In every town that calls itself an art center…"** San Francisco Chronicle, March 15, 1953
86	**"One of the most extraordinary things about this…"** Lyrical Vision, p.45
87	**"I'M DREAMING OF DADA!"** Lyrical Vision, p.38
87	**"The artists remember the gallery…"** Lyrical Vision, p.38
87	**"it was easy. I mean, all we had to do was…"** "Wally Hedrick Interview - His Place - Bodega - February 4, 1998"
88	**"babysitting"** "Oral history interview with Jay DeFeo"
88	**"Art is busting out all over west of Van Ness avenue"** San Francisco Chronicle, February 11, 1955
88	**"Things are cooking in the Fillmore-Union…"** San Francisco Chronicle, May 15, 1955
89	**"gave focus and stability to the area"** Beat Galleries and Beyond, p.132
89	**"avantgarde and primitive art"** Oakland Tribune, November 2, 1952, p.79
90	**"The proprietors of the gallery were delighted…"** The Alternative Society, p.101
90	**"That was the first time in my life…"** "An Interview with Wally Hedrick," by Mark Van Proyen
90	**"We all saw it coming—but what can you do?"** Kenneth Rexroth and James Laughlin: Selected Letters, p.206
90-91	**"If I'd gotten hung up with tape recorders…"** "Oral history interview with Wally Hedrick"

Notes

91	**"The spirit of Dada was very…"** Lyrical Vision, p.41
91-92	**"Hedrick liked working with junk…"** The Modern Moves West, p.107
92	**"In general, the parts are not permanently joind…"** Jess: To And From the Printed Page, p.91
92	**"Where Berman's sculptures are characterized…"** Jess: To And From the Printed Page, p.91
92	**"If you're not getting it in paint…"** The Modern Moves West, p.106
93	**"his paste-ups included thousands of fragments"** "Paste-ups," Jess Collins Trust
93	**"I would rather not be called a painter…"** The Modern Moves West, p.101
93	**"a marriage between painting and sculpture"** "Jay DeFeo	The Rose"
93	**"sculptural manipulation of paint as a material…"** The Modern Moves West, p.77
94	**"an event in itself"** San Francisco Chronicle, September 30, 1959
94	**"Poems are events of Poetry…"** The H.D. Book, p.41–42
94	**"conventional notions of aesthetic enterprise…"** Beat Galleries and Beyond, p.137–139
94-95	**"We did things cheaply in those days…"** "A selection of paintings, 1955-7"
95	**"cheap souvenirs of a disputed passage"** "A selection of paintings, 1955-7"
95	**"[T]he very smallest bit of new communication…"** Beat Galleries and Beyond, p.149
95	**"[T]here was a bunch of people there…"** "Oral history interview with Dean Fleming"
96	**"part of the thing was to get loaded…"** "Oral history interview with Wally Hedrick"
96	**"Remington pointed out that the gallery…"** Journal of Beat Studies 11, p.61
96	**"Sometimes we as a group would go somewhere…"** Journal of Beat Studies 11, p.69
97	**"he had in fact performed it on this very stage…"** Robert Duncan: A Descriptive Bibliography, p.35
97	**"excessively clever, at times impossible…"** Robert Duncan, p.60
98	**"Dear lower world, cigarettes, convertibles…"** Faust Foutu: A Comic Masque, p.2
98	**"O I know it's not absolutely first rate…"** Faust Foutu: A Comic Masque, p.56
98	**"a collaborative theater experience"** Robert Duncan, The Ambassador from Venus, p.134

98 **"At the end I did understand what you wanted..."** Robert Duncan, The Ambassador from Venus, p.134
99 **"A couple of people stood up while they read"** Lighting the Corners, p.114
99 **"Jess spoke his lines with the immense clarity"** Lyrical Vision, p.19–20
99 **"was a magical quality..."** Lighting the Corners, p.116
99 **"This is my body."** Journals Mid-Fifties, p.105
99 **"an aura of notoriety"** This is the Beat Generation, p.179

Allen Ginsberg Goes West

103 **"The most individual, uninfluenced..."** The Book of Martyrdom and Artifice, p.80
104 **"journeying into San Francisco on Mondays"** Allen Ginsberg to Kenneth Rexroth, simply dated "Tuesday" 1954
104 **"I'm glad I'm in San Jose..."** Family Business, p.29
104 **"I'll be glad to pay your way..."** Off the Road, p.246
105 **"On the way I apologized..."** Off the Road, p.247
105 **"house of prostitution"** San Francisco Examiner, Feb 22, 1953, p.3
106 **"to publish original writing of insight..."** Undated press release titled "City Lights," found in Kenneth Rexroth archives
106 **"demonstrate that intelligent people must deal with..."** Undated press release titled "City Lights," found in Kenneth Rexroth archives
106 **"Starting a magazine in San Francisco is like..."** Undated press release titled "City Lights," found in Kenneth Rexroth archives
107 **"first class assininity"** "'Reinvent America and the World': How Lawrence Ferlinghetti and City Lights Books Cultivated an International Literature of Dissent"
107 **"Oh, you're the one who sent me..."** "Take a Tour of Our Bookstore"
108 **"This is undoubtedly the first autograph..."** San Francisco Chronicle, June 8, 1954
108 **"The first paperbook store in the land."** 1961 promotional postcard, Kenneth Rexroth archives
108 **"The paperback version sold out quickly..."** The City Lights Pocket Poets Series: A Descriptive Bibliography, p.16
109 **"a remarkable first book, because it speaks..."** San Francisco Chronicle, October 16, 1955
109 **The concept was inspired by Pierre Seghers'** "A History of City Lights. 56 Years in the Life of a Literary Meeting Place"

Notes

109-110	**"When I first came to town in the early fifties…"** San Francisco Examiner, January 19, 1975, p.22
110	**"Allen's favorite spot in the neighborhood"** I Celebrate Myself, p.198
110	**"Shig more than anyone else is responsible…"** San Francisco Examiner, January 19, 1975, p.22
110	**"basically the technology of brainwashing…"** Conversations with Allen Ginsberg, p.54
111	**"to overcome a block in his writing"** American Scream, p.153
111	**"do nothing but write poetry and have leisure…"** Best Minds: How Allen Ginsberg Made Revolutionary Poetry from Madness, p.155
111	**"a voice that rises once in a hundred years"** Portable Beat Reader, p.317
112	**"not really great as writer"** As Ever: The Collected Correspondence of Allen Ginsberg & Neal Cassady, p.129
112	**"poor poet with big ego"** Jack Kerouac and Allen Ginsberg: The Letters, p.283
112	**"a nice guy…"** The Letters of Allen Ginsberg, p.95
112	**"I met Kenneth Rexroth who is the big…"** The Letters of Allen Ginsberg, p.97
112-113	**"[e]ven meeting me, and I was nothing…"** Jack's Book, p.200
113	**"When I first came to San Francisco…"** "Robert Duncan (1919-1988)," The Allen Ginsberg Project
113	**"Robert I think was the first person who…"** Allen Verbatim, p.146
113	**"probably looked at what was…"** Young Robert Duncan: Portrait of the Poet as a Homosexual in Society, p.279
113	**"smart but sort of a pathetic type…"** The Letters of Allen Ginsberg, p.94
113	**"his poetry also is no good because too…"** The Letters of Allen Ginsberg, p.103
113-114	**"As brilliant and 'major' as Rexroth was…"** Lighting the Corners, p.91–92
114	**"Poetry-function, for Ginsberg, is to reveal…"** Journal entry, November 30, 1955
114	**"Any man who can write down fifty pages…"** "Allen Ginsberg Interview with Aaron Latham"
115	**"de facto cultural minister of San Francisco"** Kenneth Rexroth and James Laughlin: Selected Letters, p.241
115	**"his home became a mecca for local…"** A Life of Kenneth Rexroth, p.145
115	**"We were all brought up on Daddy Rexroth's reading list"** A Life of Kenneth Rexroth, p.154

115	**"he set up an anarchist discussion group…"** Kenneth Rexroth and James Laughlin: Selected Letters, p.97	
115	**"between twelve and seventeen people…"** Conversations with Gary Snyder, p.213	
115-116	**"bandy bitcheries…"** Goodwin to Ellingham, May 12, 1982	
116	**"great chambers with high ceilings…"** Poets on the Peaks, p.146	
116	**"a bullshitter"** Jack Kerouac and Allen Ginsberg: The Letters, p.277	
116	**"learned eventually that sometimes he…"** Conversations with Gary Snyder, p.213	
116	**"Many times he made up things and exaggerated…"** "In Conversation: Lawrence Ferlinghetti with John Held Jr."	
116-117	**"James Laughlin, he said that Kenneth got…"** "Interview with Gary Snyder," by John Suiter, December 6, 2000	
117	**"You didn't know what to believe…"** A Life of Kenneth Rexroth, p.242	
117	**"I wouldn't say that he was exactly homophobic…"** "Interview with Gary Snyder," by John Suiter, December 6, 2000	
117	**"he was very bitchy…"** "Interview with Gary Snyder," by John Suiter, December 6, 2000	
117	**"Rexroth's paranoid fantasies…"** Jack Goodwin to Lewis Ellingham, June 9, 1982	
117	**"He was annoying to many people…"** "Interview with Philip Whalen," by John Suiter, October 28, 1997	
117	**"superficial knowledge"** Hip Sublime, p.211	
117	**"as a poet and bullshitter alike"** Hip Sublime, p.207	
117	**"you have to be tolerant of his arrogance…"** "Interview with Michael McClure," by John Suiter, December 9, 2000	
118	**"Though others picked up his mantle…"** Kenneth Rexroth and James Laughlin: Selected Letters, p.xvi	
118	**"He vigorously and relentlessly reiterated…"** A Life of Kenneth Rexroth, p.148	
118-119	**"a student of Kenneth Rexroth"** Conversations with Gary Snyder, p.222	
119	**"thirty secret rituals"** The Collected Poems of Philip Lamantia, p. xxxvii	
119	**"fell in love with Allen…"** Lamantia interview with John Suiter, December 2000	
119	**"For years the Poetry Center was in fact…"** Gary Snyder and the Pacific Rim, p.303	
120	**"We felt simpatico at that moment"** Lighting the Corners, p.161	

Notes

120-121	**"Art is a community effort…"** Journals: Mid-Fifties, p.19
121	**"got into a big, interesting, artistic"** Straight Hearts' Delight, p.111
121	**"Oh, that's Peter"** Straight Hearts' Delight, p.111–112
122	**"I can't stand life…"** Jack Kerouac and Allen Ginsberg: The Letters, p. 317
122	**"SF is empty"** Jack Kerouac and Allen Ginsberg: The Letters, p.284
122	**"[t]he first time in life…"** I Celebrate Myself, p.194
122	**"a very dark, Russian, Dostoevskian…"** Straight Hearts' Delight, p.116
123	**"egocentric slop"** I Celebrate Myself, p.199
123	**"[t]he lines are not yet free enough"** Journals: Mid-Fifties, p.125
123	**"Ginsberg had been a rather conventional…"** American Poetry in the Twentieth Century, p.141
124	**"I've lost too much time…"** I Celebrate Myself, p.200
124	**"monstrous nightmare"** Jack Kerouac and Allen Ginsberg: The Letters, p.297
124	**"Great art learned in / desolation"** Wait 'Til I'm Dead, p.32
124	**"a beauty […] with droop sinister…"** Journals: Mid-Fifties, p.229
125	**"A drunken night in my house with a…"** Reality Sandwiches, p.48
125	**"the bullet in her brow"** Reality Sandwiches, p.48
125	**"stilted & somewhat academic"** Howl: Original Draft Facsimile, p.xii
125	**"Baudelaire remarked on this when he…"** Dharma lion, p.198
126	**"I saw the best mind angel-headed hipsters…"** Undated journal entry. Allen Ginsberg archives.

Writing Howl

127-128	**"I sat idly at my desk by the first-floor window…"** Howl: Original Draft Facsimile, p.xii
128-129	**"Dr. Hicks, his therapist, said many years later…"** American Scream, p.xiv
129	**"I thought I wouldn't write a poem…"** Casebook on the Beat, p.27
129-130	**"writing in a new style now…"** Howl on Trial, p.31
130	**"came as a surprise solution…"** The Letters of Allen Ginsberg, p.138
130	**"Hebraic-Melvillean bardic breath"** Casebook on the Beat, p.27

130   **"I realize how right you are…"** Jack Kerouac and Allen Ginsberg: The Letters, p.319
131   **"more or less Kerouac's rhythmic style of prose"** The Letters of Allen Ginsberg, p.121
131   **"Started a poem, came to me like inspiration…"** This comes from the second known typed draft of "Howl," titled "Strophes" and sent to William Burroughs. This was written in what appears to be the start of a letter but is scored out. It is cut from the version that appears in Howl: Original Draft Facsimile but can be seen at the start of the second manuscript hosted digitally at Stanford: https://purl.stanford.edu/cq952mh6350 (It is "image 15.")
131-132   **"I've pressed up girls in Ashville saloons…"** Naked Angels, p.216
132   **"a 1960 reading from Mexico City Blues"** This is from an untitled audio cassette, digitally preserved here: https://searchworks.stanford.edu/view/wj640qd7451
132   **"[t]hese long lines or Strophes as I call them"** The Letters of Allen Ginsberg, p.138
133   **"want it arbitrarily negated…"** Jack Kerouac and Allen Ginsberg: The Letters, p.318
133   **"one of the great seminal books of poetry…"** The Best Minds of my Generation: A Literary History of the Beats, p.260
133   **"to get piano and study basic music…"** Jack Kerouac and Allen Ginsberg: The Letters, p.317
133   **"I have been looking at early blues forms…"** The Letters of Allen Ginsberg, p.121
134   **"sketching language is undisturbed flow…"** Portable Jack Kerouac, p.484
134   **"You might think of [the lines] as a bop…"** "Introduction" to Allen Ginsberg at Reed College, Omnivore Records
134-135   **"It was [in the 1940s] that William Carlos Williams…"** The Best Minds of my Generation: A Literary History of the Beats, p.36–37
135   **"a long catalogue"** Ginsberg used this phrase many times throughout his letters and writings. To give but one example, it appears in The Letters of Allen Ginsberg, p.120.
135   **"keep the beat"** Casebook on the Beat, p.28
136   **"who poverty and tatters and hollow-eyed…"** Collected Poems 1947–1980, p.126
136-137   **"Rejoice in God, O ye Tongues…"** The Religious Poetry of Christopher Smart, p.32
137   **"The form is exactly the same…"** The Best Minds of my Generation: A Literary History of the Beats, p.401

Notes

137	**"these forms developed out of an extreme..."** Casebook on the Beat, p.29
137	**"a lament for the Lamb..."** Casebook on the Beat, p.29
139	**"art is a community effort..."** Journals: Mid-Fifties, p.19
140	**"a tragic custard-pie comedy of wild phrasing..."** Casebook on the Beat, p.28
140	**"crazy poetic juxtapositions within..."** The Best Minds of my Generation: A Literary History of the Beats, p.397
141	**"who threw potato salad at CCNY lecturers on Dadaism"** Collected Poems 1947–1980, p.130
141	**"the tower of Baal or Azriel..."** Journals: Mid-Fifties, p.61
141	**"saw Moloch Molochsmoking building..."** Jack Kerouac and Allen Ginsberg: The Letters, p.319
141	**"Moloch! Moloch! Whose hand ripped..."** Howl: Original Draft Facsimile, p.58
141-142	**"What sphinx of cement and aluminum..."** Collected Poems 1947–1980, p.131
142	**"The more he performed the poem..."** American Scream, p.171–172
142	**"I used poetic license"** The Best Minds of my Generation, p.426
143	**"the poem itself is an act of sympathy..."** The Letters of Allen Ginsberg, p.131
143	**"The poet articulates the semi-known..."** The Real Work, p.5
143	**"Three generations of infants..."** In Defense of the Earth, p.57
144	**"You killed him, with your 90-cent jugs..."** Jack Goodwin to Lewis Ellingham, September 6, 1983
144	**"You you dirty son of a bitch..."** Journals Early Fifties, Early Sixties, p.154
144	**"not very classy, not very strong as poetics..."** Jack's Book, p.198
144	**"Rexroth told Ginsberg never to mention"** Allen Ginsberg to Kenneth Rexroth, October 2, 1959
145	**"Rexroth in his poem also used the word..."** Conversations with Allen Ginsberg, p.125
145	**"[e]legy for the generation"** The Letters of Allen Ginsberg, p.121

Assembling Another Six

147	**"big college professor savant about literature..."** Jack Kerouac and Allen Ginsberg: The Letters, p.318
147	**"it's a Buddhist, AN EASTERN FUTURE ahead"** Jack Kerouac and Allen Ginsberg: The Letters, p.306

A Remarkable Collection of Angels

147	**"a Shakespearean Arden cottage…"** Jack Kerouac and Allen Ginsberg: The Letters, p.315
148	**"small magazine in Southern California"** Jack Kerouac and Allen Ginsberg: The Letters, p.320
148-149	**"much laughter and applause…"** Allen Ginsberg to Robert LaVigne, September 26, 1955
149	**"a flop"** San Francisco Examiner, September 18, 1955, p.6
149	**"Hey wow, that was real nice, that thing…"** Secret Exhibition, p.47
149	**"I've been asked to set up a poetry reading…"** Jack's Book, p.195
149	**"the Six Gallery reading was probably given…"** Lighting the Corners, p. 119
150	**"An art gallery here asked me to arrange…"** Jack Kerouac and Allen Ginsberg: The Letters, p.316
151	**"Hendrix [sic—Hedrick] asked me if…"** The Letters of Allen Ginsberg, p.122
152-152	**"Rexroth as introducer McClure reading…"** The Letters of Allen Ginsberg, p.122–123
154	**"Gary's tiny doghouse"** Poets on the Peaks, p.195
154	**"infinitely expandable space"** "Interview with Gary Snyder," by John Suiter, December 6, 2000
154-155	**"Japhy lived in his own shack which was infinitely…"** The Dharma Bums, p.12
155	**"At that time…"** "Interview with Gary Snyder," by John Suiter, December 6, 2000
155	**"early heroes [were] Indians & frontiersmen…"** Journal entry, November 5, 1955
155	**"I did a lot of forest work…"** "Interview with Gary Snyder," by John Suiter, October 26, 1997
155	**"half camper, half worker"** "Interview with Gary Snyder," by John Suiter, October 26, 1997
156	**"religious practices and austerities"** "Interview with Gary Snyder," by John Suiter, October 26, 1997
156	**"metaphysical bookshop near Union Square"** "Interview with Gary Snyder," by John Suiter, December 6, 2000
156	**"What I really should be doing is…"** "Interview with Gary Snyder," by John Suiter, December 6, 2000
157	**"he grew unhappy with…"** Journal entry, November 5, 1955
157	**"Kenneth Rexroth tells me you write poetry…"** "Interview with Gary Snyder," by John Suiter, December 6, 2000
158	**"He's a head, peyotlist, laconist…"** The Letters of Allen Ginsberg, p.122

Notes

158	**"Allen had respect for Gary in a way..."** "Interview with Michael McClure," by John Suiter, December 9, 2000
158	**"the first thing I noticed was how middle-class..."** "Interview with Gary Snyder," by John Suiter, December 6, 2000
158	**"All of us were into it"** Philip Lamantia interview with John Suiter, December 11, 2000
158-159	**"Japhy Ryder was a kid from eastern..."** The Dharma Bums, p.6
159	**"I used to worry about that..."** The Beat Vision, p.9–10
160	**"witty, articulate, engaging, a way cut above..."** "Interview with Gary Snyder," by John Suiter, October 26, 1997
160	**"He had wanted to live in San Francisco..."** Off the Wall, p.9
160	**"portly poet laureate of the school"** He, Leo, p.40
160	**"It was always very educational talking..."** "Interview with Gary Snyder," by John Suiter, October 26, 1997
160	**"great teacher"** Off the Wall, p.13
160	**"He's not physical..."** "Interview with Gary Snyder," by John Suiter, October 26, 1997
161	**"It's not too hard to get there..."** "Interview with Gary Snyder," by John Suiter, October 26, 1997
161	**"This town and these new people..."** Journal entry, October 2, 1955
161	**"the lightning storms around Sourdough Mountain"** Off the Wall, p.20
161	**"[Y]ou must come as soon as possible..."** Gary Snyder Reader, p.151
162	**"a poetickal bombshell"** Gary Snyder Reader, p.151
162	**"[F]rom about 1949 until early 1955..."** Off the Wall, p.22
162	**"Poetry is shit..."** Poets on the Peaks, p.158
163	**"the first people I thought of as..."** Off the Wall, p.22
163	**"anti-poet"** Hip Sublime, p.212
163	**"150 bloody poetic masterpieces"** Jack Kerouac and Allen Ginsberg: The Letters, p.318
163	**"about the closest you have to subtle..."** "Meditation and Poetics – (Mexico City Blues)"
163	**"nothing is as great as Mexico City Blues"** "Interview with Michael McClure," by John Suiter, December 9, 2000
163	**"Snyder recalled the manuscript..."** Gary Snyder interview, by Gerald Nicosia, Tape 92, Side 2
164	**"had become old to him..."** Door Wide Open, p.5
164-165	**"Hopping a freight out of Los Angeles..."** The Dharma Bums, p.1

165-166	**"The old rotten porch slanted forward…"** The Dharma Bums, p.11–12
166	**"Someday I'll buy that cottage…"** Poets on the Peaks, p.144
166	**"Jack was wearing a red windbreaker…"** Poets on the Peaks, p.146
166	**"like Tweedledum and Tweedledee…"** Off the Wall, p.20
166	**"affable clarity, and funny little phrasings…"** Poets on the Peaks, p.146
166-167	**"the two best men [he] ever met"** Jack Kerouac: King of the Beats, p.245
167	**"Regulars were also allowed up to…"** Jack Goodwin to Lewis Ellingham, May 12, 1982
167	**"the favorite bar of the hepcats around…"** "The life and times of North Beach's renowned Beat dive the Place"
167	**"the Deux Magots of Frisco"** "The life and times of North Beach's renowned Beat dive the Place"
167	**"a freak joint, poets of all the sizes…"** "The life and times of North Beach's renowned Beat dive the Place"
167	**"The Place was like a cultural center…"** "The life and times of North Beach's renowned Beat dive the Place"
168	**"a brown lovely bar made of wood, with sawdust…"** Desolation Angels, p.122
168	**"more than a whiff of the anti-intellectual to it…"** Jack Goodwin to Lewis Ellingham, May 12, 1982
169	**"I flashed that he was Jean-Louis…"** Poets on the Peaks, p.147
169	**"some chicks showed up"** Journal entry, October 2, 1955
169	**"Everybody in San Francisco is a Buddhist…"** Memory Babe, p.541
169-170	**"Jack scorned Rexroth's ego-centric…"** Memory Babe p.541
170	**"Allen Ginsberg has arranged for me…"** Selected letters, 1940–1956, p.519
170	**"No, not me. I can't do that…"** Empty Phantoms, p.45
171	**"we typed up a postcard that I wrote most of."** Conversations with Gary Snyder, p.214
171	**"John Suiter points out that…"** Poets on the Peaks, p.303
172	**"seven million"** Crowded by Beauty, p.10
172	**"Poetry will get a kick in the arse…"** Journal entry, September 19, 1955
172	**"I suppose I'll wake up to find myself famous"** Journals: Mid-Fifties, p.186

Notes

A Subterranean Celebration

175	**"McClure doubts this was true…"** "Interview with Michael McClure," by John Suiter, December 9, 2000	
175	**"tiny little car…"** Jack's Book, p.194	
176	**"Ferlinghetti claiming there were only about 30…"** The People vs Lawrence Ferlinghetti, Kindle edition, no page number	
176	**"Rexroth suggesting a figure of roughly 250…"** Kenneth Rexroth and James Laughlin: Selected Letters, p.214	
176	**"a figure also suggested by Whalen"** Off the Wall, p.26	
176	**"A surprisingly large number of people…"** Poets on the Peaks, p.148	
176	**"[e]veryone was there"** The Dharma Bums, p.9	
176	**"a hundred eager Raskolniks…"** Jack Kerouac: Selected Letters 1940–1956, p.524	
177	**"The Six Gallery reading was open…"** Scratching the Beat Surface, p.23–24	
177	**"There were elderly women in fur coats…"** Lighting the Corners, p.163	
178	**"David Simpson was sleeping…"** Interview with author	
178	**"Hayward King had left for the University of Paris…"** San Francisco Art Association Bulletin - 1955–05/1955–06	
178	**"If Spicer had been there…"** Lighting the Corners, p.117	
178	**"may not have agreed to…"** "Interview with Michael McClure," by John Suiter, December 9, 2000	
179	**"the detritus of an Oakland dwelling…"** "Vision Become: The Artists of the Six Gallery, San Francisco 1954-1957"	
179	**"curious and haunting series of…"** San Francisco Chronicle, September 18, 1955	
179	**"considerable number of paintings…"** San Francisco Chronicle, September 18, 1955	
179	**"a lot of insulting black blotches…"** Jack Goodwin to John Allen Ryan, October 8, 1955	
180	**"The October show at the Six Gallery…"** "Beat Generation," John Natsoulas Center for the Arts	
180	**"This is a lectern for a midget…"** A Life of Kenneth Rexroth, p.244	
180	**"immediately strove to dissociated…"** Jack Goodwin to John Allen Ryan, October 8, 1955	
180	**"to defy the system of academic poetry…"** Deliberate Prose, p.239	
182	**"the culmination of twenty years…"** American Poetry in the Twentieth Century, p.161–162	

182   "I was the one who got things jumping..." The Dharma Bums, p.9
182   "got drunk [and] the audience got drunk" Deliberate Prose, p.240

Philip Lamantia and John Hoffman

183   "probably be our greatest living poet..." Beat Generation FAQ, p.86
183   "highly regarded by avant-garde connoisseurs" Howl: Original Draft Facsimile, p.130
183   "Tell him I have eyes only for Heaven..." "Jay DeFeo | The Eyes," Whitney Museum of American Art
183   "He didn't harp on his background..." "Gerd Stern Remembers Philip Lamantia"
184   "Carl Solomon was so impressed by him..." Philip Lamantia interview with John Suiter, December 11, 2000
184   "the deepest friendship I've ever had..." Retrievals, p.123
184   "was a very religious person" Retrievals, p.123
184   "I hated the Church" Philip Lamantia interview with John Suiter, December 11, 2000
184-185 "Lamantia's poetry is illuminated, ecstatic..." Poets on the Peaks, p.304
185   "all hung up on being a cabalistic type mystic..." As Ever, p.123
185   "Ineffable Blissful Realm" Howl: Original Draft Facsimile, p.124
186   "I was paralyzed for about twelve hours..." Philip Lamantia interview with John Suiter, December 11, 2000
186   "Okay now, the reason I didn't read..." Philip Lamantia interview with John Suiter, December 11, 2000
186   "persistent urging of Rexroth and Ginsberg" Collected Poems of Philip Lamantia, p.xxxviii
187   "eaten too much peyote in Chihuahua..." The Dharma Bums, p.10
187   "He was using [peyote] all the time..." Junkie, p.149–150
187   "Lamantia believes he had been picked..." Philip Lamantia interview with John Suiter, December 11, 2000
187   "Lamantia thought nothing of condemning..." Retrievals, p.111 [In the text, I mentioned this was from a collection of poems by Hoffman and Lamantia, which is where the essay was originally published, but here I have cited another book, *Retrievals*. This is because Caples expanded and edited his essay for the latter publication.]

Notes

188	**"how Berne [sic] Porter still hasn't..."** Jack Goodwin to John Allen Ryan, October 8, 1955
188	**"Lamantia seems to have pulled it..."** Retrievals, p.134
188	**"a young priest..."** The Dharma Bums, p.10
188	**"certainly is a work of art..."** Jack Goodwin to John Allen Ryan, October 8, 1955
188	**"beautiful prose poems that left orange..."** Scratching the Beat Surface, p.12
189	**"According to Snyder, he was more commonly..."** Gary Snyder interview, by Gerald Nicosia, Tape 90, Side 1
189-190	**"I had never heard any of the Hoffman..."** Jack Goodwin to John Allen Ryan, October 8, 1955
190	**"the first one"** Philip Lamantia interview with John Suiter, December 11, 2000
190	**"Between poets..."** The Dharma Bums, p.11
190	**"I play back tapes and shudder"** A Life of Kenneth Rexroth, p.221
190	**"Everybody had a Kenneth Rexroth imitation"** "Interview with Michael McClure," by John Suiter, December 9, 2000

Michael McClure

191	**"The next poet was one Mike McClure..."** Jack Goodwin to John Allen Ryan, October 8, 1955
191	**"very nervous"** Jack's Book, p.196
191	**"a more formal style than the others..."** Jack Goodwin to John Allen Ryan, October 8, 1955
191	**"It was then that he met naturalist Sterling..."** Lighting the Corners, p.3
191	**"I had fallen into the rich art..."** Lyrical Vision, p.25
191	**"It is not possible that in the end the miracle..."** Scratching the Beat Surface, p.24
192	**"Point Lobos: Animism has a tight, small sound..."** Scratching the Beat Surface, p.26
192	**"There was no further title..."** Scratching the Beat Surface, p.28
192-193	**"In high school I had written cadenced..."** Scratching the Beat Surface, p.28
193	**"I did not fear obscurity in my poetry..."** Scratching the Beat Surface, p.26
193	**"They are all broke and stay high all the time"** John Allen Ryan to Allen Ginsberg, February 14, 1957
194	**"sounds a little tightassed to me"** The Letters of Allen Ginsberg, p. 123
194	**"relatively sober mystical poetry"** Deliberate Prose, p.240

194	**"very intense poem about working..."** "Interview with Michael McClure," by John Suiter, December 9, 2000
194-195	**"This year the largest packs of killer whales..."** "ICELAND: Killing the Killers"
195	**"horrified and angry"** Scratching the Beat Surface, p.30
195	**"I read a poem [...] of outrage and anguish..."** Lyrical Vision, p.25
195	**"broken ballad"** "Interview with Michael McClure," by John Suiter, December 9, 2000
195	**"Communication was not as important..."** Scratching the Beat Surface, p.28
195	**"fourth-dimensional counterpoint"** Memory Babe, p.543
195	**"he kept a kind of chanted..."** Jack Goodwin to John Allen Ryan, October 8, 1955
195-196	**"friendly drunk [...] sitting on the floor..."** Jack Goodwin to Lewis Ellingham, July 4, 1983
196	**"Sometimes Kerouac would flake out..."** Jack's Book, p.195
196	**"Mark Linenthal recalled Kerouac lying..."** Memory Babe, p.543
196	**"Perhaps the most strange..."** Deliberate Prose, p.241
196	**"Meanwhile scores of people stood..."** The Dharma Bums, p.10
197	**"over in the corner, beating time with that jug..."** Gary Snyder interview, by Gerald Nicosia, Tape 92, Side 1

Philip Whalen

199	**"big fat bespectacled quiet booboo..."** The Dharma Bums, p.8
199	**"a strange fat young man"** Deliberate Prose, p.240
199	**"he's almost always been overweight..."** "Interview with Philip Whalen," by John Suiter, October 28, 1997
199	**"distributed in an unflattering way"** Crowded by Beauty, p.13
199	**"a large, strange, openly hedonistic man..."** Crowded by Beauty, p.12
200	**"Standing there on the low wooden dais..."** Lyrical Vision, p.21
200	**"At first you think he's slow and stupid ..."** The Dharma Bums, p.8
200-201	**"It was interesting and exciting..."** Off the Wall, p.26
201	**"I was surprised that people would..."** "Philip Whalen talks to Steve Silberman"
201	**"a funny man from the northwest"** Jack Goodwin to John Allen Ryan, October 8, 1955

Notes

201	**"[f]unny and dry, his usual style…"** Poets on the Peaks, p.152
201	**"the little audience, 150 or so…"** Lyrical Vision, p.21
201	**"too incomprehensible to understand"** The Dharma Bums, p.10
201	**"None of it [was] terribly sensational"** "Interview with Philip Whalen," by John Suiter, October 28, 1997
202	**"aridly unemotional"** Poets on the Peaks, p.159
202	**"Damn you […] Listen to me…"** Poets on the Peaks, p.161
203	**"with a mock seriousness that was…"** Scratching the Beat Surface, p.21
203	**"a series of very personal relaxed…"** Deliberate Prose, p.240
203	**"The base of Whalen's poetry is not…"** "To hunt for words under the stones"
204	**"[a] new poetickall effusion"** Poets on the Peaks, p.118
204	**"When Philip started reading his poetry…"** Poets on the Peaks, p.152
204	**"comically and crankily read[ing] both voices"** Lyrical Vision, p.21
204	**"As I watched him read…"** Scratching the Beat Surface, p.21
204	**"concise, powerful, and humorous"** Scratching the Beat Surface, p.23
204-205	**"For all its wit and elegance…"** Crowded by Beauty, p.11
205	**"wicked sarcasm wrapped…"** Poets on the Peaks, p.117

Allen Ginsberg

207	**"a small and intensely lucid voice"** Scratching the Beat Surface, p.13
207	**"precise, intense, perfectly cadenced…"** "Howl," Witness History
208	**"I saw the best minds of my generation…"** Collected Poems 1947–1980, p.126
208	**"a long descriptive roster of out-group…"** Jack Goodwin to John Allen Ryan, October 8, 1955
208	**"who poverty and tatters and hollow-eyed…"** Collected Poems 1947–1980, p.126
209	**"what he sent to William Carlos Williams…"** Howl: Original Draft Facsimile, p. 150
209	**"with a greek chorus of visible…"** Howl: Original Draft Facsimile, p.18
209	**"who disappeared into the volcanoes…"** Collected Poems 1947–1980, p.127

210	**"who disappeared into the volcanoes..."** Jack Goodwin to Lewis Ellingham, July 4, 1983
210	**"up to a thrilling jeremiad at the end..."** Jack Goodwin to John Allen Ryan, October 8, 1955
210	**"What sphinx of cement and aluminum..."** Howl: Original Draft Facsimile, p.62
211	**"felt that they could participate..."** Journal of Beat Studies 11, p.67
211-212	**"Bespectacled, vulnerable and almost..."** "Beat Generation," John Natsoulas Center for the Arts
212	**"quiet brilliant burning bohemian..."** Scratching the Beat Surface, p.15
212	**"Ginsberg was real drunk and he swayed..."** This is the Beat Generation, p.181
212	**"The reading was delivered by the poet..."** Deliberate Prose, p.241
212-213	**"Ginsberg was pretty drunk by this time..."** Jack Goodwin to John Allen Ryan, October 8, 1955
213	**"I was very drunk and I gave a very wild..."** Allen Ginsberg in America, p.48
214	**"Ginsberg's main number was..."** Jack Goodwin to John Allen Ryan, October 8, 1955
214	**"Ruth in some ways liked to behave..."** Robert Duncan, The Ambassador from Venus, p.161
214-215	**"The reading of Howl was like..."** Lyrical Visions, p.26
215-216	**"In all of our memories no one had been..."** Scratching the Beat Surface, p.12–15
216	**"It was a breakthrough for everybody..."** "Philip Whalen talks to Steve Silberman"
216-217	**"It wasn't an obtuse thing..."** Journal of Beat Studies 11, p.68
217	**"like bringing two ends of an electric wire..."** The Birth of the Beat Generation, p.187
217	**"I've never seen him unbend..."** Jack Goodwin to John Allen Ryan, October 8, 1955
217	**"My only regret is that I am too old..."** Jack Goodwin to Lewis Ellingham, July 4, 1983
217	**"clapped & cheered and wept"** Kenneth Rexroth and James Laughlin: Selected Letters, p.214
217	**"At the end of the reading..."** Lyrical Vision, p.26
218	**"Allen, m'boy, I'm proud of you!"** Conversations with Allen Ginsberg, p.79
218	**"No, this poem will make you famous..."** Allen Ginsberg in America, p.48
218	**"it just blew things up completely..."** Kerouac: A Biography, p.235

Notes

Gary Snyder

219	**"the grand finale"** Jack Goodwin to Lewis Ellingham, July 4, 1983
219	**"My first thought…"** This is the Beat Generation, p.182
219	**"it was the unlikely blending of their styles…"** Poets on the Peaks, p.155
220-221	**"The other poets were either horn-rimmed…"** The Dharma Bums, p.7
221	**"The last poet to appear on the platform…"** Deliberate Prose, p.241
221-222	**"Then Japhy showed his sudden barroom…"** The Dharma Bums, p.9–10
222	**"You know, when you're working on…"** "Interview with Gary Snyder," by John Suiter, November 12, 1998
222	**"propitious"** Journal entry, September 19, 1955
222	**"my feeling is very simple…"** Journal entry, October 2, 1955
223	**"one of Snyder's very early mature poems…"** Understanding Gary Snyder, p.77
223	**"All I know is that I read selections…"** "Interview with Gary Snyder," by John Suiter, December 6, 2000
223	**"in 'A Berry Feast' there are some passages…"** "Interview with Gary Snyder," by John Suiter, November 12, 1998
223	**"the first poems that [he'd] heard…"** Beat Galleries and Beyond, p.70
223	**"scholarly and ebullient nature poem"** Scratching the Beat Surface, p.15
223	**"there was no pouty literariness"** Beat Galleries and Beyond, p.74
224	**"The Chainsaw falls for boards of pine…"** The Back Country, p.13
224	**"presence on stage and his words had the…"** Beat Galleries and Beyond, p.74
224	**"[e]qually well received"** Beat Generation FAQ. p.90
225	**"I have been brought back to the…"** Gary Snyder to Kenneth Rexroth, Wednesday (undated) 1954
225-226	**"What makes Snyder's poetry difficult…"** Understanding Gary Snyder, p.12–13
226	**"Murphy identifies three major areas…"** Understanding Gary Snyder, p.13–14
226	**"the distinguished audience […] howl with joy.."** The Dharma Bums, p.14
226	**"Snyder sees written poetry as arising…"** Understanding Gary Snyder, p.16

227	**"Snyder often depicts the thing in itself…"** Understanding Gary Snyder, p.17
227	**"San Francisco 2x4s…"** Myths & Texts, p.4
228	**"prefaced with a Biblical quote that warns…"** Myths & Texts, p.4
228	**"The Bible […] is outrageously irrelevant…"** Journal entry, August 11, 1955
229	**"the characteristically Snyderian voice…"** Understanding Gary Snyder, p.33
229	**"He also said in that same interview…"** "Interview with Gary Snyder," by John Suiter, December 6, 2000
230	**"Let me tell you, it moved people…"** "Interview with Michael McClure," by John Suiter, December 9, 2000

After the Reading

231	**"Save the invitation. Some day it will…"** Gary Snyder: Dimensions of a Life, p.77
231	**"[i]t succeeded beyond our wildest thoughts…"** The Real Work, p.162
231	**"curious kind of turning point…"** Dharma Lion, p.216
231	**"walking away [and saying] 'Poetry will…"** Beat Generation FAQ, p.90
231	**"It was very immediately a revelation…"** Beat Generation FAQ, p.90
231	**"the poets were left with the realization…"** Deliberate Prose, p.240
231	**"breakthrough to public consciousness"** Conversations with Allen Ginsberg, p.88
232	**"with abandon and delight"** This is the Beat Generation, p.181
232	**"gaiety"** Allen Ginsberg in America, p.48; The Dharma Bums, p.10
232	**"reminded everybody that the excitement…"** Gary Snyder and the Pacific Rim, p.23
232	**"inaugurated the new wave of poetry…"** The Best Minds of my Generation: A Literary History of the Beats, p.423
232	**"All of us were interested in…"** Lighting the Corners, p.162
232	**"Ginsberg emphasized the reading's unconventional…"** Deliberate Prose, p.239
232-233	**"Their approach was purely amateur…"** Deliberate Prose, p.240
233	**"had been deflated, sunk, in disarray"** "Howl," Witness History

Notes

233	**"The academy, with its tinkly-page poetry..."** Lighting the Corners, p.165
233	**"for a poetics that would go beyond..."** "Beat Generation," John Natsoulas Center for the Arts
233	**"That year [1955] everyone was desperately..."** Jack Goodwin to Lewis Ellingham May 12, 1982
233	**"subterranean celebration"** American Scream, p.9
233	**"voice to a constituency..."** "Interview with Michael McClure," by John Suiter, December 9, 2000
233	**"We did not dream that we were speaking..."** "Interview with Michael McClure," by John Suiter, December 9, 2000
233	**"were hungry for what we had to say..."** "Howl," Witness History
234	**"[T]here was something about the city..."** American Scream, p.9
233-235	**"That night the Beat Generation was made..."** The Typewriter is Holy, p.104
235	**"the world's rudest waiter"** LA Times, April 21, 2012, p.21
236	**"a big fabulous dinner"** The Dharma Bums, p.11
236	**"big happy orgies of poets"** Ginsberg in America, p.48
236	**"I wasn't one of his group at all..."** "A 'Howl' That Still Echoes: Ginsberg's Poem Remembered," by Paul Iorio, San Francisco Chronicle, October 28, 2000
236	**"I was leading a perfectly conventional..."** The People vs Lawrence Ferlinghetti, Kindle edition, no page number
236	**"an interaction with a Chinese chef at Sam Wo's..."** Selected Letters, p.584

The Beginning of a Great Career

239	**"it seems unlikely..."** The People vs Lawrence Ferlinghetti, Kindle edition, no page number
239	**"the Thoreau of the Beat Generation"** The Beat Generation FAQ, p.16
240	**"Bern Porter or City Lights bookstore..."** Jack Kerouac and Allen Ginsberg: The Letters, p.320
240	**"City Lights bookstore [...] will put out Howl..."** Jack Kerouac and Allen Ginsberg: The Letters, p.320
241	**"as well as significant younger writers"** San Francisco Examiner 29 August 1955
242	**"his plan for 'Howl' was to print it on..."** Kerouac: A Biography, p.260
242	**"claiming years later that he'd offered..."** "Phil Nurenberg's Bern Porter Interview"

243	**"Bespectacled, intense…"** Howl on Trial, p.xii
243	**"Howl is essentially a poem to be read aloud…"** Howl on Trial, p.47
244	**"lingual spontaneity or nothing"** Jack Kerouac and Allen Ginsberg: The Letters, p.318
245	**"It was a success…"** John Allen Ryan to Jack Spicer, November 2, 1955
246	**"fits well with Goodwin's"** John Allen Ryan to Allen Ginsberg, December 20, 1955
246	**"I just wrote a huge letter to Burroughs…"** Jack Kerouac: Selected Letters 1940–1956, p.524
246	**"Allen Ginsberg read a terrific poem…"** Kenneth Rexroth and James Laughlin: Selected Letters, p.214
246	**"Rexroth lead [sic] a party howling…"** Allen Joyce to Jack Spicer, mid-October, 1955
247	**"[t]he reading at the Six Gallery…"** American Scream, p.154
247	**"It was 'sufficient' to scrape by"** Allen Ginsberg to Robert LaVigne, September 26, 1955
247-248	**"indefinite leave of absence…"** Certificate of Honorable Dismissal or Leave of Absence, Allen Ginsberg Papers
248	**"I didn't have the brains or the mind…"** Journals: Mid-Fifties, p.168
248	**"giddy literary-theatrical show"** San Francisco Examiner, November 18, 1955
248	**"come down from their towers to poke…"** San Francisco Examiner, March 31, 1957
248	**"The first show occurred on January 22…"** Vanished Act, p.228
248-249	**"During the following year…"** Manuscript version of "Dress Rehearsal: Or, Life Among the Founding Fathers," by Jack Goodwin
249	**"After the Six Gallery, poetry readings…"** American Scream, p.7
249	**"The printing press has made poetry…"** Ferlinghetti: An Artist in his Time, p.88–89
250	**"1) a spontaneous method of composition…"** I Celebrate Myself, p.210
250	**"I Allen Ginsberg bard out of New Jersey…"** Journals: Mid-Fifties, p.207
250	**"No, no, that's enough"** Dharma Lion, p.218
251	**"According to Whalen…"** Off the Wall, p.21
251	**"who made all the readings [and] digs the scene"** Jack Goodwin to John Allen Ryan, September 21, 1955
251	**"He traumatized [her] with his reading…"** Jack Goodwin to John Allen Ryan, December 3, 1955

Notes

251	**"Rexroth's doings, no doubt..."** Journal entry, September 19, 1955
251	**"SUNDAY I had a poetry reading..."** Journal entry, November 2, 1955
251	**"a square trick"** Journal entry, November 14, 1955
251	**"He had been monitored by the F.B.I...."** Poets on the Peaks, p.90
251	**"on December 5, after much effort..."** Journal entry, December 5, 1955
252	**"to encourage young poets..."** Journals: Mid-Fifties, p.201
252	**"[t]he Poetry Center readings at the..."** Robert Duncan, The Ambassador from Venus, p.144
252	**"such talents as Louise Bogan, Gary Snyder..."** San Francisco Chronicle, December 18, 1955
252	**"had banned alcohol from her events."** Jack Goodwin to John Allen Ryan, December 3, 1955
252-253	**"asked [him] not to say any of the 'dirty words'..."** Journals: Mid-Fifties, p.168
253	**"a small school-sponsored affair..."** Journals: Mid-Fifties, p.200
253	**"Allen's huge bawling evening"** Journal entry, November 21, 1955
253	**"These Sunday nights after the readings..."** Jack Goodwin to John Allen Ryan, December 3, 1955
254	**"Ginsberg really gave them their money's..."** Jack Goodwin to John Allen Ryan, December 3, 1955
254	**"eventually becoming an atheist Buddhist..."** Philip Lamantia interview with John Suiter, December 11, 2000
255	**"Between 1948..."** Journal entry, November 5, 1955
255	**"I felt I learned a lot from him..."** Gary Snyder interview, by Gerald Nicosia, Tape 92, Side 3
255	**"I've seen somebody..."** "Interview with Michael McClure," by John Suiter, December 9, 2000
255	**"I felt very close to Jack..."** "Interview with Michael McClure," by John Suiter, December 9, 2000
256	**"Lamantia largely disappeared from both..."** The Collected Poems of Philip Lamantia, p.xxxix
256	**"I became the old man telling tales..."** Journal entry, November 3, 1955
256	**"running meditation"** "Interview with Michael McClure," by John Suiter, December 9, 2000
256	**"I want to see what this mountain..."** "Interview with Gary Snyder," by John Suiter, December 6, 2000
256-257	**"see the whole thing is a world full..."** The Dharma Bums, p.73–74

437

257	**"We'd have parties at the cottage…"** Allen Ginsberg in America, p.47
257	**"a discipline in generosity and non-attachment"** Journal entry, November 27, 1955
258	**"The fruit of the tree…"** Journal entry, November 13, 1955
258	**"restraint from cunt & drink"** Journal entry, November 5, 1955
258	**"Ginsberg that you mean love…"** Journal entry, December 5, 1955
258	**"He would remove his clothes…"** Ginsberg: A Biography, p. 199
259	**"misbehaved […] very badly"** Jack's Book, p.198
259	**"very superficial and largely factitious"** Alternative Society, p.102
259	**"dirty German"** A Life of Kenneth Rexroth, p.246
259	**"told Rexroth that 'Thou Shalt Not Kill' was inferior"** Jack's Book, p.198
260	**"took it very badly"** Jack's Book, p.198
260	**"Rexroth had wanted to be a popular poet…"** Jack's Book, p.199
260	**"stealing San Francisco"** Allen Ginsberg to Kenneth Rexroth, October 21, 1959
260	**"The envy Rexroth must have felt…"** A Life of Kenneth Rexroth, p.258–259
260	**"three times a day to talk to us about…"** "Interview with Michael McClure," by John Suiter, December 9, 2000
261	**"You sons of bitches…"** A Life of Kenneth Rexroth, p.259
261	**"I heard that you and your friends…"** A Life of Kenneth Rexroth, p.259
261-262	**"In the last three years Jack Kerouac…"** New York Times Book Review, November 29, 1959
262	**"[w]e were all carpetbaggers…"** The Beat Generation FAQ, p.70
262	**"I am indeed in Ginsbergenlandt"** An Open Map, p.101
262	**"like an invasion"** Jack's Book, p.200
262	**"It was really like a mess…"** Allen Ginsberg in America, p.160
262-263	**"Returning to the City after these events…"** Poet Be Like God, p.78
263	**"pretentious ignoramuses"** Jack Goodwin to Lewis Ellingham, February 6, 1983
263	**"Dionysian homosexual 4-letter-word poetry…"** Jack Goodwin to unknown person (greeting appears to say "Doris or Boris"), June 13, 1957

Notes

263	**"[t]o some extent the remainder..."** Poet Be Like God, p.78
263	**"a real broadside attack on the Beat"** Lawrence Ferlinghetti to Kenneth Rexroth, March 14, 1959
263	**"he felt Ginsberg looked down on him..."** Lawrence Ferlinghetti to Kenneth Rexroth, April 27, 1961
263	**"united front"** Allen Ginsberg in America, p.160
264	**"had there been a united front..."** Allen Ginsberg in America, p.160–161
265	**"brainwashing technology"** Conversations with Allen Ginsberg, p.55
265	**"harder to get things, if not published..."** American Scream, p.175
265	**"a blitzkrieg"** Crowded by Solitude, p.18
265	**"conducting a regular propaganda campaign"** American Scream, p.176
265	**"Ginsberg was probably the first poet..."** A Map of Mexico City Blues, p.25
265	**"before the poem was even completed"** San Francisco Chronicle, January 8, 1956
266	**"lecher"** Jack's Book, p.192
267	**"These Eastern boys finally got out here..."** "Interview with Michael McClure," by John Suiter, December 9, 2000
267	**"5 old ladies ran out screaming"** As Ever, p.183
268	**"Do you want to read 'Howl'?"** Track #8, At Reed College: The First Recorded Reading of Howl & Other Poems
268	**"he started out like he was kind of drunk"** "When The Beats Came Back," by John Suiter
268	**"I still hadn't broken out of the classical..."** "When The Beats Came Back"
269	**"I don't really feel like reading anymore"** Track #11, At Reed College
269	**"reconsidering rhetorical poetry"** "When The Beats Came Back"
269	**"Was Moloch the embodiment..."** "When The Beats Came Back"

A Repeat Performance

271	**"specialize[d] in in the performances"** Berkeley Gazette, April 24, 1956, p.11
271	**"The theater has been completely redecorated..."** Oakland Times, August 21, 1955, p.67
271	**"smash hit"** Stockton Evening and Sunday Record, December 16, 1957, p.18

271	**"the Guild disbanded due to a combination..."** Oakland Tribune, December 28, 1958, p.80
272	**"Good-time poetry / Nobody goes home..."** The Selected Letters of Allen Ginsberg and Gary Snyder, p.3
273	**"CELEBRATED GOOD TIME POETRY..."** Allen Ginsberg to Kenneth Rexroth, March 13, 1956
274	**"lit mostly by candles"** Brother-Souls, p.249
274	**"cheap red California wine..."** Brother-Souls, p.249
274	**"a naked lady throwing her arms about..."** "Philip Whalen talks to Steve Silberman"
274	**"festooned with Chinese brush orgy..."** "Flashback: Allen Ginsberg's 'Strange New Cottage in Berkeley'," by Tom Dalzell
274	**"cheering modestly"** Memory Babe, p.569
275	**"You need a goddam passport..."** Gary Snyder: Dimensions of a Life, p.76
275	**"poet who objects to everything"** The audio recordings of all poets except Ginsberg are on a digitized tape hosted at Stanford. URL: https://searchworks.stanford.edu/view/fg667wg6291 Meanwhile, Ginsberg's section is hosted separately: https://searchworks.stanford.edu/view/wz608kc4019 These are erroneously listed as having been recorded at the 6 Gallery.
276	**"elaborate throne-like wooden chairs"** Kerouac: A Biography, p.271
276	**"a small row of lights that could be..."** Kerouac: A Biography, p.271
277	**"Bearshit-on-the-trail poetry"** "Interview with Gary Snyder," by John Suiter, December 6, 2000
278	**"This was a reference to Spicer's..."** Poet Be Like God, p.57
279	**"Nobody speaks Martian..."** Poet Be Like God, p.63
279	**"almost booed off..."** Gary Snyder: Dimensions of a Life, p.76
280	**"Expressionists impatient / wanting..."** Gary Snyder: Dimensions of a Life, p.76
281	**"unnerved by the drunken wildness..."** Women of the Beat Generation, p.336
282	**"wearing a ragged sweater..."** Brother-Souls, p.271
283	**"It was, in a way, sort of scary..."** "Philip Whalen talks to Steve Silberman"
283	**"When Ginsberg finished with..."** Brother-Souls, p.249
284	**"I remember Kerouac drunkenly..."** Kerouac: A Biography, p.255–256
285	**"a book full of representative work..."** Howl on Trial, p.38

Notes

Infamy! Infamy!

287 **"The reading was pretty great..."** The Letters of Allen Ginsberg, p.129
287-288 **"there appears to be, according to Rexroth..."** The Letters of Allen Ginsberg, p.128
288 **"[t]he term [...] shows that..."** Poet Be Like God, p.78
288 **"Poetry had no need to be reborn..."** Kerouac: A Biography, p.249
288 **"Just as a show it was a wowser..."** Evergreen Review #2, p.13
288 **"came on like Elvis..."** John Allen Ryan to Allen Ginsberg, February 14, 1957
289 **"now the local poet-hero..."** The Letters of Allen Ginsberg, p.128
289 **"My teaching technique could shock..."** The Letters of Allen Ginsberg, p.128–129
290 **"That the students should develop...."** Course description of David Park's advanced painting class, c. 1948. San Francisco Art Institute Archives.
290 **"hire fourteen naked women..."** "Oral history interview with Bruce Conner, 1974 March 29"
290 **"Allen's first 'book'..."** I Celebrate Myself, p.216
291 **"sloppy and egocentric"** Howl on Trial, p.46
291 **"an article I knocked off in love of you"** Richard Eberhart to Kenneth Rexroth, May 26, 1953
291 **"he simply told Rexroth to send him anything..."** Richard Eberhart to Kenneth Rexroth, October 12, 1953
292 **"of sheer temperament"** The Letters of Allen Ginsberg, p.129
292 **"It's the nearest thing to a group..."** San Francisco Examiner 9 April 1956
292 **"I get the aura but I want the accuracy..."** Richard Eberhart to Kenneth Rexroth, April 20, 1956
293 **"a long explanatory letter"** Richard Eberhart to Kenneth Rexroth, May 30, 1956
293 **"[t]he title notwithstanding..."** The Letters of Allen Ginsberg, p.131
293 **"the Colossus unknown of U.S. Prose..."** The Letters of Allen Ginsberg, p.136
293 **"The West Coast is the liveliest spot..."** Of Poetry and Poets, p.144
294 **"The most remarkable poem of the young..."** Of Poetry and Poets, p.145
294 **"anarchist, Rexrothian poet"** Jack Goodwin to Lewis Ellingham, November 24, 1982

A Remarkable Collection of Angels

294-295   **"It is certain that there is a new..."** Of Poetry and Poets, p.147
295   **"He was a reporter, playwright, poet..."** Vanished Act, p.320
296   **"Must quit school, so as to leave..."** Journal entry, December (date unknown) 1955
296   **"It was [Snyder] who had advised..."** The Dharma Bums, p.243
297   **"by the gnarled old rocky trees..."** The Dharma Bums, p.243–244
297   **"I don't know when we'll meet again..."** The Dharma Bums, p.244
298   **"Some have suggested that he connived..."** Blows Like a Horn, p.24
298-299   **"Civil Liberties Union here was consulted..."** The Letters of Allen Ginsberg, p.130
299   **"I mean you can't tell what I am doing..."** The People vs Lawrence Ferlinghetti, Kindle edition, no page number
299   **"Everything worked out fine with..."** The People vs Lawrence Ferlinghetti, Kindle edition, no page number
299   **"Next time will take my time..."** Jack Kerouac and Allen Ginsberg: The Letters, p.328
300   **"not printed till [1984] for reasons of prudence..."** Collected Poems 1947–1980, p.xix
300   **"a square audience"** The Holy Barbarians, p.194
300   **"receptive"** Allen Ginsberg to Kenneth Rexroth, December 11, 1956
300   **"I got my howl machine..."** Allen Ginsberg to Kenneth Rexroth, December 11, 1956
300   **"I took off all my clothes..."** Allen Ginsberg to Kenneth Rexroth, December 11, 1956
301   **"a red-haired lush from Hollywood..."** The Letters of Allen Ginsberg, p.331
301   **"Artaud's mad conference..."** The Journals of Anais Nin, p.65
301   **"gave Ginsberg and Corso five dollars..."** Allen Ginsberg to Kenneth Rexroth, December 11, 1956
302   **"[p]eople are generally negative"** Allen Ginsberg to Kenneth Rexroth, December 11, 1956
302   **"I am sick of these con operations"** Howl on Trial, p.53
302   **"Spicer threatened the photographers..."** Jack Goodwin to Lewis Ellingham, May 12, 1982
303   **"it is not the poet but what he observes..."** The People vs Lawrence Ferlinghetti, Kindle edition, no page number
303   **"The words and the sense of the writing..."** The People vs Lawrence Ferlinghetti, Kindle edition, no page number

Notes

303	**"the collector has no duty to protect…"** The People vs Lawrence Ferlinghetti, Kindle edition, no page number
304	**"the raiding of bookstores…"** San Francisco Chronicle, June 6, 1957
304	**"It's disgusting…"** Jack Kerouac and Allen Ginsberg: The Letters, p.349
305	**"freeing Miller, Lawrence, and maybe Genet"** Howl on Trial, p.79
305-306	**"I do not believe that Howl…"** Howl on Trial, p.197, 207
306-307	**"purely technically, Ginsberg is…"** Evergreen Review #2, p.12
307	**"went heavily by what Allen Ginsberg…"** Blows Like a Horn, p.20
307	**"a letter Ginsberg sent in December 1956…"** Allen Ginsberg to Kenneth Rexroth, December 11, 1956
307	**"he felt their contributions were poor"** Allen Ginsberg to Kenneth Rexroth, undated letter from Venice, Italy

The End of the 6

312	**"The 6 Gallery, at 3119 Fillmore…"** San Francisco Chronicle, November 13, 1955
312	**"David Simpson seems to have lost interest…"** Journal of Beat Studies #11, p.70
314	**"there wasn't anything to do with…"** "Oral history interview with Bruce Conner"
314	**"towards the end, sitting got to…"** Lyrical Vision, p.44
314	**"by the time I got there, the artists…"** Beat Galleries and Beyond, p.139
315	**"At the end…"** Beat Galleries and Beyond, p.139
315	**"The thing was to have regular hours…"** Beat Galleries and Beyond, p.139
315	**"a commercial space […] a fabulous place…"** Journal of Beat Studies 11, p.74
315	**"immediacy. You'd jump into something…"** Manuel Neri Early Work 1953–1978, p.4
317	**"expressed his violent disinterest in…"** San Francisco Chronicle, Nov 7, 1957
317-318	**"Dear Six Gallery members…"** Lyrical Vision, p.89
320	**"Suddenly everyone was a poet"** Manuscript version of "Dress Rehearsal: Or, Life Among the Founding Fathers," by Jack Goodwin
320	**"Bay Area bohemia […] suddenly…"** Beat Galleries and Beyond, p.139
321	**"San Francisco in the middle sixties was…"** Fear and Loathing in Las Vegas, p.67–68

321 **"the Death of the American Dream"** Thompson used this phrase dozens of times. An early example is Fear and Loathing in America, p.14.
321 **"a nonliterate age…"** Contemporary Literary Criticism, p.316
322-323 **"Even if you have no intention of buying…"** San Francisco Examiner, July 15, 1984, p.357
323 **"multi-media show by Bay Area artists"** San Francisco Examiner, Aug 19, 1979, p.259
323 **"One visitor in the 1990s reported…"** "Six Gallery," Literary Kicks

Myth and Legacy

329 **"Vision of Eternity"** Journals Mid-Fifties, p.137
330 **"The most brilliant shock of the evening…"** Deliberate Prose, p.240
331 **"a run down second rate experimental art gallery"** Deliberate Prose, p.239
331 **"the poets were left with the realization…"** Deliberate Prose, p.240
331 **"was thrown into jail for…"** Empty Phantoms, p.39
332 **"Kerouac may have read the article…"** Blows Like a Horn, p.25
333 **"Japhy Ryder is not me…"** Conversations with Gary Snyder, p.209
333-334 **"Kerouac's characters are modeled…"** The Best Minds of my Generation: A Literary History of the Beats, p.232
334 **"even by 1956 he was a highly…"** Memory Babe, p.551
334 **"fairly accurate"** Off the Wall, p.53
334 **"sloppy […] really second-rate book"** "Interview with Gary Snyder," by John Suiter, December 6, 2000
334-335 **"it's pretty accurate…"** Gary Snyder interview, by Gerald Nicosia, Tape 92, Side 1
336 **"I am one of the country's most…"** The Alternative Society, p.11
336 **"that dumb Rexroth article"** Jack Kerouac and Allen Ginsberg: The Letters, p.351
336 **"evil parody"** Allen Ginsberg to Kenneth Rexroth, October 21, 1959
337 **"There were a few references…"** Santa Cruz Sentinel, June 2, 1968 (Note: It vaguely refers to the first reading of "Howl" but gets the year wrong, saying it happened in 1956. Another newspaper printed a month earlier referred to the mythical closing party at the 6 Gallery, showing perhaps some interest in that by-gone era.)

Notes

338 **"later became recognized as a historical..."** Lincoln Journal Star, Dec 30, 1971, p.4

338 **"As in painting and music the change..."** Poetry in the Twentieth Century, p.161–162

341 **"the germinating public seed..."** Naked Angels, p.104

341 **"his personal art form"** Straight Around Allen, p.59

342 **"whatever image of myself or Kerouac..."** Burroughs-Warhol Connection, p.11

343 **"it's all gotten kind of myth-like..."** Lyrical Vision, p.33

350 **"There was an actual orgy..."** The Poetry and Life of Allen Ginsberg, p.33

358 **"It is not the intention of..."** "5th Annual Art Festival"

359 **"It was restored and reopened..."** "About the Sydney Goldstein Theater"

359 **"nearly canceled this section of the event..."** Minutes of Art Commission of the City and County of San Francisco 1955, p.3249

359 **"this year's move indoors has had..."** San Francisco Examiner, September 18, 1955, p.6

359-360 **"Location of most of the stage programs..."** San Francisco Examiner, September 18, 1955, p.6

360 **"internal documents..."** Minutes of Art Commission of the City and County of San Francisco 1955, p.3261

360 **"One of the sacred precepts of our..."** San Francisco Examiner, September 22, 1955, p.32

361 **"We had an audience of about..."** Jack Goodwin to John Allen Ryan, September 21, 1955

361 **"Stern was also Angelou's boyfriend..."** "Gerd Stern: From Beat Scene Poet to Psychedelic Multimedia Artist in San Francisco and Beyond, 1948-1978," p.45

361 **"Backstage, while everyone was sweating..."** Manuscript version of "Dress Rehearsal: Or, Life Among the Founding Fathers," by Jack Goodwin

363 **"camp, camp, camp"** Jack Goodwin to John Allen Ryan, July 4, 1983

364-365 **"One of the poetry-readings I saw..."** Jack Goodwin to John Allen Ryan, September 21, 1955

366 **"They had to call a dirty-word conference..."** Jack Goodwin to John Allen Ryan, September 21, 1955

366 **"a vision of ultimate jazz eluding..."** Howl: Original Draft Facsimile, p.27

366-367 **"The result was electrifying..."** Manuscript version of "Dress Rehearsal: Or, Life Among the Founding Fathers," by Jack Goodwin

368 **"I read this poem..."** Allen Ginsberg to Robert LaVigne, Sept 26, 1955

445

368	**"read some of his breezy, funnier poems…"** Typewriter is Holy, p.101
370	**"I have 5 pages of this to read…"** Howl on Trial, p.35
371	**"I'm going to read you…"** Jack Goodwin to John Allen Ryan, September 21, 1955
372	**"[n]o more of the restraint he featured…"** Jack Goodwin to John Allen Ryan, October 8, 1955
373	**"Ginsberg's main number was a long…"** Jack Goodwin to John Allen Ryan, October 8, 1955

Index

"A Berry Feast," 222-227, 229
Abstract expressionism, 25, 26, 44, 61
Adam, Helen, 43, 99, 253
Adams, Ansel, 24, 63
"America," 243, 250, 284-285, 291, 298
Anarchism, 10-11, 12, 112, 115, 117, 177, 184, 203
Artaud, Antonin, 138, 191, 301, 331
"A Supermarket in California," 148-149, 207, 268, 284, 368-370, 372, 373-374
Auden, W.H., 119-120, 133, 188, 299
Barletta, Joel, 81, 168
Beat Generation, i, iv, v, ix, x, xv, xvi, xviii, xix, 1-2, 3, 17, 20, 34, 48, 69, 97, 103, 107, 109, 121, 125, 128, 130, 131, 140, 156, 169, 178, 183, 193, 220, 231, 234-235, 249, 259, 263, 265-266, 296, 302, 307, 308, 311, 317, 326-327, 329-332, 336-337, 339-341, 343, 356
Beatniks, iv, 3, 4, 76, 144, 145, 263, 308, 320, 332, 336, 340
Berkeley Renaissance, 69, 178
Berkeley Town Hall Reading, xiv, xvii, 178, 201, 232, 271-285, 287, 350, 352, 367
Berman, Wallace, 92, 316

Bierce, Ambrose, 18, 31
Bischoff, Elmer, 24, 26, 31, 44, 52, 55, 61, 62, 87
Black Mountain College, 97, 193, 313, 316
Blake, William, 120, 137, 138, 232, 329-330, 341
Blaser, Robin, 16, 53, 69, 178, 263, 295
Brakhage, Stan, 49, 53, 89
Brautigan, Richard, 4, 322, 356
Breton, André, 111, 162, 183
Broughton, James, 16, 49, 115, 306-307
Brown, Joan, 17, 89, 317
Buddhism, 7, 8, 10, 11, 104, 147, 156, 157, 160, 169, 225, 254, 255, 257, 262, 336
Brockway, Lyn, 43, 45, 54
Burroughs, William S., iii, x-xi, xv, 1, 2, 12, 103, 125, 131, 140, 155, 187, 235, 246, 265, 293, 301-302, 304, 331, 340, 342
Caen, Herb, iv, 76, 235
California School of Fine Arts, 23-27, 28, 31, 43, 44, 53, 60-64, 65, 68, 70-72, 79, 80, 89, 172, 289, 312
Carr, Lucien, 282
Cassady, Carolyn, 104-105, 121
Cassady, Neal, xv, 104, 112, 121, 122, 150, 152, 167, 177, 185, 217-218, 220, 255, 266, 274, 340
Circle (magazine), 18-19, 22, 25, 29, 111
City Lights Bookstore, ii, 3, 19, 32, 34, 105-110, 127, 172, 175, 240, 241-242, 244-245, 282, 298, 300, 303-304
City Lights journal, 105-107

447

Charters, Ann, xiii, xxi, 1, 145, 171, 274-275, 276, 283-284, 288, 338, 347, 352
Chinatown (San Francisco), 3, 6, 8, 31
Conner, Bruce, 89, 92, 290, 313-314, 316, 317
Conscientious objectors, 12, 109, 215
Corbett, Edward, 24, 30, 44
Corso, Gregory, iii, ix, xi, 12, 131, 175, 183, 243, 250, 265, 300-301, 326, 330-331, 339, 349
Columbia University, ix, xv, 1, 2, 103, 121, 299, 327
Creeley, Robert, 193, 260-261, 290
Dadaism, 44, 62, 80, 87, 91, 140-141
Dali, Salvador, 24, 59
Davis, Miles, 10, 65, 134
DeFeo, Jay, 17, 47, 53, 66, 78, 81, 88, 89, 93-94, 140, 168, 183, 313, 319
Diebenkorn, Richard, 24, 26, 30, 31, 62, 87, 92
Dharma Bums, The, ix, xvi, 154-155, 158-159, 164-166, 167, 182, 183, 187, 220-223, 226, 236, 256, 259, 296-297, 327, 327, 332-336, 350-351
Duchamp, Marcel, 25, 91-92
Duncan, Robert, 2, 16, 19, 29, 30, 43-50, 52-56, 64, 66-67, 69, 78, 89, 94, 97-100, 103, 112-115, 119, 120, 138, 141, 149, 157, 167, 177, 178, 184, 240, 262-264, 288, 295, 300, 306-307
Earthquake (1906), x, 31, 33, 36

East and West Gallery, 88-89, 314
Eberhart, Richard, 273, 291-295
Ecology, viii, 184, 191, 194, 223-224, 226, 228, 343
Eichel, Bill, 83, 168
Eliot, T.S., 115, 119, 188, 251, 299, 319
Evergreen Review, 223, 275, 306-307, 337
Everson, William, 12, 19, 109, 115, 118, 168, 306
Faust Foutu, 54, 56, 97-100, 103, 141, 149, 151, 167, 246-247
Ferlinghetti, Lawrence, ii, iii, iv, xi, 1, 3, 11, 18, 19, 29, 31, 32, 34, 52-53, 69, 77, 84, 107-110, 115, 116, 120, 138, 152, 175, 176, 196, 207, 236, 239-244, 248, 249, 251, 253, 262, 263, 277, 282, 285, 288, 291, 294-295, 297-299, 302-306, 307, 321-322, 328, 331, 336, 339
Forakis, Peter, 81, 172, 317, 322
Frankenstein, Alfred, 25, 52, 82, 84-86, 88, 94, 179, 311-312
Funk art, 25, 34, 139, 216
Gechtoff, Ethel, 88-89, 314-315
Gechtoff, Sonia, 16, 88, 89, 179
Genet, Jean, 169, 299, 305, 331, 341
Ginsberg, Allen, i, ii, iii, vi-viii, ix, x, xi, xiii, xiv, xv, xvi, xvii, xx, 1, 2, 11, 12, 16, 22, 30, 33-34, 49, 67, 69-70, 103-105, 110-115, 118-126, 127-146, 147-154, 155, 157-160, 162, 163, 165, 166, 167, 168, 169, 170-171, 172, 175, 177, 180,

Index

182, 183, 184, 185, 186, 192, 193-194, 196, 199, 203, 207-218, 219-220, 221, 224, 229, 230, 231, 232-233, 234-235, 239-269, 272-276, 277, 280-285, 287-295, 297-309, 311, 313, 315, 316, 319, 325, 326-332, 333, 334, 335, 336-337, 338-339, 340-343, 349, 350, 351, 352-353, 355-357, 361-375

Gleason, Madeline, 43, 119

Gold Rush, x, 5, 11, 13

Goodwin, Jack, vii, xv, 12, 15, 32, 47, 54, 67, 68, 117, 148, 168, 177, 179, 180, 184, 188, 189-190, 191, 195, 201, 207-211, 212-213, 217, 233, 245-246, 248-249, 251, 253-254, 320, 337, 347, 356-357, 360-374

Grachis, Dimitri, 82, 89, 314

Harte, Bret, 18, 31

Hedrick, Wally, 22, 27, 28, 47-48, 55, 59-62, 63-64, 65, 66-68, 72-73, 75-77, 78, 79, 80-81, 84, 87, 88, 89, 90-93, 96, 139, 149-150, 151, 168, 178, 313, 314, 315, 319, 320, 339, 343, 352-353

Hicks, Dr. Philip, 111, 128, 247

Hirsch, Hy, 80, 84, 89

Hippies, ii, iv, v, 3, 4, 76, 308, 320-322, 340

Hode, Ida, 98-99, 214, 252, 361

Hoffman, John, xii, 152-153, 158, 183-184, 186-189, 210, 234, 353

Holmes, John Clellon, xi, 246

Homosexuality, viii, 13-16, 43-44, 69, 72, 104, 110, 117, 215, 268, 298, 340, 343, 369-370

"Howl," ii, iv, vi-viii, xv, xvi, xx, 30, 33-34, 69, 126, 127-146, 148-149, 152, 156, 163, 180, 184, 194, 207-218, 219, 229, 236, 239, 240-244, 245, 246, 248-250, 259, 260, 264-265, 267, 268-269, 260, 264-265, 268-269, 277, 280, 282-285, 287, 289, 290-291, 292, 293-294, 297, 300, 303, 305-306, 308, 311, 319, 328, 330, 337, 352-353, 355-357, 361-367, 369-375

Howl and Other Poems, ii, xx, 245, 250, 265, 285, 290, 297-300, 301, 302-306, 328

Howl obscenity trial, ii, iv, 302-306, 344

Jackson, Natalie, 121, 123, 177, 274

Jacobus, Harry, 43, 44-46, 48, 50, 52, 55, 56, 64, 66, 78, 99, 177

Japantown, 7, 8-9, 33

Jazz, 3, 9-10, 59, 62, 80, 93, 104, 110, 133-135, 138, 167, 170, 195, 248, 258, 261, 287, 288, 317

Jess (Collins), 22, 43-46, 48-50, 52, 53, 55-56, 64, 66-67, 70, 78, 81, 92-93, 99, 120, 139, 177

Kaufman, Bob, 131, 144, 307, 317

Kees, Weldon, 18, 19, 24-25, 53, 89, 115, 248, 295, 349

Kerouac, Jack, iii, v, vi, ix, x, xi, xiii, xv, xvi, 1, 2, 3, 9, 10, 12, 34, 103, 112, 113, 114, 118, 125, 128, 129, 130-

134, 138, 140, 147, 150, 152, 153, 154-155, 158-159, 163-167, 168-170, 175, 176-177, 182, 188, 190, 195-197, 199, 200, 201, 202, 203, 204, 211, 213, 218, 220-222, 226, 232, 234, 235-236, 240, 242, 244, 246, 250, 254-257, 259, 260, 265, 266, 272, 274, 288, 293, 295, 296-297, 301, 304, 306, 315, 316, 326-328, 331-336, 337-340, 342, 349, 350, 351, 352, 372
King, Hayward, 59, 61-62, 63-64, 81, 96, 178, 312, 313
King Ubu, 30, 43-57, 64, 66-67, 77, 78, 79, 81, 85, 86, 87, 91, 94, 97, 99, 138, 139, 157, 176, 177, 189, 289, 316, 319, 351
K.P.F.A. radio, 77, 150, 169, 275
Krikorian, Leo, 66, 167, 193
Lamantia, Philip, i, iii, xii, 18-19, 29, 34, 53, 64, 107, 111-112, 115, 119, 138, 152-153, 158, 162, 170-171, 175, 183-190, 199, 202, 217, 220, 221, 234, 251, 254, 255-256, 272, 276, 306, 308, 337, 351, 353
Laughlin, James, 90, 112, 115, 116-117, 261
LaVigne, Robert, 121, 122, 148, 149, 152, 168, 274, 368, 369, 370, 371
Lawrence, D.H., 114, 163, 195, 305
Leite, George, 18-19
Lehrman, Walter, 177, 287
Levertov, Denise, 265

Linenthal, Mark, 177, 196
London, Jack, 18, 31
MacAgy, Douglas, 23-27, 45, 61, 62, 63, 289
Marijuana, 71, 111, 136, 163, 189, 193, 255, 257, 258 285, 289, 316, 328
Martin, Fred, 82, 94-95, 140, 179-180, 317
Martin, Peter D., 105, 107-108, 110
McClure, Joanna, 89, 120, 149, 177, 255, 260
McClure, Michael, i, ii, x, xi, xiii, 12, 21, 32, 34, 89, 95, 99, 103, 113-114, 117, 120, 131, 149-150, 151, 152-153, 158, 162, 163, 167, 170-171, 175, 177, 178, 179, 188, 190, 191-195, 199-200, 201, 203, 204, 207, 211-212, 214-216, 217, 220, 221, 223, 224, 229, 231, 232, 233, 234, 246, 251, 254, 255, 260, 266, 272, 273, 276, 278-280, 282, 294-295, 307, 308, 313, 316, 338, 339, 347, 350, 351
McCorkle, Locke, 272
Metart, 28-29, 46, 56, 87, 189
Mexico City Blues, 132, 133, 135, 163, 261, 336
Miller, Henry, 18-19, 20, 29, 162, 183, 241-242, 299, 305, 306
Moni, Andrea, 37-38, 39
Montgomery Block, 31
Murao, Shig, 110, 304
Myths & Texts, 157, 158, 159, 221-223, 225, 227-228, 276-277
Naked Lunch, xv, 282, 327, 344

Index

Neri, Manuel, 81, 83, 85, 89, 140, 315
Nin, Anaïs, 19, 120, 300-301
Nesbit, Goldian "Gogo," 119, 188
Nourse Auditorium, 148, 355, 359-361, 364, 367, 368, 372, 375
North Beach, 31-32, 62, 77, 89, 123, 144, 156, 167, 289, 308, 320
Nudity, 90, 99, 103, 121, 179, 248, 257-258, 274, 290, 300-301
Olson, Charles, 45, 69
On the Road, iv, v, xv, 2, 9, 10, 128, 163, 167, 169, 170, 296, 306, 327, 331, 344
Orlovsky, Peter, 103, 121, 122, 124, 148, 167, 177, 218, 257, 274, 330
Pabst, Beverly, 81, 317
Pacifism, v, viii, 4, 11, 12, 117, 184
Park, David, 24, 26, 31, 44, 52, 55, 61, 62, 87, 289
Parkinson, Thomas, 22-23, 115, 168, 271-272, 337, 340
Patchen, Kenneth, 12, 19, 109, 192, 241, 294, 299
Petersen, Will, 231, 275, 279-280
Peyote, 119, 141, 158, 162, 163, 184, 187, 189, 202, 221, 316, 353
Piaskowski, Nata, 64
Picasso, Pablo, 29, 59, 62, 84, 91, 114, 139, 167
Pocket Poets Series, 108-109, 240-241
Porter, Bern, 19, 29-30, 40, 43, 44, 46, 111, 152, 177, 188, 240, 242, 361

Pound, Ezra, 113, 115, 127, 138, 166, 192, 203, 300
Reed College, 156, 160, 162, 267-269, 282, 283, 369
Religiosity, 119, 184-186, 187, 341
Remington, Deborah, xix, 16-17, 19, 48-49, 51, 53, 55, 56, 59-62, 63, 64, 65, 66, 68, 71, 75, 77, 78-79, 81, 86, 91, 96, 168, 178, 189, 211, 216-217, 312, 313, 351
Rexroth, Kenneth, i, iii, xv, xvi, 2, 7, 11, 12, 16, 17-18, 19, 19, 22, 27, 28, 29, 34, 43, 53, 77, 81, 90, 109, 112, 113, 114-119, 123, 125, 138, 143-145, 150, 151-153, 157, 161, 168-170, 171, 172, 175, 176, 180-182, 183, 184-185, 186, 190, 195, 199, 203, 210-11, 214, 217-218, 220, 225, 234, 241, 246, 250, 251, 252, 258-262, 272, 273, 275-277, 278, 280, 287-288, 291-295, 300, 302, 304-305, 306-307, 316, 328, 336-338, 339, 340, 347
Rimbaud, Arthur, 138, 194, 331, 341
Rothko, Mark, 24, 120
Ryan, John Allen, 59, 61-62, 63-64, 65, 66-67, 70, 71, 72, 77, 78, 79-80, 81, 113, 120, 124, 138, 151, 157, 167, 178, 193, 245-246, 253, 268, 278-279, 288, 313, 349, 350, 363, 369, 373-374
San Francisco Arts Festival, xviii, 75-76, 148-149, 207, 212, 251, 307, 351, 355-375

451

San Francisco Community Theater, 40-42, 43, 46, 47, 358
San Francisco Poetry Center, 56, 113, 119-120, 172, 177, 214, 248, 251-254, 277, 278, 287, 289, 292, 294, 300, 311, 328, 337, 361, 366
San Francisco Renaissance, i, ix, xvi, 3, 97, 109, 178, 266, 278, 288, 292-295, 302, 328, 330, 335-336, 338, 362, 363
Simpson, David, xxi, 59, 61-62, 63, 66, 67, 68, 72, 75, 82, 178, 312
Smart, Christopher, 135-137, 138
Smith, Hassel, 24, 30, 44, 52, 87
Snyder, Gary, i, ii, iii, ix, xi, xii, xiii, 12, 18, 28, 34, 114, 115, 116-117, 118-119, 131, 143, 150, 153-160-162, 166-167, 168-169, 170-171, 172, 175, 176, 180, 184, 188, 189, 197, 199, 200, 201, 219-230, 231, 232, 233, 234, 235-236, 246-247, 249, 251, 252, 253, 354-258, 266-267, 269, 272-273, 275-277, 278, 282, 284, 287, 293, 294-295, 296-297, 301, 307, 308-309, 313, 325, 326, 328, 333-335, 336, 338, 340, 342, 351, 352
Solomon, Carl, xv, 122, 130, 137, 142, 183-184, 185, 249-250, 283, 293, 361, 337, 361
Sotomayor, Antonio, 41, 358
Spicer, Jack, 16, 49, 59, 67, 68-73, 75, 76, 77-78, 82, 83, 99, 115-116, 167-168, 178, 245, 246, 262-264, 278, 288, 290, 295, 302, 306-306, 313, 339, 347, 350, 363
Spohn, Clay, 25-26, 63
Spontaneous composition, 53, 85, 90-91, 97, 113, 125, 128-130, 132-133, 163, 164, 244, 250, 254, 315, 372
Stein, Gertrude, 18, 29, 53, 97, 114, 160, 168
Stern, Gerd, 183, 361
Stiles, Knute, 28, 64, 66, 167, 193
Still, Clyfford, 24, 28, 44, 61, 120
Studio 13 Jass Band, 62, 87
Surrealism, 44, 62, 92, 104, 130, 140, 184
The Place, 32, 64, 66, 71-72, 103, 120, 124, 138, 144, 167-168, 172, 193, 221, 236, 253, 313, 320, 351, 363
Thomas, Dylan, 119, 143, 251, 268
Twain, Mark, 18, 31
Ubu Roi, 47, 52, 55, 97
Valledor, Leo, 81, 96
Ver Becke, W. Edwin, 40-41, 46, 56
Vesuvio, 32, 62, 172
Visions of Cody, 114, 118, 131-132, 164, 169, 183
Vollmer, Joan, xv, 125, 126
Watts, Alan, 4, 77, 274-275
Weeks, James, 52, 81, 89
Welch, Lew, 156, 160, 202, 267, 349
Williams, William Carlos, 19, 111, 119, 123, 129, 134-135, 137, 139, 162, 192, 200, 204, 209, 241, 251, 264, 301-302, 306, 331
Witt-Diamant, Ruth, 119-120, 177, 214, 250-251, 252-253,

Index

294, 295, 300, 328, 361
Whalen, Philip, i, ii, iii, xi, xii, xiii,
  3, 12, 34, 116, 117, 154,
  156, 158, 159, 160-163,
  166-167, 168-168, 170-171,
  172, 175, 176, 189, 199-
  205, 216, 220, 221, 229,
  230, 234, 244, 246-247,
  251, 252, 253, 254, 255,
  256, 257, 258, 262, 269,
  272, 273, 274, 276, 277-
  278, 283, 284, 294-295,
  301, 307, 308, 316, 326,
  334-335, 351, 363
Whitman, Walt, iii, 135, 137, 140,
  183, 232, 236, 239, 250,
  265, 268, 289, 294, 319,
  331, 341, 365, 369-370, 374
Yerba Buena, 4-5
Zen, 8, 52, 154, 156, 157, 159,
  160, 200, 204, 221, 257,
  308, 331

Also Available from Beatdom Books

Beat Poetry by Larry Beckett (2012)

Scientologist! William S. Burroughs and the 'Weird Cult' by David S. Wills (2013)

Don't Hesitate: Knowing Allen Ginsberg '73 Through '97 by Marc Olmsted (2014)

The Beat Interviews by John Tytell (2014)

The Poetry and Politics of Allen Ginsberg by Eliot Katz (2015)

Beat Transnationalism by John Tytell (2017)

Straight Around Allen by Bob Rosenthal (2018)

The Buddhist Beat Poets of Diane di Prima and Lenore Kandel by Max Orsini (2018)

World Citizen: Allen Ginsberg as Traveller by David S. Wills (2019)

Burroughs and Scotland: Dethroning the Ancients: The Commitment of Exile by Chris Kelso (2021)

High White Notes: The Rise and Fall of Gonzo Journalism by David S. Wills (2021)

Thomas Merton, Lawrence Ferlinghetti, and the Protection of All Beings by Bill Morgan (2022)

The Burroughs-Warhol Connection by Victor Bockris (2024)

The Bunker Diaries by Stewart Meyer (2025)

The Three Wives of Queer William S. Burroughs by Thomas Antonic (2026)

www.ingramcontent.com/pod-product-compliance
Lightning Source LLC
Chambersburg PA
CBHW020339010526
44119CB00048B/525